THE
POTENCIES OF GOD(S)
Schelling's Philosophy of Mythology

EDWARD ALLEN BEACH

SUNY Series in Philosophy
George Lucas, Jr., Editor

and

SUNY Series in Hegelian Studies
William Desmond, Editor

STATE UNIVERSITY OF NEW YORK PRESS

Published by
State University of New York Press, Albany

© 1994 State University of New York

Printed in the United States of America

No part of this book may be used or reproduced
in any manner whatsoever without written permission.
No part of this book may be stored in a retrieval system
or transmitted in any form or by any means including
electronic, electrostatic, magnetic tape, mechanical,
photocopying, recording, or otherwise without
the prior permission in writing of the publisher.

For information, write the State University of New York Press,
State University Plaza, Albany, NY 12246

Production by Bernadine Dawes
Marketing by Dana Yanulavich

Library of Congress Cataloging-in-Publication Data

Beach, Edward Allen, 1948–
    The potencies of God(s) : Schelling's philosophy of mythology /
Edward Allen Beach.
        p. cm. — (SUNY Series in Hegelian studies) (SUNY series in
philosophy)
    Includes bibliographical references and index.
    ISBN 0-7914-0973-2 (alk. paper) : — ISBN 0-7914-0974-0
(pbk. : alk. paper) :
1. Schelling, Friedrich Wilhelm Joseph von, 1775–1854-
-Contributions in the philosophy of mythology. 2. Mythology-
-Philosophy. 3. Religion—Philosophy. 4. Hermeneutics—Religious
aspects. 5. Idealism, German. I. Title. II. Title: Schelling's
philosophy of mythology. III. Series. IV. Series: SUNY series in
philosophy.
B2899.M9B43   1993
291.1'3'092—dc20   91-15128
                                                                  CIP

1 2 3 4 5 6 7 8 9 10

For Errol E. Harris,

whose brilliant contributions to the study and development of dialectical philosophies have been a source of inspiration

Contents

Preface / xi

Introduction: Schelling's Religious Problematic / 1
    A Fresh Search for Hermeneutical Principles / 1
    Establishing the Integrity of Religious Phenomena / 4
    Searching for an Adequate Definition of Myth / 6

PART I. HISTORICAL BACKGROUND, ISSUES AND CONTEXTS / 15

1. The Origins of Pagan Religions / 17

2. Allegory, Symbol, or Reality? / 25
    Naturalistic and Euhemeristic Theories of Religious Allegory / 25
    Schelling's Earlier Treatments of Mythology / 30
    A Final Assault on Allegorical Interpretations / 37

3. The Unconscious and the Irrational / 47
    Early Speculations about the Unconscious / 48
    From the Unconscious to the Irrational / 52

4. Toward a New Ontology of Eternity, Temporality, and Freedom / 59
    Dialectic: A Stable Law of Change / 60
    A "Groundless Activity" in Eternity / 62
    Some Preliminary Questions and Criticisms / 65

5. Three Formative Influences on Schelling: Böhme, Baader, and Hegel / 69
    Böhme: The Influx of Mysticism / 69
    Baader: Through Dialectic and Mysticism Back to Christian Orthodoxy / 75
    Hegel: A Conceptual Mediation of Time and Eternity / 83

PART II. THE THEORY OF POTENCIES / 93

6. Schelling's New Philosophical Point of Departure / 95
    A Philosophical Dilemma / 96
    *The Search for a Nonrationalistic Alternative
        to Relativism / 99*
    *The Search for a Nonrationalistic Alternative
        to Fideism / 100*
    Initial Moves toward Resolving the Dilemma / 103
    The Distinction between the Was *and the* Daß */ 107*

7. The Ontology / 111
    The Pure Potencies Prior to their Actualization / 116
    The Inverted Potencies in their State of Tension / 129
    *The Relation of the Potencies to the Functions
        of the* Daß */ 136*
    *Some Comments and Criticisms concerning the
        Potenzenlehre / 142*

8. Positive Philosophy and the Experiential
    Proof of God/ 147
    Empirical Confirmation versus Exemplification / 149
    A Logical Fallacy? / 152
    The Significance of Existential Instantiation / 154

9. Representative Issues and Controversies in Current
    Schelling Scholarship: Habermas and Schulz / 163
    Habermas: A Historicist Interpretation / 164
    Schulz: A Quasi-Rationalistic Interpretation / 169
    Concluding Comments / 175

PART III. EXEMPLIFICATION, PRIMARILY IN TERMS
OF GREEK MYTHOLOGY / 177

10. From Uranus to Cronus / 179
    *Preliminary Considerations Regarding Language, Mythological
        Consciousness, and the Names of Ancient Deities / 179*
    The Religion of "Relative Monotheism" / 186
    Zabism: The Worship of "Uranus" / 191
    The Rise of Cronus / 197

11. From Dionysus to Iakchos / 205
    The Significance of Goddesses in Mythology / 205
    The Coming of Dionysus / 209

*Divine Madness and the Strange Paradox of the
   "Dionysian" Motif / 212
Iakchos: The Archetype of Spiritual Balance / 220
Some Empirical Evidence, Ancient and Modern / 224
Secrets of the "Uncanny" Lurking beneath the
   Surfaces of Mythology / 226*

12. The Self-Overcoming of Mythology / 231

*The Origins of Ontological Ambivalence in a Displacement
   of the Potencies / 233
The Progressive Discharging of Religious Projections / 235
The Eleusinian Mysteries / 238
Toward a "Sublimated Projection Theory" of Religions / 244*

Notes / 251

Bibliography / 293

Index / 303

Preface

This book explores Schelling's philosophy of religious mythology, as he worked it out during the last two decades of his life. The topic had fascinated him since his earliest years, while still a student at the Tübingen Seminary. But it was in Berlin, at the end of his long career, that he formulated his ideas in terms of a system comprising two complementary branches: the so-called "positive" and "negative" philosophies. By examining this system critically, therefore, we shall be in a position to determine in what respects it was a culmination, and to what extent it was also a deep break, within the German idealist movement.

To treat this topic adequately requires a combination of methodologies, involving the principles of historiography, hermeneutical analysis, and comparative religion. Schelling's primary approach was always philosophical, however, and since my own interest and training are likewise philosophically oriented, I have made that the overriding emphasis of the present study.

As one of the first thinkers to probe beneath the surface layers of the often opaque mythical narratives in search of deeper psychological as well as ontological significance, Schelling helped to shape the study of religious symbolism into a respectable academic discipline. Equally important for the purposes of our investigation, he used this context as the prime case study for demonstrating his important theory of the Potencies. It is for this reason that Schelling's Berlin lectures on mythology are indispensable to anyone seeking to understand his final system of philosophy as a whole.

The successful conclusion of the research for this project owes much to the encouragement, advice, and support that I received from various sources over the past several years. Successive revisions of the draft have benefited from the helpful comments and criticisms of, among others, Van A. Harvey, Robert F. Brown, Dagfinn Føllesdal, Thomas O'Meara, George R. Lucas, Jr., and an anonymous reader for the State University of New York Press.

Financial assistance for the project came from two generous sources: first, from the Alexander von Humboldt Stiftung, Germany's outstanding fellowship program for the support of foreign scholars; and second, from a Charlotte W. Newcombe Fellowship, administered by the Woodrow Wilson Foundation.

During my two years in Munich, I had the benefit of affiliation with the Schelling Kommission of the Bayerische Akademie der Wissenschaften, which is currently engaged in the mammoth task of producing a new critical edition of Schelling's works. Professor Hermann Krings, chairman of the Schelling Kommission, and Dr. Wilhelm Jacobs, vice-chairman, went out of their way to include me in their group of dedicated Schelling scholars. I owe much to the stimulus received from the discussion and colloquia which I was kindly permitted to attend.

My thanks to the Archiv für Kunst und Geschichte, Berlin, for permission to reproduce the etching of Schelling at the front of this book.

Finally, I would like to express my appreciation for the very perceptive editorial comments and corrections offered by Mr. Wyatt Benner, proofreader and typesetter for the State University of New York Press.

Throughout the pages that follow, all renderings from the German are my own. For the convenience of readers, however, I refer where possible in the Notes to the corresponding passages in published English translations. The wording of those translations naturally diverges in places from what readers will find here, but the differences are in most cases minor.

Introduction:
Schelling's Religious Problematic

Friedrich Wilhelm Joseph von Schelling's monumental lecture series on the philosophy of mythology *(Philosophie der Mythologie)*, delivered in Berlin between 1842 and 1846, brought about a minor revolution in the philosophical study of world religions. This work provided the first comprehensive theoretical basis for a philosophy of religious psychology.

Schelling's studies on the philosophy of mythology not only issued a new point of departure for the interpretation of religions, the same works also represented the culmination of a lifetime of philosophical development. It was in these lectures, together with the parallel series on the philosophy of revelation, that he elaborated the arguments and conclusions of his final, "positive philosophy." This final position, as will be seen, sought to revitalize the prevailing patterns of German idealism and modern thought as a whole by locating them within an experiential context that, Schelling hoped, would simultaneously establish and transcend the limits of dialectical logic.

The present study will concentrate primarily on the mythological issues in Schelling's system. In order to do so, we shall need to analyze the epistemological and metaphysical foundations of Schelling's hermeneutics and explore their applications to the interpretation of paradigmatic myths. The guiding purpose throughout this book will be to evaluate and criticize the implications of Schelling's approach for religious philosophy as a whole.

A Fresh Search for Hermeneutical Principles

By examining the underlying motifs of non-Christian myths and symbols, Schelling sought to construct a model for interpreting religious experience that acknowledged the presence of a nonrational principle. Because of this principle, he argued, it was necessary for hermeneutics to recognize the struggle between rational and irrational motifs in religious symbolism. This new approach, according to him, was especially necessary with respect to the pre-Christian faiths. Through investigations into basic mythical themes, he endeavored to shed new light on the contributions of the unconscious as well as the conscious strata of human spirituality.

Even while carefully developing this psychological mode of interpretation, however, Schelling also continued to employ the dialectical method that he himself had pioneered along with the other leading lights of the German idealist movement. The logic of this dialectic was understood to be universal and necessary, as constituting the fundamental building blocks of both thought and reality itself. This applied no less to the philosophy of religion than to any other realm of experience. It was Schelling's special mission, therefore, to combine a psychological orientation emphasizing the unconscious mind with a simultaneous appraisal of the spirit as inherently rationalizable. This undertaking constituted one of the most original features of his religious thought.

Other important thinkers, to be sure, had already attempted preliminary studies of pagan faiths and proposed suggestive models for understanding them. Friedrich and August von Schlegel's translations and interpretations of religious scriptures from ancient India and Greece, published in the early decades of the nineteenth century, provided much information previously unknown in Europe concerning those remote cultures. Similarly, Georg Friedrich Creuzer's contemporaneous investigations into archaic myths and symbols, rich in philological and hermeneutical speculations, opened a wide field for scholarship. A decade later, Hegel's Berlin lectures on the philosophy of religion (1821–31) paved the way for a systematic application of dialectic principles to the new discipline, in the process galvanizing a generation of fertile research. Following Hegel, and pointing his methods beyond him in different directions, were David Friedrich Strauss and Ludwig Feuerbach, both of whose seminal works (1835 and 1841, respectively) showed how it was possible to read Christianity itself as a modern mythology.

All of these thinkers, however, were engaged in projects very different from Schelling's, and they shared a different assumption: that the presence of mythical themes in religious representations was a sure sign of illusion and error. To them, stories of gods and goddesses could not be literally true or indeed even remotely close to the truth. Critical exegesis would accordingly have to eliminate such elements from any scientific treatment of religion. Hegel, for example, regarded mythical motifs as the products of a naive and unreflective imagination. The philosopher's task was to translate religious symbols into purely conceptual terms. Feuerbach and

Strauss, applying the same methodological assumptions to the study of Christian motifs, went a step further. They denied the reality of any transcendent divinities or powers whatsoever. Meanwhile, orthodox theologians and philosophers looked on aghast at these developments and sought to defend their faith by rejecting scientific treatments altogether.

To Schelling, however, all of these approaches and the conventional reactions to them resulted from a misunderstanding of the religious objects themselves. It appeared to him implausible to regard the sources of religion either as disguised human emotions (e.g., Feuerbach), as misunderstood philosophy (Hegel), or as products of an overstimulated imagination (Strauss)—especially if one supposed that the religions in question might in some degree be "true." On the other hand, there still remained the problem of how to account for the evidently false and at times even pernicious doctrines that historically were associated with non-Christian religions, especially the ancient pagan ones. In such cases, at least, it was tempting to fall back on reductionistic models that would allow an easy dismissal of any supposed truth. Yet, as Schelling noted, if pagan faiths were to be regarded as "religions" at all, then there must be an essential continuity between them and the supposedly true religion of Christianity. Any explanation of this continuity would require a difficult balancing act among conflicting principles of interpretation. How was this balancing to be accomplished? Scholars of religion appeared to have reached a stalemate.

It remained up to Schelling to attempt a synthesis of the psychological with the logical and ontological methods of his day—a synthesis that would simultaneously do justice to the nonrational roots of religion while yet accommodating the entire field of religious phenomena in a comprehensive metaphysics. Moreover (and this goal was to prove especially elusive), Schelling also sought to explain the feasibility of a transcendent spiritual reference as constitutive of religious experience. Such transcendence, he reasoned, could also be a component of pagan faiths if it were present at all in Christianity. Yet how was one to account for it? Could fictitious narratives about false deities be of a piece with the history of God's incarnation in Christ? If so, was the Christ concept itself no more than a fiction? If not, what justified regarding other faiths as genuine "religions" at all?

Orthodox Christian theology, to be sure, could ascribe a limited degree of validity to at least one other religion—namely, Judaism, which formed a part of the same historical tradition and so could be recognized as holding an essential place in God's providential plan. But what of the many alternative cultural traditions? Might not they, too, be equally significant facets of the Divinity's self-revelatory processes? Yet how could one accord them the status of being full-fledged spiritual phenomena without casting doubt on the presumed uniqueness and preeminence of Christianity itself?

The philosophical challenge was a formidable one, but necessary to undertake. Unless these sorts of puzzles could be resolved, Schelling argued, a scientific study of religions and mythologies would never in principle be possible.

The remainder of this Introduction and much of Part One will discuss the hermeneutical principles that Schelling treated in the course of working out his own approach. At the same time, however, it will also be necessary to examine in some detail the intellectual milieu in which Schelling lived. The extent and quality of information available in nineteenth-century Europe concerning the mythological traditions of ancient pagan cultures had just undergone a vast expansion. (This was, of course, part of the explosion in knowledge precipitated by the Enlightenment.) Simultaneously, the principles of religious and philosophical criticism used for the evaluation of alien perspectives had also experienced profound changes. Each of these factors had a decisive impact on the interpretive theories that emerged during this period. The same mutually reinforcing factors were bound to have an influence on Schelling's thought as well.

Establishing the Integrity of Religious Phenomena

In the early days of his career, Schelling had been one of the groundbreaking pioneers who had established the methods of dialectical philosophy.[1] This movement flourished and reached its furthest development in the philosophy of Hegel, who succeeded in creating a comprehensive system on a scale never before achieved. Yet Schelling remained dissatisfied. For many years he worked quietly and in relative obscurity, without releasing any new publications after 1812. At length, however, more than two decades later, he was ready to bring his ideas once again before the general public.[2] His lectures, delivered first in Munich and then after 1841 in Berlin, issued a bold challenge to Hegelianism. They were a sustained attempt to transform the philosophical movement from within and to give it a more "realistic" and "empirical," as well as a less "rationalistic," orientation.

Schelling's program involved, in particular, radical revisions in the conception of the role and significance of religious ideas in human history.

These revisions necessitated, he thought, a reexamination of mythological patterns of thinking. Not content, like many other philosophers and theologians, to regard myths as either fictitious narratives or merely obscure pictorial images, he treated them rather as concrete historical phenomena, with a nature and morphology of their own. As such, he reasoned, they ought to be subsumable under definite and necessary laws—laws operative on their own irreducible level of reality.

Schelling was acutely conscious of the difficulties involved in establishing mythology as a new discipline for academic study. In the first lecture of his historical-critical introduction to the philosophy of mythology, he argued at length that myths were more than simply entertaining stories, and that their subject matter constituted an independent realm of actualities.[3] But, as Schelling pointed out, unless it is postulated at the outset that the world of mythology must possess a certain lawful coherence—and to that extent a "reality" of its own—there could be no compelling reason for seeking a scientific *(wissenschaftlich)* treatment of it. If myths were merely contingent tales, invented by imaginative individuals for purposes of entertaining (or admonishing or inspiring) their fellows, then it would be pointless to attempt a systematic analysis of them. The very possibility of a science *(Wissenschaft)* presupposes a systematic nature in its proposed object *(Gegenstand)*.[4] One might, of course, suppose that certain individual mythmakers could have developed personal "systems" of their own in order to conceptualize and arrange the contents of their fanciful narratives. This would be beside the point so far as a hermeneutical science of mythology was concerned, however, unless there were some comprehensive rationale capable of explaining the nature of mythological consciousness as such. Otherwise, it would be irrelevant whether or not there happened to have existed contingent, personal "systems" invented by a small number of individuals. A scientific treatment of myths as a whole would still be impossible.

In asserting a systematic character to the subject matter of myths, Schelling took credit for being the first thinker to have discovered the true basis on which alone the study of mythology could be established as a science. This basis, he claimed, consisted in the universal and invariable nature of human consciousness itself.[5] Whether, and to what extent, this claim was justified is a question to which subsequent chapters will return. Before launching into those critical issues, however, it will first be appropriate to review some of the alternative theoretical models that Schelling considered and either modified or rejected in the process of justifying his own point of departure. What, then, was his basic problematic, and how did he come to it?

Searching for an Adequate Definition of Myth

Throughout his investigations, Schelling was principally concerned with establishing the immanent core of meaning in different religions. His quest to determine the essential dynamics of spiritual symbols and ideas was predicated on the conviction that these representations—even if sometimes antithetical to Christian values—could still be genuine manifestations of the one true God. This conviction led in turn to the next immediately obvious question: What were myths, and what sort of "truth value" could they possess?

In the effort to resolve this question, Schelling experimented with a variety of different alternative interpretations of myths, approaching them on successively interlocking levels. A series of carefully posed hermeneutical questions resulted in an evolving definition of "mythology." In fact, this process of finding the optimal definition made up the bulk of his so-called "Historical-Critical Introduction." Schelling maintained that by means of his methodology, every possible mode of interpreting myths would be considered at its logically appropriate place.[6] These included (1) their appearance as imaginative fictions *(Dichtungen)* expressive of their creators' subjective fantasies; (2) their external, social function; (3) their role as representing struggles among competing ideological paradigms; (4) their inner, psychological effects on believers; and (5) their revelatory value, as disclosing a realm of spirit that possibly transcends the world of material existence altogether.

The following pages will touch on these issues proleptically, reserving fuller discussion until a later time. Our purpose here is simply to understand how Schelling appraised the prevailing theories of mythology in his own time, and simultaneously to see how he anticipated some of the dominant ideas of the present era.

An Inquiry into the Role of Imagination

The first theory considered by Schelling to account for the origins of myths was the very natural supposition that they were invented by certain creative individuals in the distant past and, in the course of time, became a part of the cultural tradition. On the face of it, this appears to be the most obvious explanation of the seeming contingency and arbitrariness of many mythical fabrications. It also has the advantage of recognizing the decisive role that especially gifted minstrels, poets, or dramatists have played in the development of human culture.

Schelling acknowledged a partial truth to the fictional interpretation, but he argued that on the whole it was misleading. The partial truth derived from the fact that the mythopoetic mind of early humanity was of a highly imaginative and spontaneously creative nature. The implicit error of this theory, however, was to overlook the fact that the basic materials with which the early poetic imagination worked must already have been mythological in kind prior to any individual's creative act. The cultural presuppositions, the religious belief system, indeed the very language with which the poets fashioned their images were necessary features of the mental landscape in which they and their audiences lived.[7]

A variant version of the fictional interpretation suggested that myths might have originated as the instinctive inventions of a people's collective mind, whereby commonly shared issues and problems were spontaneously pictured, but without any explicit awareness of the representational process as such.[8] In other words, the idea was that a people's collective poetic imagination might have invented their worlds of "gods" and "goddesses." Again, however, this interpretation did not account for the inextricable intermeshing of the alleged mythical products with the spiritual and linguistic tools of production. It also failed to explain the basic needs and drives that led to the representational and poetic impulses themselves. Because the original forms of the latter were always expressed in mythical terms, it was evident to Schelling that the figurative imagination of the ancients was already steeped in mythopoetic modes of thinking. He therefore concluded that the genesis of poetry and of the poetic imagination in general must have been coincident with the origins of myths themselves. Poetry might well have been a phenomenally necessary manifestation of the mythological imagination, but it could hardly have been its source.[9]

In view of these and similar considerations, Schelling argued that the fictional interpretation by itself did little to explain either the historical beginnings of pagan religions or their essential character. Instead, he argued that their symbols and myths must have a real foundation of their own, not dependent upon, or derivative from, any other realms of either individual or collective invention.

Schelling's rejection of the fictional hypothesis has been ratified by twentieth-century scholars and applied to modern treatments of religious symbolism. Ernst Cassirer, for example, credited Schelling with the discovery of "a new foundational principle for the understanding of mythology," and incorporated it into his own interpretations of symbolic forms.[10] More recently, theologians like Gordon Kaufman and Garrett Green have sought to rescue the religious imagination from the stigma attached to what is merely imaginary by arguing that the objects of figurative representation are not necessarily just fictional and illusory.[11]

Schelling's determination to treat mythological discourse as possessing an irreducible truth-content in its own right acknowledged the inner integrity of religious phenomena. But the question remained so far unanswered what their real basis was. For this reason, he felt obliged to explore other alternatives.

An Appraisal of Functional Adaptations

A second paradigm that Schelling considered for explaining myths centered on the systematic parallels between a people's religious beliefs and its social organization. In fact, he discovered several complementarities of this nature and wondered about numerous others. The chief advantage of this theoretical model was that it provided clear and unambiguous terms for the easy interpretation of most religious phenomena, which could be accounted for as various and sundry means of adaptation to the natural and cultural environment. The sheer scope of data rendered comprehensible in this manner was among the attractions that made the method so tempting.

Schelling noted, for example, that one of the earliest forms of religion in primitive times—i.e., star-worship—corresponded to early people's nomadic mode of existence.[12] Thus, the reverence they paid to the transient bodies of the heavens served to reinforce a pattern of life that involved wandering across the face of the earth. By contrast, however, the emergence of more formally articulated polytheisms, with their emphasis on the divisions of divine responsibility and hierarchical relations among the gods, paralleled the development of agriculture, civilization, and differentiated cultural institutions.[13] In the myths of these more advanced societies, the interactions and divisions of power among the various deities sanctified, and so arguably buttressed, the social institutions for which they stood.

Contemporary thinkers pose many of the same kinds of questions today about comparative mythology that Schelling wrestled with a hundred and fifty years ago. Sociologists of religion like Bronislaw Malinowski and Peter Berger, for instance, have pointed to those aspects of a culture's sacred ideology that serve, often covertly, to undergird the prestige, and thus the durability, of social institutions.[14] Pursuing a somewhat different line of thought, Robert Bellah has emphasized the role of religious symbols and rituals as adaptive mechanisms to the changing conditions of human life.[15]

Schelling, however, could not accept that the social functions of religion alone sufficed to explain the full nature and depth of its symbols, myths, and rituals. Even if functionalism represented a part of the truth, he thought, it could not be the whole truth. It was on account of such reservations that he discounted a current style of quasi-utilitarian interpretation, according to which the depictions in ancient myths were dim reflections of concrete patterns of behavior. This sort of rendering struck Schelling as superficial. Had the idea occurred to him, for example, he would certainly have rejected any suggestion that star-worship could have derived from the usefulness of stars for nomadic navigation. This was not to deny the possibility of a correlation, but he thought one should avoid putting the cart before the horse. The "utility" of the stars was a consequence of their spiritual significance, not the other way around. More specific reasons why the functionalist line of approach was rejected will be examined in later chapters.

An Examination of Dialectical Conflicts

Another feature of mythology that Schelling noted was its role in the progressive working out of felt contradictions in the worldviews of believers. These sorts of conflicts were not just products of contingent historical circumstances, he argued, but resulted from oppositions embedded in the essential structures of the mind itself. Like Hegel, Schelling posited a dialectical logic which determined the patterns of development according to rigorous principles. Unlike Hegel, however, Schelling conceived of this dialectic as embracing a domain broader even than the realm of rationality itself. The same dialectic must, he thought, additionally be capable of explaining the relations between reason and the irrational forces of existence. Indeed, it was precisely because these relations were more than merely conceptual that they demanded to be played out on the stage of world history.[16]

The essential contrasts controlling relations among the components of experience closely paralleled, according to Schelling's analysis, the structural dynamics of principles occurring also in physical nature. Primitive peoples spontaneously reacted to these principles, which they recognized as being analogous to features within their own human consciousness, by identifying them with divine powers. The dynamic properties of these powers were then responsible for all development in religious systems. Schelling maintained that early human beings inevitably must have understood conflicts in ideas or values as struggles among divine agencies. What resulted from such conflicts was a series of thematic syntheses, a commingling of natures with associated symbolic compromises. Out of their seemingly endless variety the mythical worlds were generated.[17] Hence, the task of interpreting myths required a careful identification of distinct motifs, a tracing of symbolic correspondences, and an analysis of the dialectic by which implicit conflicts could be resolved.

The above theories anticipated twentieth-century developments in several important ways. Interest in the dialectical organization and symbolic patterns of religious themes has been cultivated especially since the 1950s with the rise of the structuralist movement. Writers such as Claude Lévi-Strauss and Edmund Leach have emphasized the persistence of thematic correspondences and contrasts among the figures of myths.[18] They have also called attention to the role of myths as attempts to overcome perceived contradictions in a people's natural and social environment by depicting the struggle between thematic "opposites" moving toward resolution.

A chief difference between Schelling and the contemporary structuralists, however, turns on the ontological status attributed to these patterns of analogy and opposition. At issue is whether such perceived patterns possess an actuality that is independent of their acculturated meaningfulness and perhaps even prior to humanity itself; or whether they are merely signs—"semeiological" structures within a given species' or culture's linguistic frame of reference. If the dialectic were only a subjective phenomenon (as presupposed by the structuralist approach), then its range of applicability would arguably be limited to considerations of how the world has appeared to various peoples at different points in history. To determine the basic facts themselves would require a separate procedure. If, on the other hand, dialectic could penetrate deeply enough to describe the fundamental processes of reality, as Schelling maintained, then it should be feasible by such means to discover the true significance of human existence. Because this issue is complex, subsequent chapters will have occasion to return to it.

An Investigation of Psychological Motives

Schelling placed great emphasis on the hidden psychological stresses and motivations that produce many religious beliefs. He maintained that the hold exercised on the mind by archetypal symbols, as well as the compulsion to reenact certain motifs in often elaborate rituals, showed that these symbols and rituals must spring from the inmost recesses of the worshipper's psyche.[19] This insight led to the discovery of remarkable patterns in the ancient religious myths, patterns showing profound spiritual proclivities but also sometimes bizarre modes of expression.

Schelling further called attention to the powerful psychic energies lurking directly under the surfaces of even the most peripheral religious phenomena. The involuntary character of these emotional investments provided indirect evidence of their essential source in the unconscious mind. Especially the sense of awe inspired in religious believers when confronting divine objects made it unthinkable that their gods could have arisen from random associations, from observations of nature, or from fabricated images alone. Their origins must have been far deeper than that.[20]

Much attention has been focused in the last half-century on the psychological paradigms present in myths. Numerous psychoanalytic studies have shown that these paradigms have the ability to stimulate profound emotional reactions in their audience, providing symbolic "keys" to the expression of fundamental human conflicts and desires.[21] Schelling was a pioneer in this area and would certainly have endorsed many of the findings engendered by this approach. The studies of Carl G. Jung, Károly Kerényi, and Bruno Bettelheim in particular reflect a similar perspective.[22]

At the same time, however, Schelling was anxious to avoid lapsing into a crude psychologism, as if the significance of myths were reducible to their subjective effects alone. For in that case, he argued, neither the universality of mythical motifs, nor their irresistible power to inspire awe, nor their remarkable correspondence with the actual forces and processes of the objective universe would be explainable.[23] The truths of psychology, in other words, required location within a broader theoretical framework, in the end embracing an entire philosophical system. These issues will be explored in more detail later. For the present, it suffices to note that Schelling shared some of twentieth-century psychology's insights, but that he had significantly different ideas about their ultimate implications.

A Consideration of Possible Transcendence

In addition to the imaginative, the socially functional, the dialectical, and the psychological aspects of mythology, Schelling also explored the possibility of another dimension, beyond the field of phenomenal experience. This would be the domain of an unconditioned Causality, a pure spirit outside, and yet also immanent within, the natural world. If such a Being existed, it would presumably be transcendent to the categories of ordinary thought and experience. Schelling's willingness to conceive of the highest Godhead in this mystical manner enabled him to call into question and freely criticize the specific qualities traditionally attributed to Deity (including the Christian God), while still retaining the notion that beyond these externalia there yet might be a highest Reality.

This was a risky strategy. It ran the danger of undercutting the conventional foundations of religious faith. But although it might seem gratuitously conjectural even to suggest such a noumenal principle, no treatment of religion would be complete without at least considering the possibility. Is there, perhaps, a transconceptual Reality after all? Could it be that some or all of the various world religions have in fact been genuine reflections of such an Absolute? Are the other, empirical modes of interpreting religious phenomena dependent upon this first level of meaning, deriving whatever measure of truth they may possess from their tacit relations to that transcendent Reality? Schelling answered these questions in the affirmative. A prime objective of our investigation will be to determine whether or not he was justified in so doing.

Already in his early writings, Schelling had suggested that there might be a higher mode of being, merging subject and object in a single unity. The transcendent actuality, he thought, was accessible to a faculty which he called "intellectual intuition" *(intellektuelle Anschauung)*. This special faculty was allegedly capable of apprehending noumenal realities.[24] In his later years, Schelling rarely used this particular expression. Yet he still retained the notion of a pure Act beyond all distinction and essence,[25] an indefinable "something," utterly beyond reason and accessible only to an immediate experience,[26] a "unity" beyond unity and even beyond being itself.[27] The apprehension of this highest reality was the ultimate goal of all genuine religion and philosophy. This quasi-mystical belief never disappeared from Schelling's thought.

Similar attempts to eliminate the contingent elements of religion, while retaining a transcendent reference as their inner nucleus, have been characteristic also of religious thought in the twentieth century. One of the most challenging developments in contemporary theology, for example, has been the effort to "demythologize" religious themes by means of peeling away the contingent cultural materials through which they happen to be transmitted. Efforts in this direction by such thinkers as Rudolf Bultmann and Paul Ricoeur have primarily been concerned with Christian motifs, as reinterpreted in the light of modern ideas and values. But there is no reason in principle why the same hermeneutical methods could not be extended to other religious traditions as well. A basic premise underlying demythologization is that there would remain an inviolable core or essence of spiritual truth after the historically conditioned externalia have been removed.[28]

With this postulate, as we shall see in the sequel, Schelling was very much in accord. Indeed, he would have argued that the nature of mythological thinking itself leads by an inherent process of unfolding to its own "demythologization." At the same time, however, he questioned the feasibility of any attempts to distill the kernel of faith from its outer shell unless it could first be established that the religion in question itself fostered precisely that kind of distillation. This requirement was intended to prevent arbitrary revisions of religion that otherwise might tempt imaginative hermeneuts. Many crucial questions remain, however, concerning the nature of this hypothetical kernel of spiritual truth, concerning the processes mediating between it and the determinate religions of the world, and concerning its relation to the contingent features of myths.

This concludes the brief preliminary survey of some of the issues and related topics to be explored in the following work. Schelling contributes much to contemporary discussions concerning the nature of religion and its functioning in human life. He early recognized the importance of analyzing mythical motifs both in their social functions and in their structural and dialectical dynamics. In addition, he anticipated modern psychological treatments of myths as symbolic manifestations of suppressed motivations hidden deep in the unconscious mind. Perhaps most importantly, Schelling investigated the possibility of using these unconscious motives as keys for unlocking the essential core of religious experience, a core that conceivably would remain constant throughout all the surface manifestations of myth and ritual.

All of these pioneering efforts rested upon the implicit conceptual framework in which Schelling posed his guiding questions and established his criteria of judgment. It was, after all, from this basis alone that he could elaborate his interpretations and defend his conclusions. In view of this fact, it becomes incumbent on those who would understand this thinker to determine, first of all, the philosophical foundations upon which he erected his theories about religion. It is necessary to ask: To what extent and in what interlocking ways did Schelling regard the roles of social institutions, psychological drives, dialectical oppositions, transrational experiences, or still other elements in structuring symbolic activities of the spirit? How did he propose to determine the respective weight of each factor in forming the total gestalt of the religious life?

Part One of the present study will consist of four preliminary chapters, dealing with the following broad problem areas: (a) religious origins, (b) religious symbolism, (c) the psychology of religion, and (d) metaphysical issues. A fifth chapter will treat the influence on Schelling of three major thinkers: Böhme, Baader, and Hegel. This will complete the introductory portion of the book.

A primary goal of Part One will be to show that, in Schelling's mind, the ontology of a free consciousness involves a paradoxical antagonism between its will for existence and its will for self-determination. According to him, as we shall see, the struggle generated by this antagonism expressed itself in the primordial relations among deities in ancient religious myths. These relations played out their interactive dynamics primarily within the regions of the unconscious, where the mind's symbol-making powers were not subject to the individual's, or even to the group's, collective will, but were rather molded by dark, irrational impulses. Schelling's explorations particularly probed this boundary zone. In doing so, he staked out new positions and proposed models which greatly influenced his contemporaries and continue to challenge students of religion even today.[29]

Part I
Historical Background, Issues and Contexts

– 1 –
The Origins of Pagan Religions

The relation of Christianity to other world religions was an extremely controversial issue in Schelling's day. A corollary issue concerned the ultimate source and historical development of those other religions. It was a general assumption that they could not have derived directly from God. On the other hand, their resemblance in many significant respects to the "one true religion" posed a puzzle with potentially troubling implications. For how could the sublime worship of God appear even remotely similar to the pagan idolatries?

It is worthwhile to consider briefly what some of the alternative positions were. The often heated polemics accompanying the disagreements are especially revealing of the operative pre-understandings as to what would constitute religious truth. There were at least five clearly distinguishable views.

The nonreligious hypothesis. Perhaps the most widely held view denied that the original impulse of pagan myths was of a religious nature at all. In the course of time, it was conceded, the gradual accumulation of popular superstitions might have assumed a religious or quasi-religious character. But in order to determine the root meanings of myths, one would have to penetrate beyond these later interpolations.

What, then were the "root meanings" of myths supposed to be? According to this view, they originated in the observation either of seasonal variations, historical events, geographical features, linguistic peculiarities, or numerous other empirical phenomena. Noticing these things, the early peoples allegedly looked for patterns and principles of order that could help to make the diversity of phenomena more readily comprehensible. Myths, then, originated as primitive "theories" about the natural or social worlds. They were attempts to codify and organize what the senses perceived. The other typical characteristics of myths—including their anthropomorphism, the liberal use of fantasy, symbolism, exaggerations, dreamlike associations, otherworldly speculations, etc.—resulted simply from the undisciplined and immature quality of the mythmakers' minds. They were not, however, essential or necessary features of myths, and could safely be eliminated from consideration.

The task of the scholar, therefore, was to get to the core of myths by paring away all such peripheral details. In the following chapter, I shall return to some of the proposed interpretations that emerged out of this approach. But for now let us turn to those other thinkers who insisted on seeing myths as fundamentally religious in character.

The corrupted truth hypothesis. A second, very prevalent position maintained that myths represented confused and corrupted relics of the divine revelation bestowed by God on humankind at the beginning of time, a faithful preservation of which was recorded in the Pentateuch. But the pagan remnants, preserved in garbled form by the descendants of Ham (the disrespectful son of Noah whose offspring, as recounted in Genesis 9, were accursed and base), had lost the original monotheistic teaching and fallen prey to false beliefs and idolatry.

The interpretation of myths as deriving from an original monotheism goes back to St. Martin of Braga (c. 560).[1] This theory has the advantage of recognizing the religious significance of myths, but at the cost of radically misconstruing their import. Martin, for example, insisted that the deities of ancient Greece and Rome were actually apostate angels who had fallen from Heaven along with Lucifer and the other demons. In the seventeenth century, John Milton included a dramatic representation of the same theory in his *Paradise Lost.* Among the angels cast with Satan into perdition, according to Milton,

> The chief were those who, from the pit of Hell
> Roaming to seek their prey on Earth, durst fix
> Their seats, long after, next the seat of God,
> Their altars by his altar, gods adored
> Among the nations round, . . . [2]

Other variants of the same basic idea can be found in the writings of Gerhard Voß and Hugo Grotius, who derived pagan mythologies from perverse distortions of the primal revelation.[3]

Schelling was scornful of such theories. He pointed out that they resorted to the notion of "revelation" (*Offenbarung*) in an entirely arbitrary manner. Not only did the word by itself explain nothing, but it also presupposed an original receptivity to divine influences on the part of the ancestors of the human race. The possibility of this receptivity, by Schelling's time presumed lost, was uncritically assumed and surely no less in need of explanation than the revelation itself. Indeed, inasmuch as the

– 1 –
The Origins of Pagan Religions

The relation of Christianity to other world religions was an extremely controversial issue in Schelling's day. A corollary issue concerned the ultimate source and historical development of those other religions. It was a general assumption that they could not have derived directly from God. On the other hand, their resemblance in many significant respects to the "one true religion" posed a puzzle with potentially troubling implications. For how could the sublime worship of God appear even remotely similar to the pagan idolatries?

It is worthwhile to consider briefly what some of the alternative positions were. The often heated polemics accompanying the disagreements are especially revealing of the operative pre-understandings as to what would constitute religious truth. There were at least five clearly distinguishable views.

The nonreligious hypothesis. Perhaps the most widely held view denied that the original impulse of pagan myths was of a religious nature at all. In the course of time, it was conceded, the gradual accumulation of popular superstitions might have assumed a religious or quasi-religious character. But in order to determine the root meanings of myths, one would have to penetrate beyond these later interpolations.

What, then were the "root meanings" of myths supposed to be? According to this view, they originated in the observation either of seasonal variations, historical events, geographical features, linguistic peculiarities, or numerous other empirical phenomena. Noticing these things, the early peoples allegedly looked for patterns and principles of order that could help to make the diversity of phenomena more readily comprehensible. Myths, then, originated as primitive "theories" about the natural or social worlds. They were attempts to codify and organize what the senses perceived. The other typical characteristics of myths—including their anthropomorphism, the liberal use of fantasy, symbolism, exaggerations, dreamlike associations, otherworldly speculations, etc.—resulted simply from the undisciplined and immature quality of the mythmakers' minds. They were not, however, essential or necessary features of myths, and could safely be eliminated from consideration.

The task of the scholar, therefore, was to get to the core of myths by paring away all such peripheral details. In the following chapter, I shall return to some of the proposed interpretations that emerged out of this approach. But for now let us turn to those other thinkers who insisted on seeing myths as fundamentally religious in character.

The corrupted truth hypothesis. A second, very prevalent position maintained that myths represented confused and corrupted relics of the divine revelation bestowed by God on humankind at the beginning of time, a faithful preservation of which was recorded in the Pentateuch. But the pagan remnants, preserved in garbled form by the descendants of Ham (the disrespectful son of Noah whose offspring, as recounted in Genesis 9, were accursed and base), had lost the original monotheistic teaching and fallen prey to false beliefs and idolatry.

The interpretation of myths as deriving from an original monotheism goes back to St. Martin of Braga (c. 560).[1] This theory has the advantage of recognizing the religious significance of myths, but at the cost of radically misconstruing their import. Martin, for example, insisted that the deities of ancient Greece and Rome were actually apostate angels who had fallen from Heaven along with Lucifer and the other demons. In the seventeenth century, John Milton included a dramatic representation of the same theory in his *Paradise Lost.* Among the angels cast with Satan into perdition, according to Milton,

> The chief were those who, from the pit of Hell
> Roaming to seek their prey on Earth, durst fix
> Their seats, long after, next the seat of God,
> Their altars by his altar, gods adored
> Among the nations round, . . .[2]

Other variants of the same basic idea can be found in the writings of Gerhard Voß and Hugo Grotius, who derived pagan mythologies from perverse distortions of the primal revelation.[3]

Schelling was scornful of such theories. He pointed out that they resorted to the notion of "revelation" (*Offenbarung*) in an entirely arbitrary manner. Not only did the word by itself explain nothing, but it also presupposed an original receptivity to divine influences on the part of the ancestors of the human race. The possibility of this receptivity, by Schelling's time presumed lost, was uncritically assumed and surely no less in need of explanation than the revelation itself. Indeed, inasmuch as the only evidence in support of this original receptivity was the existence of mythology itself, one might with as much justice use mythology to explain the possibility of revelation, as the other way around.[4]

The developed superstition hypothesis. Stimulated by the recent discoveries in Africa and America of tribal societies that were rife with animism and fetishism, some observers proposed that the classical forms of paganism in ancient Greece and Rome might have descended from similarly "primitive" antecedents. Charles de Brosses was among the first to put this view forward in his *Du culte des dieux fetiches* (1760).[5]

Since this interpretation of myths anticipates the general outlook that still prevails today, it may seem especially attractive to us. Yet Schelling voiced a number of reservations. Observing that many "primitive" peoples throughout history have entertained superstitious beliefs concerning the nature and properties of physical objects in their environment, he asked whether such false beliefs also qualify as being "religious." Does the presumption, for example, that dryads or fairies exist really suffice to make one religious, or would this belief not be more aptly classified as a crude misconception about the nature of reality?[6]

These are indeed penetrating questions. If the concept of "religion" entails the notion of an actual encounter with the divine—even if only a misguided or inadequate encounter—then this definition does appear to involve two presuppositions: (a) that there does exist something divine to be encountered; and (b), that this something can be encountered in and through a human, cultural phenomenon. The real issue with which Schelling grappled concerned the question: When does a human belief or activity qualify as genuinely religious? Even if supernatural beings or paranormal powers were real, would belief in them necessarily suffice to constitute a religious faith? If not, then what would? On the other hand, if fetishism, etc., are not religious phenomena, then what are they? Clearly, the answers to these questions depend upon one's prior set of ontological commitments as to the true nature of religion and its objects. Schelling's decision to treat as fundamentally irreligious those theories of pagan religions which attempt to derive them from animism or fetishism must be understood on his own terms.

The progressive revelation hypothesis. With the Enlightenment came a number of new theories seeking to mediate between the presumptive truth of Christianity and the alien contents of paganism. Since the Renaissance, it had become increasingly agreed upon that even these religions possessed much wisdom and spiritual insight. Further complicating matters was the discovery of evidently "mythical" elements within the Bible itself.[7] This discovery threatened to undermine the comfortable distinction between "natural" and "revealed" religions. If pagan religions were as capable of containing spiritual truths as the Christian faith was of containing myths—if there were demonstrable historical and cultural connections between them—then how was one to maintain the conviction that the latter was indubitably superior to the former?

In 1780 Gotthold Ephraim Lessing published *Die Erziehung des Menschengeschlechts,* a daring and remarkable proposal for the reconciliation of Christian with pre-Christian religions.[8] In essence, his idea was to interpret God as standing in the role of a religious educator *(Erzieher)* vis-à-vis the human race. Because early humanity lacked the requisite maturity and moral sophistication to comprehend a fully developed monotheism, God revealed his nature and principles in a step-wise fashion: Divinely inspired prophets began with the notion of a stern national deity, then progressively imparted the loftier values of forgiveness, love, the brotherhood of all peoples, the immortality of the soul, as well as the singularity and universality of God. Lessing affirmed, moreover, that all religious truths originally communicated by God via special acts of revelation would ultimately be recognized as truths of reason, accessible to the unaided power of rational reflection.[9] In this way, Lessing sought to establish a continuous line of development running through all the world religions and, at the same time, to bridge the gap between "revealed" and "natural" theology.

Schelling greatly esteemed Lessing's work, acknowledging that this "wonderful man" had had a considerable influence on his thought.[10] His primary criticism was that the *Erziehung* essay remained a preliminary sketch, leaving unsolved major difficulties concerning the nature of religious truth and the content of mythology.[11] In particular, Schelling objected to Lessing's typically rationalistic assumption that the essence of religion consists in a doctrine, be it moral or theoretical. But, as Schelling was at pains to demonstrate, the religion of our prehistoric ancestors was not of a doctrinal nature at all; whereas that of more developed cultures always consists of an inseparable synthesis between doctrine and actuality *(Eigentlichkeit).*[12] What sort of "actuality" was Schelling thinking of here? This is a question to which we shall frequently have occasion to return, because it goes to the very heart of Schelling's entire philosophical program.

The primordial revelation hypothesis. A final development of great importance for Schelling's thought regarding the origins and nature of pagan religions was the translation, at the close of the eighteenth century, of Vedic texts from India. These ancient scriptures had mythical elements often strikingly reminiscent of the Greco-Roman as well as Hebrew traditions. At the same time, they also contained passages of deep mystical speculations, tending toward either a monistic or, alternatively, a monotheistic worldview. Because the sudden appearance of these texts was so important for setting the basic tone of the discussion and establishing the problematic that Schelling and his contemporaries faced, it is worth mentioning their early publication history.

As early as 1784, William Jones, founder and first president of the Asian Society of Calcutta, had published some of the Vedic myths and pointed to their affinities with familiar Western motifs.[13] Jones also translated the *Iśa Upanishad*, which features meditations on the nondual "Atman" believed to pervade all finite beings.[14] Then, at the turn of the century, Anquetil-Duperron released a stilted Latin translation, which in turn was based on a Persian translation, of the original Sanskrit versions of principal Upanishads.[15] (It was this edition, incidentally, that was to have such a decisive impact on the thought of Arthur Schopenhauer.) In 1808, Friedrich Schlegel issued a ground-breaking philological and philosophical study, including translations of excerpts from the *Ramayana* and *Bhagavad Gita*, both strongly monotheistic in flavor.[16] One year later, M. E. de Polier brought out a work entitled *Mythologie des Indous*, based on Sanskrit texts obtained by her uncle, A. de Polier, during his tour of duty in India. This book, which called attention to similarities between the Hindu and biblical traditions, exercised a great influence on many scholars in the early part of the nineteenth century.[17] Still further translations from the Upanishads were provided by the Indian scholar Rammohun Roy[18] and by the famed British philologist, Henry Thomas Colebrooke.[19]

The sudden infusion of all these religious documents from the East, happening as it did during the height of the Romantic period, brought about a virtual revolution in the attitudes and theories of numerous thinkers. According to Schelling, William Jones was the first to elaborate the idea that all the ancient mythologies, including the Hebraic, were merely fragments of an originally far more inspiring and complete religious system: the primordial revelation *(Uroffenbarung)* of God. The primary content of this religion was supposed to consist in the affirmation of the Supreme Being's absolute unity and in the repudiation of any doctrines or tendencies that conceivably could lead to polytheism. Jones's theory bore obvious affinities to the corrupted truth hypothesis described earlier on pages 18–19, but with the essential difference, according to Schelling, that even the books of Moses were treated as neither more nor less privileged than were other sacred scriptures as witnesses to a lost golden age.[20] The human beings of those times, ancestors of all the diverse peoples and nations that came after (following the "Fall" from Paradise), were originally divided by neither linguistic nor cultural differences. In his enthusiasm for the Indian religions, Jones was inclined to locate the ancestral home of all humanity somewhere between the Ganges and Indus rivers.

Closely analogous ideas were held by Friedrich Creuzer, whose massive study, *Symbolik und Mythologie der alten Völker, besonders der Griechen* (1st ed., 1810–12), was to exercise a profound influence on Schelling, as well as on Hegel.[21] Indeed, no writer would be cited with anywhere near the same frequency in Schelling's lectures on the *Philosophie der Mythologie,* and it is clear that Creuzer provided the major foundation of empirical data on which Schelling later drew to support his own theories.[22] Creuzer's basic thesis about the origins of Greek mythology was that their deities and sacred myths had been transmitted from the Orient to the (proto-Greek) Pelasgians via missionizing priests from Egypt and the Orient. All of this supposedly happened in prehistoric times. In order to make their esoteric doctrines assimilable by the primitive Pelasgians, moreover, the priests from the East had veiled their doctrines in a rich but obscure symbolism.[23] Myths were told in order to represent on an esoteric level the symbols' deeper meanings.

Creuzer theorized that the original revelation of God must have presented him in his sublime unity. However, our prehistoric ancestors had understood this doctrine in a vaguely pantheistic manner, identifying God as the organic unity pervading the cosmos as a whole. Although very near to the truth, thought Creuzer, this doctrine was subject to a progressive erosion and loss of meaning, as the subordinate aspects and powers of God's order gradually came to be seen as separate deities in their own right. In this way, the primordial monotheism was lost, the popular myths diverged increasingly from their original symbolic meanings, polytheism was born, and in the process diluted traces of the ancient wisdom spread in numerous versions across the face of the earth. Hence, although no single historical culture possessed the whole truth of God, and although the different cultures' myths had all but lost their once-profound purport, scholarship could retrieve the meanings of the symbolism now lost in these myths and thereby reconstruct the originally revealed monotheistic faith.[24] Other notable figures who espoused similar or indirectly supportive positions were Henry Thomas Colebrooke[25] and especially Johann Joseph von Görres.[26]

Collectively, all of these theories contributed to a rising interest in, and enthusiasm for, ancient Eastern religions. The notion that these religions pointed back to the original revelation of God, as transmitted to the ancestors of the human race, had gained much currency in Schelling's time and decisively shaped the intellectual environment in which his study of mythology developed.[27] Nevertheless, the other, rival ideas about the origins of pagan religions remained popular among nineteenth-century scholars. Particularly strong contenders were theories that attempted to derive the pagan religions from nonreligious sources, such as fear of the unknown, confused attempts at explaining natural phenomena, or hero-worship. These will be explored in the next chapter. Schelling considered them all to be important alternatives and he devoted much effort to resolving the controversies of his day.[28]

Moreover, he saw and drew attention to an underlying issue that most of his contemporaries either ignored or took for granted. Each of the presented options presupposed a Christocentric set of assumptions concerning the essential nature of religions in general—that is, concerning what the other faiths could teach and by what methods they typically inspired belief. Thus, for example, it was the unquestioned assumption of Christianity's preeminence as alone being true that led to easy speculations about paganism as deriving from brute ignorance and superstition or, worse, from the corrupting influence of the devil and his cohorts. Similarly, the speculations about a primordial monotheism or pantheism were rooted in seemingly axiomatic ideas about both the essence of religion and the nature of early humanity. But how, Schelling asked, could any of these theories be upheld except on the prior basis of a definitive understanding of religious meaning as such?

Schelling early recognized that questions concerning the origins and nature of pagan religions and their relations to Christianity could not be resolved satisfactorily through mere reliance on scriptural or institutional authorities. For, as the rationalists had long been at pains to point out, the possible validity even of suprarational authorities could only be established and upheld, if at all, by appeals to the bar of reason. This entailed that a sound theory of knowledge was necessary. Furthermore, inseparable from epistemology and equally necessary was a fundamental ontology. Schelling was fully cognizant of this. For only in terms of an established conception of being as such was it feasible to think of erecting any theory purporting to deal with that special kind of being (or privileged way of apprehending being) which would belong to the objects of religion. In order to deal with mythology in a systematic manner, therefore, it was incumbent on thinkers first of all to work out and defend a comprehensive philosophical basis.

– 2 –

Allegory, Symbol, or Reality?

Is mythical narrative to be understood essentially as allegory—that is, as an encoded system of representational signs whose true meaning is radically different from its ostensible sense? If so, then what other level of discourse or what realm of objects were myths intended to stand for? And why had the original mythmakers chosen to veil their actual intentions in the first place? These and related issues were some of the most hotly debated topics among historians, philologists, and other students of religion in the early nineteenth century. The various positions taken up in this debate did much to define the theoretical dimensions within which Schelling's problematic developed.

As indicated in the previous chapter, one prominent group of theories concerning pagan mythologies sought to explain their genesis out of nonreligious origins. Many of these theories interpreted myths as elaborate allegories, of which the two primary subcategories were the naturalistic and the Euhemeristic.

Naturalistic and Euhemeristic Theories of Religious Allegory

Theories of naturalistic allegorism have sought to interpret myths as being, in reality, graphic depictions of important or impressive natural events. A prime example of naturalism would be the claim that the story of Persephone—her "rape" at the hands of Hades, her descent into the underworld, and her subsequent return to the upper earth—represents the death of vegetation in winter and the renewed planting of seeds in the spring. Such theories have an ancient lineage. As far back as the sixth century B.C., Theagenes of Rhegium sought to explain the Greek gods wherever possible as ciphers for the physical elements, heavenly bodies, etc.[1] A century later, Anaxagoras of Clazomenae advocated the same line of interpretation. He treated the myth of Phaëthon, for example, as a poetically embellished account of the fall of a daytime meteorite.² The controversy provoked by this theory continued through the classical period. In the first century C.E., one finds Plutarch discussing naturalistic interpretations with evident familiarity and seeking to combat them with vigorous counterarguments.³

The popularity of naturalistic allegorism reached its heyday in the seventeenth and eighteen centuries. Charles de Brosses' attempts to explain Greek and other myths as outgrowths of a primitive fetishism have already been mentioned. Other scholars of similar persuasion who were quite influential and of whom Schelling took special note were Christian G. Heyne and Gottfried Hermann.⁴ Hermann, for example, claimed to find in the myth of Io an elaborate description of how a rain-swelled stream ("pursued by the love of heavenly Zeus") breaks its dams ("escapes the watch of Argus") and becomes a mighty river.⁵

Naturalism, when carried to its furthest development, has sometimes even claimed to discern a primitive natural science in such representations. In the twentieth century, scholars like Frank Byron Jevons, Paul Ehrenreich, and Robin Horton have continued to espouse variations on this sort of theory.⁶ According to their principles, the proper method for interpreting a myth would be to seek out the physical phenomena to which the fanciful and admittedly spiritualistic language refers, and then to eliminate such language, reducing the terms down to their mundane meanings. It would be a mistake, on this model, to suppose that the primary significance of any myth could be aimed at metaphysical or transcendental issues (though these might have been superimposed by later generations); for such interpretation would be to miss the exclusive concern of the early mythmakers: to describe and explain the course of natural phenomena.

Another allegoristic perspective on mythology that had many adherents was Euhemerism, the claim that myths recounted in exaggerated terms the exploits of former heroes, geniuses, or chieftains. For example, it has often been suggested that the Egyptian god Osiris was originally an ancient pharaoh, murdered by his enemies and subsequently divinized by the people. Similarly, Herakles and Achilles can be viewed as actual heroes, idolized for their physical prowess by the people and ultimately attributed with superhuman powers. In the same way, Hermes can be seen as a gifted individual who once really existed, made some remarkable inventions and later came to be worshipped as the god of intellectual creativity.

Euhemerism has been extremely popular from ancient times until the present day. Euhemerus of Messene (c. 340–260 B.C.) wrote a *Sacred History*, purporting to show that the gods were, in fact, simply idealized historical individuals. He drew evidence for this claim from his travels to the East and the mysterious "Islands of Panchaea" (identity unknown), where he found magnificent temples dedicated to three conquering heroes of the past. Linking these with Zeus, Cronus, and Uranus, and perhaps thinking also of the recently instituted cult of Alexander the Great, Euhemerus drew the sweeping conclusion that all deities must have originated in a like manner. Thus, a rationalistic and completely atheistic explanation of religion was born.[7]

In the Middle Ages, Snorri Sturlason made use of the same theory in order to establish facile, pseudohistorical connections between the classical and Norse divinities.[8] Closer to Schelling's own time, Samuel Bochart attempted in his *Geographiae sacra* (1646) to prove by means of learned but farfetched etymologies that the Greek gods were actually ancient Jewish chieftains, whose names and reputations had been transmitted in garbled form by Phoenician emigrants.[9] Bochart anticipated Max Müller by two centuries in suggesting that the flights of fantasy embodied in myths arose from simple linguistic confusions. Thus, for example, the soldier-spawning dragon's teeth in the myth of Kadmos originated, according to Bochart, with the similarly sounding Phoenician word for "iron spear." It followed that, by means of resolving these verbal confusions one should, in principle, be able to reconstruct the straightforward historical occurrences (e.g., arming with iron weapons) that came to be mistaken for supernatural events.

Another seventeenth-century scholar, Pierre Daniel Huet, proposed an ingenious, if also rather eccentric, blend of both naturalistic and Euhemeristic allegorism. In his *Demonstratio evangelica* (1679), Huet argued that the same pagan divinity could alternately stand for a natural object, such as the sun or moon, or for a historical personage, depending on the momentary whims of the mythmakers. These fanciful associations, thought Huet, eventually fused in order to produce deities combining cosmic as well as personal attributes.[10] Euhemerism, however, always remained foremost in Huet's interpretations. He even made use of wildly arbitrary etymological "derivations" in order to demonstrate that the Phoenician deity Taaut, the Syrian Adonis, the Egyptian gods Osiris, Anubis, Set, and Apis, the Persian prophet Zoroaster, the Greek heroes Kadmos and Danaus, as well as the god Hermes—all these were but reflections of one and the same historical figure: Moses.[11]

Of course it need not follow, from the mere fact that both natural and historical models have often been overused or abused as explanatory principles in the past, that in themselves they are totally mistaken or absurd. One could well imagine, for example, that in a religion's formative period certain allusions to physical nature or social motifs might have crept in from time to time and been assimilated into a broader mythological framework. Yet the point is to find exactly what, if anything, is the basic thematic framework or tonic key around which tangential subthemes could be and were assimilated. That fundamental vision is precisely what naturalism and Euhemerism have claimed to supply. It is not a matter just of acknowledging possible natural or historical subplots in myths. Peripheral observations do not define a unique domain of phenomena, but that is just what naturalism and Euhemerism purport to do. What stands in debate in these theories is whether the reduction of myths to descriptions of nature, or alternatively to descriptions of events in social history, should be treated as paradigmatic.

The basic hermeneutical strategy linking Greeks from the time of Theagenes and Anaxagoras to late-Enlightenment figures like Hermann was their commitment to seeing the description and celebration of nature as the root impulse of religions. For just this reason they felt justified in applying the naturalistic model in all contexts and circumstances. Similarly, what distinguished the approach shared by Euhemerus, Bochart, et al., was their universally historicizing slant, i.e., their taking the adulation of historical heroes as the central motif of myths. The general legitimacy of such interpretive reductions is the question at issue.

There is still another angle that should be considered in this context: namely, the possibility that the original religious impulse took the realms of nature or social history as being miraculous zones in which divinities characteristically revealed themselves. Perhaps the creators of myths evaluated natural wonders and/or human heroes as being inherently marvellous, and therefore as potential revelators of divine powers. In that eventuality, there would arguably be no reductionism involved in, for example, interpreting myths "Euhemeristically."

A religious theory of Thomas Carlyle's comes to mind here as a case in point, even though he postdated Schelling by several decades. Carlyle proposed two related hypotheses: first, that both nature and humanity are in fact essentially numinous existences, that their being can be regarded as an epiphany of the divine; and second, that the artless minds of our ancestors possessed a far more vivid sense of wonder in the face of this universe than we moderns do. It was therefore entirely to be expected that myths and cults would have sprung up that were inspired by the sublimities of nature, and awestruck as well by certain world-historical individuals, i.e., "heroes." Moreover, Carlyle made the very telling observation that Christianity itself is "the highest instance of Hero-worship."[12] It would be difficult to deny that at least some other peoples in the distant past might likewise have taken the lives of actual human beings as the material for religious narratives. And then of course the same argument could also be made, *mutatis mutandis,* for enraptured contemplation of natural phenomena.

However, it is significant that in Carlyle's hands nature and history were no longer treated reductionistically—i.e., as showing that myths were at base "nothing more" than allegorical descriptions of common human experiences. The whole thrust of Theagenes' and Euhemerus's interpretations had been to explain away religious phenomena, to show that they resulted from superstitious confusions or misapprehensions of ordinary facts. From this, existence of anything "divine" was thereby called into question. Quite otherwise with Carlyle's arguments. They rest, rather, on the premise that the divine is truly immanent in nature and especially in history's "great heroes." But at just this juncture the old dilemma returns. In what, exactly, would such immanence consist? That is the basic problem we set out to solve, after all. As soon as one goes so far as Carlyle did, as soon as one posits human history as the zone of a divine epiphany, the original questions reassert themselves: namely, what is the nature of the "divinity" that reveals itself? And what is it that makes a myth or ritual specifically religious in character?

In the twentieth century, some of the most penetrating students of mythology have argued vigorously against reductionistic styles of interpretation. Even granting that natural phenomena or dramatic human events might occasionally have provided the raw materials for certain aspects of myth to be taken up into, and reconstituted by, the religious consciousness, these scholars point out that this is still far from proving that these phenomena exhaust the meanings of myths. Ernst Cassirer, for example, as well as Paul Ricoeur and Jan de Vries, have taken this position in strongly repudiating Euhemerism, naturalism, and indeed any form of allegorism as a general hermeneutical principle in the study of mythologies.[13] What then is the problem with allegorism? What are the major objections that can be made to it? Most importantly for our purposes, what specific objections did Schelling make?

In pursuing answers to these questions, it will be useful first to consider briefly the development of Schelling's thinking about the significance of mythology, the first phase of which was represented by an adolescent essay written while he was still a student at the Tübingen Seminary. A second phase followed a decade later in Jena, where the now-famous twenty-eight-year-old sought to apply the principles of his philosophy of identity to the interpretation of myths. The passage of still another dozen years would find him in Stuttgart, engaged in a study of the mystery cult of Samothrace with a very different approach, marking a transition to his final views on the meaning of mythology.

Schelling's Earlier Treatments of Mythology

The essay *Über Mythen, historische Sagen und Philosopheme der ältesten Welt* (1793),[14] written when Schelling was only seventeen years old, contains sophisticated reflections on the current state of philological and hermeneutical knowledge. The main purpose of the work is to explore different models of interpretation with a view to determining which approach is most satisfactory. His approach is to divide myths into two general types: (1) those which are "historical," or at least contain the germs of a true historical content; and (2) those which seek to convey a doctrinal message, theory, or teaching in a "quasi-historical" *(geschichtsähnlich)* guise.

(1) With respect to the former type, the main hermeneutical problem is to distinguish narratives with genuine historical contents from those which have merely received a pseudohistorical facade in order to enhance their popular appeal. Schelling recognizes the tremendous obstacles that stand in the way of correctly interpreting prehistorical oral traditions, and he elaborates many reasons for caution, if not outright skepticism, regarding the alleged historicity of mythical narratives (including biblical ones).

With these qualifications, however, Schelling is prepared to admit the validity of Euhemeristic modes of explanation in certain cases, especially for those myths that relate a heroic overcoming of manifest threats to a people's lives or country (e.g., Noah), those that provide genealogical or other legitimizing "evidences" of tribal connections to the cosmic origins (e.g., Methuselah), or those that recount the making of great discoveries or inventions fundamental to their way of life (e.g., Daedalus). The ascription of a real historical core lying at the base of such narratives is, of course, nothing unusual in itself: this was standard practice in the nineteenth century and remains so today. But what is notable for our purposes is the complete about-face that Schelling would later make on this score. In his final theory of mythology, he would repudiate Euhemeristic hermeneutics unequivocally for all genuine myths (i.e., all myths expressive of a people's fundamental beliefs). Instead of tracing "pseudohistories," the later Schelling would insist on treating myths as the records of ongoing struggles in a collective religious consciousness. In 1793, however, he still accepted the rationalistic conjectures inherited from the hermeneutics of the Enlightenment.

(2) Regarding the second class of myths, those containing rudimentary philosophical doctrines, or "philosophemes," Schelling's youthful views differed even more strikingly from those he would ultimately adopt. For

example, he subscribed to the predominant romantic notion that myths were created by certain wise geniuses—thinkers or poets—whose brilliant insights then provided the cultural framework used by their posterity for millennia. Homer, Hesiod, and Plato were the primary paradigms here: original mythmakers who employed pictorial language to express ideas on the verge of true abstraction. Schelling maintained that these original mythmakers must have struggled mightily to express thoughts that the common language of the times could scarcely encompass; hence they were forced to resort to sensuous images for lack of any better conceptual tools.

In line with this presupposition, it is not surprising that the young Schelling further accepted one of the most popular models for interpreting mythology inherited from the Enlightenment: naturalism. To read myths as primitive attempts at explaining natural phenomena seemed a legitimate and useful approach. Schelling's essay cites H. E. G. Paulus, G. Hermann, and especially C. G. Heyne with approval.[15]

Already in his early work, Schelling was concerned with the distinction between symbol and allegory, a distinction to which he would return again and again in his later years. At this initial stage, he adopted a distinction derived from the biblical scholar, Georg Christian Storr, between myths, on the one hand, and allegorical representations, on the other.[16] An allegory or parable, Schelling explained, works across different types of principle, in that it clarifies an abstract concept by means of a simile or metaphor borrowed from sense experience. A myth, by contrast, works within a single type of principle, in that it embodies an experience of the same fundamental character as the principle it illustrates. The point is that allegories only appear in the history of human culture when the mind has gained sufficient autonomy to range freely over its experience and knowledge, picking out features of similarity for comparison *ad libitum*. Myths, however, take as their subject matter paradigm cases or archetypical examples of the same realities they are seeking to explain. Thus, for example, Jesus' parable about the "sower's seeds" (representing the kerygma) that land on either fertile or barren soil (representing receptive versus unreceptive souls) would count as an allegory; whereas the story of Demeter's withholding life from nature (representing winter, sterility, death, etc.) would count as a myth in the strict sense.

A decade later, in his Jena lecture *Über die Methode des akademischen Studiums* (1802), Schelling used the same basic distinction in contending that historical allegories alone were capable of serving as vehicles for expressing the insights of the true religion (i.e., Christianity). The advantages of allegories, he maintained, derived from their metaphorical character (in that the religious histories served as images of eternal ideas), and from their ephemeral quality (in that the events recounted faded into the past as soon as they occurred). Precisely because the finite signifiers used in historical allegories had disappeared from the world of immediate experience, they were ideally suited to point beyond themselves toward an infinite reality. Natural symbolism, on the other hand, utilized objects having a mundane character quite apart from their role as tokens of the infinite (in that they entered into the normal course of everyday experience), while they also appeared to be permanent representatives of the meanings they expressed (in that the physical signifiers remained present in the worshippers' world). For example, if one were to compare the fable of Atlas (a myth) with the story of Samson (a historical allegory), one would find that the symbolic meaning of the former (a huge mountain representing the power sustaining the cosmos) has less spiritual potential than the allegorical meaning of the latter (a mighty hero representing the inscrutable will of God). Schelling concluded that the more superficial, exoteric symbols of myths did not sufficiently transcend their literal significance, or direct the mind as effectively toward the infinite, as did the more esoteric historical allegories; and hence, that allegories were more suitable for communicating the highest religious truths.[17]

In the same year, another lecture series on the *Philosophie der Kunst*[18] also dealt in part with mythology. In this treatise, Schelling sought to supplement the subjectivism of Fichte's transcendental idealism with a corrective dose of realism derived from Spinoza's substance monism. Instead of eliciting the forms of the phenomenal world purely from the principle of *das Ich,* as Fichte had done (and as Schelling himself was still doing in 1800), his new approach was to take the "indifference point" midway between subject and object as the fundamental principle. These lectures on art were thoroughly Spinozistic in both content and style, even to the extent of being organized in terms of numbered "Propositions" followed by rationalistic deductions, with occasional "Elucidations" and "Corollaries," etc.

In that work, we find one of the earliest definitions of a "Potency," the conception of which later was to prove so central to Schelling's thought.[19] In the formulation of 1802, a "Potency" looks like nothing so much as one of Spinoza's "attributes": it is, says Schelling, one of the "various determinations . . . under which *one* essence, *one* absolute reality [i.e., the universe as an indivisible whole] . . . is posited."[20] These determinations, appearing in innumerable permutations throughout nature as well as human history and culture, are of three basic types—the "affirmed condition" or "real Potency" (roughly equivalent to Spinoza's *natura naturata*), the "affirming activity" or "ideal Potency" *(natura naturans)*, and the "indifference point" that unites both.

Noticeably absent from this theory is one of the hallmarks of Schelling's middle and final periods: namely, the notion of a primordial and recurrent conflict between a form-giving and a form-destroying power. Although a principle of "chaos," defined as pure formlessness, does appear in the *Philosophie der Kunst*, it has the character rather of being the bounteous and inexhaustible source of forms than the all-consuming and insatiable power that seeks to annihilate forms. This chaos does not struggle against differentiation and light (as in the later theory), but is already immediately one with it. Hence the young philosopher could write: "that chaos within the absolute is not *mere* negation of form, but rather formlessness within the highest and absolute form."[21] (In his later period, Schelling would depict the principle of chaos in much more somber, even tragic, hues. Evidently yet to make itself felt in 1803 was the influence of Jakob Böhme, of whom more later.)[22]

Within the framework of his philosophy of identity, Schelling interpreted mythology as a mode of representing concretely, in the medium of imagination, ideal principles of paradigmatic human values or experiences. Gods are objectified prototypes of typical faculties or feelings— embodying in sensuous form the synthesis of the universal and the particular. "These same syntheses of the universal and the particular that viewed in themselves are ideas, that is, images of the divine, are, if viewed on the plane of the real, the *gods,* for their essence, their essential nature, = god."[23]

An important consequence of the linkage between ideas and deities was that one could not properly interpret either aspect simply by means of referring to the other aspect. To "explain" the nature of a god or goddess as signifying some idea or doctrine would be as misleading as to "explain" the doctrine as signifying the god. Rather, each aspect should be seen within its own proper context and independent sphere of operation. This thesis marked a further step in Schelling's progressive abandonment of allegorical interpretations of myths.

In his mature works, Schelling would come more and more to insist on sharply differentiating abstract ideas, possibly illustrated by means of pictorial analogies, from concrete ideas derived from immediate experience. Only ideas of the latter type, the later Schelling would argue, could constitute genuine myths. Increasingly he would become convinced that the function of myths in religions was not to impart information or to reach an intellectual understanding of the world, but rather had something to do with stimulating a special kind of psychological response within the listener. In his final period (as we shall presently see), this distinction led him to exclude "philosophemes" and "teachings" *(Lehren)* altogether from the realm of myths.

Yet to dispense altogether with allegorism was no easy matter. It had been among the most popular approaches to mythology among intellectuals for many centuries, and had not always been limited to one-dimensional, reductionistic accounts like naturalism and Euhemerism. By means of analyzing structural parallels between the ostensive events in myths and the relationships among important ideals or principles, scholars had had considerable success at uncovering hidden significance of apparently profound spiritual import. The history of spiritual allegorism as a hermeneutical method was, moreover, quite ancient, extending at least as far back as Plutarch's interpretation of the Egyptian religion as a mystical allegory representing the conflict between matter and soul.[24] Similar applications of allegorism had continued to bear fruit, as for example, in treatments of the clearly didactic story of Eros and Psyche, or of the cosmological speculations at the beginning of Hesiod's *Theogony* about the origins of the universe. This approach reached its heyday in Europe in the nineteenth century.[25] It was hardly surprising, therefore, when Schelling's colleague and friend, Friedrich von Schlegel, affirmed that every work of art—and, by implication, every myth—must contain an allegory.[26]

Schelling, however, remained skeptical. To interpret myths as no more than elaborate metaphors portraying abstract general principles seemed to overlook the concrete and affective character that is a hallmark of mythical narratives. If myths were only figuratively expressed ideas, one would expect the figurative elements to lose their power to charm once people grasped the true principles they had been used to express. Yet mythological narratives continued to exercise an artistic vitality and expressive intensity far in excess of their ostensible doctrinal meanings.

Schelling drew support in his dissenting opinion from the work of Karl Philipp Moritz, who had recently argued that one must attribute an autonomous significance to myths and read them as treating their own unique objects rather than as implied references to some completely different class of objects. Every myth, argued Moritz, had a meaning in its own right, and did not need to be rendered in other terms. On this, Schelling agreed completely.[27]

There was one further respect in which Schelling's interpretation of mythology moved a substantial distance away from his early position. This change concerned the question of the authorship of myths. Whereas in 1793 Schelling still shared the prevailing opinion among scholars that myths were the creation of gifted individuals who used them as vehicles to express bold new insights, a decade later he had abandoned that view. Instead, he now affirmed that myths were the products of a people's collective spirit, which acted spontaneously as a single individuality.[28] Moreover, they were not at all the result of conscious reflection, but sprang immediately and unbidden from the deepest regions of the soul.

The reader will recall that the Introduction, above, identified this doctrine as among the innovative ideas in Schelling's interpretation of myths.[29] The fact that he arrived at this theory at such an early date and retained it throughout all the subsequent modifications in his metaphysics testifies to the importance that he placed on this principle of religious hermeneutics.

Yet, although Schelling came to reject allegoricizing interpretations of mythology, this did not entail advocating the treatment of myths on a simplistic literal level. Instead, he sought to create a new theory of meaning that would synthesize both the "real" moment of a lived actuality and the "ideal" moment of conceptual signification. But in what could such a synthesis consist? Schelling found an answer in a new theory of symbolic meaning.[30] A genuine (as opposed to merely "schematic") symbol, he now explained, is a "representation of the absolute with absolute indifference of the universal and the particular."[31] In other words, it simultaneously represents a particular object or image as standing for some universal idea, while it also represents the universal idea, in turn, as being concretely active in some particular object or event. (An allegory, by contrast, achieves only the first of these ends—using the particular to stand for a universal. This difference explains why allegories are always pale abstractions compared with the richness of symbols.) Since the constellation of meanings emerging out of the symbol's polyvalent unity is inexhaustible, it cannot be reduced to a single allegorical interpretation.

Nevertheless, so long as one continues to conceive of the function of symbols as representational, a potential gap reopens between the representation and the represented. With this gap, and the questions of "accuracy," or at least "appropriateness," that it brings in its wake, a subjectivist bias could reenter through the back door. In 1802, Schelling was able to assert that the singular "charm" of myths consists in the fact that their objects were "meant as real." But might not this meaning itself perhaps be a misunderstanding of the true state of affairs? Could it be that there exist meanings in themselves, as it were, lying beyond the suppositions and attributions of human symbol-makers?

It was the search for more objective meanings, as constitutive of reality, that propelled Schelling into the next phase of his philosophical development, from about 1806 to 1820, customarily identified as his "middle period." During this time, his metaphysical thinking received a decisive influx of theosophical ideas from reading Jakob Böhme and discussing them with Franz von Baader. During the same period, Friedrich Creuzer's mammoth study, *Symbolik und Mythologie der Alten Völker* (1st ed., 1810–12) also appeared, immediately becoming and remaining Schelling's primary source of information about ancient mythologies. The confluence of both these streams of influence gave rise to the major works of his middle period: *Die Weltalter* (1811–13), in which he elaborated an early version of the *Potenzenlehre* (theory of Potencies), and *Über die Gottheiten von Samothrake* (1815), in which he pursued his explorations of the significance of myths.[32]

Schelling prefaced the *Weltalter* with a discussion of a mysterious form of higher thinking that proceeds by what is intimated *(das Geahndete)*, rather than by what is merely known *(das Gewußte)*. This was a clear reference to symbolic meaning as transcending what the finite, discursive understanding could comprehend.[33] But although Schelling continued to regard symbols as the implicit coin of the realm of mythology, from his middle period onward he would write less and less about "symbols" as such, and more and more about "Potencies"—real and independent powers inherent in both nature and spirit.

No doubt this significant change in hermeneutical terminology stemmed from reservations about the hazards, just noted, of using representational language to describe and interpret religious experience. To persist in characterizing religious discourse in terms suggestive—if only by connotation—of signs and images standing for other things (as symbols stand for their referents) would be to reinforce the notion that mythology is about something other than what it *thinks* it is about. (Such a possibility should not, of course, be precluded *a priori*, but neither should it be presupposed by the investigation. We shall return to this issue in the next section.)

Schelling's study of mythology in the *Gottheiten von Samothrake* constituted a new point of departure. Encouraged by Creuzer's example, he drew on extensive philological evidence from the ancient Greek, Hebrew, and Phoenician languages to establish obscure historical connections in the prehistoric past. Probably little of this evidence would be acceptable today, but Schelling's use of it is interesting and instructive.

For example, one of the four most important Samothracian deities was "Axieros," whose name, according to Schelling, harks back to the Hebrew roots *yrs**, "to take possession," and *rys**, "to be in want." Since cognate words in Phoenician also meant "hunger," "poverty," and "craving," it followed that Axieros must be a goddess of insatiable longing, of lack and craving on both the physical and spiritual levels:

[It is] that primordial nature, whose entire essence is desire and yearning *(Sucht)*, . . . the consuming fire which, though itself in a way nothing, is in essence only a hunger that draws everything into itself *(ein alles in sich ziehender Hunger)*.[34]

What deity was this? What goddess was it, in classical Greek mythology, whose unquenchable yearning once caused the entire world to suffer famine? Obviously, it was Demeter, at the time when she was searching for her lost daughter, Persephone. Schelling credited Creuzer with having made the crucial discovery "on which this systematic interpretation rests"—the identification of Samothrace's Axieros with the classical Demeter/Persephone complex.[35] Since, moreover, the reunion of Demeter with Persephone was a central motif of the Eleusinian Mysteries, this suggested that Axieros, too, was the subject of a corresponding mystery cult in Samothrace. (In the nineteenth century, it was widely believed that the Mysteries were the prime locus where the hidden meanings of religious myths and symbols were revealed.)

Schelling also took obvious satisfaction (though without explicitly saying so) in the circumstance that the above characterization of Axieros resonated with Jakob Böhme's doctrine of the world's creation in an original fire of longing *(die Sucht, in sich zu ziehen)*, as well as with his own theory of the first Potency, whose "inward-drawing, collapsing power" *(zusammenziehende Kraft)* formed the basis for the Potencies that followed.[36]

Thus, at a single stroke, Schelling was simultaneously able (1) to establish his credentials as a competent empirical mythologist and practitioner of the prevailing philological methods, (2) to draw support from the researches of one of the most eminent classicists of his day, (3) to show the utility of philosophical analysis for hermeneutical studies, and finally (4) to illustrate the explanatory power of his own newly developed doctrine of Potencies. All four characteristics would prove enduring features of his deliberately interdisciplinary approach in the decades ahead.

A Final Assault on Allegorical Interpretations

Schelling was, as we have seen, among the first thinkers to question the validity of allegorizing interpretations of myths. In his final period, his arguments for rejecting that approach had reached a new level of hermeneutical as well as historical sophistication.

There was a common thread of error, he contended, in all the attempts to treat mythical narratives as ciphers or signs for other things, whether for natural phenomena, for great historical events, for moral principles, for esoteric metaphysical doctrines, or whatever else.[37] All these interpretive strategies, he thought, mistakenly presupposed that the contents of myths, once properly "deciphered" and translated into straightforward concepts, could thenceforward be dispensed with as mythology. Yet this notion of "translatability" amounted to a flattening and trivialization of the infinite richness of myths, overlooking their emotional intensity, their compelling realism, and the necessary laws of their development. Borrowing a term from Coleridge, Schelling insisted that "mythology is not allegorical, it is tautegorical."[38] In other words, the content of mythology is identical to its form.

Schelling argued that it was implausible to suppose the primitive tellers of myths could ever have intended complex and abstract metaphysical ideas to be the hidden contents of their narrations. Such ideas might have sprung up later and been grafted onto the myths, he contended, but they could not account for the myths' origins.[39] Secondly, Schelling criticized reductionistic interpretations of myths that brought in farfetched "historical" or pseudoscientific explanations to account for religious practices and beliefs. He noted, ironically, that in that case the creators of the myths must have stood on a far higher level of intellectual development and culture than the great mass of believers. Not only was there no empirical evidence to support such an elitist hypothesis, but it was also a mystery how the supposed geniuses of mythology could ever have prevailed on the ordinary people to accept their representations.[40] Thirdly, Schelling argued that the tremendous power exercised by myths on the popular mind, and the absolute conviction they elicited, was only understandable if one assumed a kind of objective necessity to be operative in them.[41] Hence one must reject the notion that myths could have arisen as the products of invention *(Erfindung)* or fantasy, whether of individuals or groups. For no function of human conscious life which was subject to the free decisions of intelligence and will could ever have produced the irresistible hold myths have exercised on whole peoples and cultures.[42]

It is important also to notice the strategies of argument that Schelling directed specifically against naturalism and Euhemerism, for these strategies shed much light both on the central reasons for his rejection of allegorism and on his conception of how genuine symbols function.

Against Naturalism

Schelling never denied that natural objects, heavenly bodies, seasonal cycles, etc., assumed a religious significance in many ancient and modern cultures. What he did deny was that these physical objects or qualities had furnished the original and continuing motives that inspired worship and the telling of myths. The naturalistic mode of explanation effectively put the cart before the horse. In fact, Schelling maintained, it was the religious impulse already present in the human mind that caused people to take these external objects as indicators of, or references to, higher spiritual realities. For example, in the case of the Eleusinian Mysteries, Schelling disputed the familiar naturalistic contention that the descent and subsequent return of Persephone from Hades symbolized the planting of grain. For it was not that Persephone symbolized grain, but rather the reverse, that grain symbolized Persephone, which endowed the Mysteries with such pronounced religious intensity.[43] In just the same way, Schelling added, St. Paul himself frequently used agricultural images to symbolize spiritual things. And yet no one supposed that Christianity was for that reason a nature religion.

Against Euhemerism

A parallel argument could also be made with respect to the presence of historical (or quasi-historical) figures in some religious stories and myths. The point was not so much whether such figures were or were not "historical," but whether their alleged historicity had provided the original impulse of spiritual awe that led to the development of religious ideas around them. Was it not at least as plausible, Schelling suggested, that the people of those times already possessed certain compelling spiritual archetypes, fundamental values and motifs which they then might have superimposed onto the stage of human history? Schelling interpreted the Roman legend of Romulus, Remus, and Numa, for example, as instantiations of the three universal Potencies (of which more later) that appeared in all the great world religions. Once worshipped as deathless gods, the three could later have been assigned "historical" roles as founding fathers of Rome.[44] This, then, was Schelling's theory of "reverse Euhemerism": It was not the case that history had become mythologized, as Euhemerus had taught, but rather that mythology had become historicized.[45]

Schelling's criticisms of both naturalism and Euhemerism implicitly presupposed that the true essence of religious experience consists in the encounter with an actually divine being or beings. The premise is open to question. Is it not possible, for instance, that the reductionists are correct—that the core of religion is illusion and self-deceit? Might it not be the case, after all, that the superstitious fancies of naive peoples invested commonplace phenomena with a significance and value not truly theirs? We must take this possibility more seriously than Schelling did, reserving the right at the conclusion of this investigation to set aside his system of "positive philosophy" as untenable.

In the latter half of the nineteenth century, many scholars assumed that the reductionist camp had thoroughly routed the romantic "symbolist" camp (within which Schelling could loosely be numbered). Because the symbolists often indulged in speculations of dubious historical plausibility, the reductionists had a field day in debunking their theories. Any inclination to attribute a higher spiritual significance to ancient pagan myths and religious beliefs was immediately suspect.[46] This attitude is still prevalent in many quarters today.

Nevertheless, perhaps one should concede at least this much justice to Schelling's position: Naturalism, Euhemerism, and any other atheistic theories of religion should only be considered strong options if and when the religious interpretations have been exhausted. Prior to that determination, it would be question-begging to presuppose the validity of nonreligious hypotheses and reductive hermeneutics. Instead, a critical study of religion would do better to explore religious phenomenology without presuppositions one way or the other. Guided by this methodological precept, which is more limited than Schelling's outright rejection of the above hypotheses, one can appreciate his alternative treatment of mythology as a point of departure.

The basic objection to the atheistic methods of hermeneutics was that they misconceived the essence of religious symbolism. Schelling observed that a symbol was always a sensible thing or sign that represented something else; but in the particular case of religion, the represented object was supersensible. A religious symbol therefore served to direct the mind from a lower reality to a higher one, never the other way around.[47] This assertion again presupposed a religious worldview, and Schelling was aware that its justification would require a systematic inquiry into ultimate ontology. That ontology will receive a fuller treatment later. For the time being, however, we shall merely note his central claim that the mistake of Euhemerism and naturalism lay in their failure to appreciate the supersensible orientation of religious symbolism.

Against Moralistic or Doctrinal Readings

The above critique did not by any means exhaust the full extent of Schelling's objections to the allegorical treatment of myths. He also took issue with attempts to read into them moralistic or doctrinal allegories, neither of which committed the "fallacy" of materialism, and yet both of which managed to be reductionistic in other ways. Let us briefly consider these two alternatives.

Against the axiological approach, which interpreted pagan myths as illustrative lessons in moral behavior, Schelling had little to say. Presumably he did not think it necessary, inasmuch as the view had few defenders anyway. Besides, it appeared glaringly obvious that many ancient myths and associated rituals were positively immoral in their content and were experienced as such by the ancients no less than by moderns. (Recall the wild Maenads, for example, whose mad orgies and savage rites nobody, least of all the Greeks themselves, would have designated as moral.) Accordingly, much of Schelling's effort in interpreting such religious motifs would be spent in seeking to recover and explain the powerful emotional conflicts that could have led to such excesses. But even granting that it was possible to see in some myths the presence of ethical teachings or guides to moral behavior, it still did not follow that these uses were the primary *raison d'être* for such myths. Schelling observed that moralistic metaphors could easily have been superimposed upon the myths as later strata of meaning. In order to determine the root meanings of myths, however, it would be necessary to discover the principles of their morphological development from the very earliest times.[48]

Against Hegelian Interpretations

Hegel introduced a more sophisticated variant of the conceptual approach to mythology. On the one hand he criticized the one-sided abstractness of many allegorical interpretations, yet on the other hand he was convinced that spiritual truth must be inherently rational.[49] Hegel's theory of the concrete universal, as the infinite self-realization of Reason, enabled him to synthesize the organic ontology of Romanticism with the intellectualism of the Enlightenment. Recognizing that the inexhaustible wealth of images in works of art and mythology could not be captured by any single doctrine or set of doctrines, Hegel looked for another way of characterizing the implicit rationality of myths. He proposed that the meaning of such works consisted in a creative subjectivity that was pregnant with endless new potential insights. By means of this theory, he effectively replaced one-dimensional doctrinal allegory with multidimensional rational symbolics as the hermeneutical key to mythology.

According to Hegel, mythical narratives in all the great religions contained a truly infinite content, but represented it in an inadequate, sensuous form. This inadequacy of the form to the content constituted the fundamental disequilibrium and ultimately spelled the doom of mythical consciousness. What, then, was this infinite content, the kernel of truth that lay hidden behind the outward representational forms? It was no less than Absolute Reason, the self-determining concrete universal, whose eternal reality totally transcends the finite media of space and time. Hegel emphasized that the very representation *(Vorstellung)* of divine "histories" as events occurring in particular places and times was a limitation that philosophical analysis must remove.[50] And he pointedly included Christianity within the compass of this critique.

The true content of mythology, therefore, was thought.[51] From this realization, one needed only to go one step further in order to see that myths were essentially representations of ideas, even if not intended as such by their originators. Therefore the divine essence implicit within the mythical narratives required to be translated out of the narrative form into the true determinations of philosophical reason. Only in that way could the obscure intuitions of the ordinary religious consciousness realize their full maturity as the explicit knowledge of, and unity with, God.[52]

Schelling, however, never accepted the Hegelian interpretation of religious content. In particular, he objected to a central principle of the absolute idealist position: the thesis that myths are but pictorial representations *(Vorstellungen)* of a content that only philosophical reason can adequately grasp. This assumption about the nature of religion, which Hegel shared with most of the spiritual allegorists, Schelling undertook to oppose with a full arsenal of arguments. In the process, he also came to distance himself increasingly from all interpretations of religion as *standing for* something else, something which in itself would (supposedly) be without a divine nature.

In attacking the Hegelian interpretation of religion as representation, Schelling objected that, if myths were only to be construed in that way, then their original creators must either have been philosophers and theoreticians (a patently implausible supposition), or else they could have had no notion at all of what their own myths "actually" were intended to convey. Schelling pointed out that if pagan religions were nothing more than subjective representations, the same must also hold for the presumably highest faith that had crowned their development—Christianity itself.[53] This was a consequence that few outside the Left-Wing Hegelians were prepared to accept. Finally, Schelling charged that even Hegel not infrequently fell into the very mode of thinking which he himself had characterized as *Vorstellung*.[54]

Schelling's main point was that the cognitive approach followed by the Hegelian and allegorical schools left unexplained how a *real* as opposed to merely *ideal* relation with God was possible. For, as Schelling maintained, all concepts were circumstantial in the sense that they might or might not be present in any given consciousness at any particular time. Since the mobilization of conscious thoughts (as contrasted to the submerged promptings of the collective unconscious) always involves an act of free human decision, it was an enigma how such contingent connections could explain the possibility of religion as a real connection to an infinite, all-powerful deity: Just the bare act of thinking about God could not create a relation to him. And by the same token, the absence of conceptual thinking would not extinguish such a relation.[55]

Schelling did not hesitate to apply the same arguments to the divinities of polytheistic religions. Even granting that their gods were formally "false," they might still have possessed some kind of connection to the one true God. In fact, Schelling reasoned, one must suppose their cults to have had such a connection in order to recognize them as "religions" at all. The generic principle of religion involved an immediate linking of the finite spirit to a divine reality. Hence, although the precise nature of that reality in itself was doubtless misconceived by primitive minds, the genuine character of the linkage itself could not, he thought, be denied. Its authenticity proved itself on an intuitive level that was altogether prior to rational consciousness. Schelling was thus convinced that God must be the foundation of even the supposedly "false gods" of mythology.[56]

A further argument, developed in another context, hinged on the principle that the *revealed religion* of Christianity could itself only be real if it brought about a factual change in the nature of the relationship between the human and the divine. Such a change could not result, Schelling maintained, from learning new religious *doctrines* alone, for in that case "salvation" would consist in a bare conceptual reappraisal of the prior status quo: it would amount to nothing more than a "waking up" to eternal verities that always had been, and always would be, true regardless. To the contrary, Schelling insisted (in striking anticipation of Kierkegaard) that human salvation, if it were to be possible at all, would have to involve a real transformation of the prevailing relationship between God and the human soul, a transformation grounded in concrete historical events. These events, receiving their impulse from a divine providence, must have taken their point of departure from a naturally existing, prior relationship to God. It was precisely this relationship, genuine but destined to be superseded, that the religions of mythology had embodied.[57]

Schelling's conviction therefore remained unshakable that pagan myths were narratives of real historical events. The same conviction reinforced his opposition to all allegorical or merely doctrinal interpretations of myths.

It must be acknowledged that the facility with which Schelling accepted the reality of the relationship between the pagan divinities and the "true God" of monotheism was somewhat uncritical. Only very briefly did he consider, but without analyzing carefully enough, the possibility that the religious consciousness, pagan or Christian, might stand in no relation whatsoever to a true God. Schelling maintained that the intensity and sincerity of feeling present in the worshippers' hearts—ancient and modern —ruled out that theoretical option. As for the many perplexities attending the correlation of mythical deities with a Supreme Being, these led Schelling not to the conclusion that skepticism or atheism required closer examination, but rather that the nature of the primordial relation to God must lie deeper than consciousness itself.[58]

Modern readers may take exception to the seeming imprecision of Schelling's concept of "relation" *(Verhältnis)*, as used in these discussions. While he recognized the obstacles in the way of connecting "authentic monotheism" with polytheistic religions hitherto regarded as idolatry, he seems to have been insufficiently mindful of the vagueness of his thesis. For even if monotheists should grant that the Supreme Being was "related" to the pagans in and through their multiple divinities, what might this mean beyond the very general claim that God is present in all things? On many of these issues, Hegel was the more critical philosopher.

A subsequent chapter will address the continuing controversy between the Schellingian and Hegelian positions. For the present, suffice it to note that Schelling's occasional vagueness was often only provisional. He emphasized that in order to deal with these topics adequately the hermeneut required a precise metaphysical theory, one that would specify in detail the essential aspects of God's nature and connect them point for point with the basic principles of pagan theologies. Accordingly, Schelling set out on a carefully coordinated plan to realize just such a metaphysics. Once he had established systematic connections between the essential ontological Potencies and the divinities of ancient religions, he reasoned, it would then be possible to show through exhaustive historical-critical studies how the actual myths of these religions substantiated his interpretation.

This chapter, having begun with a discussion of hermeneutical issues concerning the nature of allegory and symbolism, has ended with a consideration of issues in metaphysics. This development is by no means accidental. It reflects Schelling's whole approach to the study of mythology. In his endeavor to determine the origins of myths and the principles of their continuing development, he saw the need to alter the long-established tradition in Western scholarship of treating myths as either imaginative fictions or as elliptical representations of something else. Naturalism, Euhemerism, even spiritual allegorism and the representation dialectic of Hegel—all tended in Schelling's view to explain myths away by means of superimposing their contents onto a radically different sphere of experience. In opposing this tendency, he argued that the only way to understand myths correctly was to approach their contents as genuine and real in their own right. He also knew that, in order for this approach to succeed, it was incumbent on him to establish first and foremost what "reality" involved.

– 3 –

The Unconscious and the Irrational

Virtually all the theories of mythology developed since early Greek times through the nineteenth century were essentially rationalistic in their orientation. From the naturalism of Theagenes through the dialectical symbolics of Hegel, the whole effort of interpretation had consistently been to discover and lay bare the hidden logic responsible for mythical motifs.[1] The same orientation continues to this day—for example, in the modern "materialist" and "functionalist" schools of thought.

As Schelling was among the very first thinkers to see, this whole approach begged the more basic question as to whether the point and contents of myths really were rational in the first place. Perhaps, he suggested, a substantial proportion of mythical themes originated in the obscure promptings of unconscious desires and fears—promptings that might well be irreducibly irrational in nature. With this insight, Schelling brought about a radical shift in the horizon of possibilities open to scholars of religion.

Jan de Vries has observed that the discovery of the unconscious as a generative power was a major factor in making the age of Romanticism one of only two brief periods in the history of Western scholarship that have been receptive to the real nature and sense of ancient religions. (The other period, according to him, is the current one.) As de Vries points out, the discovery of unconscious processes in human experience led to a breaking away from the rationalistic assumptions that had previously blocked access to a genuine understanding of myths.[2]

Somewhat surprisingly, however, it happened to be a pair of arch-rationalists, Leibniz and Kant themselves, who first opened the way for this development. At the close of the seventeenth century, Leibniz proposed a theory of *petits perceptions*—undetectable perceptions and feelings that reside in the hidden recesses of the mind, often without ever coming to consciousness.[3] Almost a century later, in 1798, Kant included in his *Anthropology* a brief discussion of the "obscure representations" *(dunkele Vorstellungen)* that remain just below the surface of consciousness. This was especially true, Kant observed, where feelings of a sexual nature were concerned.[4] It is clear from the context, however, that Kant was thinking less of repressed feelings than of socially disavowed ones.

From these tentative beginnings, the nineteenth century burst upon the intellectual scene with an agenda of revolutionary approaches to the darker regions of the human psyche. Schelling must be credited with having played a major role in the creation of this new climate. For it was his revision of Kant's and Fichte's transcendental idealism, as well as his philosophy of nature *(Naturphilosophie)* and philosophy of identity *(Identitätsphilosophie)*, that produced one of the first systematic theories of the unconscious. What, then, were the main lines of reasoning that led to this theory?

Early Speculations about the Unconscious

In his *System den transzendentalen Idealismus* (1800), Schelling transformed the Kantian idea of a "thing in itself" *(Ding an sich)* into that of a transcendental psychical agency. He did this, following Fichte, by abandoning the dualistic Kantian model of a noumenal "object" impinging upon a noumenal "subject," replacing these with the conception of a single, transcendental activity which produces both the subjective and the objective poles of experience. Admittedly, however, this allegedly unitary, generative activity does not appear in ordinary experience. Instead, the empirical consciousness finds itself confronted with an intractable disparity between the two poles of subjective and objective being, between thought and a seemingly external reality, and this disparity in turn engenders severe limitations to the subject's range of knowledge and power. Schelling sought to explain how these phenomenological limits could have come into being.

Now, in order for the primordial activity to be capable of achieving the consciousness of itself as unlimited, it is necessary first of all for it to be confronted with provisional limits and then to overcome these. Only in the experience of an infinite becoming, a perpetual going beyond and overcoming of limits, can the implicit infinitude of the generative activity be realized. Hence the original unity has to become a temporary duality in order ultimately to return to itself as a higher unity. Conversely, Schelling maintained, in a striking anticipation of Hegel, that the very fact of confronting limits, and experiencing them *as* limits, already entails their implicit overcoming.[5]

The idea behind this argument was as bold as it has been controversial. Without doubt, it was among the most hotly contested doctrines in the entire German idealist tradition. Basically, Schelling's claim was that the determinative boundary between consciousness and its enveloping background (including both the outer and inner worlds) defines the nature of those worlds just as much as it does the nature of consciousness itself. In other words, consciousness and its opposite are mutually implicating aspects of a single totality. Each aspect needs the other in order to be what it is, and the limitation that separates is no less a tie that binds together. Hence, what remains "beyond" or "beneath" consciousness is intimately interwoven with its nature; and conversely, the nature of consciousness pervades what lies "beyond" it.

The same idea can also be expressed in terms of function: Just as consciousness, through its cognitional and volitional activities, continually extends the limits of its domain, in the same way, what lies beyond consciousness is retroactively engaged in reshaping the contents of consciousness. According to Schelling, this mutual interpenetration of essences and functions is necessary, so that each aspect joins in constituting its own opposite as a mutually implicating component of a greater totality.

An example may help to clarify the point. Suppose that a person places himself in a situation that tests his mathematical skills, and finds that they are limited. Unable to grasp a certain theorem, he turns it over in his mind, wondering at the lawful character of what eludes his comprehension. This is a humbling experience, and yet it also contains in germ the source of an expanded capacity. For the ability he has to experience his ignorance and identify a specific lack within himself provides the context and the means to overcome those limits. If he were endowed with no mathematical potentials at all, he could not even recognize his own incompleteness. But the very fact that he can be aware of his personal finitude in this respect demonstrates that at least he does possess the endowment to know what he is missing. A lesser being could not even have had the experience of failing to understand the theorem in question. This experience of a failure, therefore, is a sign of his being able, in principle at least, to rectify it. It is a gauge, so to speak, of the interpenetration of his mind with the world of mathematics.

Exactly the same sort of correlation obtains, so Schelling claims, in countless other types of interaction between the subject and object of experience, especially those involving creativity and insight. In each case, closer scrutiny reveals that the differences between the mind and its objects are not absolute, but are qualified by relations of mutual dependency. What is within the range of consciousness and what is without it are two sides of the same coin, neither side being definable or even thinkable except in terms of the other. Thus, what lies on the surface of explicit awareness is indissolubly linked to what escapes cognizance, just as, by the same token, the subterranean depths of all the unknown in the world and in human nature are interfused with the known. Taken together, the synthesized unity of these various aspects constitutes a single, organic whole. And this whole is in fact nothing other than the greater "Self."

Such were the arguments that Schelling developed in the opening years of the nineteenth century, in which he pushed back the frontiers of the mind in its relations to a more encompassing system. This dialectically achieved expansion of the "Self," however, was purchased at the price of recognizing that a large part of its contents do—and in principle must—remain hidden from explicit consciousness. Schelling theorized that the generative source of both objective and subjective being cannot in itself possess the characteristic predicates of either—indeed, it really cannot have any determinate predicates at all. Like a pure, undifferentiated light which obscures all else in the heavens, this "eternally Unconscious" *(ewig Unbewußte)* transcends the specific nature of finite consciousness.[6] Thus Schelling's earliest, classic theory of the unconscious was born.

This theory can be criticized on the score of at least two problems, one apparent and the other real. The apparent problem is that Schelling's account does not seem to distinguish adequately between (a) what is "unconscious" in the sense of a logical principle or physical reality not yet present to rational thought, and (b) what is "unconscious" in the sense of a repressed psychical energy. There are many laws of physics and mathematics, for example, of which scientists today are "unconscious" (in sense *a*), though this does not mean that those laws are necessarily playing an "unconscious" role (in sense *b*) in the inner lives of human beings. This seeming conflation of terms, however, simply indicates Schelling's belief in an inherent connection. He did tend to treat these two types of "unconsciousness" analogously, because his organic view of nature and insistence on the continuity of existence prevented any sharp separation of mind from matter. Yet even without positing a sharp separation, he still did recognize their relative differences in degree of development. A primary goal of his philosophy of nature, in fact, was to show exactly how and why each stage of physical and organic evolution passed into the next. This topic, however, lies outside the bounds of the present study.

A more serious problem was Schelling's implicitly equating the unity of conscious and unconscious thought with a transcendental Unconscious, posited as the ultimate source of both. The former sort of "unconsciousness," as explained above, is that which parallels consciousness, presupposing the latter no less than being presupposed in turn by it. This is an unknown truth with the potential for becoming known, a darkness with the capacity for becoming light, just as knowledge and light can revert back again to their opposites. Yet at the root of both, Schelling postulated a transcendental Unconscious, which in principle would always continue to be unknown *(unbewußt)* on account of constituting the ground of knowledge itself. Herein lies the difficulty. For even if one were provisionally to grant Schelling's contention that the ground of knowledge must transcend knowledge, the question remains whether this "transcendence" need be of the same nature as the ignorance that envelops what is known on an empirical level. Is it not equally plausible to suppose that the transcending principle would resemble empirical consciousness more than it would empirical unconsciousness, knowledge more than ignorance, light more than darkness?

Furthermore, in holding the point of "indeterminacy" between subject and object to be the absolutely Unconscious, Schelling effectively removed that point from the polarity of oppositions which alone (according to his own principles) could explain the transition from that Unconscious to the finite structures of consciousness. To suggest, as Schelling did, that this Absolute had to enter the realm of finitude and opposition in order to become self-conscious, and thereby infinite for itself, is really to beg the question.[7] For why should the primordial Unconscious need to become self-conscious? One detects here an unresolved tension in Schelling's early thinking about the Absolute, a tension which much of his subsequent work was concerned to remove.

In any case, the identification of the Absolute with the Unconscious brought important consequences in its wake. It led to an emphasis on the intuitive, the aesthetic, and the affective as opposed to the logical, the discursive, and the analytical. What the latter must strive to realize through deliberate effort, Schelling contended, the former would be able to apprehend spontaneously. Hence emotion and imagination, instinct and blind desire, were seen as more immediate manifestations of the same powers and drives as the articulated processes of rational thought.

The presence of the psyche's unconscious faculties is characteristically revealed, according to Schelling, in the intuitive creations of the artistic imagination. By means of its symbolic representations, art (including mythology) is uniquely capable of bringing to light the hidden, preestablished harmony of the unconscious with the unconscious mind. Hence, the young Schelling elevated the artistic faculty to the pinnacle of human capacities. In one especially eloquent passage he wrote of art as the fulfillment of an "Odyssey of the spirit," wherein the mysterious unity long hidden in unconscious nature, like the meaning of an encoded text, finally uncovers its inner significance.[8]

In his *Naturphilosophie* and *Identitätsphilosophie,* also written around the turn of the century, Schelling continued to draw out the implications of his position for psychology, and in particular for the psychology of religion. Here he elaborated in detail his thesis that the essential nisus of the soul consists in the drive to bring its unconscious potencies to fulfillment in the form of human consciousness. This idea was to prove extremely fruitful for several generations of German thinkers. The "Schellingian school" of psychology developed his insights in a number of different directions, but it shared in common a commitment to his basic program.[9]

From the Unconscious to the Irrational

Closely connected to the above theory was the conviction that the unconscious contains a force of irrationality with the ability to resist, and at times even overturn, the conscious mind's drive toward clarity and reason. The doctrine of such an irrational power was to have tremendous repercussions, especially in Schelling's later philosophy.

This corollary theory is far from obvious, however, even assuming the validity of the former. For one may well ask whether the presumed existence of an unconscious region in the mind suffices by itself to establish the reality of any primitive, irrational urges lurking there. But clearly it does not suffice to establish this. The unconscious is not necessarily irrational, any more than the irrational is necessarily unconscious. Indeed, several metaphysical theories have been proposed which treat the unconscious as operative entirely on rational motives, even if these differ from those of the conscious mind.

One need only reflect, for example, on the Judeo-Christian idea of a divine *Providence,* or alternately on Hegel's notion of the "cunning of Reason," in order to realize that what is hidden or obscure to human consciousness does not have to be thought of as necessarily irrational. Perhaps Schelling's unconscious might be supposed to operate in similarly recondite, yet eminently rational, ways.

As a matter of fact, in his early period Schelling tended to conceive of the unconscious in precisely such a manner. His *System* of 1800 does, to be sure, occasionally qualify the unconscious as a "blind" power, but on the whole this "blindness" involves simple ignorance, rather than a positive opposition to reason.[10] Yet increasingly, as Schelling passed into his middle and later periods, he came to emphasize the presence of a primordially irrational power which serves as the "basis" or "ground" *(Grund)* of all existence. This irrational power was, moreover, to be closely identified with the unconscious. How did Schelling reach this position, and how did he proceed to justify it?

A central tenet of his philosophy was that rational thought must lead as far as it can go, up to the final point where it postulates that which transcends reason itself. Like Kant, Schelling maintained that it is reason's own critical self-examination which proceeds to the recognition of the faculty's inherent limits. Unlike Kant, he also held that there must be a going beyond these limits, whereby the mind directly encounters the nonrational. Nevertheless, even this enigmatic experience transcending thought can and must return from the far side of reason's limits in order to relate itself freely to the conceptual order. One of the purposes of Schelling's final system was to explain the possibility of this return from the incomprehensible back to comprehensibility.[11]

The above prescription may look perplexing initially; at the present undeveloped stage of our discussion it could scarcely be otherwise. A closer examination of Schelling's epistemology will be required in order to determine how well he succeeded in combining these divergent aims. In this introductory chapter, however, it is only possible to adumbrate the broad dimensions of the issue and touch upon some of the theoretical considerations that motivated his efforts.

One of Schelling's principal concerns throughout his life was to establish the possibility of human freedom in the face of God's all-encompassing law. This posed a difficult problem. Since God's law must be reasonable, and since the one, absolute Reason—for Schelling as for the other post-Kantians—could not be thwarted, rationalism seemed to threaten the possibility of individual, human freedom.[12] On the other hand, the concrete experience of freedom was not to be denied, nor was the sense that each person has of being able to oppose the dictates of reason or even to commit evil. Added to this was the obvious fact that much in the universe appears to be disorganized and contrary to the divine order. In an important essay, *Über das Wesen der menschlichen Freiheit* (1809), Schelling sought to account for these conflicting observations by positing a fundamental principle of chaos:

> After the eternal act of the divine self-revelation, everything in the world as we now see it is according to rule, order, and form. But still there always lies in the ground *(im Grunde)* that which is unruly *(das Regellose)*, as if it could someday break through again; and nowhere does it appear as if order and form were the original condition of things, but rather it seems as if an initial state of unruliness had been brought to

order. This is what constitutes the incomprehensible basis of reality in things . . . [13]

In the same essay, Schelling defined this original ground of reality as "the irrational principle" *(das irrationale Prinzip)*,[14] and he located the primary zone of its present activity in the most primitive centers of the human mind. Although he took this irrational principle to be the indispensable basis of individual freedom, he insisted that it must be subordinated and disciplined by reason in order to fulfill its ultimate purpose.

A year later, in his *Stuttgarter Privatvorlesungen* (1810), and again in his ambitious but unfinished study in cosmological history, *Die Weltalter* (1810–13), Schelling elaborated further on the psychological aspects of this irrational principle. It subsists, he maintained, in all sentient creatures as the unintelligent basis of the higher, conscious life. In its proper role as a subordinate power, the irrational principle is "relatively nonexistent" (i.e., in a condition of mere potentiality as opposed to actuality, in the Aristotelian senses of those terms). If, however, the irrational substrate should rebel against the controls of consciousness and seek to achieve an independent authority within the mind, the inevitable result is madness. Schelling drew the conclusion that a controlled potential for madness lurks within all souls, and especially in creative individuals:

> What is the spirit of the human being? Answer: a being, but one emergent out of nonbeing, that is, the understanding out of the unintelligent. What is, then, the basis of the human spirit, in that sense in which we take the word? Answer: the unintelligent. . . . The deepest essence of the human spirit therefore—n.b., *if* it is regarded in separation from the soul, and thus from God—is madness *(Wahnsinn)*. Madness therefore is not something that arises new, rather it merely emerges into view, when that which is properly nonexistent—i.e. the unintelligent—actualizes itself and seeks to become essence, being.
>
> The basis of the understanding itself is therefore madness . . . [15]

Decades later, in the "Historical-Critical Introduction" to his *Philosophie der Mythologie* (1845), Schelling made an explicit link between this chaotic principle and the foundation of religion. At the same time, he also offered a further argument to explain why the earliest religion must have been grounded solely in the unconscious. This argument hinges on the idea that the original religion had its source in the most basic stratum of the psyche. It could not have arisen, as subsequent religions could, out of the struggles of the conscious mind to comprehend and come to terms with previous stages in cultural history. Hence, the only conceivable starting point for the whole development lay in the mind's own primordial "substance," in the blind impulses of its subterranean nature. This, Schelling maintained, was the religion of the "primordial consciousness" *(Urbewußtsein)*.[16]

In order for this deduction to be plausible, one must already have accepted the notion that there was a definite "beginning point" in human history and that this beginning preceded the genesis of all deliberative, conscious thought. A second premise is that the structurally layered order of relations among the mind's constituent parts as they exist today corresponds to the order of progressive unfolding in the development of the human race—in other words, that whatever structures are presumed "lower" in an existing individual must have preceded those that are "higher" in the development of the species as a whole.

Neither one of these premises is obvious. The first is closely linked to the esoteric theory that time itself must have had a starting point—what he called a "beginningless beginning." Because this beginning of time could not itself have been part of the temporal continuum, Schelling located it in eternity.[17] The conception that the eternal beginnings of things must have constituted the enduring foundations of their nature pervades his entire system. By means of it he was able to argue that the original religion of primal humanity remains latently present in the deepest strata of modern religious experience.

The second, related premise derives from Schelling's doctrine of temporal/ontological parallelism, the principle that a living organism's essential nature (in particular including its consciousness) not merely descends from, but recapitulates the genealogy of its kind. If the macrocosm, consisting of the universe as a whole, has unfolded in a specific pattern of evolutionary development, he reasoned, then by the same token every natural organism—insofar as it, too, is a microcosm mirroring the totality—must pass through an identical, or a very similar, series of stages. This model of inherent progression had already enabled Schelling in his early *Naturphilosophie* to cast light on the organic interconnections of many natural phenomena.[18]

A critical analysis of both these premises will be necessary if one is to understand Schelling's later philosophy.

All these variously intertwined ideas about the irrational and the unconscious converged, in the *Philosophie der Mythologie,* on the interpretation of ancient cultures and religions. For example, in his treatment of the early Greeks, Schelling emphasized that the surface humanism, clarity, and worldliness of their civilization concealed a dark underside: namely, a wild emotionalism as reflected in their art, their myths, and their Mystery cults. The fact that these features left little imprint on the enduring works of Greek literature and philosophy—e.g., the fact that Homer never mentioned the Mysteries—proved nothing about the inner experiences of the people who lived in those times. More than likely, Schelling surmised, the Greeks simply repressed those elements of their collective experience that seemed to them too fantastic, bizarre, or socially unacceptable.[19] Scholars must always remain alert to the possibility of masked significances in mythical symbolism.

In addition to shedding light on the ambiguity of religious symbolism, Schelling also probed deeply into the subject of emotional ambivalence. He proposed a theory of opposed archetypal images, between which streams of hidden psychic energies perpetually flowed. The result, according to him, was that mythical figures often assumed a dual character. For example, Schelling found it extremely significant that Dionysus was simultaneously worshipped as the "wild god" and as the "mild god."[20] How, he asked, was such a radical dualism of roles to be understood? The predatory mammals in Dionysus's train, especially the felines, manifested the same sort of ambivalent symbolic value: On the one hand, the intelligence, gentleness, and almost human personalities of these animals were striking, yet their penchant for wanton cruelty and even occasional madness was also a frequent motif.[21] Schelling further noted that, because of the potentially shattering effect that this ambivalence can have on the mental balance, it is generally kept hidden away in the unconscious. This explains why Dionysus, especially in his chthonic form as Zagreus, was treated as such a dark and fearful power in the Mysteries.[22]

The recognition that mythical figures might sometimes be associated symbolically with their psychic opposites has proved extremely fruitful in subsequent scholarship. G. H. Schubert, for example, an early writer on psychological imagery who strongly influenced Freud, echoed Schelling's thought in his *Symbolik des Traumes* (1814). The same example of predatory mammals as representations of emotional ambivalence again appears.[23]

We shall return to a detailed examination of these and related issues in Part Three. In order to treat the subject effectively, however, it will first be necessary to examine (in Part Two) Schelling's epistemology and metaphysics, for it was there that he developed the principles which guided his theories about the unconscious. Critical questions need to be asked: What is the nature of the "irrational power" that allegedly constitutes the "ground" of human existence? Why is such a ground held to be necessary if individual freedom is to be possible? How does Schelling go about establishing the criteria of judgment in terms of which his theory of the irrational is to be evaluated? Are these criteria rationally justifiable, or are they, after all, themselves irrational? Further, what is the optimal relation, according to him, of the conscious intellect to the irrational elements that make up the realm of the unconscious? Ought consciousness to cede the place of priority to the limitless unconscious, as some thinkers have argued? Or ought the unconscious, rather, to defer to the rational powers of thinking? More generally, on the basis of what fundamental, underlying ontology of the mind can any of these issues be resolved?

– 4 –
Toward a New Ontology of Eternity, Temporality, and Freedom

Among the problems that Schelling faced in seeking to work out a systematic philosophy of mythology, by far the most difficult concerned the ontology of human and divine freedom in their respective relations to thought and temporality. Included in this set of issues were all the old questions concerning divine predestination as compared to simple prescience, the origins and cosmic purpose (if any) of evil, and the possibility of a genuinely free will. The familiar answers to these questions, however, no longer seemed viable. Schelling was deeply dissatisfied with the traditional metaphysics of time and eternity, which in his view either shipwrecked on the Scylla of static immutability or else fell headlong into the Charybdis of relativistic flux. In order to create the philosophical foundations for an adequate theory of mythology, therefore, he deemed it necessary first of all to work out a satisfactory account of the relations between permanence and change.

The need for an ontology of mutability. Schelling saw compelling reasons for positing a changeable nature in both God and human beings. One of these reasons stemmed from his conception of dialectic as a developmental method of thinking. An evolutionary worldview seemed already built into the very presuppositions of his method, and accordingly Schelling sought to take account of mutability in his interpretations of natural and cultural phenomena. This project necessitated, among other things, a new approach to logic, for in his view the old substance ontology reduced nature—and in particular human nature—to the status of a mere formula.

Further considerations along the same lines came from reflections on the meaning of freedom. The possibility of autonomy seemed to require that the individual spirit should be capable of altering previous decisions so as to take control of a personal destiny. Even God, presumably, would have to be free in this sense. Yet how was that thinkable, Schelling wondered, if the unfolding of history, including cosmic history, were determined by inflexible laws? A typical substance ontology such as that elaborated by the rationalist school—Descartes, Spinoza, Leibniz—was obliged to derive the qualities of things as well as their interrelations from a static conception of essence. Yet even the best efforts of Leibniz had been unable to restore the meaning of genuine freedom.[1]

The need for an ontology of permanence. On the other hand, there was the need to avoid the pitfalls of blind historicism and relativism. For Schelling, a philosophical system was the indispensable locus of truth. This meant that there must be some verifiable and stable structures in the universe, structures which philosophy had to discover. But how was this possible if the constituent parts were themselves supposed to be continually evolving? Or what if the premises of all theoretical reasoning rested on nothing more than arbitrary assumptions?[2] Schelling was convinced of the need to establish a clear and comprehensive system delineating the nature and order of first principles. Otherwise, a crude relativism would inevitably result.

These considerations seemed to lead back in the direction of the older, more familiar metaphysics concerning the need to posit eternal realities of some kind or other. For one thing, there was the problem of God's role as the author of time. It was a rather compelling argument that if God is the source of space, time, and even causality itself, he must in his essential nature be beyond them. For only in terms of certain fixed milestones and changeless criteria could the nature and meaning of time itself be determined. Therefore, Schelling affirmed that God in his divine self cannot enter into the developmental process.[3]

In opting to retain the conviction that a genuine ontology had to grapple with those eternal truths which transcend time, Schelling took upon himself a weighty theoretical dilemma. For how could the need for an enduring reality be plausibly reconciled with the equally compelling need for a developmental worldview? How could the flux of time be reconciled with eternity?

Dialectic: A Stable Law of Change

A partial answer to the above difficulties, to be sure, would be provided if one had the assurance that the world's evolutionary process is determined by absolute laws of logic. The laws themselves could then be seen as fixed and therefore ascertainable, even though the particular objects embraced by them would be in a state of flux. But while Schelling did in fact adopt this position, he still maintained that this idealist dialectic offered only a partial solution to the root problem. For if the very principles of change and of cosmic evolution are themselves immutable, wherein does the alleged freedom reside? The suggestion made by several of Schelling's idealist colleagues—viz., that "freedom" consists in being self-determined rather than other-determined—seemed to him but a portion of the truth. Self-determination alone, he argued, even if it exists, would still only be "formal freedom"; and although this is indeed a *sine qua non*, actual freedom requires much more.[4] Yet what else might philosophy invoke in order to make the theory of freedom more concrete and believable? Or what other principles are needed in order to make the theory more coherent?

All of these problems became especially acute in regard to God and his Creation. No less than Leibniz before him, Schelling was obsessed with the question of how God's freedom was possible. This issue, indeed, seemed of even greater moment than the related one of human freedom, for unless God were free, how could any of his creatures be? Yet God's freedom appeared *prima facie* more problematic than that of finite beings, inasmuch as the presumably infinite scope of his knowledge and wisdom made all the familiar notions of freedom—e.g., choosing among equipollent options or acting in accordance with the moral law—scarcely thinkable. Thus, Schelling perceived a pressing need to explain how God could be a free agent in his act of Creation, unlimited by the requirements of any merely rational system of eternal truths.

This general problem in religious philosophy also had immediate implications for the philosophy of mythology. For suppose it were true, as Schelling maintained, that previous world religions represented necessary dialectical phases along the way toward God's complete self-revelation. Suppose that the diverse forms of polytheism, etc., were the essential stages of a divine unfolding process which inevitably culminated in the highest form of monotheism. Where is the possibility of freedom to be found here? The whole dialectical structure we have just assumed for the sake of argument wears the *prima facie* appearance of being just another variant of dialectical determinism.[5] Had, then, the historical development of pagan myths, rituals, and symbols been necessitated by a bloodless series of logical categories? Were all the sufferings and horrors experienced by humanity in the long course of worldly time fated to happen? Had there never been an exception or any kind of release from this inflexible system? Was even the rise of Christianity itself the product of an *a priori* law?

Schelling thought the solution of these difficulties called for the formulation of a radically new ontology capable of satisfying a number of important requirements. Firstly, it would have to be grounded in an undetermined fiat of the divine will. Secondly, this new ontology would also have to explain the possibility of a correlative freedom for human beings. Thirdly, there would have to be provision made for the determining reality of a lawful, dialectical process. Fourthly, since freedom is inherently a volitional concept, this ontology would have to achieve all these various ends based on the fundamental principles of consciousness.

> There might well be others, too, who believe themselves incapable of combining the requirement of such a process in human consciousness with the divine Providence. In just the same way one also finds, in view of much else that is repulsive and somewhat shocking in the world of nature, that an excuse and justification are needed. Yet it should be noted that if the process productive of mythology is involuntary in its course, and if it appears even in its origin as in a certain sense inevitable (as the emergence of the human being out of God also does in a certain way—namely, when taken just naturally—appear inevitable), nonetheless the first beginning and occasion of this movement is only consciousness's own act, even if this act is to consciousness itself unfathomable *(unergründlich)* in its consequences. And so we come to the real beginning of the *theogonic* process, i.e., of that which produces mythology. In coming to this point we are placed at the beginning of a genuine philosophy of mythology.[6]

A "Groundless Activity" in Eternity

The initiatory "act" that sets off the whole theogonic process may, Schelling held, appear "groundless" or unfathomable *(unergründlich)* to consciousness, in that it follows from no law of dialectical necessity. The reason it can follow from no such law is that this "act" is by hypothesis what has brought the law into existence in the first place and at the same time has given it a field of application. In other words, the first "act" of a free consciousness is that which posits the transcendental framework of experience and worldly rationality itself.

Like Kant, Schelling believed that God and all finite free spirits must, as ends in themselves, have an eternal existence in the "Idea-world" *(Ideenwelt)*. He further theorized that it was consequent to a Primordial Fall out of the latter that the sense world came into being. Again like Kant,

Schelling supposed that God himself could not have created this sense world directly, with all its contradictions and imperfections, but instead must have created the noumenal realities alone. These noumenal realities, in turn, projected in their capacity as free spirits the representations of space and time, and all the natural beings within the world. Schelling explained:

> Each individual ego is—not, to be sure, the absolute Substance, for this hasty expression cannot count as correct. But rather, it is the unfathomable *(unergründlich)* act of each individual's egoity which simultaneously *(zugleich)* posits this world for each one—the world outside of the Idea.[7]

It might be asked, however, whether it is plausible to imagine that any consciousness which was still residing in the pure Idea-world would have, or ever could have, effected the transition to sensible nature. For does not the very concept of a "transition" already presuppose the principles of space, time, etc.? And would not such parameters be absent, *ex hypothesi,* from a pure Idea-world, consisting exclusively of ideal relationships? But in that case, how could one invoke the possibility of a "transition" *from* a realm where transitions are meaningless *to* a different mode of existence where transitions are feasible? Would this not amount to *petitio principii?* Schelling's ontology seems to court the danger of assuming those same features of phenomenal existence which it was intended to explain.

Still more problematic is the assumption that prior to all specific predicates there must have been some determining act which, as such, was itself indeterminate. The immediate question arises, how is it possible to conceive that something, which has in itself no determinations whatever, would take on the role of a causal agency? Is not the attribute of "being a cause" a form of determination, which therefore would contradict the presumptive indeterminacy? Moreover, even if one granted this possibility for the sake of argument, how would such an indeterminate act be *relatable* to the determinate things in the sense world if, as Spinoza already observed, all relation is a form of determination?

That these are difficult puzzles is undeniable, and Schelling would be the first to admit it. But he would not concede that they are therefore insoluble. The key to their resolution, according to him, lies in the recognition that objective necessity, even purely logical necessity, depends upon the prior assumption of an already subsisting, extralogical context. (This "context" could perhaps be remotely compared to the unformed character of an infant, whose undeveloped disposition and absence of any determinate characteristics would make it devoid of any specific personality. Yet it would have the original, impredicable foundation from which a real personality would later emerge.)

Provisionally granting the possibility of an extralogical context through and from which the principles of logic must derive, the next question is, of course, what if anything would establish the basic orientation of the context? Again, Schelling would urge that this context could not itself have been objectively necessitated, otherwise freedom would be impossible.[8] Hence, the nature of the "priority" attributable to the grounding context must be of another kind. The only conceivable alternative seemed in Schelling's mind to lie in the direction of a preconceptual antecedence that was somehow endowed with an inherent, developmental nisus toward the logical and conceptual. The possibility of explaining this nisus, in turn, demanded a temporal, or rather a proto-temporal standpoint, one that would contain at least in germ the values of "before" and "after."

Just how Schelling proposed to justify these novel ideas may appear perplexing. The notion of an extralogical dimension of being, so central to his philosophical project, has always been among the most controversial, and least understood, in the literature. Some scholars have been inclined to dismiss the whole subject as metaphysical mystification. Yet it is essential to come to terms with such problems if one is ever to appreciate Schelling's system of mythology. Chapter 7 will undertake a critical analysis of these and related issues as formulated by Schelling in his final system of philosophy. At present, however, the objective is limited to simply laying bare some major themes in the historical development of his thinking on these subjects.

In the *Weltalter* (1811–13), Schelling announced as one of his principal philosophical objectives the thorough investigation of time.[9] The same objective remained central to his project throughout the long decades devoted to the philosophy of mythology. This temporal orientation induced him to weave history into ontology and ontology into history in a manner that had never before been attempted. In order to do so, he sought to explain how a dialectical synthesis of time and eternity is thinkable.

It was not enough, in Schelling's view, to treat these two principles as merely coordinate concepts, as in the well-known Platonic epigram—"Time is the moving image of eternity."[10] This way of representing the interconnection, while correct insofar as it showed the dependency of time on the eternal, failed to bring out the converse side of the relationship: viz., the inherent tendency on the part of eternity to unfold itself as time.

The great fallacy of previous theories on this subject, according to Schelling, consisted in the assumption that the eternal must be a pure negation of time, and that therefore it must be "timeless." But from a "timeless" eternity there could never be a transition to actual time, nor any way of explaining the essential distinctions between past, present, and future. Therefore the true eternity must be proto-temporal,[11] i.e., it must include within itself the noetic structures which, though transcendent to phenomenal time, would yet be the foundation of it. Furthermore, there must be an "eternal past," an "eternal present," and an "eternal future" within eternity itself.[12] Only out of these essential structures of the eternally proto-temporal could the order of empirical time have ever come into being.

Based on this new conception of eternity, Schelling drew conclusions about the nature of human and divine freedom. Freedom cannot, he argued, consist in mere contingency, nor is the bare arbitrariness of choice equivalent to genuine autonomy. Such superficial conceptions of freedom result from the error of regarding phenomenal time and the empirical causes operative within it as things in themselves. The error becomes compounded when the absence of natural determination is equated with volitional independence. Yet neither determination by blind chance nor the illusion of undetermined "choice" is the same as real freedom of the will.[13] The latter must at least involve actual self-determination, but that can only occur on a level of being that transcends the phenomenal altogether—namely, in eternity. On this level of eternal proto-time, Schelling argued, an individual spirit creates its own inherent character, whether for good or evil, and this supratemporal "act" establishes from then on the predisposition to behave in certain ways.[14] The same principle, moreover, applies to God no less than to finite spirits.

Some Preliminary Questions and Criticisms

It is possible to raise substantial objections to Schelling's theory of a proto-temporal eternity. One may wonder in particular how any sort of "activity," whether free or unfree, is conceivable outside of phenomenal time. Does not every "act" involve a transition from one state of affairs to another, and does not the very concept of transition already presuppose changes within the empirical world? Many philosophers would argue that it makes no sense at all to talk of a being outside of time.

On the other hand, to reject Schelling's theory solely on the grounds that activity presupposes temporal change would be to beg the question. If the concept of an "act" can be defined broadly enough, then it might not necessarily be limited to situations involving changes of state. Aristotle, for example, distinguished between "activity" and "movement." Only the latter, with a motivating principle outside itself, would imply transitions of state. But "activity" in the full sense, according to Aristotle, contains its own purpose or end within itself, and as such it neither seeks nor requires any alteration of conditions.[15] This classical concept of activity was doubtless in the back of Schelling's mind when formulating his theory of the spirit's transcendental, premundane act.

Another theoretical precedent was Kant's well-known distinction between "intelligible causality" and "sensible causality."[16] Operating with the assumptions of Germany's post-Kantian philosophy, Schelling was convinced that human freedom could only exist, if at all, in a noumenal realm beyond the reaches of space and time. This conception of freedom was already present in his *System des transzendentalen Idealismus* (1800) and also in the *Freiheitsschrift* (1809).[17] In his final works, the same idea of autonomy recurs, as consisting in a purely spiritual act of creation, whether this was the primary Creation of God or the secondary creations of human beings.[18] Both these kinds of creative activity Schelling understood as being wholly transcendent to the ordinary processes of natural phenomena.

Modern readers may nevertheless be skeptical of these ideas. Even leaving aside the tangled issue of verifiability, there are problems concerning the internal coherency of Schelling's theory of freedom. In particular, one might object to his paradoxical conception of the agency responsible for determining an individual's character in eternity. This agency presumably would have to be either (a) the same as, or (b) different from, the individual self.

(a) On the former hypothesis, there apparently could be no other being with an independent basis by which, or out of which, the intelligible world of eternal characters could have come into being. Yet how can the *determinandum* be nondifferent from the *determinans*? How can a cause be identical to its effect? This model of volitional agency would appear to be on logically shaky terrain.

(b) On the latter hypothesis, taking the cause or causes of the eternal characters to be separate and distinct from the characters themselves, it is difficult to see where autonomy and self-determination would enter into the picture at all. For an effect has no independence over against its cause. Hence, the effect would owe its character entirely to the cause or causes that had shaped it, so that the possibility of autonomy would seem to be in doubt.

In view of these conflicting principles, Schelling's position might appear to be faced with the equally unacceptable alternatives of either affirming an implausible conception of volitional autonomy or else settling for a more plausible, but less palatable, conception of heteronomy.

These are serious criticisms, to be sure, but it would be premature at this stage to conclude that they irremediably undermine Schelling's theory, or that he had no good answers to them. He could have replied, in the first place, that the above puzzles are endemic to the notion of autonomy and did not by any means originate with his philosophy. To the extent that this philosophy was an attempt to deal with these difficulties, it was only to be expected that it would have to confront such challenging conundrums concerning agency, responsibility, and freedom.

In the second place, it should be noted that a large proportion of Schelling's efforts were dedicated to making the concept of a *causa sui,* or self-determined causality, comprehensible. This was a bold undertaking. The theories of previous thinkers had often foundered on just this issue. It was, in fact, because Schelling recognized the virtual impossibility of accounting for freedom on the basis of traditional ontology that he was led to propose a new ontology and to develop his theory of Potencies *(Potenzenlehre).*

– 5 –
Three Formative Influences on Schelling: Böhme, Baader, and Hegel

More than any other philosophers, Jakob Böhme, Franz von Baader, and Georg Wilhelm Friedrich Hegel exercised a profound influence on the final decades of Schelling's thought. The three of them presented problems and raised critical questions to which Schelling sought answers. This was especially true in those areas of metaphysics concerned with problems of mysticism versus rationalism, time in its relation to historicity, and the nature of God's creation. The following pages will examine some of these issues insofar as they impinge on the ontological foundations of Schelling's religious theories.

Böhme: The Influx of Mysticism

Jakob Böhme (1575–1624) combined in his thought a deep Lutheran piety with abstruse theosophical ideas derived from several mystical traditions. One probable influence was the Jewish Kabbala, from which he apparently borrowed the notion of a cosmic evolution via progressive precipitations of the Divine Unity.[1] Another major source was hermeticism, as transmitted through writings of Paracelsus, a tradition which used alchemical symbols and allegories in the search for occult knowledge of the Deity.[2]

Unlike most kabbalists and hermeticists, however, Böhme regarded the deliberately obscurantist character of much occult literature as being, not a sign of spiritual superiority, but a symptom of pride and pretension. As part of his campaign against learned humbug, Böhme sought to restore the language of religious discourse to a purer, more accessible form.[3] He disavowed any claims to a scientific knowledge of nature, leaving this to the natural philosophers. What he sought, rather, was "to write according to the spirit and meaning (of things), and not according to the outer appearances."[4] Refusing to allow his metaphysical insights to sink beneath the dead weight of philosophical or theological jargon, he combined plain, everyday terms into elaborate metaphorical images. Despite their deceptive simplicity, these images served to express innovative, often profound, ideas.

The result was an original and poetic, if also idiosyncratic and at times apparently naive, system of mystical Christian speculation. The mythic realism of Böhme's method lent his work a visionary quality which occasionally could give rise to striking religious and philosophical insights.

To what extent Böhme's ideas could have exercised a direct influence on Schelling's thought has been a disputed topic, because the latter was often rather negligent about crediting his sources. Harald Holz, in his study of Schelling, has claimed that Böhme's importance was in fact negligible.[5] Yet the many correspondences and congruities between Böhme's theosophical principles and Schelling's later *Potenzenlehre* are too striking to dismiss. Frederick O. Kile and Robert F. Brown have marshalled impressive evidence to show that Böhme's impact on Schelling was indeed considerable.[6] Werner Marx also concurs in this judgment, as do most other Schelling scholars.[7]

In what ways, then, did Böhme's thought lend itself to assimilation with Schelling's ideas? And which of the Silesian mystic's doctrines were to have the greatest effect on the Swabian philosopher's development?

Böhme's primary theological project was to attempt to think through the transition from the Godhead's illimitable oneness to its self-imposed aspect of limitation. This limitation was necessary, Böhme maintained, in order for the Godhead to be able to apprehend itself as God. The Deity needed to experience his epiphany in nature in order to become fully self-conscious. "In his depth (i.e., in the *Ungrund*)," Böhme wrote, "God himself does not know what he is. For he knows no beginning, and also nothing like himself, and also no end."[8]

In the finite creature, however, God found his own revelation reflected as in a mirror. Böhme reasoned that because God desired to reveal himself to himself, and because revelation required a sensible (i.e., experienceable) embodiment, therefore God had to become sensible in order to satisfy his need for self-revelation. Thus, the dialectical drive toward self-awareness within God's originally inchoate will was what gave rise to the spiritual as well as the material universe.

Böhme elaborated a rudimentary form of dialectic, consisting of positive and negative polar principles. These principles, he said, emerged out of the Godhead's originally undifferentiated nonbeing *(das Nichts)*, also described as the primordial Abyss, or *Ungrund,* and then developed through ordered stages of manifestation toward complete self-revelation. In a vivid, often dramatic, style, Böhme portrayed the development from

God's quiescent eternality toward his creation of, and active embodiment in, the physical universe:

> In the non-natural, uncreaturely Godhead *(Gottheit)* there is nothing more than a single will, which is also called the One God, who wants nothing else except to find and grasp himself, to go out of himself, and by means of this outgoing to bring himself into visibility *(Beschaulichkeit)*. This *Beschaulichkeit* is to be understood as comprising the threefold character of the Godhead, as well as the mirror of his wisdom and the eye by which he sees.[9]

One of Böhme's most daring conceptions was that God's emergence out of pure oneness into differentiated actuality required a confrontation with opposition. It was out of this creative struggle that the sensible universe issued forth. Böhme held that it was inevitable and even desirable that conflict and suffering should have arisen. These negative elements were the motivating spurs that stimulated the production of all the manifold phenomena of nature. Moreover, it was solely through the struggle with negativity that the minds of finite creatures could become aware of themselves, their world, and ultimately God:

> If the natural life had no opposition *(Widerwärtigkeit)*, and were without a goal, then it would never ask for its own ground, from which it came; then the hidden God would remain unknown to the natural life . . . there would be no sensation, nor will, nor activity, nor understanding . . . [10]
>
> If the hidden God, who is but a Single Essence and Will, had not of his own will gone forth out of himself, if he had not issued out of the eternal knowing . . . into a divisibility of the will *(Schiedlichkeit des Willens)*, and had not the same divisibility into comprehensibility *(Infaßlichkeit)* conducted to a natural and creaturely life, and were it not the case that this same divisibility in life consisted in strife—how else then could he have wanted the hidden will of God, who in himself is but One, to be revealed? How might a will within a Single Unity be a knowledge of himself *(Erkenntnis seiner selbst)*? [11]

In God's quest for self-manifestation, however, there lurked an implicit dilemma. On the one hand, his eternal purity and freedom consisted in the condition of the *Ungrund,* which transcended all limitations. On the other hand, the very absence of oppositions within this *Ungrund* meant that it was incapable of either manifesting or apprehending itself—it was, in fact, a "nothingness" *(ein Nichts)*. In order to manifest himself, then, it seemed that God had to negate his own essence and eternal freedom. But even assuming such an act were possible, how would it qualify as a true revelation? Would it not rather be a distortion of what it was seeking to make manifest? Consequently, as the will of the unmanifest Godhead sought to reveal itself in its primordial freedom—that is, as containing no other features or attributes than the mere will to become sensible—all that this will could possibly bring forth was the "quality of hunger, which it itself . . . [was]."[12] This will, by means of becoming desire, could find and feel itself, and in so doing it had taken an important step toward self-manifestation. Yet what this will-as-desire initially revealed was only an imperfect reflection of its inner essence. The spiritual hunger began as a "darkness," obscuring the purity of the *Ungrund.*

Yet how, one might ask, could the eternal "no-thing" experience longing in the first place? Evidently, this primal Abyss was only relatively, not absolutely, "unreal." Its "no-thingness" was somewhat analogous to the indeterminate Void in Buddhism, or to the *ain soph* in the Kabbala. Although undifferentiated, the Abyss possessed the inherent potentiality to become something actual and concrete; and the first manifestation of this potentiality, according to Böhme, was the experience of a "hunger" or, as he otherwise expressed it, a "longing."

Once having established the existence of a primal "darkness," Böhme next proceeded to elicit a series of developmental stages through which, as he maintained, the world-creative process necessarily had to pass. The impetus came from the contradictory character of a situation that could not endure, inasmuch as the "darkness" covering the will conflicted with the purpose that had first given rise to it. Consequently, a second will came into being, whose aim was to return again into the original condition of unity, while at the same time keeping hold of the darkness, which thus far had been the only product of God's will toward manifestation.[13] The result was a movement of drawing in upon itself, a contraction into a core of being. This core then became the ground *(Grund)* of all subsequent stages.

Now, because the introverted "longing" appeared to be incapable of ever finding satisfaction, it took the form of a fierce and chaotic "fire" that burned without giving light. This was the quality of divine wrath or bitterness *(Grimmigkeit),* which perpetually turned in upon itself and consumed its own substance.[14] This self-destructive activity caused tremendous pain and anguish within the divine nature, the first suffering that the universe had ever known. Böhme described this first principle as "the craving to draw into itself" *(die Sucht, in sich zu ziehen)*—a phrase strikingly similar to one that Schelling would later use.[15]

Yet despite the destructive aspect of the divine wrath, it was, according to Böhme, essential as the foundation for all subsequent developments. Without it, there could have been neither light nor life nor joy of any kind. Hence, the *Grimmigkeit* could in a sense be described as the generator of all things: as God the Father. When the first principle turned its primordial bitterness upon itself, there transpired a dramatic reversal. The anguished negation of free self-manifestation was itself negated: with a violent thunderclap, the harsh first principle overcame its own harshness, and a joyous light supervened.[16] This symbolized the emergence of harmony and order out of the original chaos. Triumphant was the second principle, that of divine love, which Böhme also characterized as God the Son.

Böhme taught that the interaction between these two principles of the divine wrath and love produced the creative impulse out of which the manifold universe evolved. Moreover, the two cooperative forces did not cease to be productive after the universe's creation, for both are necessary also in order to sustain it. All things consist of positive and negative aspects, the divine Yes and No.[17] In the present age, however, the first principle is no longer violent or chaotic, having been transmuted by the influence of the second principle. Indeed, Böhme's third major principle, identified with the Holy Spirit, is precisely the continual movement between the first two: it is the living breath of the cosmos.[18]

If one makes allowances for the fanciful quality of Böhme's modes of expression, one can see him wrestling with a classical philosophical problem: namely, how to understand the relationship between God's timeless unity and the multiplicity of the actual universe. Part of what made this problem so formidable was that it involved trying, in a way, to "conceive" of a connection between the conceivable and that which (by hypothesis) is beyond conception.

It is perhaps useful to recapitulate briefly Böhme's main problematic in more standard philosophical terminology. Since God was the inconceivable essence par excellence, it was a riddle to comprehend how or why this essence could have rendered itself understandable, even if only to a degree. The question was, why should the Deity not far rather remain inscrutable, forever wrapped in absolute mystery? The originality of Böhme's approach consisted in giving the problem a self-referential twist—in the claim that God would have no knowledge of himself *(Erkenntnis seiner selber)* if he did not reveal himself to himself.[19] Inasmuch as revelation consists in a kind of experience, it must require a structural subject/object polarity. Hence, it would follow that God's self-revelation simultaneously implied the existence of a creation and creatures to whom, and through whom, the revelation would take place.

Böhme's speculations led him to the idea that the first schism within the will of God had to materialize in the form of a concrete self-alienation.

He argued (in effect) that there must be a transition between (1) the potential polarity involved in positing an unmanifest nonbeing's need to become manifest to itself, and (2) the coming-into-existence of a being that was manifest, and yet also contrary to itself. The unmanifest Godhead was prior to all existence and as such absolutely homogeneous; and yet—this was the first paradox—it included an inherent tendency to differentiate itself into contraries. Thus the undifferentiated unity passed into the self-differentiating unity. The latter, like the Logos of Heraclitus, contained *in posse* the germs of a balance of opposites, whose hypothetical contrariety was of such a kind—and this was the second paradox—that their transition into concrete actuality was necessary. In this way, the hidden dialectic of God issued forth into the manifest dialectic of nature, and with that, the sensible universe was created.

One can appreciate how repugnant these ingenious but unorthodox reflections must have been to the church authorities![20] But the same features that outraged many of his contemporaries were qualities that ensured his continuing appeal for posterity. Although Böhme's manner of reasoning was far from rigorous, yet viewed as an attempt to account for the emergence of multiplicity out of unity, and existence out of possibility, his thought is richly suggestive.

Schelling was sympathetic to Böhme's conception of a transition from an undifferentiated, eternal "no-thing" to an active, inwardly conflictual "something" (a transition Schelling would later characterize as that between the pure *Daß* and the inverted First Potency). He also praised Böhme's attempts to account for the progressive evolution of things out of God as a real occurrence, which, being the product of an absolute need within the Deity himself, was at the same time the consummated "birth of God" *(Geburt Gottes)*.[21] The theory of three distinct "wills" within God's nature—wrath, love, and the unifying movement between them—bears remarkable affinities to Schelling's doctrine of three Potencies (as will be seen in Part Two). However, he strongly criticized Böhme for his tendencies to mistake visionary images for clear concepts, to treat spiritual principles as if they were substantial entities, and to substitute intuitive leaps for rational arguments. The unscientific and often mythical manner in which he expressed his insights rendered them vague and confused, hence unacceptable for inclusion in a coherent philosophical system.[22]

Recently, there has been a growing appreciation of Böhme's importance in the history of philosophy. His emphasis on the primary of the will led him to sketch out the principles for an innovative metaphysics, an alternative to the mechanistic determinism that became dominant in Europe for over two centuries. By focusing on the experience of lack, need, striving, and conflict as fundamental dimensions of both human life and the divine life, he paved the way for modern philosophies of the will. One scholar, John Joseph Stoudt, has for this reason called Böhme "the first significant voluntarist" in Western thought.[23]

Notable also were his efforts to work out a theogony which was simultaneously a cosmogony—an equivalence based on the principle of the close interrelationship between God's self-consciousness and his self-revelation. This principle has since played a pivotal (and controversial) role in modern religious thought. Böhme's thesis that God's coming to self-consciousness was a genetic process led to a new model for revelation, one involving the mediation of successive creations through premundane as well as worldly time. Jürgen Habermas was scarcely exaggerating when he credited Böhme with having been the first to attempt thinking through the historicity of the Absolute.[24]

To sum up, Böhme's elaboration of a theosophy based on the interactions of divine wrath, love, and movement lacked rigor and consistency. His writing had an ecstatic, visionary style. It is evident that he conceived of his divine principles not as objective laws but as the supernatural fusion of psychological and alchemical properties. Their nature was, to him, dynamically volitional rather than formally logical. Yet no doubt it was partly for these very reasons that Böhme's principles did much to inspire Schelling, who thoroughly revised them and sought to incorporate some of their chief insights into his final system. In doing so, Schelling had to wrestle with many of the same ontological difficulties and paradoxes that Böhme had raised. There is no question that Böhme's thought had a very significant impact on the development of Schelling's problematic, particularly concerning the nature of God's inmost being in relation to the external universe.

Baader: Through Dialectic and Mysticism Back to Orthodox Christianity

The thought of Franz von Baader (1765–1841) bears many points of striking similarity to Schelling's. As a holistic thinker and dialectician of considerable skill, Baader for many years enjoyed Schelling's and Hegel's respect.[25] Both appreciated Baader's efforts to synthesize Christian theology with a comprehensive system of science and philosophy.

Trained as a physician and also as a mining engineer, the devout Roman Catholic directed his attention to establishing the theoretical foundations for such a synthesis. Baader realized that this aim could never be accomplished so long as religion continued to ignore modern science, while science, for its part, gingerly sidestepped the implications of its discoveries for religion. Active collaboration between Schelling and Baader began in 1806, when both were living in Munich. Thomas O'Meara notes that, of all Catholic thinkers affected by Schelling's ideas, only Baader also had in turn a decisive impact upon him.[26]

In order to understand the reasons for, and the consequences of, Baader's singular influence on Schelling, it is helpful to compare their respective styles of dialectic. Baader's worldview emphasized the dynamic interplay between the unity and multiplicity inherent in all things. He developed an organic model of reality and forcefully opposed the growing tide of mechanism in physics and philosophy. All things, to Baader, are fundamentally alive, and life always involves a constant movement of exchange between the variety of externally directed functions and the synthesizing activity within. In a passage remarkably reminiscent of Schelling and Hegel, Baader wrote:

> Every living thing is a one-in-many *(Vieleins)*, consisting of the double drive . . . on the one hand, to sublate *(aufheben)* the multiplicity of its powers and qualities, etc., into itself as unity, and on the other hand to sublate itself as unity again in them, so as to maintain itself in the middle of both.[27]

Despite these similarities in his argumentative style, however, the central principle of Baader's dialectic diverged significantly from both Schelling's and Hegel's. While he shared their conviction that a single, all-pervasive identity must underlie the world's differentiation, Baader was concerned lest the postulation of this unity might obscure, in the minds of some people, the absolute distinction between God and the finite creature. There was no idea more harmful, in Baader's judgment, than to suppose that the phenomenal world has proceeded by a sort of "emanation" or evolutionary "effulgence" out of God's eternal nature, as if God and creature were ultimately of one essence *(einwesig)*.[28] This theory of a single essence was the root error of pantheism.

Instead, Baader proposed that the stuff out of which God created nature was and is external to himself. This outward aspect of God is, as it were, his divine "glory," a kind of pleroma consisting of the interwoven network of all his potencies and qualities. God's "outer being," therefore, supplies the dialectical moment of multiplicity, which in turn has been transmitted to the creatures, whereas the moment of unity remains forever ensconced in God's essence alone. Baader drew what seemed to him the inescapable conclusion:

> Now since the creature proceeded immediately out of this multiplicity as a one-in-many, and since each of the creative principles was peculiarly active thereby, it is understandable that this peculiar mutability had to remain also in those transmitted principles that were constitutive of the creature. Further, since the creature was able neither to ward off this inner multiplicity [i.e., of the principles], nor to bring them to a unity for itself, we can see that it became the creature's duty to win this unity by means of a turning back and return into the one-and-only unity (Logos).[29]

It is clear from this passage and others like it that Baader rejected the principle of the post-Kantian idealists concerning the ultimate identity of the finite and the infinite. Rather than viewing the unity of the Logos as continuous with the identity of each phenomenal being, Baader conceived of the divine unity as standing essentially apart from the multiplicity of the created world. And yet, insofar as the unity is absolutely necessary for the continued existence of each and every thing, it constitutes the eternal axis on which the creature depends. Baader invoked scriptural authority to prove that the proper functioning and fulfillment of each finite being requires its total submission to the will of God. This is particularly true for humanity, the preeminent crown, but also the potential Achilles heel, of all nature.

Baader's method of thought may perhaps be most usefully characterized, in contrast to the approaches of Schelling and Hegel, as a "dialectic of cooperation" *(Kooperationsdialektik)*. What this term (coined by the present author) seeks to bring out is Baader's sense that the ethical as well as metaphysical ideal consists in a harmonious interaction between essentially different natures. Only if this difference is accepted, and the fundamental Otherness of God is acknowledged, can the true dynamic of the dialectical process emerge.

The goal of religious faith, for Baader, is to turn oneself into an instrument *(Werkzeug)* of the Deity.[30] The individual can aspire, in his capacity as such an instrument, to represent *(stellvertreten),* but never to assume authority over, the providential activities of God. Here one sees clearly how Baader treated the moment of dialectical unity as separate from, and wholly beyond, the moment of multiplicity. God's Logos, in other words, utterly transcends nature, and to forget this is to fall back either into pantheism, or worse, into naturalism.

Despite these significant differences in the treatment of dialectic, however, the similarities between Schelling's and Baader's general methods and goals were sufficiently great to stimulate for many years an active exchange of ideas. Two features of Baader's theology were of particular importance: his emphasis on mysticism and his theory of radical evil. These themes as developed by Baader helped to set the framework and define the problematic for Schelling's final philosophies of mythology and revelation.

Emphasis on Mysticism

Baader's entire theological approach was steeped in the ideas of late medieval and Renaissance Christian mystics: people such as Tauler, Meister Eckhart, Paracelsus, Böhme, and Saint-Martin. Like the alchemists of old, Baader was convinced that the divine presence permeates and inhabits all material nature, which should therefore be viewed in its entirety as the holy sacrament of God:

> In this way, the human being becomes aware that the external is, after all, by no means such a small and insignificant thing (in which case it would be capable neither of the danger stemming from misuse nor of the blessing coming from good use), as both the spiritualists and materialists suppose. The latter, being alike ignorant of the secret of matter, fail to recognize the hidden, immortal power that lies enclosed as the deepest mystery within the outer body, and without whose disclosure the paradisiacal human misses his essence and hence is incapable of receiving revelation.[31]

To Baader's mind, it was Jakob Böhme who, more than any other European thinker, had opened the way for the disclosure of the divine truth concealed within nature. Baader devoted much of his work to the clarification and explanation of the theosophist's cryptic texts. Even today, Baader is generally regarded as the foremost interpreter of Böhme. On this subject, his writings have the status of a definitive source.

This enthusiasm for Böhme transmitted itself to Schelling. It is more than likely, though not quite certain, that Baader was the one who pointed the way to Böhme and encouraged Schelling's decisive turn to Christian mysticism.[32] The period of the two men's collaboration in Munich brought about deep intellectual changes in Schelling. By the time he published his essay *Über das Wesen der menschlichen Freiheit* (1809), his language and methodology were already heavily tinged by characteristically Böhmean categories. Much of this was probably due to Baader's influence.

Yet Schelling's appropriation of Böhme's ideas went even farther in some respects than Baader himself thought wise. Schelling took much more seriously than Baader the paradoxical teaching (especially prominent in Böhme's *Morgenröte*) that God could not have been self-conscious prior to his creation of the world; hence, that the Creation was an essential stage in God's coming to consciousness, etc. To Baader, all such speculations amounted to heresy.

Sin as a positive perversion

Baader had considerable impact on Schelling with respect to the doctrine of evil and its relation to the underlying world order. Prior to knowing Baader, Schelling had been inclined to treat the natural world as an incompletely developed, but otherwise intrinsically good, manifestation of God's perfection. To Baader, however, this theory dangerously misrepresented the fallen condition of the present state of nature, which in no way accorded with the purposes of God. Evil, he insisted, had never been included in God's original plan: not even a provisional "evil," as proposed by the foolish doctrine of *felix culpa* (the fortunate fault).[33]

It was a central proposition of Baader's—indeed, this was his *idée fixe*—that human nature is utterly fallen and that the entire natural world has been spoiled as well. In consequence of this cataclysmic rift, so Baader argued, the current relationship between God and humankind is an abnormal one.[34] Idealistic thinkers who minimized the extent of this rift did so at the cost of obscuring the radical transcendence and perfection of the Deity. Baader wrote:

> It is well known that those who ignore evil in the human being, as in nature, take the lack of the revealed glory in both for nothing more than ... a still innocent condition of childhood. But if it is true that a treasure already lies in the earth (matter), yet there also lurks a poison in it.[35]

Schelling's view of this subject, by the time of his move to Munich in 1806, had moved significantly closer to that of his colleague. He praised Baader for his concrete conception of evil as a "positive perversion or inversion of the principles," analogous to the condition of disease.[36] In both cases, Schelling now agreed, the underlying principle is that good moral character, like good health, consists in an organically functioning system, such that each part would perform its own special service to, and in turn receive its nourishment from, the whole. Perversion, however, results when one of the vital forces throws off its proper role of subordination to the higher order and seeks to become an end in itself. Disregarding the complex, delicately balanced array of interacting principles, the perverted force strives to take for itself a disproportionate share of the available resources and power. In so doing, however, it undermines the environing order that has made its own existence possible.

In his *Freiheitsschrift*, Schelling explained this inversion of organic relations as an "elevating of the ground *(Grund)* above the cause *(Ursache)*" of existence.[37] The precise meanings assigned to the terms were Schelling's own, but the language and general conception were heavily tinged with traces of Baader. The same concept of a radical disruption of an organic order, and even the same linguistic nuances concerning "ground," "cause," "inversion," and so on, continued late into Schelling's final philosophies of mythology and revelation.

Nevertheless, there were profound differences between the two thinkers. Schelling continued to search for a dialectical reconciliation of God's infinitude with the apparent rupture of his divine plan. To urge that free human actions were the sole causes of this rupture did not seem adequate to Schelling, since God presumably must have foreseen their misdeeds as well as the consequences of them—and yet he had willed this specific universe into existence. Why? For Schelling, this stubborn fact was a powerful argument in favor of the *felix culpa*. Thus, whereas Baader bemoaned the "poison of life," Schelling saw it as being (with qualifications) dialectically necessary.[38]

Baader, on the other hand, could not accept as being in any sense necessary this present brute mode of existence in a corruptible matter, in a misshapen nature. Baader dreamed of what might have been, if only Adam and Eve had not made their fatal mistake. The morose theologian emphasized the diametrical opposition between existence in this present, fallen world and existence as it ought to have been. To him Schelling's (as well as Hegel's) failure to see, or to take seriously enough, this breakdown in the world order was the reason why their thought constantly verged on the edges of pantheism. Unless the current situation were posited as abnormal, reasoned Baader, God would have to be considered at least co-responsible, if not totally responsible, for the evil and depravity of this world. And once theology has gone that far, the next spurious conclusion would be to suppose that God *had* to redeem the world in order to actualize his own perfection.

Another significant point of difference between Baader and Schelling concerned the question of the Deity's relation to the changes and developments in the phenomenal universe. Does God participate in all these temporal transformations, or does he not? If he does not, then arguably, like Aristotle's God, he would not even be aware of them (since awareness is a kind of participation, and subject to change). On the other hand, if he does participate in change, his eternal perfection would seem to be undermined. Schelling took this dilemma seriously, contending that God must in one sense share the same developmental process as the phenomenal world, even though in another sense he must also be beyond it. Having suggested this idea, of course, it was the philosopher's responsibility to show how such diverse aspects could even in principle be joined together.[39]

No such paradoxical subtleties were necessary, in Baader's opinion. He argued strongly against the notion that God is part of the world process, and he denied that God could be subject to any development at all. The perfection of the Deity should not be diluted, he thought, with the vicissitudes of the moment. This applied *a fortiori* to the relation between the Christian faith and the pagan idolatries.

In a short sketch, "Mein Cursus philosophicus in München auf der Ludwigs-Universität," Baader described with biting sarcasm his attendance at Schelling's lecture series on the philosophies of mythology and revelation. One interpretation of Christian doctrine to which Baader took particular exception was Schelling's theory of the Son as actualizing himself in and through world history. This doctrine, Baader objected, would be tantamount to the Arian heresy, denying the divinity of Christ.[40]

As for other religions, Baader vigorously disputed the idea that the history of world mythologies, with their strange practices and beliefs, could have played any role in God's own theogony: "Schelling gives us to understand that all these will-'o-the-wisps, gathered together over the broad swamp of mythology, were necessary in order to bring into the world the light of the world, i.e., Christ."[41] This supposition Baader thought would mean that the Christian faith must be dependent on other religions.

As Schelling was well aware, one of the main reasons Baader and others so bitterly opposed his ideas was for fear of admitting any alteration whatever in the divine nature.[42] By taking the risk of proposing this thesis, Schelling made his own problematic far more difficult: Now it was indeed incumbent on him to demonstrate how the "swamp of mythology" (in Baader's words) had somehow played a role in bringing about the final emergence of the "light of the world." Schelling also needed to explain why and how human ignorance, error, and relative evil were essential to the world process. Yet at the same time, he was determined to avoid falling into the trap of supposing that God himself was co-responsible for the existence of evil. How was philosophy to accomplish this balancing act?

Schelling faced a further delicate task in seeking to harmonize the developmental perspective fundamental to his approach with the traditional teleological requirement that God's guiding spirit must in some sense "precede" the entire process. Whereas Baader's God could avoid responsibility for the present abnormal course of the universe, Schelling sought to prove that God must have planned it, and yet that he could not have been the direct cause of the intrusion of evil. But if God, in his infinite fullness, really did precede and plan the creation, then in what sense was his creative activity free? Was he bound by an inflexible logic to create what he himself wished to avoid? How else could one explain the manifest imperfections of the present world order? And how could any room be left for the freedom of finite agents?

Much of Schelling's later theoretical work would be dedicated to the solution of these kinds of issues. For Baader, by contrast, they were merely pseudoproblems arising from the confusion of Creator and creature.

Given the divergencies between Schelling's and Baader's philosophical orientations, it was perhaps inevitable that their collaboration would come to an end. Around 1820, when Schelling moved to Erlangen, the relationship with Baader was already showing signs of severe strain. The patience of each wore thin as the implicit differences that had always divided them increasingly became sources of friction. Baader found Schelling's ideas too unorthodox, too heretical. Schelling, for his part, considered Baader narrow-minded and bigoted. The final break came in 1824, when Baader was said to have given some fiery sermons condemning "the Godlessness of all recent philosophy." Schelling, acting on hearsay reports of the indirect slur, promptly ended the relationship.[43]

Although the friendship between the two men ended badly, their intellectual influence on each other endured. The issues raised and criticisms made by Baader were provocative in their own time and remain pertinent today. They serve to point up important tensions in Schelling's religious thought—concerning the problem of evil, the conception of Deity, and the relation of freedom to history. In his efforts to formulate a new ontology that would emphasize the temporal and immanent dimensions of God's existence, Schelling ran afoul of the long-standing tradition insisting on the Supreme Being's eternity and transcendence. Yet, as noted at various points in the course of this discussion, Schelling also sought to accommodate the transcendent aspect as well. His God was to be "the transcendent made immanent," hence neither the one nor the other by itself.[44] The vociferous objections of Baader and other religious thinkers gave testimony to the novelty and daring of Schelling's enterprise.

Hegel: A Conceptual Mediation of Time and Eternity

We have already had occasion in chapter 2 to discuss Hegel's interpretation of religion in connection with questions concerning the nature of religious allegory and symbolism. The following pages will concern themselves with an associated set of issues—namely, the interrelationships between time and eternity insofar as these are embraced together within dialectic. Our goal will be to see in outline how Schelling's and Hegel's philosophical presuppositions concerning the nature of dialectical development—presuppositions on which they partly concurred and partly diverged—affected their respective approaches to religious phenomena. If one assumes that the divine order is eternal, and also grants the obvious point that human religions represent finite episodes within historical time, it is evident that one's view about the relationship between worldly time and the eternal order must be significant. If one further understands dialectic as a process of rehearsing, in thought, the internal dynamics of those ordered, temporal-*cum*-eternal relationships, it follows that the interpretation of dialectic must have important implications for the nature of religion as well.

Hegel's understanding of development and temporality was in many ways close to Schelling's. Like his colleague and former friend, Hegel saw religious truth as consisting in the gradual unfolding of God in the processes of nature and history. Also like Schelling, Hegel sought a philosophical principle that would render comprehensible the puzzle of the divinity's eternal aspect vis-à-vis the historical religions. But for Hegel, unlike Schelling, the only way to make thinkable this eternal aspect was to approach it as a "concept" *(Begriff)*.

Hegel's approach tended to be cognitively oriented and was aimed primarily at apprehending universals. His thought proceeded by systematically examining the meaning of each hypothesis, perspective, or worldview in search of its logical implications. Even when treating the noncognitive areas of human life, including emotional, aesthetic, or religious experiences, Hegel insisted that the inherent purpose of philosophy must be to render these in terms of their conceptual determinants.[45] In support of this approach, however, he undertook to broaden and deepen the traditional understanding of what a "concept" is. This process of redefinition had ramifications for ontology as well as for epistemology, because it involved importing "conceptual" aspects into the very core of being itself.

Compared to Hegel's orientation, Schelling's was decidedly more voluntaristic. A characteristic feature of his ontology was the conviction that the will is the most basic constituent of all reality—that in fact nothing can exist in the absence of will. From this it followed that the ultimate substance of things could not be discovered by means of logical deduction alone. Schelling maintained that the nature of every finite entity consists, at least on a rudimentary level, in its being a product of the will. "Willing is primordial being" *(Wollen ist Ursein)*, he wrote in his ground-breaking *Freiheitsschrift* (1809).[46] By placing volition at the center of ontology, Schelling emphasized the distinction between what is thinkable and what is existent, between what is logically possible and what is empirically actual. Without denying the validity of universal laws of reason, Schelling sought to do greater justice than Hegel to the roles of contingency, particularity, and the free acts of individuals.[47]

For Hegel, however, it would be inherently self-defeating to attempt any explanation of the world that does not rest squarely on logic. Although the foundations of logic must involve principles which would appear on a preliminary level as presuppositions, this does not imply, in Hegel's judgment, that logic is groundless, but rather that the system as a whole must eventually turn back around to justify its own premises. The notion of a recursive process of self-justification, however, involved paradoxes that Schelling could never accept. A key point of difference here was that, whereas Schelling thought in a linear mode, Hegel reasoned in terms of conceptual circles. Much of Schelling's work in the final decades of his life was concerned with criticizing Hegel's method of reasoning and trying to find viable alternatives.

Lying at the root of the differences between Hegel's and Schelling's philosophical systems is a basic divergence in their ways of understanding "dialectic" as a method of thinking. This divergence in styles is perhaps best characterized as that between a "dialectic of sublation" *(Aufhebungsdialektik)* and a "dialectic of production" *(Erzeugungsdialektik)*. These names (which are the present writer's invention) refer to technical terms, *aufheben* and *erzeugen,* as characteristically employed by each philosopher. The purpose of the distinction is to bring out subtle, at times scarcely perceptible, yet always significant, disparities in the two thinkers' procedures. Let us briefly look at each in turn.

Aufhebungsdialektik[48]

Hegelian dialectic typically operates by subjecting each concept to a series of "thought-experiments" or tests for internal coherency. In the course of these tests, the concept's manifest purport becomes "sublated" *(aufgeho-*

ben)—that is to say, the surface significance, which gives rise to incoherencies, is cancelled, while at the same time the deeper kernel of truth is retained. This double activity of *Aufhebung* is essential to Hegel's dialectic. The discovery of logical antinomies is never a final result, but one uses the errors themselves as stepping-stones along the way toward a more complete and adequate comprehension.

For Hegel, moreover, the series of successive derivations is not intended to give rise to altogether *new* principles that would or could have been absent previously. Rather, the idea is that the subsequent phases must have been already present, implicitly, in the foregoing ones; and that their "deduction" is therefore just a matter of making logically explicit the thought-determinations that were always there, though in an undeveloped and inadequate form.[49]

Erzeugungsdialektik[50]

Schellingian dialectic, by contrast, seeks to infuse the process of reasoning with a strong volitional component, so as to be capable of recovering the willing that allegedly precedes rational thought itself. Proceeding from this perspective in structured stages, the thinker must then elucidate how this willing guides the development of determinate being. The emphasis on volition is directly coupled with a call for experience; for willing and experiencing alone can *produce* a truth that goes beyond the abstract demonstrations of logic.

Schelling's treatment of dialectic obtains its successive forms not as though implicitly contained in the foregoing ones, but rather as produced or reproduced *(erzeugt)* by a kind of procreative causality which is supposed to reenact the processes by which the outer universe itself has evolved. The proper aim of philosophy is to find the path of conative (re)production *(Erzeugung)* by which the universal forms of volition sequentially emerge in poses of mutual reinforcement or conflict. Furthermore, inasmuch as this "reenactment" depends upon causal influences as well as logical inferences, any conclusions that it yields must remain incomplete until they can be exemplified in direct historical experience.

Because the truth, for Schelling, emerges in this process of (re)production, subsequent phases in the dialectic can supplement and perhaps subordinate, but by no means cancel or reconstitute (as for Hegel), what the previous phases have revealed. Each succeeding development is conceived as bringing something more than its predecessors have done into the dialectic chain, a "something more" which originates precisely in the volitional dimension of a procreative will. It is not just a question of finding more adequate expressions for the same inherent content. At issue, rather, is the systematic genesis of new thought-determinations emerging out of the old. The principle of *Aufhebung* has here been supplanted by that of *Erzeugung*.[51]

Especially significant is a passage in the *Stuttgarter Privatvorlesungen* (1810) where Schelling attacks the Hegelian method of effecting transitions by means of *Aufhebungen:*

> This transition from Identity into Difference has very often been regarded as a sublation *(Aufheben)* of the Identity. This is not the case, however, as I shall presently show. It is far more a doubling of the essence, that is, an augmentation of the unity. . . . Neither [i.e., of the reduplicated principles] should be cancelled out *(vertilgt)*.[52]

Schelling's notion of a "doubling" *(Doublierung)* of the essence—a clear instance of his *Erzeugungsdialektik* at work—led to the conception of a generative order which must be ontologically prior even to dialectical logic itself. The successive (re)production of Schellingian principles, unlike the successive sublation of the Hegelian ones, always presupposes a context or medium of the progression, within which the principles, so to speak, *occur*. Thus, whereas the logic of Hegel's dialectic turns its activity in upon itself so as to reconstitute continually its own presuppositions, that of Schelling remains enveloped within a preconceptual, existential framework which no logic can in principle establish or modify. For this reason, the dialectic of (re)production *(Erzeugung)* necessarily disclaims the ideal of a logically autonomous and self-conditioned totality, as Hegel's dialectic of sublation *(Aufhebung)* aspires to be.

The divergences between Hegel's dialectic of sublation and Schelling's dialectic of (re)production culminate in their respective interpretations of the significance of "concepts." For Hegel, the essence of reality—what he called sometimes "the concept" *(Begriff)* and at other times "the concrete universal" *(das konkrete Allgemeine)*—is an organic unity of form and content. He conceived of this unity in such a way that formal properties defining the nature of a true essence are inseparable from the content, just as, by the same token, the content is inseparable from the form. In other words, Hegel tried to show that the ideal nature of a thing (its essence or "form") and its concrete embodiment (its makeup or specific "content") are so interdependent as to be virtually identical. Thus the "thought" of a thing and its "reality" are not truly different.

This was a principal axis of Hegel's absolute idealist philosophy. He rejected the still influential Aristotelian theory, which conceived of a thing's *essence*, or "intelligible form," as needing a separable "material substrate" in which to inhere. Hegel rejected as well the notion that an identical "form" could be imposed upon different instances of "matter." On Hegel's account, the familiar old examples of universals—e.g., "man," "house," and "animal"—no longer should count as such. These he considered merely abstract class names. The genuine universal, on the other hand, he regarded as being itself an "individual" in the truest sense, while it is yet at the same time a systematic whole.[53]

One example of a concrete universal, frequently used by Hegel, would be a specific national identity. The French nation, for example, consists of a cultural unity, linked by a common language, history, and artistic heritage, which pervades every aspect of its people's lives. "Being French" is clearly a universal, because it involves a set of characteristic qualities shared in common by a broad range of particular persons. (Up to this point, even the traditional Aristotelian conception of universality would concur.) But for Hegel, the French national identity is more than an abstract class concept; it is also itself a concrete individual. Thus, *France,* acting as a totality, has a unique life of its own, and it can perform actions and engage in relations with others in a manner distinct from the actions or relations of any of its citizens, including its government officials. (This, incidentally, is why the French nation, as such, can have a collective responsibility for its actions on the world stage which is distinguishable from the responsibilities of its citizens.)

The same principle of concrete universality can be found at work in innumerable other fields, ranging from physics and biology through the arts and literature. Moreover, according to Hegel, a concrete universal is, as a single totality, simultaneously self-specifying and self-particularizing, and thus capable of "grounding" itself. On the highest and most comprehensive level, the concrete universal manifests itself as being at once the objective substance of knowledge and the knowing subject itself.[54] This absolutely self-knowing subject is, in the final analysis, the same reality that religious persons worship under the name of "God."

This is not the place to enter into a sustained discussion of the Hegelian epistemology, which I have done elsewhere.[55] Sufficient for our present purposes to see how the argument of Hegel's dialectic led to the conclusion that the inner nature of each and every thing—and most especially the nature of the Deity—consists in its "concept." Using this word in a novel and unconventional way, Hegel wrote the following:

> It is in this nature of what is—to be in its very being its own concept—that the *logical necessity* really consists. That alone is the rationality

and the rhythm of the organic whole; it is just as much a *knowing* of the content, as it is the content which is concept and essence. . . .[56]

Schelling, however, rejected Hegel's notion of the "concrete universal." Whatever its intentions, the theory struck him as far too abstract and narrowly logical. A complete philosophy, he thought, required ways of accounting for the development of order and rationality without reducing the richness of experience to mere entailment relationships. He charged that Hegel deceived himself in supposing any experience to be possible which did not include a nonconceptual element. Thought, by its very nature, is always an informing or structuring of something else that, in itself, precedes thinking. Since, however, thought does require this nonconceptual foundation, Schelling also found that Hegel was bound to import it unconsciously into his system. Hence, absolute idealism covertly relies on modes of experience (including that of representation) whose fundamental differences from conceptual thinking it refuses to acknowledge. However (Schelling's critique continued), Hegel sensed the need for some way of recognizing the nonconceptual aspect of experience, and therefore sought to "deduce" it by means of his dialectical logic. The "deduction," however, amounted to nothing more than a sophistical superimposition whose hidden purpose was to win back the nonconceptual reality which, as a matter of fact, could never have been truly absent. Even Hegel's pseudodeductions, according to Schelling, would have been impossible without the presence of precisely that element of experience which he initially claimed to exclude. Therefore the "deduction" of an objective moment standing over against the subject, though professing to be a necessary transition from pure thought to the self-externalized "Other" of thought, actually presupposed the very thing that it claimed to derive logically.[57]

The result of these accumulated errors, in Schelling's judgment, was to generate a vicious circle which the system of absolute idealism could never overcome. Especially symptomatic of the problem was Hegel's abstruse dialectical transition from the domain of Logic to that of material Nature. This bogus transition tacitly betrayed the fact that even Hegel could not rest content with bare logical thought alone. Schelling's scathing critique anticipated by decades very similar objections made by Feuerbach, Marx, and others.[58]

Schelling went further, however, in arguing that Hegel's idealistic reductionism was particularly inappropriate when applied to the explication of religious phenomena. To treat the gods of polytheistic religions, for example—or worse, to treat the One God of monotheism—as mere

"Ideas," or even as "the Absolute Idea," was to miss the personal dimension that underlies and sustains the divine order. Once again, Schelling found the crux of the problem in the mistaken theory of "concrete universals."

To correct this alleged mistake, he proposed an alternative theory of "actual universalia" *(wirkliche Universalia)* which, unlike Hegel's *konkrete Allgemeinen*, were conceived as living powers endowed with wills and purposes.[59] Schelling insisted that these *wirkliche Universalia* were not to be understood as abstract concepts, although they might, like human minds, use and appropriate concepts to their own ends. (A detailed exposition of this theory will be explored in Part Two.)

It would be greatly oversimplifying Hegel's position, however, to interpret it as an abstract system of static, formal categories. Such a system he explicitly and repeatedly rejected as a product of the "mere understanding" *(bloßer Verstand)*, as opposed to what he identified as "reason" *(Vernunft)*. The latter, he maintained, is necessarily synthetic and progressive.

Hence, despite his insistence on the conceptual determination of the system, Hegel also fully recognized the vital role of temporal development. Indeed, for him the essential nature of a thing, and especially of the universe as a whole, is solely realizable in terms of the gradual unfolding of its individual character through time. Invoking the principle of the inseparability of content from form, Hegel insisted that the inner nature (content) of the Absolute Idea—or in other words, of God—must in the normal course of time emerge from the preliminary immediacy of changeless identity and manifest itself through concrete actions in the world.[60] Hegel's celebrated play on words, *Wesen is was gewesen ist,* (Essence is that which has been), conveys this strong emphasis on historical development as the key to every being's nature, including God's.[61] The notion of a static infinite essence, of an unknowable Deity residing in the precincts of an inviolable eternity, would be foreign to Hegel's system. His whole approach to religion was radically historical.

Clearly, Hegel's views on this point were very similar to Schelling's. The latter, indeed, had himself pioneered the developmental approach to being that Hegel was later to employ.[62] Yet Schelling in his later years took pains to distance himself from the other's position. Again and again, he accused Hegel of espousing an essentially lifeless conception of temporality and of God's activity in particular.

It may be asked: What, then, was the basic difference on this point between these two thinkers? And what main objections did Schelling have to Hegel's theory of a historical dialectic? The answers to these questions again turn on the crucial relationship of time to "the concept."

Hegel regarded time as a phenomenon that in principle is contained within the eternal concept—i.e., as a necessary mode of the concept's self-manifestation. "Time itself," he wrote, "is in its concept eternal."[63] Accordingly, even while he emphasized the developmental character of both nature and history, Hegel was nonetheless able to assert that "temporal difference has no interest at all for thought."[64] It was precisely this reduction of time qua "mere" representation *(Vorstellung)* of the self-contained concept that Schelling found most objectionable. As an alternative to the Hegelian conception of the ultimate level of thought as *der absolute Begriff,* Schelling proposed a still higher level where truth would appear as *das absolut Vorgestellte.*[65] Criticizing Hegel for having, as he believed, fallen into a sterile panlogism, Schelling charged that he had hypostatized the concept in a vain attempt to assimilate the movement of development and process. But, Schelling argued, genuine movement can only be experienced by individual subjects. It cannot be deduced by logical means alone.[66] Partly paraphrasing, partly parodying his rival, Schelling wrote that Hegel's God

> is the God of eternal, perpetual activity, the incessant restlessness that never finds Sabbath; he is the God who always does only what he has always done, and therefore can accomplish nothing new. His life is a circulation of forms, in which he perpetually externalizes himself in order to come back to himself again, and ever again comes back to himself just in order to externalize himself anew.[67]

In opposition to Hegel, Schelling sought to formulate an even more thoroughgoing developmental view of God and the universe. We saw in the previous chapter how he proposed the theory of a temporal or proto-temporal medium, with a primordial polarity between a "before" and an "after." This theory combined naturally with the conception of an *Erzeugungsdialektik* producing the framework of progressive dialectical stages. Schelling insisted that this proto-temporal framework could never be absorbed into the logic of concepts, for the very reason that the logic of concepts always presupposed the proto-temporal framework. It seemed to him a confusion to argue, as Hegel did, that the character of noetic successiveness could ever be replaced by a logic of atemporal entailment relationships. On the contrary, Schelling contended, even eternity must include in its nature the structural equivalent of time. To be sure, the eternal is prior to the temporal, yet this "priority" itself includes the senses both of subsisting before and of continuing after. According to Schelling, "That is the [true] meaning of the proposition that 'in the Idea all is simultaneous.' But this being 'simultaneous' does not annul *(hebt nicht auf)* the fact that the one moment is noetically earlier than the other."[68] Hence, whereas Hegel regarded time as ultimately *aufgehoben* in the concept, Schelling maintained that the meaning of the concept must always depend on a quasi-temporal order.

This, in essence, was the core of the philosophical debate between the two thinkers on the subject of temporality and its relation to eternity. The issue was complex, with far-reaching consequences for the theory of autonomous action and in particular for the philosophy of religion. Schelling maintained that Hegel's principles undermined the possibility of freedom. The conceptual determination of events appeared to preclude a significant role for individual character and volition. Yet again, it must be borne in mind that to Hegel the term "concept" signified something quite different from its meaning in ordinary usage. To the extent that Schelling's own position understood the "concept" as a purely formal structure superimposed upon a material substrate, he missed his rival's point. Hegel's purpose was not to reduce movement and volition to a formal set of categories, but rather to expand and concretize the meaning of "concept" so as to include within it volition, movement, and historicity. On the other hand, Schelling arguably was justified in questioning the standpoint of a philosophical system for which "differences in time hold no interest." Did Hegel's attitude betray an insufficient regard for the contingency of history and the facticity of human experience?

Such were the issues that swirled about in the atmosphere of mid-nineteenth-century Germany: Was Hegel's program for assimilating and sublating temporal differences in favor of a developmental logic feasible? Or did Schelling's strategy for treating temporal (or proto-temporal) relations as prior to logic hold more promise? Did Hegel's notion of the eternal infinite threaten to swallow up the finite creature entirely? Or was Schelling's attempt to portray God as mutable rather in danger of collapsing into a finite conception of the Deity? Finally, in terms of actual practice, which of the two approaches yielded more fruitful interpretations of concrete historical developments? And which was better able to grasp the true nature of religious experience?

Part II
The Theory of Potencies

– 6 –
Schelling's New Philosophical Point of Departure

The previous chapters have reviewed the historical and intellectual forces in nineteenth-century Germany that influenced Schelling's treatment of religions and mythologies. They have also examined some of the most controversial issues during that period concerning the origins of religion, the nature of religious symbolism, the role of the unconscious, and the relation of freedom to time and eternity. In each case, we found that a sound appreciation of Schelling's project requires an understanding of his metaphysics, and in particular of his ontology. It was always in terms of an underlying metaphysical worldview that this philosopher formulated his interpretations of the available data and worked out his solutions to problems. The next three chapters, therefore, will focus specifically on Schelling's ontology as it took shape during the final decades of his life.

For Schelling, ontology was the core of mythological thought, just as mythology, conversely, was a concrete embodiment of ontology. His "doctrine of the Potencies" *(Potenzenlehre)* was designed partly in order to prove that the content of all the narratives about gods and goddesses in the various world religions was a true theogonic process—a history of real events that took place among distinct, living divinities. The Potencies were these divinities qua purged of everything accidental or circumstantial.[1] As such, a critical discussion of their origination and development should not be understood as preliminary to, but rather as the purest distillations of, pagan religions in general.

Accordingly, Part Two (chapters 6 through 9) will deal primarily with the *Potenzenlehre* and its significance for religion and mythology. Part Three, entitled "Exemplification" (chapters 10 through 12), will take up specific applications of the teaching in order to see how Schelling employed his theory for the interpretation of certain specific myths, notably from ancient Greece. The reader must not suppose, however, that the examples to be discussed there would, by themselves, be very illuminating.

In order to be in a position to interpret Schelling's hermeneutical project, it is first necessary to understand his broader philosophical project, in particular a critical puzzle that had simmered in Schelling's consciousness for decades.

A Philosophical Dilemma

Throughout his long career, one of Schelling's most persistent problems had been how to account in rational terms for the existence of concrete nature and particularity *as such*. The brute facticity of existence seemed inexplicable: this was a miracle which mere thought, with abstract ideas alone as its medium of exchange, could never hope to fathom. And yet, what foundation could reason have, or what purpose in extending the reach of its theoretical system-building, if the world's reality itself eludes comprehension?

To Schelling, the solution to the problem could not consist in a blanket affirmation of existence as opposed to the idea, or of the idea as opposed to existence. Somehow, it seemed clear, the opposition between these extremes required mediation, and the method for achieving it would have to be dialectical. But exactly how to conceive of this mediation remained a puzzle.

Assuming that every idea already presupposes an existence of some kind—whether that of the objective reality being referred to or simply that of the thinking mind itself—it was evident that immediate existence as such must be prior to all thought-content. Hence the "idea" of this pure existence could not be an idea of the ordinary kind, but must rather be a conceptual anomaly, what Schelling at one point called "the inverted idea" (*die umgekehrte Idee*).[2] Yet even to affirm the possibility of this "inverted idea" is in a way to attempt to conceive of it, and so perhaps to contradict oneself. What makes this problem difficult to resolve or even to state coherently is that the terms of its formulation are themselves logical universals. The very concept of "particularity," for example, is not itself a particular but a universal; and the same applies to the related concept of "contingency." To speak and to think about "contingent particulars" is, after all, to deal just in universals, and thus precisely *not* what the quest for the particular *as* particular was supposed to capture. This is the case of an idea reaching out to grasp the non-ideal—indeed, the diametrical opposite of an idea—and discovering that even its wished-for aim seems to be itself just another idea.

This dialectical paradox involving the elusiveness of the particular was well known to Schelling's contemporaries. Hegel called attention to it in his *Phänomenologie des Geistes* (1807), where he argued that any attempt to apprehend a particular object, or "this," necessarily negates itself and becomes instead the positing of a universal "Thisness."[3] Hence, Hegel concluded, the proper course for philosophy is to recognize that all existence and all meaning is comprised of ideal principles. Particulars survive, in his analysis, only as "sublated" *(aufgehoben)* aspects of what remains intrinsically universal.

Like Hegel, Schelling saw the problem of particularity as a crucial one for philosophy, but he differed radically as to its solution. For him, the putative absorption into universal principles of the particular as *individuum ineffabile* represents a loss in content which no amount of rationalizing could restore. If ideas inevitably tend, through incestuous reversions upon themselves, always to see and to find only more ideas, then the conclusion to be drawn is not that all existence is ideal, but rather that there must also be an extra-ideal reality. How to explain this extra-ideal reality and relate it to the world of thought would later become one of Schelling's most persistent projects.

Already in 1804, with the publication of his *Philosophie und Religion*, Schelling had raised the question as to how an existence outside of the pure world of ideas could possibly have originated. He argued that the eternally perfect ideas (conceived at that time in more or less Platonic terms) could never by themselves have generated an extra-ideal, corruptible reality. Consequently the only explanation for the existence of this material universe must be to postulate an utterly contingent, yet primordial, leap *(Sprung)* out of ideality and into corporeal finitude.[4]

With the *Freiheitsschrift* of 1809 and the *Weltalter* manuscripts of 1810-13, Schelling went a significant step further toward his final position. He theorized that there must exist an irrational "Ground" *(Grund)* which is "other than" God and in eternal opposition to him. Yet at the same time, Schelling also maintained that God as the infinite reality must contain all things, including the Ground, within himself. Obviously, these two views seemed *prima facie* inconsistent, but Schelling thought he had found the solution:

> Since, however, nothing can be outside of God, this contradiction can only be resolved if things have their Ground in that within God which is not he himself.[5]

Exactly how it would be possible for God (as the highest ideal) to contain within himself what is "other than" himself (i.e., the non-ideal), the

Freiheitsschrift does not quite succeed in making clear. This would, in fact, be a continuing problem throughout Schelling's later philosophy, to which he would keep returning again and again. The relation of the ideal to the non-ideal would also be a major puzzle of his philosophy of mythology. In any case, this much at least is certain: Schelling from 1809 onward held that it was necessary to postulate this Ground in order to provide for creaturely independence of God and to lay the basis for the possibility of human freedom.[6] He suggested, further, that this same principle of the "Ground" was the source in finite creatures of egoity *(Egoität)* and instinctual will *(Wollen)*.[7]

One of Schelling's principal aims in elaborating this theory was to provide a systematic and philosophically sophisticated reinterpretation of Jakob Böhme's principle of the "wrath within God."[8] Another equally important goal was to incorporate his own discoveries and theories concerning the unconscious.[9] Both of these purposes merged with each other and became fused as well with his more general intention to provide a theory of the particular *as* particular.

Let the foregoing suffice to briefly set the background against which Schelling's metaphysical program developed. We now turn to consider an important logical dilemma which it occasioned: namely, how could one hope to provide a coherent account of the relation of rationality to the irrationality which, by hypothesis, is the "Ground" of reason itself? And yet, if one should fail to provide such an account, of what use would be theorizing (i.e., rationalizing) about anything at all?

An identical problematic confronted Schelling in the two related areas of epistemology and religious philosophy. In epistemology, one of the central issues was how to account for the evolution and ultimate triumph of a rational world order without already presupposing the principles of that order as operative prior to their realization. (Recall that, for Schelling, to presuppose Reason as the sole source of being would undermine the possibility of particularity, of creaturely independence, and of genuine freedom.) Yet if—Hegel to the contrary—Absolute Reason did not and does not realize itself, then through what has it come into being? By the same token, what would guarantee that a finite thinker's apparently rational system of ideas is not founded upon baseless suppositions?

In the philosophy of religion, a parallel issue occurred in relation to the nature and knowability of the divine: viz., how to explain the possibility of the Deity's self-revelation in history without assuming that all the processes and events leading to that revelation were themselves necessarily attributable to the divine nature. (And again, to assume this would, in Schelling's view, make God directly responsible for all that is imperfect and corrupt in the sensible universe.) But if the creative agencies operative in the world did not themselves originate from God, then how, if at all, would they be related to him? And how could one be certain that the final form in which the Deity has been "revealed" is not, itself, just another transient phase in the history of human projections?

The Search for a Nonrationalistic Alternative to Relativism

To take up first the epistemological side to this problematic, we observe that certain aspects of Schelling's argument resembled that of the classical relativist. The linear/causal model of his *Erzeugungsdialektik*[10] required that any chain of reasoning, and so any worldview resulting from it, must begin with a nonrational starting point. Once having determined that the basis and origin of reason is itself nonrational, it might seem to follow that the entire theoretical system to evolve out of it would be arbitrary and relative.

In raising these questions, Schelling put his finger on a dilemma that casts doubt on the feasibility of any rational derivation for the transcendent source of existence and rationality: for is it not the case that any such derivation (should there be one) would already presuppose the *being* of the criteria by which the proffered deduction is to be made? And must one not therefore draw the conclusion that human reason requires an extrarational ground, that consciousness finds itself "thrown," as it were, into a context of existence which defies rational justification? Is not existence itself radically "unthinkable" *(unvordenklich),* in the sense that thought always presupposes it in a manner which precedes reason?[11]

Affirmative answers to these questions would not be without problems of their own, however. What made this issue particularly tricky was the paradox of attempting to provide a rational explanation as to why there must be a nonrational basis of existence. One might object: If the explanation should succeed, then the purported "nonrational basis" would presumably have a rational foundation after all (as provided by the explanation), in which case the seeming nonrationality of it would be nullified. On the other hand, if the explanation should fail, then there would evidently be no sound reason for positing the nonrational basis in the first place.

Schelling was fully aware of the paradoxes and contradictions to which relativism would lead. He pointed out, for example, that a system of knowledge based upon merely assumed premises—whether these are the putative "givens" of a sense-data empiricism or the axioms of a mathematical logic—can produce only a "contingent knowing" which is devoid of certainty.[12] Unless a firmer basis for philosophical thought were found, even the very attempt to criticize the excessive claims of rationalism would be futile. Schelling sought to avoid these sorts of pitfalls at all costs. In order to do so, however, he had to establish a means of erecting a rational and coherent system on the basis of a nonrational Ground. The crucial puzzle was how to conceive of such a project.

Contemporary scholars have differed greatly in their reactions to Schelling's problematic. Such interpreters as Martin Heidegger, Jürgen Habermas, Walter Kasper and, more recently, Alan White have celebrated him for pointing beyond the ideal of a philosophy modeled on logic and beyond the necessity of dialectical determination toward a new conception of freedom as the root and foundation of being itself.[13] For these writers, freedom is incompatible in principle with a comprehensively rational world-system, because a free agent must be capable of acting in ways unpredictable by any logic. From the opposite side of the hermeneutical spectrum, on the other hand, Györgi Lukács has been equally emphatic in condemning what he regards as a reactionary "irrationalism" in Schelling's thought.[14] For Lukács, this irrationalism is symptomatic of the sickness of modern bourgeois values as a whole.

As a matter of fact, however, Schelling by no means entertained a negative attitude toward rationality, dialectical determination, and so on. His apparent undercutting and dethroning of their absolute pretensions was meant to be provisional only.[15] The ultimate purpose of his philosophical undertaking was precisely to demonstrate the *reestablishment* of these principles as the outcome of the dialectical process. Schelling realized that any attempt to go beyond a rationalistic methodology and ontology must propose either a plausible substitute or a return route back to reason. A failure to do either of these would run the risk of sabotaging one's own basis of argument. This is a lesson which contemporary relativists, too, would do well to bear in mind.[16] The problematic facing Schelling—of trying to find, as it were, a "metaphilosophical" framework upon which to erect a self-critical system of reason—is one that modern thinkers are no less obliged to wrestle with.

The Search for a Nonrationalistic Alternative to Fideism

Turning now to the religious dimension, we find precisely the same kinds of issues and dilemmas concerning the knowledge of God. On the one hand, Schelling followed Kant in rejecting the ontological proof of God's existence: for no mere definition or set of attributes, however sublime and perfect these might be, could guarantee the existence of its object. Even granting (as Schelling did) that the attribute of necessary existence must belong to God's nature, this only proved that the concept of God includes the concept of existing necessarily. Yet all this is still only hypothetical. Schelling wrote:

> But out of the essence, out of the nature, out of the concept of God (for these are merely equivalent expressions) there follows in eternity no more than this: that God, *if* he exists, must be the *a priori* existent being, else he cannot exist at all. But *that* he exists does not follow therefrom.[17]

Indeed, Schelling went even further and repudiated any attempt to reach God via reason alone (even "practical" reason *à la* Kant). For any purely rational approach could only result in a fatal "hypostatization of the concept," hopelessly confusing the roles of reason and experience. According to Schelling, this very confusion was Hegel's worst mistake. His doctrine of pure thought as capable, through its own resources, of establishing the actuality of nature, spirit, and God effectively reversed the true relations of thought and being: "For it is not because there is thought that a being exists; but rather, it is because a being exists that there is a thought."[18]

Schelling's skepticism about the capacity of bare reason to apprehend the reality (as opposed to the abstract possibility) of God compelled him to look elsewhere for a solution. But what other means of access was there to the absolute source of all existence? The best option seemed to lie in the direction of a purely intuitive insight, modeled on the theory of Νοῦς in Aristotle.[19] Only such an intuition, thought Schelling, would be capable at once of grounding reason without itself requiring to be grounded.

In his earlier years, Schelling had characterized such a transcendental insight as "intellectual intuition." Although he later abandoned the phrase as being needlessly subjective in its connotations,[20] he nevertheless adhered to the doctrine of an intuitive act, which he sometimes described as an "experience" or as an "immediate knowing," and which in any case must be the highest mode of communion with the Pure Actuality of the Godhead.[21] To the spiritually sensitive mind, this suprarational "experience" would take the form of a profound awe, constituting the bedrock on which all religions have been founded.[22]

Even Kant, Schelling observed, had experienced the shuddering of awe when confronted with the notion of the absolute source of all existence, but he had erred in placing this experience outside the bounds of philosophy.[23] Like Jacobi, Schleiermacher, and other noncognitivist theologians of the period, Schelling regarded this intuitive apprehension as the single most compelling sign of the reality of religious objects. For no one would feel such awe toward the logical deductions of the intellect.[24] The ultimate referent of religious experience, therefore, must transcend reason altogether.

Yet, although Schelling refused to accord unaided reason access to the reality of God, he was equally concerned to avoid the quagmires of theological fideism. Any attempt to erect the edifices of religion solely upon such uncertain foundations as human experience would, in his eyes, be bound to collapse into psychologism. If, for example, the conviction that a deity exists were to rest upon merely empirical phenomena—whether the phenomena in question were the magical powers attributed to an extraordinary individual or, alternatively, the presence of certain remarkable feelings in the hearts of believers—in either case the knowledge-claims based on such data would be circumstantial. One could, moreover, pose questions as to why such data should ever have been interpreted as evidence for the existence of divine, supramundane reality.[25] Clearly, the way people might happen to feel about religion at any particular point in time is a product of changing personal and historical circumstances. Hence, if the proof of religion depends upon evidence of this nature, then conclusions drawn from such evidence must necessarily be unreliable and arbitrary.

Schelling's principal opponent here was his lifelong antagonist, Jacobi, but also by extension Schleiermacher and others who shared a like approach. These noncognitivist theologians had made the mistake, in his view, of supposing that the foundations of religion are not subject to rational scrutiny or criticism. This was the core issue of the so-called *Pantheismusstreit,* which revolved around the question whether all holistic philosophies—that is, philosophies which attempt to interpret reality in terms of a single, comprehensive system—are inherently "pantheistic" (and thus, by implication, actually atheistic). Jacobi, especially, represented this position, and he launched a blistering attack on Schelling for his alleged advocacy of a "Spinozistic" holism.[26]

Schelling, however, insisted on the indispensable role of reason in the organization and testing of religious hypotheses. Unless it could be shown that the variable forms of feeling and experience are determined by rational laws, then, he thought, the whole enterprise of treating religion as a genuine and coherent confrontation with Deity must fail.[27]

The desire to avoid both the extreme of religious rationalism and that of noncognitivism created serious theoretical difficulties. For if reason is not the source of our knowledge of God's reality and yet constitutes an indispensable feature of mature religious faith, if nonrational or prerational intuition is a necessary, but not sufficient, component of religious "knowledge," then the crucial question becomes how to justify our assertions about God. What would make possible a transition from the ineffable "experience" of an initially indeterminate Deity to the reasoned comprehension of that Deity's essential attributes? On the other hand, what guarantee could there be that the suprarational "experience" (if there were such a thing) could ever be more than a contingent psychological phenomenon? Finally, assuming that some means were found to validate an intuitive leverage point for a systematic treatment of religion, how was one to conceive of the relation of that intuition to the transcendent Cause of the universe?

Initial Moves toward Resolving the Dilemma

As a preliminary step to resolve these puzzles, Schelling argues that the contingency of ordinary empirical experience results from the division of the particular subject pole from the equally particular object pole. Because particularity as such involves an element of arbitrariness, the evidence of finite experience cannot yield absolute knowledge. Yet the transrational insight mentioned above would not, properly speaking, be an "experience" in the usual sense, but rather a unique kind of "ecstasy" transcending the subject/object polarity.[28] If that polarity could be overcome, then perhaps the limitations characteristic of ordinary experience could be superseded as well.

Accordingly, Schelling suggests that the "ecstasy of reason" would only occur, if at all, when the mind has pressed to the absolute bounds of rational thought. The reason must first lead as far as it can go, up to the final point where it is obliged to postulate that which transcends reason itself. Like Kant, Schelling maintains that it is reason's own critical self-examination which proceeds to the recognition of the faculty's inherent limits. Unlike Kant, however, he also holds that there can be a going beyond those limits, whereby the mind directly encounters the transrational ground of all existence. This idea has been among Schelling's most influential contributions to modern religious thought.[29]

Significantly, Schelling hypothesizes that the supreme reality apprehended in this manner could not in itself be an existent entity at all, but rather must be that "Over-being" *(Überseiendes)* which is the source of all existence.[30]

Schelling obviously intends this theory to circumvent the major liability of emotivist and fideistic theologies in general. In maintaining that the "ecstasy" would dissolve the subject/object polarity, he can argue that it is not susceptible to the vicissitudes of individual personality or historical circumstance. At once the consummation of reason and its supreme negation, the "ecstasy" would be free of conceptual determinations altogether. And because the contingent components of both the objective world and the individual's psyche would be momentary suspended, the uncertainties of psychologism would be avoided as well. Lifted beyond those circumstantial features of experience by an act of immediate insight without any trace of discursive thought in it, the mind finally might be able to realize the unfathomable nature of Being that precedes all differentiation.

This is what could be called the "existentialist dimension" of Schelling's thought. The theory of an indeterminate identity from which all finite entities derive their existence has obvious affinities with Heidegger's doctrine of the Being in which all determinate beings have their ground, or with Sartre's notion of the existence which precedes essence. No doubt this affinity explains why Heidegger would call Schelling "the actually creative and most deeply penetrating thinker" of the German idealist movement.[31]

There are, however, certain problems with this doctrine, problems tracing all the way through its developmental history, from the times when it was variously described as an "intellectual intuition," as an "indifference point" between subjectivity and objectivity, or as an undifferentiated "ecstasy of reason." Precisely to the extent that this ineffable experience is beyond the discursive intellect, it also is unverifiable by either formal or (ordinary) empirical means. If skeptics questioned the possibility of such an experience, Schelling could at first only answer that perhaps these persons lacked the capacity for having it.[32] Thus there develops a curious combination of apodeictic certainty mingled with structural indeterminacy, and this combination can even lead to the claim that the content of such transrational insight is beyond the range of criticism.[33] But how is this sort of claim to be taken seriously by those who may lack the alleged special insight, or who lack the talent for a "transrational experience"? If words and concepts cannot attain to the Supreme Reality, how can one rely on the vague notion that one has reached it via an immediate act going beyond discursive thought? Might not this "ecstasy of reason" be an exercise in self-deception? Could it be that Schelling has, after all, fallen into just that sort of romantic obscurantism which Hegel once caustically labeled "the night in which all cows are black"?[34]

It is true, to be sure, that Schelling already attempted to distance himself from the latter kind of objection as early as 1802, when he cautioned that "most people see in the essence of the absolute nothing but empty night, and they can distinguish nothing within it; it contracts for them into a bare negation of differentiation, and it is for them a purely privative experience . . ."[35] In his later years, Schelling would continue to deny any suggestion that his philosophy was based on emotivism: "I do not belong to those who seek the wellspring of philosophy in bare feeling," he would assert.[36] Clearly, therefore, he would resist the charge of having fallen into a blank, featureless monism. But the question here is *how,* given the positions to which he has committed himself, he could plausibly avoid such a charge.

Other possible lines of defense for Schelling could be to dispute the seeming fallacy of intellectual exclusiveness or esotericism stemming from his reliance on intuition as a criterion of ultimate truth. Firstly, it might be said, perhaps the real issue is just that he has opted to supplement the standard philosophical methods of verification with another method more suitable for evaluating experiences at the boundary of religious illumination. Secondly, the mere fact that a given viewpoint may refuse to accept philosophical criticisms of itself, or may go so far as to treat these as unintentional illustrations of its (the same viewpoint's) own inherent correctness, does not by itself suffice to prove the falsity of the view in question. Even a true position could be "logically rude" in this equivocal sense.[37] Therefore, Schelling's taking refuge in the claim to a faculty of insight beyond the ken of his critics need not necessarily undermine his theory. If, thirdly, he also makes provision—as he tries to do—for the eventual attainment by such critics of the higher insight from which the rightness of his theories would someday be manifest to all, then maybe the charge of esotericism might also be met.[38]

Yet, on the other hand, the skeptics' objections need not, in order to be effective, establish the outright impossibility of achieving a transrational insight or experiencing something like an "ecstasy of reason." Their main point is simply to call into question the *trustworthiness* and *reliability* of a theory to the extent that it resists rational scrutiny. Although neither intellectual exclusiveness nor "logical rudeness"—if these are indeed imputable to Schelling—would be enough to invalidate his position, their presence would certainly be a legitimate cause for concern. One might well wonder whether the ultimate perspective given in the "ecstasy of reason" is genuine or deceptive.

In any case, even if Schelling's transrationalistic strategy worked, by itself it still would not achieve the full aim intended. For it is one thing to establish the feasibility of an ecstatic encounter with the ineffable divine, but quite another to demonstrate that this encounter can yield any usable results for the philosophy of religion. Conceivably, the attainment of the quasi-mystical, nondual awareness might be a dead-end street leading nowhere, without any purchase on the universe's order, the ideals of ethics, or the spiritual destiny of humankind.

In view of all these considerations, therefore, Schelling recognizes the need to bridge the theoretical gap between the noncognitive Truth apprehended in the "ecstasy of reason" and the lower-order truths of discursive thinking. He refuses to abandon reason or to leave it in a condition of impotence vis-à-vis the Absolute. Instead, his goal is to show why that Absolute, which in itself is inconceivable, must nevertheless mediate a determinate content to thought. Equally necessary is to show how such a mediation is possible. Referring to the actuality *(Wirklichkeit)* which must precede all thought and all logical possibility, Schelling argues:

> One could object: an actuality that precedes all possibility is *unthinkable*. This one may concede in a certain sense, and say: precisely therefore it is the *beginning* of all real thought—for the *beginning* of thought is not yet thought itself. An actuality that precedes possibility is, to be sure, also an actuality that precedes thought; but precisely therefore it is the first genuine *object* of thought (*quod se objicit*). So much the more important is the question what relation this [object] could have to reason, when it [reason] bows before it. To be sure, it already has *for itself* a relation to reason, but as indicated by the expression just used, a negative relation.[39]

Thus, even the enigmatic experience transcending thought can and must return from the far side of reason's limits in order to relate itself freely to the conceptual order. One of the purposes of Schelling's final system is to explain the possibility of this return out of the transrational back to rationality. His "positive philosophy" must recognize the essential finitude of reason and do justice to the principle of the nonrational, yet without falling into the quagmires of relativism or irrationalism.[40]

The need to transform this initially negative relation into a positive relation provides the driving force for Schelling's final philosophy. Having established that the highest actuality is not directly graspable by reason (i.e., is "negatively related" to it), the goal of thought must be to find some means whereby that actuality still can and does render itself at least indirectly comprehensible through its effects, so as to become "positively related" to reason. Otherwise, one would be left only with the negative result of a blind noncognitivism, at which the entire philosophical enterprise would collapse. A qualified noncognitivism might indeed supply the beginning stages of thought, but it could not be the final standpoint.

Accordingly, Schelling's complex purpose is to construct a rationally coherent metaphysics, but to do so on the basis of a transcendent reality that lies beyond both concepts and ordinary experience altogether.

The Distinction between the *Was* and the *Daß*

The next important step towards this goal is to distinguish between abstract essence *(quidditas)* and concrete "thatness" *(quodditas)*.[41] As we have seen, it is Schelling's position that the essence, logical structure, or "whatness" (*Was*) of the universe—and even of God himself—is, in principle, a bare possibility, which either could exist or not exist. The "thatness" (or *Daß*), on the other hand, Schelling defines as the pure fiat on which being, as well as the very possibility of being, depends. The *Daß* he regards as the transcendent Cause of existence and therefore as standing at the pinnacle of the universal chain of being. Thus, although Schelling argues (in his critique, along Kantian lines, of the ontological proof) that the *Daß* of God is not deducible *a priori* from his essence, yet this still leaves open the option of establishing God's essence by *a posteriori* means and on the basis of his *Daß*.

This consideration suggests to Schelling a new line of approach to the philosophies of religion and mythology. Corresponding to the distinction between the essence and the *Daß*, he divides his system into two separate, yet complementary, branches: the "negative" and the "positive." The task of the negative philosophy is to define and order the various possibilities of things—that is, to determine their formal structures considered exclusively *as* possibilities, but without reference to whether or not they actually exist. The highest order of possibility is that of a pure actuality which (as we just saw) transcends the very limits of thinkability—if indeed it exists at all. This is the possibility of the *Daß*. But the actuality of the *Daß* must be intuited directly. The positive philosophy, accordingly, begins with the "experience" of immediate existence in and through the *Daß*, and proceeds from there, in tandem with the negative philosophy, to establish when and how the bare possibilities become concrete actualities.

Schelling characterizes the negative branch as "rational philosophy," insofar as it deals with the purely possible. Yet the term "rational" is somewhat misleading, for among the possibilities to be considered are those of a nonrational ground (i.e., blind nature, or chaos) and of a suprarational, ordering directive (the will of God). Both of these, for different but related reasons, are supposed to escape rational determination; indeed, they are literally inconceivable. And yet the thought of their being inconceivable can and must be conceived. Thus, the negative philosophy, as understood by Schelling, paradoxically includes within itself the concept of a reality transcending all conceptual determinations, as well as the rationale of a struggle with the powers of unreason. Similarly, the positive philosophy represents the actuality of that struggle as revealed in human history, a process hopefully leading to the final triumph of reason over blind nature. In this way, the positive and negative philosophies are mutually to reinforce each other in the search for truth.

The ontological principles charged with this dual mission are the Potencies. Schelling conceives of these as mediators between the necessary laws of the rational, on the one hand, and the creative forces of the suprarational, as well as the irrational, on the other hand. Simultaneously rational "laws" and volitional "drives," according to him, the Potencies are defined as individual agencies, each with its own internal nisus. Schelling argued that their endowment with will would obviate the fault of panlogism, which resulted in the "shipwreck" of the Hegelian philosophy.[42]

The next chapter will focus specifically on the details of the theory of Potencies *(Potenzenlehre)* and reveal how Schelling endows them with concrete individualities, enabling them to assume innumerable relations among each other and the Over-being. According to him, this variety of possible roles constitutes the cosmic "script," as it were, from which the "drama" of the world mythologies has been continuously played out.

Schelling's approach to religious philosophy, diametrically opposed to the regnant Hegelian approach, was extremely controversial in his own time and remains so today. It should be expected that a project heading so boldly against the stream would be susceptible to considerable criticism. The mid-nineteenth century saw a spate of publications weighing the pros and cons of Schelling's versus Hegel's philosophy. In the twentieth century, Schelling's intention to grasp the necessity for, and development of, a suprarational framework of metaphysics (within which being and rationality would assume subordinate positions) has been the subject of ongoing debate.

Some scholars, such as Manfred Schröter, Walter Kasper, and Walter Schulz, have regarded Schelling's division between negative philosophy and positive philosophy as a natural, internal development within German idealism: a final working out of its self-mediating project that led inevitably to that project's self-overcoming.[43] Others, such as Horst Fuhrmans and Xavier Tilliette, have maintained that Schelling's fundamental impulse underlying the positive philosophy was basically unrelated to the idealistic problematic, but stemmed from a different set of concerns touching the possibility of radical spiritual freedom and redemption.[44]

According to these commentators, the separation of the positive from the negative philosophy represents more of a breaking away from the idealist movement than it does an immanent continuation of the same.

Even more difficult than the quest to understand the theoretical motivation for the bifurcation of philosophy is the evaluation of Schelling's efforts to weld the two branches into complementary aspects of a single system. Opinions are again divided on this topic, with some commentators endorsing the project as a promising alternative to Hegel's, and others repudiating it as entangled in contradictions of its own.[45] Certainly it cannot be denied that Schelling set himself a formidable dilemma, which a simpler and more conventional approach would have avoided. One wants to ask: if the two branches are to be integrated in the end anyway, are the principles of their harmonization contained within the negative philosophy, or the positive philosophy, or both? The first two alternatives, which regard one or the other approach as holding the key to their essential unity, seem difficult to reconcile with the repeated claims that each branch is theoretically independent of the other.[46] The third alternative, which suggests that the same basic principles would be found in both branches, appears inconsistent with the emphasis on their sharp separation. Hence, the problem of how to reconnect the severed disciplines gives the impression of being intractable. Tilliette states the paradox with trenchant irony: "Once the caesura has been firmly sliced between the negative philosophy and the positive philosophy, how shall one throw across a bridge between the two banks?"[47]

Much of the continuing controversy among Schelling scholars has centered on his efforts to create a new ontology of freedom while still maintaining the philosophical goal of constructing a complete dialectical system. The side of freedom, represented by the positive philosophy, and the side of systematic completeness, represented by the negative philosophy, were to converge in a synthesis of dovetailing strategies. The root question remains whether these two aims can be combined, or whether they are, in principle, irreconcilable. This issue has important implications for religious thought as well.[48]

– 7 –
The Ontology

The theory of Potencies *(Potenzenlehre)* is the most original and certainly the most conceptually difficult aspect of Schelling's final system. This theory makes up the central core of Schelling's "negative philosophy." Basically, it is an attempt to replace abstract logic with another kind of structured thinking that would be capable of doing better justice to the processes of concrete being and evolution. If this project should succeed, it would amount to a major revolution in Western ontology. And the ontology, in turn, would provide the fundamental framework from which to analyze and interpret the significance of world religions.

Before launching into a discussion of the *Potenzenlehre*, it will be useful to recall three features of Schelling's methodology that have decisively influenced his conclusions. The first is his radical temporalization of thought and being, an innovation that culminates in the placement of temporal (or quasi-temporal) determinations "prior" to those of essence and even of logic. Second is the development of what I have called Schelling's *Erzeugungsdialektik,* or dialectic of production, as the principal mode of philosophical reasoning. The third decisive feature is the emphasis on will, leading to an infusion of volitional characteristics into areas and issues that previously were thought to be the domain of impersonal, invariable laws. Let us examine these characteristics in a bit more detail.

The Temporalization of Essence

According to Schelling, traditional Western philosophy committed the error of treating the essences of things as changeless and fixed in eternity. As a consequence, time was relegated to a merely representational status and treated as the phenomenal medium in which the static, essential verities would appear.

With the dawning of the nineteenth century, a new, organic conception of time began to emerge. But this did not immediately penetrate into the deep structures of ontology. Temporal change, for example, could still be viewed as a phenomenal transition from one timeless essence to the next. Or one could think of future possibilities as quasi-mathematical forms into which the shifting configurations of empirical existence successively would move. But the paradox, as ancient as Zeno, remained: How could one account for movement and change on the basis of theoretical categories which were themselves motionless and static? How could a series of point-events, be they ever so close together, produce the continuity characteristic of real time? The root problem evidently stemmed from the attempt to combine a dynamic conception of change with a static essentialism.

None of these ways of viewing the matter, in Schelling's opinion, would succeed in accounting for the developmental patterns and principles implicit even in the forms of possibility. In order to accomplish that, he argues for incorporating genetic principles into the very core of ontology. This further entails, he thinks, that some prototype or analogue of temporality must be discernible within the eternal essences themselves. Specifically, there must be an "eternal Past," i.e., a past that was never present, as well as an "eternal Future," or future that will never become present.[1] For if, as Plato saw, "time is the moving image of eternity," then by the same token eternity must be the immutable image of time.

Schelling's writings show a persistent wrestling with these and related problems, to which he keeps returning. Unlike Hegel, for whom time is ultimately *aufgehoben* in the concept of the eternal,[2] Schelling's approach is to show how the principle of temporality can be incorporated into that of eternity. Arguing against the notion of a timeless eternity, he insists that there must be a "past," a "present," and a "future" within the eternal itself.[3]

The attempt to introduce time-like qualities into the interpretation of eternal essences brings with it a whole new range of problems. If one supposes, in the first place, that there is such a thing as eternity and that it is accessible to human knowledge, then the question is what role this concept serves in either metaphysics or epistemology. Schelling argues that the traditional concept of a timeless eternity, consisting merely of an "eternal Now," fails to relate itself to temporality and is therefore vacuous.[4] Yet even conceding the point, would this be enough to establish the validity of a still more esoteric doctrine of eternity? Does the failure of theories about an eternal present suffice to prove that there must be an eternal fusion of past, present, and future? Not without more evidence, surely.

Again, the concept of a "past" that never existed in the present is rather mind-boggling. Even if one granted Schelling's claim that this concept would resolve the old Kantian antinomy concerning the unthinkable limitlessness of past time,[5] would that happy result by itself establish the truth of the hypothesis? Clearly not. Yet there is validity to the point that, if there should be eternal essences of some kind, they would have to be concretely relatable to the flow of phenomenal time and not be cut off from the latter. This is already a significant insight.

The Erzeugungsdialektik

This is a method of reasoning which proceeds by successive stages to demonstrate the necessary production of one dialectical principle or phase out of another. In chapter 5, it was noted that Schelling's method is significantly different from Hegel's *Aufhebungsdialektik*. Unlike the latter, Schellingian dialectic seeks to derive successive forms not contained in the foregoing, but rather produced *(erzeugt)* by a kind of teleological necessity. At every stage of Schelling's reasoning, he posits a new level or principle of being that is not just entailed, but actually caused, by the preceding elements of the system.[6]

To arrive at such a progression, Schelling typically employs a three-tiered argument:

(a) He first shows the *lack of means* to realize a state of affairs or goal which is found to be an absolute *desideratum* under the given conditions. This lack is conceived as more than a bare absence of something. It is rather an apprehended lacking-to or lacking-for, however undeveloped and dim this apprehension may often be. The operative premise here is that either the presence or the absence of essential dialectical structures must, to the extent that they are thinkable, always be seen in relation to some purposive activity or power, which would be their ground.

(b) Then Schelling elicits the inevitable experiencing of a *definite need (Bedürfnis)* to fill this lack in order to complete the dialectical phase under consideration. The identification of such a need presupposes, of course, that one has already established, at least in a provisional way, the determinate goal or goals for which the entity or structure in question would be needed.

(c) Finally, Schelling identifies the principle capable of acting as a *(re)productive cause (erzeugende Ursache)* in order to bring the needed means into being. This (re)reproductive cause must be teleological, in the sense of acting for the sake of satisfying those wants which the foregoing reflections have shown to be fundamental. Ultimately, the highest (re)productive cause would be that for the sake of which the entire universe exists.

It is easy to see that the methodology of the *Erzeugungsdialektik* goes hand in hand with the temporalization of essence. This is not the same as an abandonment of the logic of essences (though it is a significant modification of that logic.) But the dialectical production of successive principles does not, for Schelling any more than for Hegel, take place in empirical time. If it did—that is, if each new principle of thought and being were produced according to no other rule than the exigencies of the moment—then the so-called "dialectic" would soon fall into relativism. As we have seen, however, Schelling rejects relativism. The principles educed via the *Erzeugungsdialektik* are not supposed to be either ephemeral or arbitrary, but rather they are understood as eternally true and demonstrably necessary according to the immutable laws of thought. So the dialectic of (re)production is by no means to be confused with a doctrine of Heraclitean flux.

More serious difficulties, however, concern the transition from a recognized ontological need *(Bedürfnis)* to the posited fulfillment of such a need. A number of questions suggest themselves. First, a need to whom or a need for what? Schelling is not always clear on these points, leaving it up to the reader to fill in the gaps on the basis of context. Second, how compelling is the need, and what would be the consequences if it failed to be met? In order for this mode of arguing to be persuasive, it is necessary to prove in each case that no alternative provisions could have satisfied the conditions equally well. Third, is not the notion of "need" intrinsically subjective and for that reason unfit to serve as an objective category? Many philosophers today would argue that "needs" are wholly contingent features of contingently existing creatures. In that case, it would be futile to attempt a dialectic based on the teleology of needs. Perhaps so. Yet it is precisely this assumption—that need is always subjective and that its resolution is determined entirely by contingent circumstances—that Schelling's philosophy calls into question. He claims that certain metaphysical potentials and their associated needs are fundamental to the natures in which they inhere; and further, that in a holistic universe, where no feature exists in isolation from the rest, every genuine potential must possess the means to its eventual actualization. This principle explains why Schelling's method of arguing regularly starts by identifying what next higher principle the dialectic at each stage would need *(bedürfen)* as teleologically requisite *(erforderlich)*, and then goes on from there to establish the reality of that principle as being the goal *(Zweck)* of the preceding moments.[7] There will be ample opportunity in the following pages to witness the application of this procedure and to evaluate its results.

Ontological Voluntarism

A characteristic feature of Schelling's ontology is his conviction that will is one of the most basic constituents of all reality, that in fact nothing can exist in the absence of will. "Willing is primordial being" *(Wollen ist Ursein),* he wrote as early as 1809; and in his later works he continues to maintain the same fundamental thesis.[8] Volition must, on his analysis, be logically irreducible because it transcends logical determinations altogether. Indeed, he insists that the transition from pure possibilities to actualities can only come from an act of the will, whether that of an infinite being or a finite creature.[9]

One scruple that might be raised at this juncture is the following: Who or what was it that brought the primordial Will into existence in the first place? Though this is a good question, it misses the point if it supposes that the answer must point to some entity or principle that would itself be nonvolitional. The whole thrust of Schelling's ontological voluntarism is to deny the traditional assumption that will is a derivative quality supervenient upon a more fundamental stratum of being. Indeed, one of his central arguments is that the will alone is capable of acting as a *causa sui*, of bringing itself and its encompassing world simultaneously into concrete existence.[10]

Schelling opposes both the standard materialist and idealist views about the nature of the will. Concerning the former, he criticizes reductionistic attempts to explain purposiveness as merely the result of a combination of physical forces and conditions. Materiality itself, he argues, already presupposes a rudimentary will, inasmuch as the essential attributes of matter—force, resistance, inertia—are themselves only thinkable in volitional terms.[11] This contention is debatable, of course. Does Schelling lapse into anthropomorphism? There are times that he may—as, e.g., when he suggests, echoing Baader, that the genesis of the sense-world was a consequence of humanity's Fall from the Idea-world.[12] On the whole, however, the main point of Schelling's attack on materialism is just that the way one understands such terms as "force," etc., is rooted in the lived experiences of a body endowed with a will.

As for idealism, to this position Schelling is more favorably inclined. He agrees with its central claim that a subjectivity is indispensable for the possible existence of objects. But he faults thinkers of the idealist school for treating the will as if it were merely the product of a preestablished set of impersonal laws. In espousing this theory, he thinks, they have only gotten hold of a necessary, not a sufficient, condition of experience. The universal principles of pure reason are indeed logically deducible; but no less indispensable are the particular experiences of an individual self.[13] Wherever selfhood appears, however, there must already exist the prior reality of a living will. Schelling therefore concludes that the will must be the ultimate source of all thought, just as it is of matter.

The theory of a volitional foundation for both material being and ideal being is debatable. One may wonder especially how plausible is the thesis that inanimate objects are endowed with a rudimentary will. One may also criticize the concept of a *causa sui,* whether it be supposed infinite or finite. And one may further question the notion of a primordial fiat (the *Daß*) which, as Schelling alleges, must have "preceded" in proto-time any determinations of intelligible structure.

Paradoxical and abstruse as these ideas undeniably are, a major share of their obscurity derives from the fact that they revolve about some of the deeper issues in fundamental ontology: How has Being come into being after all—was it determined by an accident, by a logic, or by an unfathomable Will? Although Schelling's answer in favor of the last alternative is less than wholly convincing, he does offer intriguing insights and clues that together make the primacy of volition at least a thinkable metaphysical option.

Taken all together, the *Erzeugungsdialektik,* the emphasis on the temporality of essence, and the ontological voluntarism constitute the hallmarks of Schelling's approach to philosophy. The following pages will show how these methodological commitments have specifically determined the metaphysical theories contained in the *Potenzenlehre,* the core of his religious thought.

The Pure Potencies Prior to their Actualization

Schelling conceives of an era prior to the beginning of worldly time, during which the generative Potencies would subsist in a state of quiescence. During this primordial, first "time" within eternity (or "proto-time," as we might rather say, in order to distinguish it from worldly time), motion and change would not yet exist, for there would be no physical matter or energy present to serve as the bearers of change. Instead, there would only be the pure dialectical relations of the Potencies in their original condition, a condition marked by total harmony and a mutual codetermination by each of the others' essential natures.

(We may note that implicitly, according to Schelling's theory, these three Potencies are identical to the three Personae of the Christian Trinity. He would argue that it was and remains their inherent function to guide world history from the beginning of the universe until the end of time. Their deeper significance, however, would only become manifest when God's full revelation in Christ emerged. At the present stage of our discussion, it would be premature to elaborate further on this most esoteric aspect of Schelling's doctrine.)

In their state of quiescence, as they were before the creation of any concrete existence, the three Potencies would be defined as follows:

The first Potency, which Schelling symbolizes variously as -A or as A^1, is the sheer, unlimited possibility of being, *das sein Könnende*.[14] As such, it is also the principle of pure subjectivity (for even in his late period, Schelling remains faithful to the basic idealist tenet that objective being presupposes a subject *to which* the object presents itself).[15] Because this original subjectivity is entirely self-contained and undifferentiated "in itself" *(an sich)*, and because the defining concept of it need refer to nothing outside the first Potency as such, it can also be described as the primordial "being-in-itself" *(an-sich-Seiende)*.[16]

However, the pure principle of possibility by itself is proto-temporally indeterminate. As including all possible forms of being, it discriminates among none, so that the ephemeral is equally represented along with the durable, the contingent along with the necessary. The first Potency is thus wholly unlimited and indefinite. As such, it is devoid of objective being, since objectivity requires definite structure. Schelling describes the first Potency at one point as "the infinite lack of being" *(der unendliche Mangel an Sein)*,[17] which needs to be provided with limits of some kind in order to acquire a specific content. This indiscriminate totality therefore requires to be brought under control, or "subjected," by other principles so that it can obtain the determinate structure necessary to real being.[18]

The notion that there are degrees of reality and degrees of contingency among possibilities is one of the presuppositions of Schelling's thought. It underlies the method, characteristic of his *Erzeugungsdialektik*, of winnowing out the more contingent from the less contingent forms. In this manner, the idea is to establish a progressive series of possibilities, which gradually phase into partial actualities and lead toward the highest (and absolutely necessary) principle. This highest principle, thinks Schelling, will then finally stand revealed as the unconditioned actuality that contains nothing of potentiality within it. But again, in order to reach this ultimate principle, the progressive series of its partly real, partly unreal and provisional way stations will first have to be fully traversed in both thought and experience.[19]

At this point, however, three related objections spring to mind regarding Schelling's somewhat unusual employment of the terms "potentiality" and "actuality." The first objection concerns the concept of degrees of reality, the second concerns the parallel concept of degrees of possibility, and the third concerns the infusion of value terms into the discussion.

Against "Degrees of Reality." In the first place, one might question the principle that there can be degrees of reality, in such a way that some entities would count as "more real" than others. Is not "reality" an all-or-nothing category, so that any given object must be either "real" or "unreal," but nothing in between? Furthermore (to approach the problem from another perspective), would not the very fact of an entity's being within the field of experience suffice to establish its place in the real world, thereby rendering any doubts as to the given entity's reality superfluous?

This latter way of posing the objection, however, soon reveals its question-begging character. For it is not obvious that all objects of experience are equally real. Even leaving aside illusions, hallucinations, and the like, there still remains the distinction between more and less accurate, as well as between more and less profound, modes of experiencing phenomena. Advocates of the "all-or-nothing" school bear the burden of proving that degrees of experienced reality are, in principle, reducible to a single pair of mutually exclusive alternatives (i.e., real versus unreal). But Schelling, for his part, belongs to the long tradition of philosophers, extending from Plato through the post-Kantians, for whom the notion of degrees of reality is an acceptable, and indeed a preferable, model.

Against "Degrees of Possibility." What of the doctrine of degrees of possibility? This conception of Schelling's appears to be rather more dubious. Is not "possibility," at least, an all-or-nothing category, allowing no degree of variation between itself and its opposite, "impossibility"? (Bear in mind that possibility is different from probability, which clearly does admit degrees.) But one might still maintain that the possibility, for example, of scaling an imaginary mountain of gold would be "less" than that of scaling a publicly observable mountain of earth and stone; and that the latter possibility, in turn, would be "less" than that of experiencing either mountain (whether sensible or imaginary) as three-dimensional (which is *a priori* necessary). The point here is not that one is "more likely" to scale a sensible than an imaginary mountain—this suggestion would be patently false—but that the order or type of possibility is different in each case: Lower-order possibilities are dependent on higher-order possibilities in a manner that the latter are not, in turn, dependent on the former.

So much may perhaps be accepted. Yet Schelling often writes as if a mere possibility could independently promote itself into existence, as if its need for self-completion or self-manifestation would alone be enough to transform a potential being into an actual being. This approach is not without difficulties. The main problem stems not from Schelling's conception of possibility as such, but rather from the general method of the *Erzeugungsdialektik*. The transition from a bare possibility's perceived need for ontological completion to the posited actualization of its inner nature sometimes appears tenuous. Final judgment on this matter, however, must await the conclusion of Schelling's application of the method.

Against the Admixture of Value Terms. A third set of scruples concerns the introduction of valuational terms into the discussion. Readers may be puzzled at first on finding such frequent references in Schelling's texts to the "consummate being" *(das vollendet Seiende)*, to the "most desirable object" *(der am meisten begehrenswerte Gegenstand)*, to "the perfect object" *(der vollkommene Gegenstand)*, etc.[20] Supposing that these labels may be legitimate enough in themselves, one can still be skeptical as to their validity when applied, as here, to sheer possibilities. What, indeed, do notions of value have to do with the totality of all forms, when these are considered just in their capacity as pure possibilities? Even if one grants that some states of affairs may possess a higher degree of ontological stability, coherency, or potentiality than others, what should all that have to do with better or worse? And on what grounds can Schelling maintain that an ordered series of possible entities or states of affairs would necessarily lead up to something allegedly perfect and complete—the so-called "highest Being"?

In order to appreciate Schelling's theory of the Potencies, it is necessary to understand that he is thinking not only about what is logically possible in the sense of abstract mathematical relations, but primarily in terms of what is volitionally possible.[21] As Xavier Tilliette observes, Schelling's conception is that "the possible pushes toward the act, and freedom is the force that actualizes the possible."[22] One may understand this doctrine in the following way. Real volitional possibility is that which a being originating in particularity and grounded in egoity *(Egoität)* might conceivably entertain as desirable for itself. (Note how different this conception of the "possible" is from a merely logical one.) A volitionally possible state of affairs is any condition of being, distribution of resources, allocation of pleasure or pain, etc., which some agent (or derivatively, some collectivity of agents) might aspire toward as a worthwhile goal. The point is to emphasize the role of the will as a determinator of possible realities based more on their perceived values for individuals than on their abstract structural characteristics in general.

At this preliminary stage of the dialectic, however, there is no question yet of any particular objects of desire or volition. For nothing specific has taken shape within the horizon of the pure *sein Könnende*. Schelling describes it as the "wantless will" *(der nicht wollende Wille)*, which has the innate capacity to will, but which has not yet assumed determinate form.[23] In this state of indeterminacy, the first Potency is devoid of concrete actuality *(Wirklichkeit)*, although it does possess a lesser degree of being *(Sein)* qua potentiality. The capacity to become specified through definition, in other words, and to assume a determinate volitional form, confers on the as yet amorphous, inactive A^1 a qualified condition of being, even though it does not yet "exist" in the full sense of the word.

Schelling refers, in this connection, to the distinction in Greek between absolute nonbeing (οὐκ ὄν) and relative not-being (μὴ ὄν).[24] Only the former denies any reality whatever to its subject; but the latter, μὴ ὄν, simply states that the subject lacks some particular predicate or set of predicates. Thus, for example, the color green would count as a relative not-being with respect to red, since green is not red. But green is still not absolute nothingness by any means. Similarly, Schelling maintains, the premundane condition of A^1 is a relative not-being (since it is not yet anything specific), but this is still different from absolute nonbeing (since A^1 does possess the infinite potentiality to become specific).

Despite this distinction between μὴ ὄν and οὐκ ὄν, however, it may not be enough to extricate Schelling's theory from its difficulties. For the fact remains that A^1, unlike the color green, is by hypothesis at this stage a not-being in every specific relation. The universal character of its supposedly "relative not-being" therefore seems to verge on absolute nonbeing after all. The ascription to A^1 of the capacity to become determinate appears fairly vacuous when that capacity itself is described as wholly indeterminate. In other words, unless this Potency has at least some definable character already inherent in its nature, something definite and specific, there would seem to be a total absence of means to transform the initial indeterminateness into something that "subsequently" (even in prototime) could become determinate.

Here Schelling's method shows itself at something of a disadvantage. He cannot argue (as Hegel, for example, could) that the concept of determinate being is already implicitly contained in the concept of the indeterminate. Because the *Erzeugungsdialektik* treats each successive phase in the unfolding of thought and being as an entirely new production, the "provisional" lack of determinacy within A^1 has no logical purchase on the next succeeding phase, and so the indeterminacy risks becoming a permanent condition. This first Potency in itself seems unable to provide a theoretical "chisel," as it were, by which to sculpt the "uncarved block" of indeterminate potentiality into the determinate structures of an actual universe.

Schelling, however, thinks he can resolve this problem by finding the source of determinations in another Potency, as we shall presently see. As for A^1, the content of its "willing" remains at this preliminary stage completely indeterminate.[25] Yet this very indeterminacy, he says, constitutes the ideal material for all the future beings and projects that might conceivably someday traverse the world scene. This is why the first Potency in its initial mode appears as a "magical power," encompassing infinite realms of possibility in amorphous guise.[26]

The second Potency, symbolized as +A or A^2, provides the principle of order. This is the source of objectivity, whose role it is to impart determinate structure to the limitless possibility of A^1, and in that way to enable the formation of a concrete world. Basically, A^2 is the principle of specification, whereby a limited subset of all possible predicates is assigned to each particular thing. For, Schelling reasons, there must be in reality (i.e., in any possible reality) a sufficiently lawful character to ensure that the predicates of every entity are definite and fixed.

An example may help to clarify Schelling's point. A piece of coal is typically hard and not soft, black and not white, brittle and not elastic, . . . and so on through the list of possible predicates. Otherwise, no determinate character would be attributable to the coal, in which case its being as coal would be nullified. Furthermore (to continue the example), the specific nature of the coal must stand in systematic relation to all other entities in the universe, thus forming a network of interconnected determinations. That which fixates the hardness of coal, in other words, must be integrally related to that which determines the softness of chalk, the greenness of grass, the swiftness of light, etc., etc. Determinate facts and principles are not isolable; necessarily they belong together as a system. Schelling therefore concludes that an ontology of concrete being requires a general principle of differentiation, and this is just what his second Potency provides. The definiteness and fixity of A^2 contrasts with the indefiniteness and fluidity of A^1 in approximately the same way that, in grammar, the indicative mood contrasts with the subjunctive. The former (indicative mood: A^2) represents the world of possible determinate facts, while the latter (subjunctive mood: A^1) pictures all that might have been or could have been. For Schelling, both principles are equally indispensable components of any possible universe.

Now because the second Potency is all order and without any capacity in itself for indeterminacy, Schelling characterizes A^2 in its original, premundane state as "the pure being" *(das rein Seiende)*, as opposed to A^1, which is the pure possibility of being.[27] It is the "bare object" *(bloßes*

Objekt) as opposed to the subject. This Potency contains no portion of the infinitely variable potentiality *(potentia pura)* allocated to A^1, but is instead a fullness of being so completely determinate that it can be nothing other than precisely what it is. Schelling maintains that A^2 is necessary in order to supply the storehouse of qualifying properties with which the inchoate formlessness of A^1 can "clothe itself" so as to acquire the specificity of particular thinghood.[28]

The second Potency accordingly constitutes the "pure act" *(actus purus)* which serves as the "formal cause," in Aristotle's sense, over against the "material cause" which is the first Potency.[29] This "pure act" or "pure being" functions as the container bounding A^1, the "being-in-itself" *(an-sich-Seiende)*. Since the defining boundaries provided by A^2, however, are supervenient, and in that sense "outside" of that which they limit (whereas A^1 as the "inside" constitutes the actual "self" of the *definiendum*), Schelling characterizes A^2 as the "being-outside-itself" *(das außer-sich-Seiende)*.[30] In still other contexts, in order to emphasize the obligatory aspect of the second Potency's activity, he defines it as "being-that-must-be" *(das sein Müssende)*.[31]

The somewhat mystifying flavor of the above characterizations results partly from Schelling's abstruse terminology, but partly also from the nested layers of ideas that have been packed into his argument. Readers may wonder, in particular, why it should be necessary to posit a single principle, containing each and every determination to be distributed among all the individual entities composing the universe. Why not rather postulate a large number of different principles or causes, whose interactions among each other might then be supposed to bring about the specific determinacies of this world? What motivates the notion that the totality of all defining limitations must emanate from just one original source?

Schelling does not address this question directly, but based on his general philosophical orientation we may be fairly certain what he would say. In the first place, he would maintain that, prior to the derivation of A^2, the principle providing the possibility of multiplicity had not yet arisen. In fact, it was precisely in order to account for the being of differentiation and multiplicity that he has proposed the theory of the second Potency. Even the very distinction between A^1 and A^2 stems, in the terms of the Schellingian vocabulary, directly from A^2 itself. From his perspective, then, it would be begging the question to attempt to explain the genesis of logical pluralities in terms of predicates already posited as plural.

In the second place, Schelling would argue that the concept of multiplicity rests upon a more elementary notion of the single, connecting context in and through which the distinguishability of all things has its source. Thus, regardless of whatever properties or relations one might wish to ascribe to a hypothetical array of separately grounded first principles, inevitably some form of implicit, overarching unity must creep back in. At the very least one would need to explain how this array could collectively constitute a single, intermeshing system. Schelling is convinced that thought necessarily strives for a comprehensive unity.[32] And in terms of the *Potenzenlehre,* it is A^2 which has the role of the unitary principle underlying the totality of determinate attributes comprising Thinghood as such.

So much of Schelling's argument may perhaps be provisionally accepted. But there remains the issue as to the manner of A^2's objectifying activity vis-à-vis the infinite potentiality of A^1. Just as the latter principle was seen (in terms of Schelling's ontological voluntarism) to have a primordial nisus transcending bare logic, so its counterpart would presumably also have a volitional aspect corresponding to it. Yet Schelling claims, somewhat surprisingly, that the second Potency cannot immediately possess a will of its own, for the reason that A^2 has been defined as pure objectivity without any subjectivity whatever. This position creates new problems. What kind of a "volitional character" is thinkable in the absence of a will?

Likewise puzzling is how A^2 can exert any determining influence at all upon A^1. This function allegedly cannot take the form of imposing negative barriers or restrictions on A^1 (as Schelling did hold in his early, Fichtean period), because there is nothing positive as yet within A^1 to be restricted in the first place. Insofar as A^1 has been defined as the "infinite lack of being," its determination would require something capable of bringing a positive content to it. But where would such positive content come from? This is not an easy question to answer.

The central dilemma here is that A^2 must be a limiting activity, although without possessing—at least initially—anything specific to impose limits upon. And it must perform this function as an objective volitional activity that nevertheless has no determinate goals as yet to aim at. How is such an activity, how is such a "drive," conceivable? Schelling attempts to resolve these difficulties by theorizing that the second Potency must be a kind of involuntary motivation, or "unwilled wanting" *(willenloses Wollen),* which constantly strives to satisfy the indeterminate propensities of the first Potency.[33] This "motivation" would supply the appropriate volitional content on which A^1, as the inchoate drive or "unwanting will" *(nicht wollende Wille)* can direct its energies. Thus, A^2 constitutes (in this originally ideal condition) a moment of "objectivity" not, as in subsequent dialectical stages, via opposition and negation, but just by providing the infinitely pliable material for A^1 to do with as it might will (that is, if the latter were to exercise its will, which as yet it does not). Hence, reasons Schelling, A^2 provides a nonrestrictive framework (anticipatory of "limiting activity") for future acts of will by the subject; and yet it does so without imposing any specific limits on its counterpart, A^1. In this way, although willing nothing in particular, A^2 proleptically belongs to a volitional system.

As a figurative example of A^2's *willenlose Wollen*, Schelling cites the superabundant generosity of a being whose giving nature is so inexhaustible as to be incapable of denying the wishes or needs of another.[34] Insofar as such a being's total resources would be available for the use of the other, the donor's wish to satisfy would not reflect any will of the donor's own. However, insofar as these same resources would supply the wherewithal for the recipient to mold and manipulate *ad libitum*, they would form the objective means for all the latter's subjective intentions.

The point of the analogy is to help make thinkable a principle of "objectivity" as it would appear prior to the determination of any specific objects per se. In a similar manner, by ceaselessly providing objective means in accordance with the promptings of the subjective moment, A^2 fulfills its role as the infinite determining activity. It is the pure object, giving itself completely to the pure subject.

The obscurity of the above reasoning stems, according to Schelling, from the very nature of the investigation itself. Critics may suspect that part of the problem lies in the method of the *Erzeugungsdialektik*. Perhaps. But even so, it is evident that the philosopher has brought out some formidable issues in a crucial area of metaphysics. The outstanding difficulties noted above would lead Schelling to the next phase in the development of his system.

Each of the first two Potencies, A^1 and A^2, is incomplete by itself in that it requires the cooperative influence of the other in order to be what it is. We have already seen that A^2, as the objective moment, depends upon A^1 as the subjective moment, because no object can be in isolation, but only insofar as it stands in relation to, and is experienced by, consciousness. On the other hand, A^1 is equally dependent upon A^2, the principle of determinate being, because no subject can be, except insofar as it has an object. Thus, each moment presupposes its other.[35]

Yet, paradoxically, according to Schelling, neither can coexist simultaneously with the other in its pure condition, for the reason that their essential natures are inherently incompatible. Where the sheer potentiality of *das sein Könnende* presides, there is a perpetual process of self-negation, of transforming and thereby in a sense annihilating that which immediately is (or was). The reason why A^1 possesses this self-transformative character is precisely because, in its capacity as the wellspring of all potentialities, it is the pure power of assuming any and every other possible form besides what it immediately is. The very nature of this first Potency consists in nothing else than its ability to be different from itself, to negate itself. Hence, A^1 cannot remain fixed in any condition of static self-identity. Quite otherwise is the character of A^2, *das rein Seiende,* whose solid determinacy remains just what it is, without the ability to be anything else. The self-identical stability of A^2 endows it with an enduring self-sameness, and only for that reason can it serve as the principle of objective actuality. The two Potencies therefore stand opposed like Heraclitean flux against Parmenidean being, despite the interdependency that inextricably binds them together. To be conscious, and to be an object of consciousness, can never pertain to the same mode of being at the same time, and yet neither one is thinkable apart from the other.

The determination that two mutually implicating principles are nevertheless incompatible with each other would have led, in the hands of an *Aufhebungsdialektik,* to the conclusion that one or both must be redefined. Schelling's *Erzeugungsdialektik,* however, takes him in a different direction. Noting the logically untenable relation between A^1 and A^2, he reasons that an oscillation ensues between the two Potencies, such that A^1 transforms itself into A^2, and A^2 thereupon reverts directly back to A^1 again.[36] This "oscillation," he says, does not exist in actual time, but transpires in the "noetic" medium constituting the deep structure of eternity.[37] (Again, it is notable how significant for Schelling is the idea that dialectical conflicts require a proto-temporal dimension in order to work themselves out. This idea will bear further examination.)

The next step is crucial for the development of Schelling's argument. He maintains that the oscillating movement between the first and second Potencies "is not what we want," nor can it be the final resting point for a teleologically oriented metaphysics. The noetic "movement" in proto-time is untenable because each pole undermines, even while requiring, its dialectical opposite. What one wants, and what the cosmological system of the universe itself truly "wants," is the infinite range of possibilities open to a free subject while at the same time retaining objective being; and conversely, one wants the complete determinacy of a concrete objectivity which nevertheless possesses the capacity for self-negation and transformation.[38] This "need" for a more adequate principle of being therefore produces the third Potency, symbolized as $\pm A$ or A^3.

The third Potency is the ideal fulfillment and balance of the first two Potencies. As the mediating interface between subjectivity and objectivity,

A^3 is the principle of "being-with-itself" *(das bei-sich-Seiende)*, which rises above the other two.[39] Like A^1, it represents the totality of possibilities, but without being for that reason indefinite. At the same time, like A^2, it accommodates the determinate, but without losing its inner spontaneity. In other words, whereas A^1 is the Unlimited and A^2 is the Limiting, A^3 is the purely Self-Limiting, and this constitutes its perfection.[40] Consequently, A^3 is the highest of the three Potencies. Schelling describes it as the "subject-object" *(Subjekt-Objekt)*.[41] In order to clarify its relation to the first Potency, *das sein Könnende,* and to the second, *das sein Müssende,* Schelling defines the third Potency as *das sein Sollende.*[42] For it is here that the dialectic of ontological principles reaches its highest culmination and final goal.

Again, the genesis of A^3 out of the first two Potencies does not proceed through any dialectical absorption or "sublation" *(Aufhebung)* of logical contradictions found in its predecessors.[43] Such a deductive procedure (if Schelling were to use it) would be much like Hegel's *Aufhebungsdialektik,* but it does not accord at all with the method of the *Erzeugungsdialektik.* Instead, Schelling characterizes the third Potency as a supplementary principle that continues to depend on the cooperation of the first two Potencies. The model here is distinctively Aristotelian: just as the first Potency has supplied the material and the second Potency the form, so the third Potency constitutes the synthesizing purpose that integrates the whole.[44]

The essential function of A^3 in terms of this dialectical analysis is to furnish the pattern for an ultimate ontological synthesis of selfhood (as foreshadowed by A^1) and an objective world (presaged by A^2). Unless the principle of such a synthesis were determined in advance as a pure possibility, Schelling maintains, there could be no concrete phenomena of existence. For the being of a self is unthinkable apart from the encompassing horizon of experience; just as, conversely, the being of a world requires the presence of a self or selves to which it can appear. The role of A^3, then, is to serve as the buffer and mediating interface between the other two moments. To draw a simile from the field of mechanics, one might compare A^1 and A^2 to a pair of gears that need to mesh and yet, because of their different shapes, sizes, and movements, cannot do so. A^3 would then be the analogue of the transmission gear, working to connect the other two and bring their discrepant motions into harmonious fusion. It is what enables selfhood and worldhood to "mesh" productively.

However, the third Potency is much more than just a means to an end; it is rather the final cause or purpose toward which the whole ideal organism of the universe is striving. Because A^3 is able to maintain the unity of A^1 and A^2 without permitting either to cancel out the other, it is the self-possessed principle par excellence, combining the assets of the other two. In its provision of material for motivation, or "wanting" *(Wollen)*, A^3 yet remains a will *(Wille)*; while in its state of willing it is still a fundamental source of motivation. For these reasons, then, Schelling declares that the third Potency alone is the true essence of spirit *(Geist)*.[45]

Nevertheless, the concept of such a synthesis is, as we have seen, problematical. Schelling's reasoning has led to the conclusion that pure subjectivity and pure objectivity are not logically compossible; but at the same time he has insisted that they are mutually entailing and inseparable. The solution he offers to this dilemma is to postulate A^3, which supposedly overcomes all the inadequacies noted in the case of the first two Potencies. A critical reader might object at this juncture that the procedure of the *Erzeugungsdialektik* appears in this case to be an exercise in wishful thinking. Granted that we philosophers might well *want* to derive a principle which would unite the qualities of subjectivity and objectivity into one, does this suffice to establish that such a union is indeed a possibility? Or might it not rather be the case that an ideal of human thought—be it ever so desirable and praiseworthy—could be an idle phantasm of the imagination, some sort of "transcendental illusion"? Even if A^3 were deemed necessary for the construction of a complete philosophical system, is there not still a danger that this Potency might contain elements of inconsistency within itself?

To these objections Schelling or his defenders might reply that they stem from an inadequate appreciation of his unique dialectical method. For the conception of A^3, in its relation to the other two Potencies, is no merely theoretical construct designed to meet the logical inadequacies of its predecessors. The progressive emergence of A^3 out of its preceding moments is not supposed to be something that was determined through concepts alone. It was, rather, the result of archetypal "events" occurring in eternity prior to the generation of anything else. The abstractness of the *Potenzenlehre* should not, according to Schelling, obscure the inherent historicity imbedded in its very foundations. The principle underlying this doctrine involves the idea of proto-temporal syntheses whereby initially incompatible states of affairs are conjoined as past, present and future. Thus, the notion of A^3 as a "subject-object," for example, only seems unacceptable if one forgets that it presupposes the previous Potencies, A^1 and A^2, as having been retained in a noetically sequential, proto-temporal order.[46] This noetic medium, says Schelling, provides the ideal matrix for a synthesis of moments that logic by itself could never completely explain or justify.

Yet even if one provisionally grants these points to Schelling, the fact remains that his arguments adduced so far to prove the necessity for a third Potency are less than conclusive. More compelling reasons for accepting the *Potenzenlehre* may be forthcoming, and until then the best that his readers can do is to withhold judgment.

It is, in any case, evident that Schelling's theory of the pure Potencies, as elaborated so far, resembles a Hegelian triad. This is no accident, and it is important to notice the similarities as well as the differences. A^1 is similar to the Hegelian moment of universality, in that both are unitary, comprehensive, and general; A^2 parallels Hegel's moment of particularity, in that both provide the differentia distinguishing entities from each other; and A^3 corresponds to Hegel's moment of individuality, in that both involve a self-determined synthesis of unity and differentiation.

Hegel himself noticed the correspondences, but he rejected the *Potenzenlehre* in stinging terms. Although the following passage does not mention Schelling specifically by name, it is obvious who the primary target of criticism must be.

> In recent years, there has been a tendency to use especially the *Potency relation* as applied to *conceptual determinations*. The Concept in its immediacy has been named the *first* Potency; in its other-being or difference, in the determinate being of its moments, it has been labeled the *second* Potency; and in its return into itself, or as totality, it has been called the *third* Potency. —Against this it is at once apparent that Potency, as used in such a manner, is a category that essentially belongs to the quantum. . . . [Yet] differentiations, so far as they pertain to the quantum, are superficial determinations for the Concept itself. They are still far from being determinate in the manner which is appropriate to the Concept. It belonged to the childhood of philosophy to employ numbers, as Pythagoras did, for the definition of universal, essential differences. . . . The retrogression to a method using numerical determinations is indicative of a thinking which feels its own inadequacy. In opposition to the present level of philosophical culture, which has accustomed itself to thought determinations, this approach now even goes to the ridiculous length of attempting to pass off its weakness for something new, admirable, and progressive.[47]

For his own part, Schelling likewise disagrees with Hegel's understanding of how the three dialectical moments should relate to each other. Whereas for Hegel the moments are involved in genuine—although progressively resolvable—logical contradictions, Schelling holds firmly to the Aristotelian canons of noncontradiction and excluded middle. He refuses to accept either the reality of contradictions or the possibility of a progressive development within the realm of pure Ideas alone. For Schelling, as we have seen, logical principles by themselves are lifeless and void of real content.

This crucial difference is most clearly reflected in the two thinkers' modes of treating the first moments of their respective triads. Hegel conceives of the universal moment as something implicitly actual, that is, as an idea which contains within itself the means and the power for its own emergence into existence. In its fullest development, this idea culminates in the highest reality of the so-called Concrete Universal.

By contrast, Schelling's first Potency, being the absolutely indeterminate plenum of possibilities, is a bare abstraction without any claims on actuality whatever. Although it constitutes the universal and indispensable rationale to which any existent world must conform, A^1 does not yet exist (and the same applies as well to the other two Potencies that presuppose it). At the present dialectical stage, the status of all three is purely conceptual, and the only subsistence attributable to them is that of formal essences, which subsequently may or may not acquire concrete actuality. It is by reason of this intrinsic vacuity of the first Potency—whose ideal (but so far merely ideal) function is to supply the fund of infinite possibilities for the two higher Potencies—that Schelling feels compelled to look for the actual content of his system beyond the world of ideas altogether.[48]

The Inverted Potencies in their State of Tension

In order to understand the transition to the next stage of Schelling's ontology, it is helpful to refer back to the characteristic *modus operandi* of the *Erzeugungsdialektik*. By this method of philosophical thinking, it will be recalled, Schelling seeks to identify the nodal points where contrary dialectical principles collide and where potentially new principles may emerge to resolve the conflicts. Schelling does not pretend that the latter principles are necessarily contained in, or logically entailed by, the previous elements of his system. Their emergence is, rather, a result of experiential production *(Erzeugung)*, as determined by the familiar rhythm of first finding the lack, then establishing the need, and finally showing the causal genesis of the principles in question. The influence of Schelling's ontological voluntarism is very much in evidence here. This method of thinking is decisive in the present instance.

For Schelling, as we have just seen, the three pure Potencies described in the previous section are necessary, but not sufficient, to explain the generation of a concrete universe. Taken together with the internal dialectical relations deriving from them, they constitute a network of intermeshing essences, a kind of blueprint for all that conceivably might be. Schelling refers to this totality of possibilities as "the figure of [determinate] being" *(die Figur des Seienden)*.[49]

It is important to understand in what respect this "figure of being," consisting of $A^1\ A^2\ A^3$, is similar to, and in what respects it is different from, the first Potency considered by itself. Both are sheer possibilities. But whereas A^1 represents an inchoate mass of random and undifferentiated shapes, the "figure of being" is a coherently organized system. And whereas the first Potency by itself throws up infinite numbers of possibilities without regard to logical consistency or to the interrelations of forms, the unified complex of all three Potencies takes into account degrees of possibility, compossibility, and the order of temporal development.

Nevertheless, although the "figure of being" is a highly complex and internally coherent system, and although its laws constitute an indispensable constituent of reality, it is not yet real, for the reason that it lacks the specificity of material presence and individuality. Pure essences in themselves are sterile, defining no more than the general natures of things. Schelling maintains that these essences, by virtue of their very generality, are lacking in full actuality. For example, the essence of a horse would remain the same regardless of whether a particular horse, or any horses at all, actually existed. To this extent, therefore, the world of essences, as determined by the three Potencies, is still only hypothetical.[50]

Real existence, however, requires something more than formal essences. In addition, there is also required the immediate particularity of spatiotemporal presence, as well as the concrete involvement of specific, free agencies. Yet neither particularity nor freedom, according to Schelling, can be, or be produced, by essences alone. Indeed, even the very concepts of space and time, of particularity, of freedom, etc., are all still only hypothetical thought-determinations. How, then, is one to understand the transition from ideal being to actual existence, from formal laws to concrete facts? How, above all, is one to explain the sheer existence of particular entities as particulars?

By way of providing an answer, Schelling turns again to the first Potency, A^1, which represents the indeterminate totality of possibilities. As we have seen, ideally A^1 should subordinate itself to A^2, accepting the structural limitations that determinate being necessarily involves. According to Schelling, this means that A^1 ought to remain in a position of "relative not-being"—i.e., to keep its nature within bounds so as to provide the enabling foundation *(Grund)* for the other two Potencies to be.[51] Yet precisely because of A^1's capacity as the wellspring of all possibilities, it also possesses the ability to cease subordinating itself in the proper way. Instead, it can oppose the harmoniously rational order. Just as its original submission to the two higher Potencies has always been unconstrained and uncoerced, by the same token it is at liberty to abandon this condition. In exercising that option, however, the first Potency would thereby be expropriating for itself the preeminent position in the world system, which by rights should pertain to the third Potency.[52]

In their original condition of rest, the three Potencies have, of course, had a "being" of sorts—namely, as ideal possibilities—but without possessing concrete actuality in real space and time.[53] Hence, for A^1 to effect a transition from potential-being to actual-being *(ā potentiā ad actum)* would involve stepping outside its prescribed limits (i.e., prescribed by A^2) and taking upon itself a mode of being that would, at least in the beginning, be quite foreign to it. In other words, A^1 must cease to relate itself to the other Potencies as part of an intelligible order of thought-forms, for such forms are mere universals and as such possess no particularity of their own. But where, then, can A^1 acquire the requisite particularity since, as we have seen, no mere concept or principle by itself can confer actuality? And what will the effect be of A^1's first brush with a reality which, by hypothesis, must utterly transcend the system of ideas comprising the "figure of being"?

By way of anticipation, we may note that this other mode of being would ultimately have to derive from God, whose perfect individuality alone is free of all universality. However, the present stage in the inquiry concerns neither the point of origin nor the accomplished fact, but only the bare possibility of assimilating actual-being.[54] Now Schelling asks, what would the expected consequences be of this transition from pure ideality into concrete actuality?

The next move in Schelling's argument is quite difficult to grasp. In order to understand it, one must bear two things in mind: first, that the new mode of being which A^1 is to receive will be completely alien to that Potency's original nature; and second, that this alien type of being will be the antithesis of everything that is universal, everything that is ideal. Why should this be so? Schelling's argument takes its departure from the proposition, which he now regards as established, that the three pure Potencies comprising the "figure of being" embrace all the principles of intelligible structure any universe could possibly possess. These principles include the abstract essences of all things in every conceivable pattern of interrelation; yet they do so—be it carefully noted—in the form of ideas alone. Concrete existence, however, would still be unaccounted for, since (as Schelling never tires of repeating) existence requires something more than the bare descriptive predicates that ideal essences provide. Hence, the brute facticity of existence must be the opposite of an idea, the precise contrary of an essence. The concrete basis of existence must escape the formal structures of intelligibility altogether: it will therefore be the ultimate surd.

Now insofar as the new mode of being would be of an alien type, the first Potency would be forced to undergo a profound alteration. This change would involve a dislocation of its previously self-contained character (for which it was known as the "being-in-itself"), so that presently it would seem, as it were, to be turned inside out. (Schelling observes that the word "exist" derives from the Greek ἐξιστάμενον, which literally means "standing outside itself."[55] In any case, the result would be a total disruption of A^1, transforming it into something nonconscious and in disequilibrium with its own, implicit essence. By the same token as the pure Potency, when included in the "figure of being," previously sustained an ideal system of perfect order and harmony, so now the revolution in A^1 would result in a condition of radical confusion and disorder. According to Schelling, what was once an inchoate plenum of possibilities would suddenly become a chaotic field of conflicts, no longer receptive to the ordering influence of A^2, but positively resistive to determination in any form.

Perhaps an example will help to make this clearer. Just as an architect's designs for a new building may be perfectly rational on paper, yet fall into disarray when the attempt is made to put them into actual practice, so here the same problem occurs magnified on a cosmic scale. The limpid rationality that characterized the "figure of being" becomes subverted in the process of the first Potency's actualization and falls into the quagmire of confusion that is primal matter.

Thus, the original *sein-Könnende* would abruptly change its nature and become *das nicht-sein-Könnende,* something opposed to the acceptance of any such qualities or predicates as are necessary to the being of rule-ordered structures. Concurrently, what was once the seat of subjectivity would acquire—qua "outside of itself"—a new kind of "objectivity," but not one harmoniously attuned, as A^2 was, to the wants and needs of consciousness. On the contrary, this inverted first Potency would become an unruly substance, opaque to the penetrating light of reason.[56]

The following step in Schelling's argument is even more challenging and difficult. He maintains not only that the actualization of the first Potency would render it confused and intractable, in the sense of being passively resistive to reason; but more than that, he suggests that it must become an active power, working in opposition to the principles of rationality. Not just randomly unordered, the actualized first Potency transforms into a positive force for disorder, disruptive and tumultuous in the extreme. This new substrate, Schelling continues, would in effect be an "inversion" *(Umkehrung)*—or, more forcefully still, a "perversion" *(Verkehrung)*—of the first Potency as it was in its original state of rest. In its capacity as the material ground of a concrete, but disordered and in that sense "blind," existence, this principle would ceaselessly work against all that is systematically ordered and rational in the world.

In effect, the first Potency would now behave in exactly the opposite manner from formerly. Schelling accordingly symbolizes it with a new designation, as "B."[57] The transformation from A^1 to B involves much more than just a radical break away from the ideal world of essences. For again, whereas A^1 has been submissively receptive to the rationalizing influence of A^2, its new incarnation as B would be resolutely irrational. The primary functions of this new Potency, indeed, would be to negate the forces of order, to resist formal determinations of any kind, and to exclude the two higher Potencies from existence. For these reasons, Schelling characterizes B variously as the "negating power" *(die verneinende Kraft)*, the "inward-drawing, collapsing power" *(die zusammenziehende Kraft)*, or the "excluding power" *(die ausschließende Kraft)*.[58] All of these descriptive phrases are more or less equivalent terms. Their main point is to emphasize that real existence begins in chaos. Such a beginning is necessary, thinks Schelling, because the extra-ideal and irrational type of being which is the source of concrete existence must, initially at least, make a sharp break away from the harmonious system of pure possibilities that previously prevailed. Furthermore, Schelling insists that this principle of chaos cannot merely be passively indeterminate, but must be actively antithetical to differentiated being.

Because of B's intractably monolithic, even destructive character, it would clearly be inimical to the teleological purpose of creating a rationally articulated, harmonious universe. Assuming that there is a God, therefore, B would be a principle fundamentally opposed to the divine Providence. It would assume the aspect of "that-which-ought-not-to-be" *(das nicht-sein-Sollende)*.[59] In this capacity, then, B would take on the role of the cosmic Antagonist, the dark Other which needs to be subdued. (The alert reader will immediately note what applications this idea will have in the interpretation of myths.)

Yet although B would in this way become the counterweight poised against the good, it would not for that reason be an absolute evil, but only a relative one. For without it, without a firm foundation for self-assertiveness that would be capable of resisting, at least for a time, the grand designs of the Deity, neither independent selfhood nor real freedom would be possible. In a sense, therefore, B is a "necessary evil," for this dialectical moment is required in order to catapult the pure Potencies out of the Idea-world into an actually existent world.[60] From the very beginning, however, God's attitude would be one of merely permitting B as the means to a higher end. Schilling takes pains to show that *das nicht-sein-Sollende* cannot be a permanent or essential feature of an infinitely good Deity's universe. Hence, he concludes that B must originate as the indirect by-product of the divine will, whereby God posits B as an indispensable means to the actualization of his true purpose.[61] B as such cannot be part of either God's essence or that of his creation, but exists only provisionally, so as to satisfy the requirements of both the divine and creaturely wills as they must be prior to their voluntary assimilation into the divine order. In fact, Schelling sees the whole tendency of world history subsequent to the Creation as being precisely to bring the inverted first Potency into submission, to change B back to A^1. This, he thinks, reflects divine Providence.[62]

The radical voluntarism implicit in this argument is striking. It suggests that neither the world nor God himself can become actual except by breaking out of mere essentiality via an extrarational activity. Because such activity would result from a free determination of God's will rather than by logical necessity, Schelling claims to have avoided the error of depicting God as if bound by his own essence. At the same time, because the world's undesirable by-products (e.g., the violence and chaos of B) would not in themselves be thought of as direct objects of the divine will, but merely as things that had to be accepted as means to a higher end, the philosopher hopes to escape the charge of attributing evil to God.

Yet this theory, for all its ingenuity, contains deep conceptual difficulties. The most serious problem concerns Schelling's insistence that B must be actively opposed to the rational order of the universe. Critics may inquire whether it might not have been more moderate, as well as more plausible, just to have suggested that B could be passively resistive or inertly impenetrable to reason. The idea, however, that B would have to be a dynamic force for chaos and for positive irrationality seems to be making a very great leap indeed. One will ask: Have not Schelling's conclusions here overreached his evidence? Has he really given adequate grounds for supposing that the original Basis of existence must stand in opposition to reason and to God? Is it even possible in principle to articulate a rational and coherent theory purporting to prove the necessary existence of a radical irrationality?

These are provocative questions. In any case, Schelling continues undaunted with his elaborate exposition of the *Potenzenlehre*.

Simultaneously with the inversion of the first Potency, the other two Potencies have also undergone a corresponding transformation. The second Potency, A^2, now excluded from its proper position in relation to the first Potency, is forced to assume a subordinate position. To that extent it finds itself in the position of a relative not-being (pushed *ab actu ad potentiam*). Yet precisely in provisionally being pressed back to this position of an unrealized potential, A^2 becomes, in its turn, a "subject."[63] That is, it acquires an orientation with a positive directionality. One may compare the new condition of A^2 to the flexing of a spring: in the process it acquires a dynamism of its own, a kind of "purpose" or spontaneous tendency. Similarly, A^2 also acquires in its "tensifying process" a purpose, and thus a "selfhood" of its own: The purpose is to drive B back to its proper, subordinate position as A^1; and the selfhood consists in the will to achieve this goal.[64] (Observe in this connection, that Schelling conceives of the principle of subjectivity as essentially involving the potentiality for assuming properties and forms not immediately present. Hence, although A^2 has lost its control over A^1 and so has provisionally been excluded from existence, yet as *das sein Müssende* the second Potency retains its capacity to become actual, and to that extent it counts as a "subject" in its own right.)

One notices, moreover, that the first and second Potencies have undergone a peculiar sort of role reversal. Whereas A^1 in its original, pure condition was the primordial principle of subjectivity, in its new phase as B it is virtually a formless matter. Conversely, whereas A^2 in its pure condition was the principle of objectivity, it has now become a subject and a self in its own right. This ironic role reversal is a hallmark of the Potencies in their state of tension.[65] The struggle to return these Potencies to their proper relations in the ideal world defines the entire dynamic of concrete existence.

The third Potency does not experience a change of character in quite the same sense as the other two. As the ideal balance and synthesis of both the subjective and objective poles, A^3 is not susceptible to any distortions of that kind. Nevertheless, since the realization of A^3 presupposes a prior attainment of the proper relationships between A^1 and A^2, the third Potency cannot emerge in its full actuality until the other two Potencies have successfully completed their development. Consequently, A^3 in its state of tension no longer appears as the eternal harmony of the Unlimited and the Limiting (although on the ideal level it remains that, too); but instead it assumes the form of a future condition that will only then fully supervene when the struggle of the world process has finally achieved completion. Until that culminating point has been reached, A^3 hovers on the horizon as the final cause toward which the entire course of history is evolving.[66]

The Relation of the Potencies to the Functions of the *Daß*

It will be recalled that Schelling distinguishes between the *Was,* or essential "whatness" of things, and the *Daß,* or actualizing "thatness" of them.[67] His purpose in formulating this distinction is, as we saw, to try to establish the possibility of constructing an ordered, hierarchical ontology without presupposing an unexplained Something to exist at the pinnacle of the chain of being. Yet the inherent linearity of the *Erzeugungsdialektik* suggests that one naturally would think in terms of just such a chain.

On the one hand, therefore, philosophy apparently must seek a nonrational starting point from which reason can then proceed. On the other hand this starting point must not yet be posited as existent, lest the foundations of all thought and all reality should collapse into the merely arbitrary. Schelling's solution to the problem is to place at the head of the chain not an existing thing but an "over-existing" *(überexistierende)* principle, which is at the same time an existentializing Act—a causal agency transcending the universe of both real and ideal entities.[68]

Schelling explains that the *Was* of the universe, and even God himself, is in principle a bare possibility which may either exist or not exist. The *Daß,* on the other hand, is the pure fiat on which being as well as the very possibility of being depend. The *Daß* is neither a natural nor an ideal cause, since both of these operate *within* the universe and therefore presuppose it. But the *Daß* is the transcendent cause *(Ursache)* of the whole of existence and therefore stands above and beyond the pinnacle of the universal chain of being.[69] As *das Überexistierende,* the *Daß* is the creative breath of life that calls the Potencies, along with all the conceivable relations derivable from them, out of the void of not-being and into the realm of actual being.

It is important to look behind the esoteric vocabulary to see what actually is being said here. The argument is a subtle one. Schelling notes that the mind, in its search for the First Cause of all causes, seems to be involved in an infinite regress. For at any stage and at any hypothetical "First Cause," reason can always demand further: Supposing that this thing exists as cause, what is or was the cause of that? . . . etc. Such a regress can never reach a satisfactory conclusion, Schelling suggests, because it persists in conceiving of the highest agency in terms of existence and thinghood. The only possible First Cause, however, that would be capable of sustaining the entire causal chain must be the source of both existence and thinghood, and therefore it cannot in itself be either one.

By means of this argument, Schelling thinks he can escape the old Kantian antinomies concerning the presuppositional nature of all thinking about the regress of causes. Here one allegedly presupposes nothing, for the First Cause to be posited is a No-thing. Nor has one committed the mistake of assuming existence, since the No-thing is the transcendent *Überexistierende*. Thus, the dilemma would seem to be dissolved at a single stroke.

Nevertheless, some readers may wonder whether this neat solution does not involve a piece of verbal legerdemain. Although Schelling claims that the First Cause stands beyond all predication and so is entirely beyond the *Was*, the question remains whether a No-thing is even coherently thinkable. Likewise, when he suggests that the *Überexistierende* surpasses the world of spatiotemporal existence, this assertion itself may surpass the limits of meaningful speech. Such scruples should certainly be borne in mind as one critically follows Schelling's exposition. Yet, by the same token, it is equally important to maintain an open mind while reflecting on his ideas, for these represent nothing less than a concerted effort to reestablish philosophy on fresh metaphysical foundations.

Now, in order to appreciate the significance of Schelling's ontology, it is necessary to analyze carefully the doctrine of the transcendence of the Potencies by the pure *Daß*. This free act of the *Daß*, he says, is "spirit" in a far deeper sense than is the third Potency of *das bei-sich-Seiende* (A^3). For *das bei-sich-Seiende* is only the structural frame of a potential harmony between the other two Potencies. It is, in other words, the formal possibility of becoming the fully self-realized spirit. The pure *Daß*, however, has the capacity either to assume or not to assume the mode of being characteristic of the third Potency. It is this capacity that makes it the totally "free," as opposed to the "necessary," spirit. Thus, whereas *das bei-sich-Seiende* offered the formal possibility of spirit, the *Daß* provides its concrete realization. As such, it transcends even the powers that drive the universe, constituting the unity that runs through all of them.[70]

According to Schelling, the highest reality of the *Daß*, symbolized as "A^0," is the supreme personality of God.[71] Concerning this personality, Schelling must show: (a) that it is different from, and transcendent to, all finite determinations, including those of rational thought and even being itself. For any definable quality or property is in principle a universal, applicable to more than one individual, and for that very reason different from the unique character of God. This requirement nudges the philosopher's thought in the direction of mysticism. Yet at the same time, he also wishes to show (b) that God's personality can still possess a definite character, even though logic would seem to dictate that whatever possesses a definite character must lie within the realm of the finitely determinable. And whatever is finitely determinable must be derivative. This requirement seems to push Schelling in the direction of theological arbitrariness.

Both alternatives, however, are equally unacceptable to his basic position. Indeed, the conflict between these two requirements is another manifestation of the same basic dilemma discussed in the previous chapter. Again, if God's character is composed of statable predicates of any kind, then it would seem to be an assemblage of universals. But what is it, then, that assembles the universals? Just another universal? That would seem capricious. Always the same questions return: Why this predicate rather than that, or indeed why any predicates at all? And yet, unless God's character possesses determinate features in some sense, his attributive personality threatens to dissolve into a void. So the issue becomes whether a knowledge of God's character is possible even to himself. What we see here is the thinker groping to conceive of an altogether different mode of being from that which "is" in the predicative sense of either being some particular quality or being constituted by a congeries of such qualities. This latter kind of predicative being, when conceived as a totality, Schelling calls *das Seiende*. It consists of the three divine Potencies together with all the permutations of form and activity derivable from them. And yet, Schelling insists, God's personality cannot itself be a "whatness," in the sense of having shareable predicates; for again, any such predicate would be a universal *(das Allgemeine)*, and hence subsumable within *das Seiende*. But *das Seiende* has been defined as just the ensemble of those ideal relations which God, as their ultimate First Cause, necessarily stands beyond. How, then, can God be conceived as possessing a character or distinctive personality?

Closely connected with this issue is Schelling's voluntarism. The logical codeterminations of factors in a rationally ordered system of ideas *(das Seiende)* would appear to be a limitation on freedom of the will. Yet neither God's creative activity nor the responses of autonomous creatures could, thinks Schelling, be the consequences of "merely" logical entailment relations. Hence, the final goal of religious philosophy must be to see how God has revealed his personality *through* (rather than *in*) the determinations of concrete being.

In order to make such a relation thinkable, Schelling has recourse to a distinction adapted from Aristotle between *das Seiende* (τὸ ὄν), on the one hand, and "that which IS *das Seiende*" (τὸ τί ἦν εἶναι, literally "that which was to be"), on the other. While the former is the totality of predicative being, the latter, says Schelling, provides the transcendent Causality responsible for bringing *das Seiende* into being and existence.[72] As such, precisely because "that which IS *das Seiende*" is the mode of being which both precedes and enables (as the αἰτία τοῦ εἶναι) the emergence into predicative being, it allegedly escapes the limitations attaching to *das Seiende* itself. Thus, referring contrastively to the three Potencies, Schelling writes as follows:

> Subject, object, subject-object: these are the prime material of *das Seiende*. However, not *das Seiende*, but that which IS *das Seiende*, is the object *(Gegenstand)*, is the desired, the goal, is the *principle*, that it actually is (the others are only the possible). For that being, *by virtue of which* alone it IS *das Seiende*, is independent of its being-qua-*das Seiende (das-Seiende-Sein)* . . . It is that being which it has within *itself*, and so independently of those preconditions which proceed only in thought . . . It is that being by virtue of which it is the πρῶτοσ ὄν, the first being, which is preceded by no other, and which already for that reason is an individual.[73]

This divine Causality, however, cannot possibly operate as a single event in time. True to his *Erzeugungsdialektik*, Schelling argues that it must occur as a developmental process passing through several distinct stages along the way. The theory of these developmental stages was first stated in *Die Weltalter*. In a somewhat changed form the same theory reappears in the *Philosophie der Mythologie*.[74] According to both formulations, each stage represents one of the constituting functions of the *Daß*, and only when all are finally seen together can the true meaning of Creation be fully comprehended. (In this way, Schelling will later seek to connect the pre-Christian, mythological religions in a single line of succession with the consummating realization of Christianity. Here in the negative philosophy, however, he is simply concerned with establishing the formal possibility of three successive stages in the unfolding of the *Daß*.)

In the first stage, then, the divine *Daß* projects the three Potencies in their primordial, paradisiacal unity. Because this unity is based upon an indeterminate unity of principles without any awareness of contrast or opposition, the finite spirits can dwell in an undisturbed, completely innocent relation with God and with the eternal Ideas. Schelling describes this original fiat of a premundane harmony as the creative interaction between God and the finite soul *(Seele)*.[75] However, the relation which obtains here is vegetatively passive rather than self-consciously active. Hence there can be no genuine revelation or *knowledge* of God at this stage.

The next stage of development is not a direct result of God's own activity, but is rather an act of withdrawal, on the part of finite spirits (e.g., human beings), from the divine order. This act of withdrawal is a positing of individual selfhood, whose immediate effect is to precipitate the struggle among the inverted Potencies in their state of tension. Yet the positing of a separate selfhood *(Ichheit)* is not itself a function of the Potencies, according to Schelling. This creative act "has nothing at all in it of a *Was*, but is pure *Daß*, without any Potency, and to this extent is in fact like God . . ."[76] Here the individual volition tears itself loose from the condition of primordial unity in a quest for freedom and independence. In the process, however, the Potencies become distinct and independent powers in their own right. This stage is accordingly marked by an active, often desperate effort on the part of finite spirits to hold together the Potencies and bring them back in relation to each other.

With the third stage of development, that of *Geist* proper, the Potencies will be reconciled and spirit will at length come into its own, full personhood. Because the Potencies will finally have achieved their true and destined relations to each other, opposition and conflict will reach an end. Thus the good spirit can achieve both a reconciliation with God and, at the same time, a reunion with its own soul. In effect, the self-positing *Ichheit* will be able to realign itself with its divinely posited *Seele*, leading to a condition of final blessedness.[77] Moreover, the individual will no longer misidentify either herself or God with one or another of the Potencies, but instead the personality of all spirits can emerge as fully self-conscious in their *Daß*, ready for a free communion with one another.

The relations among the various modes of creative *Daß* and the three informing Potencies can be represented schematically as in table 1.

Schelling sometimes depicts the relation of the Potencies to the *Daß* as being analogous to that of clothing to the body.[78] So long as one fails to distinguish the outer vestments from the inner reality, it remains impossible for the naked truth to emerge. But once having overcome the false pretensions of the outer vestments, finally the way is opened for self-mastery, as well as for a genuine person-to-Person relationship with God.[79] Schelling accordingly characterizes the revelation of God's Spirit as a progressive "elimination" *(Ausscheidung)* or "separation" *(Absonderung)* of the *Daß* from the Potencies along with their derivative attributes.[80]

Table 1

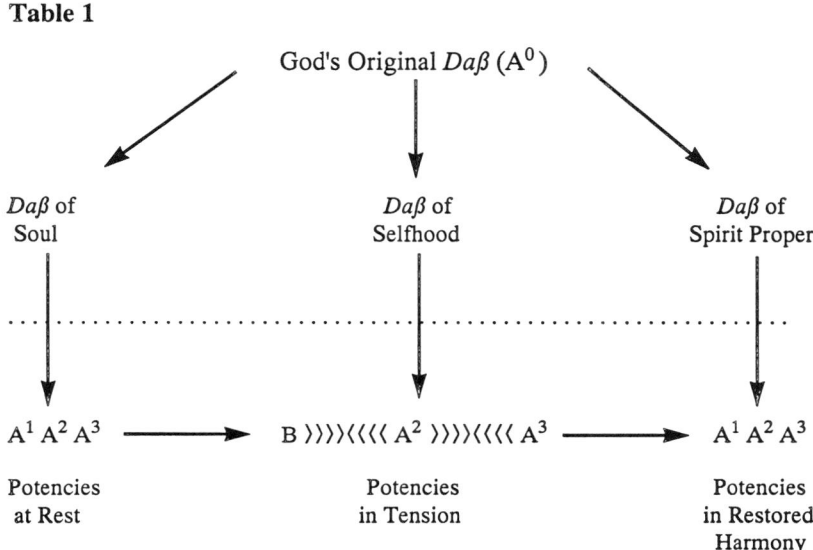

> For the Potencies are equivalent to him, yet are not He Himself. Thus, when he places them in tension, so that they are no longer equivalent to him, then he appears as Himself and, having as it were expelled the material of his being from himself, stands there in his utter nakedness. ... Monotheism is in this sense directly opposed to Spinozism, where God is the universal substance or *the* One. Indeed, for as long as God is posited as mere absolute, for just so long is the God himself (*He* himself) still covered, as it were, by that being which he possesses as a hiddenness in himself. There he is equally the πᾶν (the All): he must, then, be able to free himself of this, in order to appear in his true individuality (*Einzigkeit*).[81]

Such an *Absonderung* and revelation of God's inwardness can, however, only take place to the extent that the finite spirits are able to achieve the proper ordering of active and passive relations among the Potencies. Because these finite spirits also have a free will, this confers on their activities a certain degree of independence from God's plan. The Potencies can, therefore, temporarily act in opposition to the divine will; but the purpose and destiny of the universe is, as already explained, for the first Potency, B, to subordinate itself completely to the second Potency, A^2.

Some Comments and Criticisms Concerning the *Potenzenlehre*

At this point in our study, it is appropriate to look back on the terrain covered and also to raise some critical questions concerning Schelling's methodology and ontology. Having seen in what direction his *Erzeugungsdialektik* has taken him, we can begin to evaluate the significance of his thought.

On the positive side, let us review what are perhaps the three most significant contributions made by Schelling to modern philosophy, especially religious philosophy:

(1) Most influential among subsequent generations of philosophers have been his efforts to clarify the distinction between essence and existence, and to draw out the consequences of this distinction as applied to the ontology of freedom. Going beyond his predecessors, Schelling's later works represent a systematic attempt to think through the implications of the insight that, in Kant's famous phrase, "'Being' is . . . not a real predicate." Taking this as his starting point, Schelling asks, in effect, what then "being" (or existence) might be. If the totality of predicable qualities, the *Was*, still fails to account for the sheer facticity of existence, and if reason is able to deal only with the *Was,* then how shall consciousness confront its own actuality? Schelling, as we saw, argues that it is necessary to posit an extrarational "leap" by a creative *Daß* in order to account for the transition from essence to existence. The precise nature of this "leap" remains, to be sure, rather obscure, despite all the ingenious arguments. Nevertheless, Schelling's endeavor has certainly drawn attention to a vital and persistent set of problems. Such twentieth-century thinkers as Heidegger, Jaspers, Tillich, Habermas, as well as numerous others, have continued to draw inspiration from these efforts.

(2) Equally noteworthy has been Schelling's emphasis on the volitional dimension of experience. His relentless attacks on the sterility of formal/mechanistic reasoning have opened the way for a reexamination of several of the most deeply held metaphysical presuppositions. At the same time, this reorientation has also made possible a new perspective on the significance of religions. Voluntarism has given a new impetus to teleological modes of thinking. Schelling's doctrine of the priority of the

will suggests the possibility of a nisus toward self-realization in the very structure of things.

(3) Perhaps most importantly, Schelling's investigations into the role of the irrational and unconscious have had a revolutionary impact on the philosophy of mind. He has explored the possibility that this component of experience might be more than just the slumbering darkness of a hidden system of laws—that it might in fact be a positive force for confusion, capable on occasion of acting in direct opposition to reason. This insight can serve as a useful antidote to the sometimes excessive rationalism of much of Western philosophy. Certainly it does seem to be the case empirically that the power of unconscious irrationality can be a formidable antagonist to order on both the personal and social levels. So despite the risks of this approach, it opens promising avenues for further research, particularly in the areas of psychology and mythology. Schelling's work helps lay the theoretical bases for these humanistic sciences by creating new categories for a richer analysis of experience.

On the negative side, however, there is reason to be concerned that Schelling's attempts to place ontology on a purely voluntaristic foundation fall victim in the end to arbitrariness. His efforts to avoid this outcome do not appear, in the last analysis, to succeed. We have already encountered one of the major difficulties: that the dialectically "productive" character of Schelling's methodology, although intended to explain how essence and rationality (encapsulated in the *Was*) could come to supervene upon an irrational ground (the first Potency, B), threatens to dissolve into a non-explanation. For the ultimate presuppositions of rational thinking about the foundations of reality would seem to be implicitly undercut by the insistence upon postulating an absolutely irrational starting point.

One wishes that he would instead explore the possibility of treating this starting point as perhaps only apparently irrational, or as hostile to reason in just certain aspects. Yet Schelling's program requires him to postulate at the foundation of his system an actuality that would transcend any and every form of conceptuality. This strategy creates great difficulties. To argue, with him, that the move is legitimate because the foundation is not presupposed to exist, may be intriguing, but it is hardly convincing. It is just not easy to see how the *Daß* can be described as "prior" to the *Was* and yet be supposed to develop *pari passu* with rationality toward an ultimate truth.

The arbitrariness of much of Schelling's system is especially evident in his doctrine of the inverted first Potency (B). Even granting that there might be a nonrational substratum as a basis for concrete existence, the most that could be concluded from this would be that reality includes elements of randomness, contingency, and disorder. Arguably, perhaps, the recognition of an irreducible moment of particularity in existence leads to the idea of an opacity to reason in the fabric of all things, a fundamental surd which resists even the most persistent efforts of logical thought to comprehend the world. And again, arguably there might be components of the human psyche that intuitively react to the feeling of this surd by becoming positive forces of destructiveness and chaos. But Schelling extrapolates this feature of experience to cosmic dimensions. His Potency B is more than just undifferentiated nature—it is a monolithic and suprapersonal power of opposition to reason and to formal structures of any kind. The brute principle of nonrationality thereby becomes, in Schelling's hands, a willful urge *(Wollen)* toward the irrational; it becomes a drive to consume and destroy all the appearances of order in the world.

Schelling's characterization of B as the "inward-drawing power" *(die zusammenziehende Kraft)*, which seeks to annihilate all differentiated being into a single, chthonic unity, harks back to Jakob Böhme's theosophical speculations. The derivation from Böhme enables us to trace the doctrine's intellectual ancestry. But less clear is how cogent the philosophical arguments are that lead Schelling to conceive of his B in precisely the way he does, even given his *Erzeugungsdialektik* and assuming that his arguments for an inversion of the first Potency are correct. For all Schelling's ingenious reasoning, the connection between the suprarational *Daß* and the irrational B is tenuous at best.

Similar criticisms can also be made respecting the other two Potencies. The relation between the condition of "relative not-being" and potentiality, for example, is extremely problematic in Schelling's thought. He often writes as if "relative not-being" were a kind of limbo state or realm capable of exercising real influences upon the existing world. Speculations of this kind would seem to blur the otherwise sharp distinction between essence and existence. Yet it does not occur to Schelling to worry about this problem. He repeatedly asserts that the initially non-existent Potencies A^2 and A^3 nevertheless can *act* upon Potency B in order to bring it back to its appropriate status as non-existent. How such a thing should be possible is far from obvious, and Schelling never makes himself fully clear on this point.

Eduard von Hartmann has called attention to another, related difficulty concerning the principle of subjectivity. He questions Schelling's arguments purporting to show how the second Potency, which originally was defined as pure objective being, would necessarily acquire a subjectivity and a will just by virtue of being excluded from actuality by the power of the inverted first Potency.[82] It is, indeed, more than a little difficult to grasp exactly how the denial of existence to A^2 could transform the original principle of objectivity into a subject. This strange twist in Schelling's argument is symptomatic of unresolved tensions in his thought.

If logical tensions are the major difficulty with Schelling's conceptions of the first two Potencies, a borderline superfluity seems to be the weakness in his theory of the third Potency. It was the role of A^2, after all, to bring B back into the proper relationship of cooperative subordination. How much does A^3 really add to the mix by relieving A^2, as Schelling says, of its "compulsion" to subordinate B? Or, if there is a need to posit something capable of moving through the forms of subjectivity and objectivity without being caught in the trammels of either one, why could not the pure *Daß* itself assume this function, instead of assuming another Potency on the level of the *Was?*

Schelling would doubtless reply that the *Daß* requires a form-structure within the *Was* as the instrument to fulfill its harmonizing role in being. Since the *Daß* is the form-transcending spirit, it needs something determinate within essence in order to channel its activity. But again, why could not A^2 by itself satisfy this condition? In view of the radical transcendence of the *Daß*, one wonders how compelling Schelling's argument is. Why should the *Daß* require yet another mediating variable?

These are difficult questions. But perhaps, for the sake of fairness, one should suspend judgment on these and similar critical issues until having studied his theories' specific applications.

Furthermore, even if Schelling's ontological system should prove in the last analysis untenable, it would still remain possible that his approach to mythology might provide striking insights and uncover important truths. In the history of thought, it has happened more than once with respect to theoretical premises later exposed as mistaken, that such premises have yet provided valuable perspectives for guiding subsequent research. Often, indeed, the worth of a theory or idea lies mainly in its rhetorical emphasis on certain features of experience as opposed to others. (By the same token, the rhetorical emphasis of a literally correct theory might, in some cases, have a counterproductive effect on intellectual progress.) The same principle could apply to much of Schelling's thought: even though the theoretical underpinnings of his voluntarism and his theory of the unconscious might be logically flawed, they still could lead to significant discoveries within the field of mythology itself.

The feasibility of Schelling's general interpretive approach to religion cannot, as he points out himself, be determined *a priori.* It is necessary to embark on a careful exegesis of specific religious myths and seek to unravel their inner meanings. This undertaking will form the subject matter of Part Three, to follow. However, even the appeal to empirical procedures as criteria of judgment can raise new questions concerning the epistemological relations between the *a priori* and *a posteriori* branches of philosophy. In the next chapter, therefore, we first take up Schelling's transition to the empirical science of "historical-critical interpretation."

– 8 –

Positive Philosophy and the Experiential Proof of God

The previous chapter dealt primarily with Schelling's negative philosophy, that is, with the ontological framework on which the interpretation of religions is to be constructed. Subsequent chapters will explore Schelling's application of his hard-won principles to the empirical domain of mythology proper. By means of this empirical application, Schelling intends both to uncover hidden strata of meaning in myths that previously had eluded the best efforts of hermeneutical scholarship, and at the same time demonstrate the explanatory power of his theory of Potencies. This dual purpose is sufficiently complicated and important to warrant special consideration.

According to Schelling, the negative philosophy is entirely *a priori* in its procedures and conclusions. Because it begins with an allegedly indubitable starting point—the first Potency in its state of purity as *das sein Könnende*—this first branch of the system lays claim to a radical logical necessity. As we saw, however, Schelling's methodology diverges from traditional logic in several respects: (1) the strong strain of ontological voluntarism contained in Schelling's *Erzeugungsdialektik*, as well as (2) the temporalization of essence, and (3) the explicit inclusion of irrational and suprarational elements, together significantly modify the conception of "logical necessity" as used in his system. By entering these qualities into the metaphysical equation, Schelling moves beyond the strictures of rationalistic philosophies. More importantly still, (4) by limiting his negative philosophy to the determinations of the *Was* (as opposed to the *Daß*), Schelling effectively drives a wedge between essence and existence. Insisting that there is no purely logical passage from the former to the latter, he demands an additional input from immediate experience.

In all of these ways, then, Schelling characterizes pure thought as pointing beyond itself toward a supplementary source of knowledge. This supplementary source is to be empirically verifiable, natural, and historical:

the domain of the so-called "positive philosophy." The appropriate method for this second branch of the system is thus *a posteriori*, basing itself on demonstrated facts and proceeding from these via a "historical-critical" method.

Schelling explains that this method will use documentary records where available recording the historical past, but will supplement these as needed with carefully formulated hypotheses regarding the prehistoric past. In treating these periods for which no hard data are available, he says, one must resort to a process of inductive sifting, following the principles pioneered by Francis Bacon, in search of the most plausible probabilities. "Through a successive exclusion of the demonstrably erroneous and a cleansing of the underlying truth from adhering falsehoods, this truth will eventually be enclosed within such a narrow compass as to compel one to acknowledge and declare it."[1] Significantly, however, Schelling's conception of the "empirical" is not limited to the data of sensation, but also includes the possibility of encountering the "supersensible" (*das Übersinnliche*). The proper method of the positive philosophy will therefore include a component of "metaphysical empiricism," a unique kind of reflective experience grounded in the principle of self-consciousness itself.[2]

What Schelling calls "metaphysical empiricism" is evidently something different from "experience" in the ordinary sense. As he uses this term (or other equivalent expressions), it seems to be an immediate empathetic encounter with the spirit of another being. Examples of this sort of encounter would include perceiving a person's intellectual or moral character, recognizing the difference between sincerity and hypocrisy, or perhaps even discerning the predominant ethos of a historical period or cultural group. The awareness of such things is certainly not *a priori*, Schelling observes, yet neither is it given through the senses alone.[3] The procedure of metaphysical empiricism must instead consist in a kind of spontaneous reenactment within one's own mind of the other's subjective processes. Schelling is groping for a new model of empirical understanding in the human sciences.[4] Instead of seeking merely to establish the objective data in phenomena (the aspect of "whatness"), his notion of metaphysical empiricism seeks to recover the subjective activity of volition (the aspect of "thatness"), which he regards as the actualizing principle of all experience. To recover the willing fiat through which another spirit actualizes a world for itself is not a matter of inductive inference, but rather of putting oneself vicariously into the role of the other.

Schelling states that the proper procedure is to retrace the same basic path as that forged by negative philosophy, only this time in reverse order and including all the particulars, together with the additional evidence provided by the fact that the objects under investigation are now recognized as existent (rather than merely hypothetical) agencies. Through this concrete method, Schelling means not only to unlock the secret of God's progressive self-revelation in history, but also to cast light, retroactively, on the ontological "keys" employed in this hermeneutical exercise.

How such spontaneous reenactment is to be achieved, however, or how it is to be verified, is difficult to comprehend. As we shall see presently, Schelling's theory is very problematical. Indeed, scholars have been unable even to reach a consensus regarding the meaning of metaphysical empiricism, or in what sense the positive philosophy is intended to "demonstrate" or "confirm" anything at all.

Empirical Confirmation versus Exemplification

Schelling emphasizes the epistemological differences as well as the thematic parallels between the positive and negative philosophies. Because of this dual relationship, he maintains that the positive approach serves to substantiate the conclusions first reached by the negative method. Mythological, philological, archaeological, and artistic data are all invoked to this end. Drawing on the researches of such early pioneers as Herodotus, Pausanias, and Plutarch, as well as on later ones such as Friedrich von Schlegel, Henry Thomas Colebrooke, and especially the work of Friedrich Creuzer, Schelling constructs a complex account, with systematic connections among the different world religions. Behind their outwardly diverse forms, Schelling claims to detect the signs of a single, infinite Spirit gradually growing toward self-realization.

There is a difficulty, however, concerning the nature of the relation between *a posteriori* and *a priori* knowledge: whether it is a relation of strict confirmation or a looser one of illustrative exemplification. On the one hand, inasmuch as the conclusions already reached by negative philosophy have been presented as *a priori* necessary, it would appear that confirmation by empirical means should be superfluous. "The rational philosophy," Schelling asserts at one point, "has its truth in the immanent necessity of its progress; it is so independent of existence, that it would be ... true, even if nothing existed."[5] Hence, even granting that the infusion of the *Daß* into the formal structures of the *Was* would alter their existential status, yet their nature and place within the fabric of philosophical science would presumably remain the same. Schelling frequently reiterates in the "empirical" sections of his work that every formal possibility must, without exception, find its necessary place within the actual world.[6] These indications all suggest that the positive philosophy could at most exemplify, but certainly not in any stronger sense confirm, the conclusions of the negative philosophy.

On the other hand, Schelling himself maintains that the results of historical research do offer additional evidence supporting the insights derived from the negative branch.[7] At times he goes even further and argues that, although the negative philosophy definitely requires to be seconded by the positive, yet the converse relation does not hold. In certain contexts, he claims that the results of empirical research are independent of any concepts developed by the purely theoretical, negative method.[8] Clearly, then, Schelling wants to present his empirical studies as separately grounded and significantly corroborative of his abstract theoretical system.

In the actual practice of his "historical-critical method," however, Schelling tends to treat the phenomena of religion more like ciphers to be decoded in terms of a preestablished schema than like fresh data to be analyzed by strictly empirical methods. Modern readers of his work often have the impression that he is trying to mold the material to fit a procrustean bed of aprioristic ideas, instead of proceeding by framing new hypotheses to fit the facts, as is standard practice today. This is the chief complaint of Gerbrand Dekker, for example, who attributes the source of the problem to Schelling's having superimposed the requirements of human consciousness upon the reality of God's freely creative activity.[9] Jürgen Habermas, without invoking God, objects that the so-called empirical studies of Schelling's final system "deliver nothing new," but simply repeat with specific historical instances what the negative philosophy has already proven in general terms to be necessarily true.[10]

A priori thought or *a posteriori* data—which should provide the primary source of knowledge about the meaning of religion? For the student of Schelling, this is by no means an easy question to answer. Because these two approaches are so different in nature, they seem to impose incongruent sets of criteria for the interpretation of religions and mythologies. The result appears to be two incompatible alternatives: either (1) the *a posteriori* data of positive science are to be construed as capable of providing genuine confirmation of the negative science's theoretical conclusions (in which case other data would also presumably be capable of disconfirming those conclusions); or, (2) if the propositions of the negative science are after all indubitable and secure against any disconfirming evidence, then the empirical data of the positive science could at most exemplify and supplement, but by no means confirm, the *a priori* truths.

Could there be a third alternative, however—one, for example, that strives to overcome the presupposed opposition between *a priori* and *a posteriori* thought, between the methods of rationalism and those of empiricism? Xavier Tilliette has made a convincing case, well supported by the texts, that this is exactly the sort of synthesis Schelling was aiming at with his theory of the relation between the negative and the positive modes of philosophy. Tilliette writes:

> However, to reduce the opposition to that of rationalism and empiricism would be to go against the intended goal, which is to establish a rupture between two modes of philosophizing or two philosophical directions. And Schelling sees in the transcendental dialectic or the antinomy of pure reason (à la Kant and Hegel) the attestation of the insoluble conflict of the two philosophies. Only, the duality of negative philosophy/positive philosophy requires finer distinctions than those provided by the contrast between rationalism and empiricism.[11]

A few pages later Tilliette continues:

> The negative philosophy is described with the constant concern not to trespass on the prerogatives of the positive philosophy. The latter would therefore be endowed with what is lacking to the negative philosophy. However, the contrast is not a simple contrast of black and white. We have seen that the historical and methodological distinction between rationalism and empiricism is far from accounting for the duality of negative philosophy/positive philosophy. There is not, on the one side, reason and the *a priori*, and on the other, experience and the *a posteriori!* But the diversity in their comportment with respect to experience furnishes an initial criterion of differentiation. The negative philosophy begins with what is *before* experience or, equivalently, with what is *after* being. The positive philosophy begins with what is *beyond* all being and all experience; it is concerned with that which transcends experience, with the supra-empirical.[12]

Granting the plausibility of Tilliette's interpretation, however, the crucial question remains: How are two modes of thinking so apparently diverse ever to be brought into a synthesis? The solution to this problem will be of central importance if Schelling's philosophical project is to succeed.

A Logical Fallacy?

The precariousness of Schelling's undertaking is illustrated with telling force at a crucial stage in his discussion, where he appears to fall into a logical fallacy. The background context is his critique of the ontological proof of God, which, it will be recalled, Schelling regards as inconclusive. For him, the most that bare reason can establish concerning the existence of the Deity is that "God is the necessarily existing being, *if* he exists at all."[13] Existence itself, in other words, is here still only considered as a "whatness," a pure possibility (including that of existing necessarily). In order to show that God actually exists (via the pure *Daß*), some *a posteriori* evidence is needed. Schelling spells out his clinching argument in the following terms:

> The necessarily existing being . . . *is* . . . God; and this is proved *a posteriori* in the manner already indicated, namely in that one says: If the necessarily existing *God* is, then this and that consequence—i.e., then a, b, c, etc., are *possible*. But in fact according to our experience a, b, c, etc., actually exist. Therefore—the necessary conclusion—the necessarily existing being is *actually* God.[14]

This argument seems to suffer from two related problems. In the first place, it is evidently an enthymeme—and one whose missing component admits of various interpretations. In the second place, Schelling appears to be committing the fallacy of affirming the consequent. Let us begin with the question of the enthymeme.

What makes the above argument an enthymeme is its presupposition (perhaps regarded as too obvious to state) that whatever is actual is *eo ipso* also possible. But if Schelling's reasoning were to be construed as relying on empirical data *(a, b, c)* to establish that certain hypothetical entities and states of affairs are in fact possible, then the supposed *a priori* status attaching to the negative philosophy would break down. The very possibility of *das Seiende* would be dubitable until demonstrated *a posteriori*. Yet this supposition flies in the face of virtually everything that Schelling has previously said about *das Seiende*. The prospect of empirical confirmation provided by the positive philosophy would thus be purchased at the price of undercutting the logical status of the entire negative philosophy.

On the other hand, if one insisted on the *a priori* truth of the negative philosophy qua description of a world which is at least indubitably possible, then Schelling's extended empirical discussions would, after all, be irrelevant to the above proof of God. The possibility of *a, b, c* would already be known, regardless of whether such things existed in fact. And from the establishment of this possibility, the argument could go on to deduce the actuality of God. In this case, empirical data could at most serve to exemplify the nature of the Deity, insofar as they would show that the actual world does not contradict what is *a priori* necessary. But knowledge of God's existence would be logically independent of the empirical facts. Once again, there is a tension here between the claims of exemplification and confirmation.

More critical still is the fact that Schelling's conclusion does not seem to follow logically in any case. On the face of it, he appears to have committed the fallacy of affirming the consequent. Granting that *a, b, c* (the consequent) might be true, yet in principle there could be other possible causes leading to the same result; hence the desired conclusion (the antecedent) would not be deducible on these grounds alone. Could it be that the philosopher has unwittingly fallen into so elementary a fallacy?

A fallacy it may be—that is debatable—but unwitting it surely is not. In fact, Schelling makes it clear that he has deliberately modified the ordinary canons of correct logical reasoning. According to him, the standard logical procedure is only appropriate and necessary where the "whatness" *(Was)* of things is at issue. If one seeks to define the nature of an entity, or to determine the various structural relationships it can have with other entities, then one should reason in the traditional manner from the conditioned being to its conditioning causes, mainly by eliminating those hypothetical conditions that could not possibly have resulted in the given effect. This is the method known as *philosophia ascendens,* because it proceeds by way of a logical ascent to embrace progressively more universal and foundational principles. Important as this method is, however, Schelling denies that it is the only valid mode of reasoning, for it must be supplemented by another, which he designates as *per posterius.*

> The positive philosophy does not make use of *a posteriori* proof in the ordinary understanding of the word (viz., as *philosophia ascendens*); for the progression is not from the effect to the cause, but in reverse, from the cause to the effect. Just as the cause in its own *nature* is the preceding moment, so here it also furnishes the *prius* of the proof. From this (natural) placement of cause and effect it follows that here, while the *causa* (God) is proved or demonstrated *a posteriori* or *per posterius,* the result (the world) is educed or comprehended *a priori* . . . [15]

> Negative philosophy is only *philosophia ascendens* (proceeding upward from below), from which it is immediately evident that this approach can have only a logical significance. Positive philosophy is *philosophia*

descendens (proceeding downward from above). Only both together, therefore, complete the whole circuit of philosophy.[16]

These statements do much to clarify the underlying thought implicit in Schelling's seemingly fallacious argument above. Once again, the difficulty arises from the fact that it is, as there enunciated, an enthymeme. In order to comprehend the convoluted line of reasoning, it is necessary to import an unstated premise that may reasonably be imputed to the negative philosophy: "*Only if* the necessarily existing being is God would *a, b,* and *c* be possible." Although Schelling does not explicitly make this presupposition, it is clearly implied by the context. Starting from this proposition, a valid argument can then be reconstructed. Schelling clearly believes that by following the causal order step by step in his dialectic, he has established a series of "if and only if" connections; and consequently, that the system as laid out in the negative philosophy is the only conceivable explanation of this universe, considered as a formal possibility. The concept of *das Seiende* as the blueprint of the world has far more than the status of an ordinary inductive "hypothesis." It is, rather, understood to be the sole theoretical framework that could serve to explain all entities and states of affairs considered as pure possibilities. This is what the negative philosophy has already claimed to establish; and by the same token, it also explains why Schelling can announce (as we just saw) that even in his positive philosophy "the world is educed *a priori.*"

The Significance of Existential Instantiation

At this point, however, it is necessary to ask again what contribution the "empirical" studies of the positive philosophy really can make to the philosophy of religion. If the essence of the Deity has already been determined in the negative philosophy, and if the necessary sequence of stages in God's progressive revelation has already been worked out by *a priori* means, then what can the observed actuality of the world add to the evidence? Is this is not a case, as Habermas and others have charged, of superfluous recapitulation?

There may be some truth to this critique, and it shall be resumed shortly. First, however, it is important to make sure that one has adequately understood the true goal of Schelling's project in the positive philosophy. Granting that neither the essence of God nor the nature of the world can be at issue here, the question is: What remains to be proved by the "empirical" portion of the system?

Basically, Schelling is seeking to demonstrate the pure *Daß* of the Godhead, the uncoerced fiat whereby the "Over-being" *(das Überseiende)* has the capacity of simultaneously willing both himself and the world into existence. Whether God has in fact willed to exist, whether he has determined to reveal his full personality to humankind through providential guidance of the world process, in any case his absolute supremacy and perfection as he is in himself, beyond existence, would be untouched. The positive philosophy, accordingly, is not so much concerned with determining the predicative being of God's nature as it is with evincing the transcendently causal being from which the existing universe ultimately derives. This is the point of Schelling's repeated assertions that the creative agency of God is an entirely free act, undetermined by any concept, essence, or nature.[17] Being free, the divine Act could at any point go either way, without thereby diminishing its status as the "Prius" to all that is actual or thinkable.

A question might be raised at this juncture how Schelling could assert that God's agency is a free act of volition, undetermined by any concept, since the nature of that agency has already been endowed with an eternal and unchanging essence. "How is this conceivable," the critic will remark, "especially if the interpretation given to the above-cited passages is correct: that for Schelling the observed universe is possible if and only if the absolute Prius is actual?"

In order to treat this difficulty, one must bear in mind that the essential possibilities of the universe are different from the manner of its concrete existence. Only the former follow with the necessity of dialectical logic, according to Schelling, whereas the latter must be freely willed by the Prius which precedes all essence. The point of this distinction may be clarified by means of the following illustrations.

Suppose that a logician is engaged in a long and complex proof. For any step n in the argument there are only a limited number of consistent alternatives for the succeeding step, $n + 1$. This corresponds to Schelling's conception of being qua pure possibility *(das Seiende,* or the *Was)*, which falls within the domain of the negative philosophy. Thus, in terms of this analogy, the formal determination of *what* the logician (qua logician) may write is already circumscribed within definite limits, but *that* he will write at all, and precisely *how* he will go about doing so, remain open questions. This aspect of our example corresponds to Schelling's conception of the *Daß*, for here what counts is not just a matter of formal possibilities, but of elegance and style. Perhaps the logician will terminate the exercise without completing it: such a decision would surely involve no formal error. Alternatively, perhaps he will proceed with the proof in a perfunctory and mechanical way, showing neither discernment nor any real interest in the argument: such a plodding performance could not, however, be called incorrect. Finally, perhaps the logician will produce a truly inspired demonstration, evincing at once ingenuity and a personal involvement in the outcome: such a favorable result could come not from any logic alone, but also from creativity and commitment.

Similar comparisons could likewise be drawn from the arts. One might think, for example, of a symphony orchestra's performance of a piano concerto. This too combines the elements of a formally determined essential structure together with free and undetermined volition (perhaps including opportunities for the virtuoso pianist to improvise). Again as before, *what* the musical structure is may be predetermined, but *that* it will be put into effect and *how* it will be played are other matters entirely.

> The demonstration that is at issue in the positive philosophy is not finished as soon as it comes to the main matter at hand. What concerns this demonstration (the existence of the personal God) is by no means just a question of arriving at a certain point—for example, not just to the world, which is the object of our experience. Rather, in the same way that I, even with respect to human beings who are important to me, do not find it enough to know only that they are, but demand continuing demonstrations of their existence, so it is also here. We require that the divine approach ever nearer to the human; we demand that this should become an object of consciousness not just in its sequence of appearances but as *itself*.[18]

The analogy between examples drawn from our common experience and the Deity's world-creative *Daß* is not hard to find. Just like the hypothetical logician or pianist, God can be thought of as following an essential plan (in this case, one that is both eternal and *a priori* necessary), but the precise manner of this plan's execution would depend upon his attitude toward the universe and toward humanity in particular. The chief difference between these everyday examples and God's freely willed fiat is that the latter activity must have originated, according to Schelling, in a primordial *Daß* which preceded both the universe's and even God's own existence. Only in the execution of the world's creation does this *Daß* reveal its true character. This is why Schelling insists that God in himself did not, properly speaking, exist prior to the creation, but simply had the status of the infinite Prius, or *Überseiende*.

This is a most difficult concept to grasp, because one normally assumes that a nonexistent being would be a non-entity, the same as a nothing. Not so for Schelling, however. For him, *das Überseiende* has the power either to become manifest or not to do so. The absolute Prius could, moreover, freely withdraw the universe from existence; or alternatively, it could permit the course of dialectical development to ride roughshod over individuals and nations, without care or concern. (If it should do so, however, it would not properly deserve the title of "God," insofar as that term implies a personal commitment to the welfare of finite spirits.) This is why the "empirical" proof *per posterius* of God's existence must remain an open question until the end of historical time; for it is always possible that the *Überseiende*'s will to exist, to create, and to reveal himself as the supreme *Daß* might be withdrawn at some future point in world history.

Xavier Tilliette aptly explains the relationship between the world's existential instantiation and its implications for the nature of God:

> To be sure, it is not a question of proving the existence of the world nor that of the absolute Prius—but the divinity of the absolute Prius and, consequently, the creation of the world. The proof of the deed shows retroactively the divinity of the absolute Prius.[19]

It may next be asked how this possibility would show itself specifically in concrete experience. How, that is, would one ever know the difference between (a) the case where the absolute Prius does not after all possess the quality of divinity, whether this lack is established through a somehow "insufficient" manner of agency or through a premature withdrawal from the world; and (b), the case where the Prius reveals himself as God via a complete revelation of his divinity through a providential instantiation in the world? Unfortunately, Schelling does not devote much attention to this specific question. Although he amasses a wealth of material in support of his thesis, he rarely gives a hint as to what could conceivably weigh as counterevidence.

In a few critical passages, however, Schelling provides indications as to how the master plan of Providence might be temporarily thwarted by contingent events. Both natural history and human history could get stuck at lower stages of development and be unable to regain the thread of continuing progress. This has happened to individual species and peoples in the past, and conceivably it might threaten the whole of humanity. The possibility of such setbacks is ever present, and Schelling thinks it must be so in order to give free rein to both the human and the divine agencies.[20] But even these momentary or permanent setbacks, should they occur, would have to follow the *a priori* principles set forth in the negative philosophy.

Moreover, Schelling states that the absolute Prius, *if* it is truly God, would be a magnanimous power "which has lifted humanity, as if by a divine hand, up and over the subordinate stages [of development], even though these are logically to be presupposed . . . "[21] In other words, the divine Providence may sometimes so influence historical events as to spare humanity from having to bear the full onus of conflict and turmoil required by dialectical principles, and instead ascribe these necessary stages attributively, as it were, rather than requiring them to be played out in actual fact. This affirmation stands in striking contrast to Hegel's conception of God: the purely rational Absolute whose nisus toward self-realization could show no particular regard for individuals. (Recall that the "cunning of reason," in Hegel's view, does guide the world process, but in a manner that necessarily shatters the happiness of persons and perhaps even of entire peoples.) By means of distinguishing between what is dialectically necessary and what is providentially attainable, Schelling means to avoid the sort of panlogist fallacy which, in his view, was the major fault of the Hegelian philosophy.[22]

Important to observe at this juncture is how the problem of the relation of the negative and positive branches of philosophy has shifted imperceptibly to the question of how divine Providence may, or may not, manifest itself in human history. What connects the two issues is the idea, dating back to Schelling's early period and continuing throughout his career, that the final cause of the universe is not so much a present reality as it is a future hope, one whose ultimate outcome must remain in doubt so long as human history endures.[23]

Nevertheless, with every sustaining moment in the unfolding of God's will, with each succeeding stage in the vast panorama of a providentially guided, purposive universe, with so much the more assurance can finite spirits await God's eventually complete self-revelation at the end of time. This is why the statement "God exists" is to be reinterpreted as describing not so much a present state of affairs as a proleptic anticipation, subject to verification *a posteriori*, of what the future may bring:

> The experience to which the positive philosophy is progressing is not just a *particular* one, but the total experience from beginning to end. It is the whole of experience. But for precisely that reason, this proof *(Beweis)* itself is not just the beginning or a part of the science (least of all some syllogistic proof posed at the pinnacle of philosophy); it is the whole science, namely the whole positive philosophy: This is nothing other than the continuing demonstration *(Erweis)*, ever growing and becoming stronger with each step, of the actually existing God. And because the realm of the actual in which this [demonstration] unfolds is not a completed or finished one—for even if nature now is ended and

stands still, yet in history there is continual movement and progress—because to this extent the realm of actuality is not a finished one, but is rather one continually approaching its completion, so too the proof [viz., of God's existence] is *never* finished. . . . The object of positive philosophy is the object of a proof which, to be sure, is already accessible at earlier levels of development, but which yet is not for that reason a finished proof. There could still always arise in some succeeding stage a contradiction *(Widerspruch)* to what went before. Even the present is here no limit, but there opens here the glimpse into a future which will also be nothing other than the continuing proof of the existence of that power ruling over being, [a proof] of that which is no longer merely *das Seiende* (with which the negative philosophy concerned itself), but which is *das Überseiende*.[24]

Here Schelling makes it quite clear that the "continuing demonstration" of God's existence in the positive philosophy is not at all a matter of testing alternative hypotheses and then choosing the most feasible one. He presupposes that the negative philosophy has already established the sole possible theory concerning the nature of the universe. At stake, rather, is the hopeful conviction that God will instantiate this universe in such a way as to make it meaningful and fulfilling for free finite spirits. This conviction can, he thinks, only increase in the face of a consistent and thoroughgoing exemplification *a posteriori* of its *a priori* framework.

Starting with a quasi-mystical "ecstasy of reason" which transcends the question of existence altogether, the empirical "demonstration" combines two aspects. (1) On the one hand, there is the sense of religious awe consequent upon the emergence of the *Daß* into concrete existence. Schelling emphasizes that this awe cannot be a merely psychological phenomenon attributable to natural origins.[25] It arises only when the human being has been stripped of the psyche and becomes aware of the undifferentiated Source of all being and all differentiation. Once having experienced this awe, the religious mind sees it continually "growing and becoming stronger with each step" in the development of world history. That history, experienced in its entirety, is seen as the existential instantiation and progressive revelation of divine Providence.

(2) Secondly, there is the awareness of standing in a direct and personal relationship to God. This awareness, Schelling argues, is not a function of either the theoretical or practical reason, as philosophers generally supposed. No bare regard for universal laws of logic or morality could lead any mind to postulate a real God and yearn for a rapport with him. Rationality and conscience impose their duties on the individual, to be sure, but though the fulfillment of these is necessary, it cannot be sufficient for the blessedness sought in faith.[26]

So much of Schelling's position is clear. Yet the nagging difficulty remains concerning how one is to understand his use of the word *Widerspruch* in the long passage quoted above. One might ask, what sort of possible "contradiction" is he thinking of here? It cannot be a contradiction with the structures of *das Seiende* (the *Was*), either in part or as a whole; for that is embedded forever in the essential nature of things, as something which is deducible *a priori*. Therefore, if the "contradiction" is not on the level of the *Was*, it must be on the level of the pure *Daβ*, of the fiat responsible both for the fact *that* the world actually exists as well as *how* its dialectical principles are being realized in concrete experience. The final aim of Schelling's "metaphysical empiricism," then, is not to determine the "whatness" of the universe, but rather to come in touch with the transcendental "thatness" of an infinite Creator. With his novel conception of a possible *Widerspruch*, Schelling is suggesting that the future unfolding of universal history may "contradict" not its *a priori* essence (which is fixed in eternity), but rather the idea of its standing in a personal relation to God's core as *das Überseiende* (which transcends essence altogether).

Only on the basis of this interpretation, in my judgment, can Schelling's paradoxical statements about the course of human history and religious evolution be understood. At issue is whether the instantiation of the *Daβ*, considered as a whole, reinforces or undermines the gradually awakening sense of religious awe, of standing in a direct and personal relationship to the author of the universe. Divine Providence involves much more, in Schelling's view, than the presence of a rational order controlling the course of events; such a rational order by itself could exist even in a purposeless, meaningless universe. But *if* there is any ultimate purpose underlying all the turmoil of life (something which only experience can determine), then that ultimate purpose would have to consist in the establishment of a personal dialogue between God and free spirits.[27]

It would go beyond the scope of the present study to pursue in detail this conception of the personality of God as related to finite persons. Suffice it to say that Schelling takes as his working hypothesis the presence of a providential, caring Deity directing the flow of events. The purpose of his direction is to prepare human beings for a standpoint from which they would at last be fully open to the possibility of a unique communion with the Godhead. The consummate goal of life, Schelling suggests, is to enter into a direct experience of rapport with God—a rapport that would be so intimate and personal that it would no longer depend on the mediation of either natural or rational principles. This goal is posited, moreover, on the basis of each individual's inmost identity and quest for a relationship with the author of our existence: for in the end, "person seeks person."²⁸

But let us return, in closing, to the question whether Schelling has succeeded in making precise the supposedly *a posteriori* knowledge of this goal. What he says is in many aspects extremely suggestive and rich in insights. In the last analysis, however, it does not appear that he has conclusively established his case. For although, as we have seen, Schelling tentatively broaches a new conception of empirical "falsification" and "verification," he never develops the idea clearly. It remains difficult to see in what sense the thesis that God exists could in principle be falsified. Even a total suspension of the *Daß* could hardly qualify as a "contradiction" (in any ordinary meaning of the word) to the realized manifestations of the *Daß* that went before. Both confirmation and contradiction seem to be categories more properly belonging to the structural relations within the "whatness" of the universe (its *Was*) than to the inscrutable principle of the *Daß*.

Ambiguities in the relation of *a priori* essence to *a posteriori* existence are broadly reflective of the more fundamental ambiguity in the relation of the *Daß* to the *Was*. One suspects that Schelling, after having carefully distinguished between the universal *Was* and the individual *Daß*, waffled from time to time on the distinction. This would hardly be surprising, since the concept of the *Daß* (if one may even call it a concept) is such an elusive thing. Defined as that "Over-being" which in itself escapes all conceptual definition, the *Daß* is described as "separable" *(trennbar)* in thought from every involvement with the *Was*.²⁹ Paradoxically, however, the *Was* in turn is so closely connected to the *Daß* as to be called "inseparable" from it *(nicht von ihm zu trennen)*.³⁰ Evidently the relation between the two terms is asymmetrical: the *Was* requires the *Daß*, but the *Daß*, in turn, is independent of the *Was*. Yet even the very attempt to describe the *Daß* and differentiate it from the *Was* seems to involve one in the contradictory task of stating "what" the *Daß* is.

Properly speaking, the *Daß* can neither be confirmed nor disconfirmed by experience. It can at most be progressively revealed by means of three mutually cooperative approaches. According to Schelling, it is necessary (1) to apprehend the *Daß* through an ineffable, spiritual "ecstasy"; (2) to articulate and schematize its essential *Was* via a unique kind of *a priori* thought; and (3) to exemplify and thereby reaffirm its reality *a posteriori* (or *per posterius*) by means of empirical experience. The subtle interrelations among these three approaches are as difficult to maintain as they are central to Schelling's undertaking. In effect, he is trying to develop a new, synthetic model for justifying religious faith.

Schelling's search for a comprehensive synthesis of the rational and empirical components of thought, as interpreted via the negative and positive branches of his philosophy, is at best only partially successful. As a result, his attempts to find an experiential alternative to the purely logical proofs of God are not convincing either. Instead, he ends up with a curious amalgam which satisfies the truth criteria of neither approach: The aprioristic schematicism produced by the negative philosophy comes perilously close to being a procrustean bed. On the other hand, the twin doctrines of the "ecstasy of reason" and of "metaphysical empiricism" are too nebulous to yield any definite conclusions about the nature of the Deity.

Nevertheless, these shortcomings do not diminish Schelling's very significant accomplishments in the field of religious thought. By recognizing the implications of the rational understanding's deficiencies vis-à-vis the Godhead and refusing to plaster them over with either abstract formulas or empty declarations of faith, he opened up a major philosophical problematic. Moreover, in his quest to mediate the hiatus between the discursive truths of religious beliefs and the transcendent "Truth" of an ineffable, but ultimate, reality, he bequeathed to subsequent generations a profound set of issues that continue to stimulate creative research and debate.

But this is a matter which itself eludes any *a priori* determination. The feasibility of Schelling's philosophical hermeneutics requires careful testing and evaluation in light of the interpretations he has made of actual religions and myths.

– 9 –

Representative Issues and Controversies in Current Schelling Scholarship: Habermas and Schulz

Modern students of Schelling's later thought have drawn attention to his pioneering efforts to work out a new ontology: one that would be radically developmental instead of fixed in eternity, and that would be experientially oriented instead of determined by an *a priori* logic. This search for a new ontological basis has received praise in recent years, especially in Germany, as a significant philosophical advance. Some have seen in Schelling a prophetic herald of existentialism, others of Marxism, and still others of a revitalized Christian faith. There is a measure of truth in each of these characterizations. Especially valued by a broad spectrum of scholars have been his attempts to reconstitute the notion of freedom.

This chapter offers critical synopses and evaluations of Schelling interpretations by two representative thinkers: Jürgen Habermas and Walter Schulz, chosen in order to illustrate some of the dominant trends in current Schelling scholarship. Perhaps more than any others, their analyses and arguments epitomize the reception of Schelling's philosophy—particularly that of his final period—in Germany today. As Michael Theunissen, another eminent Schelling scholar, has pointed out, "There are, in my opinion, only these two interpretive possibilities: either, like Schulz, to work out a dialectical unity which Schelling himself was unable to express, or else, continuing the work of Jürgen Habermas . . . to presuppose an essential equivocation at the basis of the positive philosophy."[1] Pursuing this observation, the following pages will seek to explain in brief compass the basic lines of thought encapsulated in the two positions. An assessment of these scholars' ideas is all the more appropriate in view of the fact that their work on Schelling remains to this day virtually unknown in the English-speaking world.

To be sure, no two representatives alone can by any means claim to cover the full spectrum of interpretive issues. Notable by their absence are such important figures as Horst Fuhrmans, Karl Jaspers, Walter Kasper, Werner Marx, Manfred Schröter, Xavier Tilliette, and many others. Nevertheless, this chapter will have served its purpose if it provides the basic outlines of the ongoing debate and indicates the broad intellectual context within which the contributions of other Schelling scholars are situated.

Habermas: A Historicist Interpretation

Few thinkers in Germany today have been more receptive than Jürgen Habermas to the influence of Schelling's ideas. Habermas has emphasized Schelling's sensitivity to the concrete conditions of human cultural development, his appreciation of the struggle and risk involved in historical processes, and his fostering of a radical temporalization of modern ontology. Furthermore, Habermas claims to see definite tendencies toward dialectical materialism in Schelling's thought. He credits the *Potenzenlehre*—in particular the theory of the first Potency—with substantial contributions toward the emergence of a more concrete, dynamic, and to that extent "materialistic," orientation in Western philosophy.[2]

At the same time, however, Habermas has also noted a deep-seated conservatism in Schelling's thought. The foremost signs of this alleged conservatism are the continuation of an aprioristic methodology characteristic of traditional metaphysics and the retention of a concept of eternity as an ontological category. According to Habermas, as explained in his study "Das Absolute und die Geschichte: Von der Zwiespältigkeit in Schellings Denken," the implicit discrepancy between Schelling's historicism and his eternalism result in deep and ultimately irresoluble tensions.[3] Let us briefly examine the background of this purported discrepancy.

In his earlier period, the time of his so-called *Identitätsphilosophie,* Schelling adopted a quasi-Spinozistic conception of nature as predetermined for all time according to the immutable laws of God. To the determinism that this worldview entailed, he fused a modified Fichtean theory of freedom as residing in a premundane, transcendental "act." True, or "absolute," freedom, therefore, pertained to individuals insofar as their original "decisions"—i.e., to assume the specific moral characters they presently possess—took place "outside" of the spatiotemporal manifold. Such "acts" must be conceived of as codeterminative of this universe in its every particularity and structure, such that even the apparent vicissitudes of chance and circumstance would be their direct consequences.

The main advantage of the early Schellingian theory above was its logical compatibility with natural determinism. But in the years between 1806 and 1834, Habermas observes, Schelling's thought was gripped by an ambition to penetrate the developmental and inherently historical character of existence. This led to the revolutionary breakthrough of his middle period, which involved an attempt to lay the foundations for a novel understanding of essence as being inherently temporal.[4]

Habermas sees in the *Freiheitsschrift* (1809) and the almost contemporaneous *Weltalter Fragmente* (1811) the dawning of a new, existential understanding of human agency as grounded in the contingent exigencies of the individual's immediate life-situation.[5] In these works, he argues, the assigned locus of responsibility for an action and its consequences shifts from the premundane, transcendental plane to the level of concrete, phenomenal experience.

Moreover, Schelling also introduces a new conception of Being itself as fundamentally volitional. Will as such becomes recognized as existentially prior even to the essential nature, or "whatness" *(das Was)*, that defined an individual's character.[6] The idea here is that Will, as the primal reality, is not in the first instance the will of any particular agency, but rather is undifferentiated and prior to all specification. Individual consciousness later emerges out of the primal Will, and for that reason alone can serve as a privileged locus within which the nature of true freedom can reveal itself. As being subject to circumstantial factors, changes of condition, and personal choices, this new model of free agency qualifies, for Habermas, as one of genuine "historical freedom."[7]

It is, however, significant that he can find but one place in the Schellingian corpus—it occurs in *Druck I* of *Die Weltalter*—where, in his words, "the essence of historical freedom is clearly highlighted and set apart from absolute freedom."[8] At issue in that particular passage is an analysis of the human moral character and the degree to which it may be changeable through time. But even this text can only with considerable strain be taken to support the highly freighted meaning that Habermas would read into it.[9] The moral character, Schelling there writes, is freely assumed by each person in a transcendental act prior to historical time (this is the part that Habermas finds patently ahistorical). But then Schelling adds (to Habermas's evident satisfaction) that this primordial character can subsequently be mastered and altered by the individual. Habermas thinks that the potential for such self-modifications implies the possibility of a "historically free act."

A careful examination of the passage in question, however, fails to substantiate the interpretation that Habermas wants to put upon it. In fact, only a few pages later, Schelling says that the secondary volitional act, whose function it can be to overcome the initial character assumed transcendentally, "is an activity dictated in no way by choice, but rather, even though most carefully thought out, yet following from the inner necessity of its nature."[10]

In general, although Schelling conceives of Will as logically prior to all particular specifications, and although he ascribes to eternity itself proto-temporal determinations (i.e., the "eternal past," "eternal present," and "eternal future"), yet it still does not follow for him that individual choices, etc., are mutable from the transcendental perspective. It therefore seems doubtful, after all, that Schelling would ever draw Habermas's sharp boundary between "absolute freedom" and "historical freedom." To the extent that they are distinguishable at all, both are regarded as flowing from a personal "necessity" which "precedes" the creation of phenomenal time altogether. For Schelling, then, freedom in the true sense would have to be simultaneously "historical" in one sense and "absolute" in another.

Nevertheless, Habermas does make a number of important observations. He points out Schelling's efforts, dating from the same middle period, to interpret even the nature of God as subject to developmental changes. This undertaking proceeds parallel to the temporalization of ontology. An inherent risk in the endeavor is, however, that it may appear to threaten the absoluteness and eternity of God's nature.[11]

During the period between 1827 and 1836, Schelling would become increasingly critical of philosophical methodologies that proceed by means of rationalistic, *a priori* deductions (like Hegel's) of the forms through which world history necessarily must pass. Yet Habermas notes that Schelling returns during the last decades of his life to the project of formulating a reconstruction of the dialectical stages through which humanity had to develop. This move corresponds, Habermas thinks, to a simultaneous shift from the "historicist" back to the "absolute" conception of freedom. What accounts for the changes?

Habermas's answer is that Schelling's final system of philosophy is "erected on the ruins" of his earlier, more promising *Weltalter* philosophy.[12] The ruination, Habermas believes, has been brought about by Schelling's equivocation, which leads him to attempt grafting his new, developmental ontology onto the traditional ontology consisting of eternal and *a priori* truths. Thus, his key insight concerning the irreducible contingency of existence has been undermined by his continued adherence to the idea of an inalterable, logically necessary world of essences. The only way of overcoming the theoretical dissonance that this occasions, in Habermas's view, would be to abandon Schelling's distinction between essence and existence—between the *a priori* necessary and the contingent acts of volition. Going beyond Schelling, Habermas suggests, one must learn to see essence itself historically, recognizing that it is changeable as well as subject to material conditions.[13] This leads to the central thesis of Habermas's interpretation: he claims that Schelling has failed to grasp and to fulfill the revolutionary implications of his own philosophical breakthrough. Habermas focuses his critique on two important shortcomings he finds in Schelling's later thought.

(1) One of the most telling criticisms Habermas makes is that Schelling's final system of philosophy seems to fall into a lifeless determinism. Whatever his dialectic dictates as being transcendentally necessary for spiritual development, the same is precisely what his historical studies always discover in fact to have taken place. Habermas complains, not without justice, that the so-called "positive" portion of Schelling's final system simply recapitulates in other terms the results of the "negative" philosophy.[14] The rhythmic pattern of aprioristic construction and empirical "confirmation" results in an invariable repetition of the same content. Can such a procedure constitute genuine historiography? Habermas rhetorically asks.

(2) Habermas's second major objection is that Schelling should have given up any claim to apprehend God in the concept or qua essence. This criticism, too, has considerable force. Habermas correctly observes that the late Schelling's conception of divinity characterizes God as "elevated above every sort of development."[15] Again, in Habermas's view, this position represents a step backward from the more daring and creative conception of a developing Deity as presented in the first draft of the *Weltalter*.

On the other hand, the latter criticism overlooks the fact that Schelling continues to espouse the theory of development in God qua manifest and operative agency in world history.[16] The sole aspect of God that he regards as transcending development is the Deity "as he is in himself," referring to his identity in eternity.

Schelling evidently wants to have it both ways—to describe both God and the world as in one sense temporally developing and yet in another sense as untouched by change. Moreover, there is evidence that this agenda is already present even in the first draft of *Die Weltalter*, though it is less prominent there. In the latter work, Schelling undertakes not only to describe the primordial past and historical present but even to predict the outlines of the eventual ages to come. Insofar as this project involves an attempt to delineate the shapes of the future by means of analyzing the implications of eternal principles, it obviously shares some of the same motives and presuppositions as in Schelling's "constructivist" approach of the final system.

Whether or not Schelling does alter his conception of the role of the "empirical" method in philosophy, it is clear that he would always think of God's and the universe's historicity as something about which definite—though always open-ended and incomplete—predictions can in principle be made. This belief does not seem, in his own mind at least, to conflict with the recognition of an element of contingency in the course of things. On the contrary, he holds that a qualified "constructive" moment in philosophy is compatible with the methods of empiricism. The central questions are, therefore, whether these apparently conflicting theoretical motives are capable of reconciliation, and whether Schelling's efforts succeed in doing so.

Habermas, however, poses the following exclusive disjunction as self-evident: either one employs the procedures of philosophical construction or one adopts the methods of historical inquiry, but not both.[17] A fusion of the two approaches he considers impossible, because he assumes that free human activity cannot coincide with determination by universal principles or "Potencies." In Habermas's view, the obvious shortcoming of Schelling's final system is that it tries to use philosophical construction as a historical method. Hence, Schelling's main project—to explain by means of a single, all-embracing framework not only the nature of God and the processes of cosmic evolution but also the sociocultural struggles of human history—in Habermas's judgment has to fail.[18]

The previous chapter has already considered this problem at some length. As we saw, Schelling does not intend his "constructive method" as a formal straitjacket, determinative of life in every detail, but rather as a heuristic guide to orient thought and anticipate certain basic, repeating patterns in experience. The details of the general pattern would, however, remain formally contingent and logically *a posteriori*. (Observe that this could arguably be the case even if an array of transcendental acts, taken in "absolute freedom," preestablished the particular factual content that this partially contingent universe would assume in space and time. The point is that spatiotemporal predetermination does not necessarily entail a formal, logically deducible version of determinism.)

Likewise open, on this alternative interpretation to that of Habermas, would be the crucial questions as to which particular individuals or cultures would assume which potential roles, or who specifically would exercise the vital options that the constructive method might previously (but only very generally) have anticipated. Walter Kasper has drawn attention to this aspect of Schelling's project. Kasper's book, *Das Absolute in der Geschichte. Philosophie und Theologie der Geschichte in der Spätphilosophie*

Schellings—the title itself, echoing Habermas, already hints at a difference of interpretation—emphasizes the centrality of religious hope rather than philosophical certainty as the axis of Schelling's later thought.[19]

It is important also to distinguish between Schelling's purposed program and his actual execution of it: for the limitations of the latter do not necessarily apply to the former. Schelling clearly wants his system to leave room for logically contingent actions and developments.[20] But his actual analyses of historical events do, admittedly, often leave the impression of stretching the data onto a procrustean bed of arbitrary and inflexible presuppositions.

In the last analysis, the fundamental issue between Schelling and Habermas concerns the relation of individual freedom to a comprehensive ontological order. For Schelling, true freedom is only thinkable within the context of a comprehensive world system.[21] For Habermas, however, the very idea of such an encompassing world system is the logical antithesis to freedom in any meaningful sense. It is because he regards freedom as consisting precisely in the ability to break out of any ostensible system that Habermas finds the Schellingian attempt at a synthesis to be incoherent. This judgment, in turn, lies at the root of his claim that there is a fundamental equivocation at the heart of Schelling's philosophy.

Schulz: A Quasi-Rationalistic Interpretation

Walter Schulz's study of Schelling's final philosophy, *Die Vollendung des Deutschen Idealismus in der Spätphilosophie Schellings,* brings out the strong rationalistic currents never far from this philosopher's thought.[22] Schulz goes somewhat counter to the mainstream of contemporary Schelling interpretations, but the solid textual evidence he marshals in support of his views has made them very influential.

More than Habermas, Schulz appreciates the centrality, and indeed the indispensability, of Schelling's systematic endeavor. He emphasizes that one cannot succeed in understanding Schelling's fundamental project without taking into account his drive to produce a comprehensive system.[23] On the other hand, Schulz also draws attention to the important parallels between Schelling's thought and that of twentieth-century existentialists, especially Heidegger.[24]

In his interpretation, Schulz undertakes to balance the rationalistic/ idealistic strands in Schelling with the incipient "existentialistic" tendencies. In fact, one of Schulz's central theses is that the internal, dialectical development of German idealism naturally produced succeeding movements such as Marxism, existentialism, etc. This important transition he finds exemplified in Schelling's intellectual history. Schulz argues that Schelling's thought is simultaneously the culminating stage of nineteenth-century idealism and the harbinger of the succeeding era. The fusion of these two tendencies is preeminently visible, on his analysis, in Schelling's theory of the relation between the "positive" and "negative" philosophies.

Schulz observes that these two branches of Schelling's system are not merely complementary, but in fact mutually entailing. While the "negative," *a priori* branch conducts thought to the point of seeing its lack of, and need for, a suprarational experience, the "positive," *a posteriori* branch leads back to the necessary principles of rationality within the phenomenal universe. Thus the positive dialectic restores the basis of the negative. Because one and the same process of internal development leads in each of these directions, Schulz concludes that a single activity of the mind must be involved in both. The whole system, then, is actually to be understood as a unitary movement of thought, proceeding from the phenomenal order to its ineffable Prius and then back again to the concrete level of its manifestation.[25]

While noting that the positive and negative philosophies are mutually inseparable aspects of a single system, Schulz himself tends to stress the negative branch. He argues against the prevailing view that Schelling's final system involves a radical turn away from the formal schemata of idealistic rationalism in order to develop a "philosophy of experience" in the modern style.[26] On the contrary, Schulz maintains, Schelling's dominant concern is always with the elaboration of a formal, *a priori* system. But if the purpose of the positive philosophy is not to develop a new variety of empiricism, then what is it? According to Schulz, the main goal of this branch of the system is specifically to treat the problem of God.[27] This key issue should therefore provide the benchmark by which to evaluate Schelling's final system as a whole.

Schulz maintains that God's fundamental character as absolute subjectivity is to be "pure mediation" *(reine Vermittlung)* or "self-mediation" *(Selbstvermittlung)*.[28] These technical terms are intended to make clear the central nerve of Schelling's religious thought: the idea that Deity is the sole principle which has the power to move through all the forms of thought and being—and in particular through the three essential Potencies—without thereby becoming attached to, or enmeshed in, any one of them. Each of these forms is possible only insofar as it presupposes and is mediated by the others. Because the mediating divine process always returns back into itself, it is at the same time also a self-mediation. Thus, the Deity is all-pervasive and yet unattached: in Schelling's words, the "penetrating Act, the indivisible unity of the process which passes through these three forms."[29]

Yet although this idea of self-mediation is undoubtedly a useful one, it hardly seems adequate to characterize Schelling's conception of God's nature. After all, it was Hegel and his school that characterized the activity of reason itself as a matter of "self-mediation" through concepts.[30] But Schelling would militate against this primacy of the mediating reason with his insistence that the true apprehension of God's spirit (qua *das Überseiende*) must be purely immediate and knowable without reliance upon logical concepts.[31] It is necessary to ask, then, in what way Schulz's description of God as "self-mediation" would differ from the Hegelian position.

Schulz does recognize, to be sure, that the "self-mediation" he attributes to Schelling's Deity could not take place wholly within the purview of human reason alone. He emphasizes that finite reason must "negate" itself in order to obtain God as free.[32] In confronting God's transcendence, human rationality must face the contingency of its own existence as grounded in the *Daß*, or "thatness," which is a pure fiat, and which our reason alone can never comprehend. Schulz compares this theory of reason's contingency to contemporary existentialist notions—in particular to Heidegger's doctrine of "thrownness" *(Geworfenheit)*.[33] The role of Schelling's *Daß*, he says, is to delimit the presumptions of human reason while at the same time, "in exemplary dialectical fashion," locating its proper functions within a broader context.[34] But even if this is so, one would still need to ask whether that broader context itself is or is not to be construed in some sense as "rational."

Schulz makes an interesting case for a paradoxical inversion of reason's abasement, arguing that the shattering confrontation with the Unthinkable could, nevertheless, be transformed into a restorative negation of the first, seemingly antirational, negation. He suggests that in and through the very experience of the Deity's "essenceless" *(wesenslos)* nature, the seeds are planted that will ultimately reveal the true essence *(Wesen)* of God. In this manner, "reason itself now completes in its self-negation the consolidation of this incomprehensibility into an essence that cancels and sublates the incomprehensibility, in that it [reason] *expressly* posits it."[35] In other words, reason's experiencing and expressly positing the Absolute as incomprehensible enables thought to take the first momentous step toward "comprehending" the Absolute after all!

Thus, despite his recognition of reason's limitations, Schulz places far greater stress on the rationalistic elements and goals of Schelling's project. He emphasizes the return of reason out of its temporary condition of impotence and its resumption of a dominant position in relation to the world.[36] This continuous movement of reason—from a condition of power to provisional impotence and then back to power again—is for Schulz part and parcel of God's own "self-mediating" process.

There is indeed much truth to this interpretation.[37] Yet, again, one must be careful to avoid overrationalizing the system in question. There is a potential danger of drifting by subtle, almost imperceptible, degrees to the point of assimilating even the transcendent and suprarational character of Schelling's God to conformity with ordinary thought and experience. Schulz seems in particular to court this danger with respect to both (1) our knowledge of God, and (2) the nature of God as considered in himself.

The Knowledge of God

Schulz maintains that God is not accessible, on Schelling's view, to either the outer experience of sensation or the inner experience of mystical insight.[38] Reason, on the other hand, as developed systematically in the negative philosophy, concludes with the concept of God as the necessary being. The status of this concept is still, to be sure, initially only hypothetical (the positive philosophy being needed to complete the evidence), but the implication is nevertheless clear to Schulz's mind: namely, that only through reason, if at all, would God's existence admit of being demonstrated. "This path of reason," writes Schulz, "can and must be taken, for reason has, after all, derived God *a priori* as its own terminal concept."[39] By extension it would also follow, for Schulz, that rational inference is the favored, and indeed the only compelling, form of evidence in Schelling's final system.

This interpretation involves several difficulties, however. In the first place, although it is true that Schelling rejects sense-data empiricism, his attitude toward the claims of mystical insight is more complex and nuanced. He criticizes theosophical approaches (like that of Jakob Böhme) as unscientific, but in the same breath he praises them for insisting on the necessity for a concrete *experience* of God.[40] Recall also that Schelling does espouse a theory of "metaphysical empiricism," which he claims is capable of affording a direct experiential access to supersensible realities. According to him, such direct, intuitive insights actually constitute the basis, by serving as implicit presuppositions, even of deductive reasoning. For example, he argues that our knowledge of other persons as self-conscious agencies depends on such "metaphysical empiricism."[41]

Moreover, as Xavier Tilliette has observed, a major obstacle for Schulz's thesis is that many of the central themes of the positive philosophy, including the possibility of supersensible experience and the primacy of the suprarational, were developed earlier in Schelling's career than the formulation of the final system, which integrated the positive and negative philosophies.[42] This circumstance suggests that an intention to reassert the priority of reason, even a reconstituted reason, as the sole adequate means of apprehending God was not a part of Schelling's program—at least not during his middle period. Although Schulz could answer that this intention was probably implicit also in the middle period, such a claim would be straining his argument. The more plausible conclusion to draw is that the primary doctrines of the positive philosophy were arrived at separately from those of the negative philosophy, and that they were then retroactively joined together. In that case, however, the significance of metaphysical empiricism as an autonomous means of apprehending truths, independently of the procedures of the negative philosophy, appears all the more likely.

The role of metaphysical empiricism is especially evident in the case of the knowledge of God. God in himself, as Pure Act, contains nothing of potentiality and hence (universals themselves being a kind of potentiality) no conceptually apprehensible predicates whatsoever. Therefore, the late Schelling maintains, the only possible mode of apprehending God directly is through intuitive insight:

> If the soul wishes to occupy herself with that which IS *das Seiende*, and to have it as posited outside of *das Seiende* and in and for itself . . . then she is no longer thinking but rather (because stripped of everything universal) *seeing*.[43]

By minimizing this idea of an immediate, intuitive "seeing," Schulz's interpretation tends to portray the doctrine of reason's impotence as merely a provisional lapse on the part of the finite intellect—a lapse which, however, can ultimately be overcome through submissive openness to the infinite intellect of God. This is partly true. Yet the "resurrected" reason which returns after its lapse includes an element of mystical illumination within it. And the God to which reason has opened and submitted itself is more than just an infinite intelligence. Schulz seems to overlook these factors. At one point, he even suggests that the reason-bending experience of the *Daß* must itself be negated in the course of the dialectical process.[44] However, there does not appear to be any textual support for this assertion.

The Nature of God in Himself

Schulz's efforts to read Schelling's Deity as a kind of rationalistic ideal culminate in his characterization of God as "pure thought" and in his deemphasizing the personhood of God. For example, in reference to the theory of the *Inbegriff*—a concept derived from Kant to signify the sum total of ideal possibilities determinative of things[45]—Schulz treats this *Inbegriff* as if it were simply identical to God as considered in himself. "The goal and principle of all philosophy," so Schulz interprets Schelling, "is *das Seiende* in itself, i.e., God as the absolute *Inbegriff*."[46] Yet Schelling explicitly states many times that neither *das Seiende* nor the *Inbegriff* is the highest principle. The rational ideal has, on Schelling's account, no actuality in itself, but only insofar as it belongs to Another and is infused with being by that Other.[47] Rationality is, as it were, the outer vestment that God freely assumes for the sake of his creation.

Schulz himself is aware that God's rationality is, for Schelling, not a necessitated condition but one taken up in total freedom.[48] However, the paramount question at this juncture concerns the transcendent nature of the Deity prior to the assumption of a rational guise; and here Schulz is at pains to suggest that God "in himself" may at least be conceived of as a distant analogue of reason. The primary limitation of reason, on Schulz's account, is due to its facticity as a mode of determinate existence—in other words, to its being a structural ordering of entities in precisely *this* universe. As existing, this ordering is contingent. But in order to apprehend God as free of this limitation, thinks Schulz, it is only necessary to posit him, qua transcendent, as subsisting outside the realm of spatiotemporal existence. He is, then, "the inexistent God, who is pure thought."[49]

Now, it is true enough that Schelling's God, as he is in himself, transcends existence altogether. Yet it is doubtful whether God's status as "inexistent transcendence" is enough to distinguish him in a meaningful way from the rational order operative within the existent world. Is this Deity, in the final analysis, simply identical to reason? Schulz himself raises this question and concedes that it is insoluble as thus formulated.[50] But in the end he seems after all to opt, by implication, for a more or less affirmative answer. God's distinction from reason consists, for Schulz, just in the fact that he is the mediating activity which sets the whole movement of reason into motion. He is the supreme power over rationality and to that extent is different from it.

The picture to emerge from all this is accordingly that of an inexistent, divine "analogue" to the existent, finite reason. Indeed, Schulz even characterizes God explicitly as the "corresponding opposite" *(der entsprechende Gegensatz)* to reason.[51] This telling expression—together with Schulz's other descriptions of God as "self-mediation," *Inbegriff*, "pure thought," etc.—effectively crystallizes both the strengths and weaknesses of Schulz's entire interpretation. The primary strength is his compelling demonstration of the systematic impulse that always motivates Schelling's thought. The primary weakness is his insufficient attention to Schelling's other great drive: to account for the role of the unconscious, the mystical, and the irrational in human spiritual life.

Concluding Comments

The reader will have noticed a fundamental difference between Schulz's and Habermas's interpretations of Schelling. For Habermas, Schelling's greatest contribution lies in his having foreseen the end of systematic idealist philosophy, in his humbling the claims of an overweening reason, and in his struggle to develop a new ontology that would be capable of doing justice to the contingency and mutability of human existence. Numerous other students of Schelling, such as Martin Heidegger, Walter Kasper, and Karl Jaspers, have emphasized the same basic theme. But while these thinkers have appreciated Schelling's formulations of the ontological issues, they have also by and large rejected his proffered solutions. Schelling's chief limitation, in the opinion of these and many other scholars, consists in his inability to free himself completely from the rationalistic presuppositions that have dominated Western philosophy up to the twentieth century. The result is an "equivocation" in his approach toward the respective claims of freedom and systematic thought.

For Schulz, by contrast, Schelling's project never ceases to be systematic in the first place, nor does his recognition of reason's insufficiency in the face of radical freedom signal an end to the legitimate operations of dialectical thought. Instead, Schulz regards the critique of rationality as a deliberate paradox. Only by means of demonstrating the breakdown of a naively "negative" style of reasoning, only by experiencing the collapse of the search for immediate, self-evident concepts, can philosophy lead in the end to a full restitution of reason's indubitable supremacy.

Habermas's and Schulz's contrasting interpretations represent two of the main lines of thinking in the continuing debate concerning Schelling's final philosophy. In many respects, Schulz comes closer than Habermas to understanding the full scale and depth of the problematic with which Schelling is concerned. There is no question that he is attempting a most paradoxical and self-consciously dialectical fusion of freedom and system, of the rational and the suprarational. At the same time, however, Habermas has made penetrating observations concerning Schelling's ontological innovations, the extent of whose implications even he does not fully realize. It is certainly true that Schelling's avowed conceptions of human and divine freedom are difficult, if not impossible, to harmonize completely with his actual practice in the explanation of cultural processes and historical events.

There is no reason, in the last analysis, why both equivocation and paradox should not be simultaneously attributed to Schelling's thought. He has grappled with formidable problems that still today remain at the center of philosophical debate.

In my judgment, the central difficulty lies in the undertaking to conceive (in some manner) of a Reality which supposedly would transcend conceptualization altogether. This project, however, could only succeed if some new mode of "thinking" were to be developed, a mode which on the one hand would be independent of concepts, and yet on the other hand would constitute the basis for conceptual reasoning. But how should such a thing be possible? For all his efforts, Schelling offers no fully satisfying answer.

Nevertheless, some of the issues he raises are brilliant ones. How, indeed, is an autonomous volition (if there even is such) to be understood except on the basis of a radical new ontology, one that would call into question the primacy of substances with their necessary logical relations? On the other hand, how should the unconscious mind's obscure intuitions of its own freedom be brought into conformity with the clear, but limited, ideas of the conscious intellect? And finally, how should the illuminations of a mystical ecstasy—which arguably might be capable of resolving these kinds of mysteries by providing insight into the Ground of all existence—cohere in a convincing manner with the discursive arguments of systematic reason? These are the sorts of guiding questions with which Schelling's thought is continually struggling; and out of this web arise the dialectical tensions that some critics would characterize as reflecting equivocation and others as deliberate paradox.

Part III
Exemplification, Primarily in Terms of Greek Mythology

– 10 –

From Uranus to Cronus

Our investigation now turns to a discussion of Schelling's interpretations of some specific mythical themes. Even this relatively limited topic might seem at first to be unmanageable on account of the sheer mass of details included in Schelling's voluminous study. Yet the ontological principles developed in the negative philosophy, and in the *Potenzenlehre* in particular, provide a sufficiently complex theoretical framework upon which the empirical data can be arranged. In order to grasp the essentials of Schelling's system of mythology, one must focus on the recurrent themes which, according to him, appear in virtually all religions.

Basically, Schelling interprets mythology in terms of three primary deities, whose changing interrelationships and corresponding degrees of activity or passivity constitute the various levels of development in world religions. These three deities are none other than the three inverted Potencies themselves: god B, god A^2, and god A^3. The critical analysis of their respective roles and interactions will accordingly make up the backbone of Schelling's interpretation of mythology.[1]

Preliminary Considerations Regarding Language, Mythological Consciousness, and the Names of Ancient Deities

Although these gods have received diverse names and forms in different cultures, Schelling insists that their identities are fundamentally the same. Consequently, he does not regard it as necessary to conform to the indigenous names for the gods as used in each separate culture, but instead he tends to use identical, mainly Greek, names throughout his analyses. This hermeneutical strategy certainly does facilitate comparisons of the different mythical systems concerned.[2] The question remains, however, whether the strategy is justified.

Is it legitimate, in fact, to identify the Babylonian deity Ishtar, Canaanite

Table 2

Schelling's Classification System of World Mythologies

	Incomplete Mythological Systems					Complete Mythological Systems				
	Zabism Relative Monotheism	Parsi Religion	Babylonian Religion	Phoenician & Canaanite Religions	Phrygian Religion	Egyptian Religion	Indian Religion	Buddhist Religion	Chinese Atheism	Greek Religion
B Material Potency	Sky God (Nature worship) Undifferentiated devotion to material being		Mylitta Feminized sky deity feeling impulse of higher god	Baal (Moloch) Material god actively resisting higher influences	Cybele (Great mother of the gods) Material deity yielding place to higher god	Set Material god conquered by and subordinated to higher god	Brahma Material god now totally subordinated to higher god		The State Religious stillbirth: Material power denuded of all higher meaning	Cronos Material god clarified into support and foundation of the higher god
A² Relatively Spiritual Potency		Mithras Monistic dualism combining matter and spirit in One	The Unnamed God	Melkart (Herakles) Relatively spiritual god struggling for recognition	The God(s) to Come	Osiris Relatively spiritual god conquering material god	Shiva Relatively spiritual god imposing form onto matter	Buddha Throwback to Parsimonism		Dionysus Relatively spiritual god in free supremacy
A¹ Liberated Spiritual Potency						Horus Triumphant resurrection of spiritual power	Vishnu Spiritual power freely incarnating into matter			Iakchos Spiritual power intimating future transcendence of all mythology

(First Kata bole — spanning B and A² rows across the Babylonian → Phrygian columns)

Moloch, the Phrygian Cybele, the Egyptian Set, Canaanite Moloch, the Phrygian Cybele, the Egyptian Set, and the Indian Brahma—all as so many forms of the one god B? (See table 2.) Schelling maintains that it is indeed legitimate.[3] The reasons given for the cross-identifications of these deities are several. For one thing, Schelling asserts that, although their names differ, still their mythological characters and functions remain essentially constant. Further, Schelling observes that the adherents of these ancient religions themselves engaged frequently in such cross-cultural identifications. Herodotus, for example, recognized the Egyptian god Osiris as being identical to the Greek god Dionysus, and he regarded their ubiquity as natural and necessary precisely because they were, to him, actual deities.[4] Third, Schelling sees a spontaneous development toward greater refinement and clarity in mythological representations. These refinements are only thinkable, however, on the assumption of a basic continuity.

What is meant by the theory of a cross-cultural identity among the ancient gods? How can Schelling—how indeed could anyone—make such a seemingly extravagant claim? Perhaps the best way of approaching this issue is to begin by excluding what clearly is not intended. Schelling does not mean that religious beliefs, customs, or values, are necessarily the same across different cultural traditions. Quite the contrary, one of the first results of his studies has been to emphasize the diversity among cultures. Not only did physical representations of specific deities vary greatly from one people to the next, but also the forms of worship, cult objects, and local associations, as well as religious dogmas, worldviews, and of course the myths themselves.

In what respect, then, might there be a common thread to bind all these diverse phenomena together? Schelling's answer points back to the arguments elaborated in his exposition of the *Potenzenlehre.* The reader has already seen (in chapter 7) how he employs this theory to explain the fundamental laws that led to the genesis of the universe. In that connection, it will be recalled, he asserted that prior to the emergence of any specific multiplicities there had to be three more basic principles on which all derivative thought-forms must depend. These were the principle of undifferentiated unity, the principle of general differentiation, and the principle of differentiated unity. Out of the interaction of these three Potencies, Schelling argued, the whole integrated system of nature and mind has been constituted.[5] The Potencies, in short, are not so much categories or laws as they are metacategories, metalaws on the basis of which all subsidiary objects and all forms of experience have been built up.

The very same idea applies in the present context, with reference to the religions of the world. Just as the universe as a whole has been predicated on the Potencies, according to Schelling, so too is human consciousness. And just as this triad of powers constitutes a set of unifying themes traceable throughout the multiplicity of nature, in the same way these powers must also play a determinative role in the depths of the human soul.

An objection might be raised, however, that Schelling's reasoning proves too much. For if his argument purporting to prove the cross-cultural identities of pagan gods hinges on the presence of these universal Potencies, then by the same token, would not all human thoughts, all theories, all cultural products in our own historical period as well be similarly identifiable? Is Schelling prepared to maintain, for example, that modern economic theory, Copernican astronomy, and the romantic movement itself are all products of the Potencies, and as such to be linked directly to the gods of old?

Yet this is clearly not his position, for it overlooks the distinction he makes between conscious and unconscious thought. The latter, in Schelling's view, is subliminally determined by the Potencies, whereas the former can be freely reflected upon and changed at will. This explains why the cultural products of contemporary civilization are so diverse. But early humanity was far more subject to the control of unconscious impulses than we of the modern age. Indeed, Schelling says it is precisely because the archaic peoples' mythmaking activity occurred in the psyche's deepest strata that the stages of development were so predictable and uniform:

> The mythological representations behave in general as pure *inner* offspring of human consciousness. They cannot come from the outside into the human being; he cannot be conscious of these as of something merely external and brought to him (as Hermann, for example, thinks they are transmitted through teaching). If they had just been brought from the outside to consciousness, then the latter (which, incidentally, is taken by the common theories to be quite similar and equivalent to our present consciousness) would have behaved toward those representations no differently from the way ours does; that is, it would have been as little able to take them up into itself as our consciousness accepts and assumes them. The human being had to become conscious of these representations as produced within himself with irresistible power.[6]

It is important to distinguish, in the above argument, (a) which aspects have been borrowed from other prominent thinkers concerning the origins of myth, and (b) which aspects constitute a breakthrough tending in new directions. In suggesting that divine representatives of certain cross-cultural paradigms may have dominated the experience of ancient cultures,

Schelling is following the lead of numerous distinguished scholars in the history of religions. Typical of the eighteenth and nineteenth centuries is an easy readiness to transfer the characteristic ideas and symbols from one religious tradition to another, finding the same motifs and esoteric doctrines even in very different cultural traditions. Usually, such interpretations would be accompanied by elaborate explanations of how the old myths and forms of worship must have been transferred in prehistoric times from one people to another.

Although Schelling is susceptible to these oversimplifying tendencies, he appears to be less so than the majority of his contemporaries. Many students of religion during this period would indulge in drawing sweeping conclusions about early humanity on the basis of little, if any, empirical evidence.

Prominent thinkers believed that there must have existed in remote antiquity a sublime, perhaps even perfect, religion, derived from the immediate contact the earliest peoples had with the Supreme Being. This theory, as old as Genesis, had recently been reinforced by the discoveries and translations of ancient religious texts from Egypt, Persia, India, and elsewhere. Encouraged by these findings, scholars launched historical and philological investigations, purporting to trace the genealogy of old religious ideas back toward their primal beginnings. The more demonstrably ancient a deity was, the closer its presumed conception to the sublime "Adamite" religion.[7] A corollary to this view was the belief that different cultural traditions—no matter how widely dispersed in geography or historical background—would still be likely to contain dim recollections of the same fundamental truths.

One of the most influential proponents of this approach was Friedrich Creuzer, who theorized that the deities and myths had originally been systematized by a caste of learned priests. According to Creuzer, these priests had deliberately veiled in obscure symbols their ancient, Oriental doctrines concerning the One in All. Traveling from the East through Egypt, Phoenicia, and Phrygia, they eventually reached the Greek subcontinent and transmitted their doctrines to the early Pelasgians who lived there.[8] Later, thought Creuzer, the Hellenic genius for vivid imagery, their storytelling powers, and above all their profound humanism transformed the ancient symbols into the features of humanized gods. This transformation was a natural by-product of the development in Greece of a powerful middle class, according to Creuzer; but it also heralded a more superficial spirituality and loss of the myths' esoteric meanings. Thus, for example, Creuzer maintained that the god Cronus's Hesiodic epithet ἀγκυλομήτης (generally rendered today as "crooked-minded" or "wily") actually referred to a mystical doctrine of long-forgotten significance, unknown even to Hesiod himself. Properly interpreted, Cronus was "the god turned back into himself, the hidden god, the *deus in statu abscondita,* the god of the immeasurably dark abyss of time, or in other words the absolute, as opposed to the intelligible, god."[9]

The above theory is an example of the historiographical methods employed by Creuzer and other contemporary scholars of religion. This method combines massive learning, brilliant philological observations, imaginative speculation, and a wholly uncritical willingness to accept hearsay evidence as true (especially if derived from the Bible). Schelling too, as a man of his times, proves to be no exception. Attracted, like Creuzer, to the idea of an original *Urreligion* at the dawn of human prehistory, he sees that this doctrine would go far toward legitimizing cross-cultural identifications and associations of mythological motifs.

Yet, to his credit, Schelling is uncomfortable with the exaggerated claims of wisdom for the old "Adamite" religion. To equate the *Urreligion* with revealed religion strikes him as facile. Such a notion not only violates his sense of historical integrity, but it also conflicts with his conviction that evolution and development are fundamentally progressive movements.[10] Most important of all, Schelling objects, the theory of an original revelation (as opposed to a subliminal, inarticulable faith) is symptomatic of a prevalent, but in his view mistaken, presupposition. This, again, is the assumption that religious ideas originate in conscious experience, in the external environment of a publicly perceivable world.

In his continuing campaign against this view, Schelling disputes Creuzer's assumption that the pagan deities and myths could have originated in self-consciously formulated doctrines of any kind. He opposes, for example, the interpretation of Cronus as an esoteric *deus absconditus,* for he finds that this view erroneously assigns the source of human religiosity to an abstract, reflective mode of thinking which did not develop for thousands of years.[11]

On the contrary, Schelling argues (anticipating Jung) that what conferred on the ancient gods their irresistible power and objective reality was precisely their origination in the depths of the unconscious, whose intuitive activities long preceded the reasoning and categorizing functions of the mind. This is what is genuinely novel in his hermeneutical approach. According to his analysis, myths could not have been the voluntary products of either fantasy, intellect, or any other partial aspect of subjective consciousness. They were not half-understood representations (as Creuzer maintained) of concepts whose origins in conscious experience had been lost or whose meanings had been obscured. Rather, the true genesis of myths predated explicitly "conscious" experience and in fact decisively molded it. The originative impulses that issued in the worship of ancient gods were inextricably interwoven with the inmost nature of the human psyche, being as inseparable from it as language itself.[12]

Schelling mounts several more arguments to support his belief in the reality of persistent, cross-cultural types of divine beings. The manifest similarities connecting the deities of different religions and peoples could not have derived from cultural contacts, he maintains, at least not in historical times. Instead, he proposes that there must have been a prehistoric period, lost in the immemorial past, when all human beings shared a single way of life, a single primitive culture, and a single form of worship. Subsequently, after what he calls the "Great Spiritual Crisis," the amorphous body of humanity separated into distinct languages and peoples.[13] It was because of their common origins, then, that the various cultures of historical times have shared so many features of religious thought and experience.

Schelling's theory of an original unity in the human race rests on rather slim empirical evidence. He finds support partly in the similarities and correspondences among different languages and mythologies. He asserts, but does not prove, that there exist a multitude of linguistic correspondences which could not possibly be explained on the basis of historical interactions.[14]

Schelling's main line of thought, however, relies in effect on the theoretical intuition that there can be no "chicken before the egg": Since a distinct people cannot exist as such without a prior language (and mythology), he argues, the linguistic and mythological divisions must have preceded the formation of separate races and cultures. Prior to the partition of languages and myths, therefore, there must have been a single human culture. Only on the assumption that there was an originally undifferentiated condition of humanity is it feasible, in his eyes, to explain how divisions into separate linguistic groups and nations might later have occurred.[15]

The argument is somewhat dubious. It would be analogous to a chemist's maintaining that, since no element can exist without electrons and protons, the existence of numerous distinct chemical elements is only possible if one assumes that subatomic particles existed before the separation of elements; and hence, that at one time there was but a single element. This line of reasoning, however, while suggestive, is hardly conclusive. There seems to be a conflation of the concept of a necessary condition (which need not precede the conditioned object in time) and the concept of an efficient cause (which does precede its effect). Schelling's merging of the two concepts is hardly unusual, however. It is typical of the method employed in his *Erzeugungsdialektik.*

One consequence of the above theory is that the specific names assigned by different cultures to the variable forms of the high gods would be of only secondary importance. Even the so-called "Unnamed God" of the Assyrio-Babylonian religion was not for that reason any the less significant—or any the more difficult later to identify and "name" on the basis of his religio-symbolic meaning.[16] (See table 2, p. 180). In this case, according to Schelling, it was the new god A^2, whose premature coming had temporarily disoriented the people of Babylon. They still worshipped a pantheon of older, more primitive deities.) But the present point is that this provisional condition of "namelessless" on the part of A^2 should not impede the student of religions from recognizing the spiritual power involved.

Schelling contends that there are solid grounds for using the Greek names of the divinities in making cross-cultural comparisons. In the first place, it was the Greeks who were able to bring these fundamental prototypes to their highest and most articulate expression. The Greek religion, he further thinks, was finally able to liberate the mind from its more irrational compulsions and therefore could bring to a free, poetical expression the same mythological impulses as were present in earlier religions. For these reasons, Schelling holds it justifiable not only to employ the Greek names, but also to rely on the Greek versions of the basic myths as the most self-consciously clarified, and therefore truest, formulations. He expressly cites Hesiod's *Theogony* as the main sourcebook and evidence for his entire interpretation of mythology in general.[17]

Modern readers will be unlikely to share Schelling's sanguine reliance on Greek religion as the key to world mythologies. Yet his conception of certain prototypical patterns as underlying the most fundamental strata of all religions is provocative and worthy of consideration.

The Religion of "Relative Monotheism"

In the first book of his *Philosphie der Mythologie,* Schelling sets out to examine the original condition of humankind prior to its division into distinct races, peoples, and nations. According to the theory just cited, there must have existed a prehistorical epoch that was dominated by the first primal Potency. This, Schelling declared, was "the inward-drawing power" *(die zusammenziehende Kraft),* a monolithically chaotic principle whose primary effect was to fuse the phenomena of experience into a relatively undifferentiated whole. The abstract philosophical reasoning for positing this principle has been discussed in previous chapters. Our current task, therefore, will be to outline its alleged manifestations in the realm of actual myth.[18]

The first Potency, in its inverted form as B, was essentially the principle of bare existence. As such, Schelling designates this Potency as "the real god."[19] This principle had already appeared at the lower levels of inanimate nature as physical matter, which subsequently had been formed by the two higher Potencies into organic life and finally into consciousness itself. Now, at the vastly more complex level of religious experience, an analogous succession of stages was about to take place. The identical logical necessity that had controlled the physical transitions from matter through organism to sentient awareness must also, by the same token, have determined the development of mythical consciousness itself. The theory, first proposed by C. F. Kielmeyer, concerning an ontogenetic parallelism among different levels of natural existence, here reaches its ultimate extension.[20]

In religion, the application of this dialectical law meant that the emergence of polytheistic religions, with all their intricate allocations of spiritual functions and spheres of influence, could only have made an appearance relatively late in the life of humanity. Prior to that, extending far back into prehistorical time, there must have been a religion of uniform monism, untouched by any specifications into diverse deities or powers. All differentiation and alteration, for Schelling, implies a previously existing substratum or "material," out of which the differences are made up. Even the very capacity to experience differences in historical time presupposes an earlier mode of "primordial consciousness" *(Urbewußtsein)* for which the awareness of temporality and historicity did not yet exist. The tonic chord *(Grundton)* of religious consciousness, he maintains, always has presupposed this sense of an underlying unity.[21] During the First World Age of humankind, this tonic chord of unity must have been so dominant as to have completely filled and overwhelmed consciousness. Schelling explains why in the following terms:

> It was a *spiritual* power that accomplished this. For the condition of remaining one, the nondifferentiating phase of humanity requires for its explanation a positive cause, no less than the subsequent differentiation does.... But if we ask, *what* spiritual power alone was strong enough to hold humanity in this immobility, it can immediately be seen that it was one *principle,* and indeed it must have been One principle by which the consciousness of people was exclusively dominated and controlled. For as soon as two principles would divide the hegemony, differences

would have to arise within humanity also, as the latter would inevitably divide itself between the two principles. But further, such a principle as gave room to no other within consciousness, permitting none beyond itself, could only have been that of an infinite being, only a *god;* a god who *completely* filled consciousness, who was common to all humanity; a god who drew this humanity, so to say, into his own unity, denying it any movement, any straying from the path at all, whether to the right or to the left, as the Old Testament often expresses it; only such a principle could bring about a duration *(Dauer)* for that absolute immobility, that standstill for all development.[22]

Notice again the implicit roles played here by the Schellingian *Erzeugungsdialektik* as well as by the temporalization of essence. These have led in turn to a conception of the Potencies as productive causes operating in succession. Just as the beginnings of organic life required a preexisting material substrate in order to evolve (so the argument goes), in like manner the development of polytheism required a preexisting monistic substrate. With these theoretical presuppositions firmly in place, then, Schelling proceeds to track down the empirical evidence for an original, primitive "monotheism."

The "historical-critical method," as Schelling describes it, consists in a careful sifting and eliminative process of evaluation, which subjects the available evidence to a "critique which gradually removes all that is historically unthinkable."[23] What remains after this process has taken place should, to the extent that it coheres reasonably with what has already been established, presumably be the true historical residue. Schelling relies for evidence on his extensive knowledge of ancient texts, as well as on archaeological and philological discoveries made in the eighteenth and nineteenth centuries. (Today, of course, much of this evidence would be regarded as of questionable accuracy.)

Not too surprisingly, his empirical investigations lead Schelling to just the anticipated conclusions. In the present instance, he contends that the First Age of humanity was characterized by an original, naive form of monotheism. He designates this as "relative monotheism," in order to distinguish it from the much later development of a spiritually differentiated "absolute monotheism."[24] The deity in question, god B, was basically a quasi-pantheistic nature god, constituted by the generalized feelings of awe people experienced when confronted by the sheer existence of natural things. Schelling claims that the pantheistic aspect of this *Urreligion* derived from the reverence paid to the pure power of Being—what he calls the "immediate *potentia existendi*"—which was worshipped without regard for any distinctions of form or function.[25] The naturalistic aspect of this religion arose from the attributive role of its object as the original starting point of all subsequent creation. The awe that this inspired was at first an entirely prereflective awareness, an inarticulate celebration of that substantial Reality out of which particular beings had emerged and into which they all most inevitably return. For this reason, Schelling sometimes describes god B as "the Nature in God" *(die Natur in Gott)*.[26]

One must be careful, however, in characterizing Schelling's conception of B as a "nature god," for this term is certainly not intended here in either of its two more familiar senses. (1) It does not refer to the worship of merely physical nature (so-called "fetishism"), an interpretation which in Schelling's view puts the cart before the horse, overlooking the inner spiritual impulse responsible for the genesis of religious phenomena.[27] (2) Nor does Schelling mean by "the nature in God" to include organic nature as such. He is referring, rather, to the generative source of inorganic nature, which in its primordial formlessness is at once the supporting "ground" *(Grund)* and the potentially destructive "cancellation" *(Aufhebung)* of the organic world.[28] The main point, then, is that god B is the original, nature-positing power, not the tame and, as it were, "civilized" nature observable in the subsequent ages.

Because both these aspects of pantheism and "naturalism" corresponded to the as yet undeveloped self-consciousness of early humanity, and because the principle of their faith sprang from the deification of a "blind impulse" *(ein blindes . . . Wollen)*, which did not include the notion of any purposeful deliberation or will *(Wille)*, the first religion tended to emphasize feelings of fatalistic necessity in the worshipper and precluded any sense of personal freedom or individuality.[29] Schelling maintains that the effect of god B's power was to prevent the development of differentiated social forms and to fuse the mass of humanity into a culturally homogeneous whole. Complex divisions of labor, as well as the divisions among national groups, such as would later characterize agricultural civilizations, were as yet unknown. The people of this era comprised a single, if relatively simple, world. Schelling believes they must have lived primarily as nomadic herders, mingling easily with one another and undistinguished by racial or ethnic differences.[30] Their speech, which at that time was uniform, consisted of a proto-language whose sentences lacked grammar and were actually not even differentiated into distinct words. Yet, wherever they wandered, these people allegedly could make themselves understood without difficulty.[31]

The ultimate destiny of this early society would be, of course, to serve as the seat and foundation for the subsequent development of civilization, culture, and the whole realm of spirit in general. Yet at this initial stage the emergence of the latter phenomena lay far in the future. People still lived in direct communion with the one god B, enjoying that power's beneficent protection so long as they remained in subjection to it. During this first age, moreover, polytheism did not exist—not because the people were spiritually evolved enough to reject the belief in a plurality of gods, but because the notion of more than one god had never occurred to them in the first place.[32]

In connection with this last point about the absence of multiple divinities, Schelling makes a telling qualification which, in the minds of some readers, may give away the whole argument. For he admits that, even in this period of "relative monotheism," people might have perceived a variety of divine shapes and spirits inhabiting the universe. This admission suggests an objection: in that case, one might ask, would not this religion already have been, by definition, a form of polytheism? But Schelling maintains otherwise. The distinction between monotheism and polytheism is not, he says, a matter of merely contingent appearances; at issue is whether there existed a sense of essential differences among contrasting deities. During the First World Age, he insists, people could conceive of only a *single type* of divine power. Hence, the circumstance that they might have experienced this single power under the guise of multiple names or subordinate aspects—as, e.g., in the form of demigods or angelic beings—is irrelevant. What counts is that they saw these entities as manifestations of the one high god.[33]

The chief virtue of this suggestion is that it emphasizes the importance of probing *behind* the superficial features of a religion in order to appreciate its inner significance. At the same time, however, the above qualification makes Schelling's theory far more difficult to evaluate or verify. It no longer suffices to consider just the empirical data (such as there is) concerning the religions of prehistory. Schelling imposes the additional demand on scholarship to interpret those ancient people's inner attitudes as well. But this seems almost impossible when there is so little evidence to begin with. In this connection, one wonders which hat Schelling is wearing. Could it be that the philosopher's theoretical preconceptions are here interfering with the would-be archaeologist's quest for empirical objectivity?

Schelling's conception of the earliest humanity's mode of living contains several arbitrary and unlikely elements. Most improbable of all, from a late-twentieth-century perspective, is his conviction that these people lived as a single race with an undifferentiated, common culture. By contrast, anthropologists today who study the surviving stone-age peoples point to the complexity of so-called "primitive" languages, to the elaborate social codes of kinship and tribal membership, to the ingrained patterns of behavior that often create impassable communication barriers between different groups. If these phenomena are any guide to the distant past, they suggest that the earliest human beings probably had less in common than the people of historical times.

Let us return to Schelling's exposition concerning humanity's first religion. Because of its undeveloped nature, he says, the original "relative monotheism" was fundamentally inadequate. In making this claim, Schelling parts company with those of his contemporaries, like Creuzer, who supposed the primal religion to have been the result of an original revelation *(Uroffenbarung)*, second only to the subsequent revelation of Christianity in terms of its profundity and truth. Against this view, Schelling maintains that the more complex ideas of full-fledged polytheism would constitute a significant advance over the first, unreflective monotheism.[34] Indeed, the level of spiritual development embodied in the worship of god B was simply incapable of manifesting the genuine One God in his true form. In order for the latter's transcendent unity to be revealed, it was first necessary for polytheism to emerge and unfold to the fullest extent.[35] Only after humanity had experienced this polytheistic phase and learned the necessity of a differentiated religiosity would the higher, "absolute monotheism" be finally capable of realization.

Zabism: The Worship of "Uranus"

At the dawn of history, according to Schelling, the previously homogeneous human species began to separate into distinct races and peoples. The cause of this occurrence, he says, was the "Great Spiritual Crisis," which suddenly irrupted into human consciousness. Basically, this was the advent of the god of the second Potency, A^2, the harbinger of the Second World Age.[36] Simultaneously with these developments (and not accidentally so), the religion of relative monotheism underwent a gradual divergence into different forms and teachings. Yet the central motif concerning the existence of a single Supreme Being lived on for thousands of years. It was, therefore, only to be expected that various religious traditions would contain still echoing resonances from the once universal faith.

In order to illustrate his thesis, Schelling marshalls a large body of mythological materials. His interpretations are often highly speculative, but always interesting. He suggests, for example, that an ancient Persian deity celebrated in the Zend Avesta scriptures, Mithras, actually represented far more than just a heroic god of courage and strength. He was, rather, the zero point of identity suspended in between the quasi-dualistic Ormuzd (god of light) and Ahriman (god of darkness). By keeping their nascent polarity in check and refusing to let them separate completely, Mithras instantiated the principle of pantheism which, Schelling insists, was never far from the heart of the Persian religion.[37]

Similarly, in the Hebrew faith, Schelling distinguishes between the designations of God as "Elohim" and as "Jehovah." Only the latter name, according to him, conveyed any sense of a definite transcendence, of a going beyond the very idea of a plurality of gods. The earlier title, "Elohim," predicated merely an indeterminate unity, as indicated already by the fact that the word itself, despite its usage as a singular, is grammatically plural in form. Although provisionally "one," the Elohim was/were capable of solicitation into being a vague plurality. ("See," he/they say(s) in Gen. 3:22, referring to Adam, "he has become like *one of us* . . .") According to Schelling, the Jews who lived in "Eden" knew their god only as "Elohim"; it was their distant descendants (the seed of "Enosh") who first conceived of the deity in a manner befitting the name of "Jehovah." Indeed, precisely because the unity of the Elohim was so weak and undeveloped, it/they would later return as the "god of wrath," as the "jealous god" pitted in earnest struggle against all rival powers.[38]

In Greek mythology, the same dramatic tension between relative and absolute monotheism reappeared in another guise. Here the undifferentiated unity of the first Potency assumed (among other aspects) the androgynous form of Persephone, the "virgin" whose primal innocence depicted a state of being prior even to any distinctions of masculine from feminine qualities. This was another manifestation of the indeterminate character attributed to god B. As long as Persephone continued in this condition of innocence, Schelling maintains, she was protected from all sources of discord, safely ensconced in a paradisiacal "garden" surrounded by high walls. But once the virgin turned outward, embracing the dangerous possibility of "seduction," she was destined to be "raped" by Hades, the spirit of the underworld. With that painful event, however, began her growth toward self-conscious maturity. Thus, the tale of Persephone was a Greek image for the idea of Original Sin. Yet a common theme is that the Primal Fall was necessary in order for humanity to achieve the capacity for real spiritual freedom. Indeed, Schelling even goes so far as to claim that the myth of Persephone, properly interpreted, contains the key to all mythology.[39]

Each of these sample narratives, according to Schelling's analysis, included two aspects contending with one another for recognition and dominance. One the one hand, there was the simple representation of a deity in his/her primordial unity, prior to any awareness of oppositions or conflicts. On the other hand, there was also an intuition that this condition of innocent contentment could not last forever, that a departure or Fall from the bower of vernal purity was inevitable. The uneasy ambivalence brought about by this realization signaled, on Schelling's interpretation, that the Second World Age of mythological development was about to begin. The religion of relative monotheism was dialectically determined to flower into full-fledged polytheism. Before that could happen, however, the darker aspect of god B would rouse itself for a final stand against the coming encroachments of the new gods.

In order for religious development to advance, thinks Schelling, it was necessary for the god of relative monotheism to make room for, and eventually to be subordinated to, a higher principle. In effect, this meant that god B would have to cede the place at the "Center" of the religious universe and assume a less important, less dominant role at the periphery. The changes needed in religious consciousness could not help but be traumatic. The transferral of allegiances would be all the more difficult in that it required people to shift their innate sense of identity and reevaluate the relations of self and others. This was so for at least two basic reasons. (1) Because the first Potency, in its capacity as the original principle of subjectivity, was also the prototype of selfhood and egoity,[40] the subordination of that principle would necessarily have to involve, by association, a conquest of the worshipper's own sense of self. In effect, humanity would have to sacrifice the inflexible spirit of selfhood by which until now it had been enthralled. (2) Furthermore, insofar as god B represented the first Potency's inverted mode as the chaotic substrate of natural being, the primal religion had been fixated on the immediate fact—the *miracle*—of existence.[41] To throw into question this pure adulation of existence could not help but appear to the primitive imagination to be a threat to the bedrock of the universe and even of human life itself.

For both these reasons, then, the hegemony of god B was a dangerous thing to question. As the exclusive "inward-drawing power" *(zusammenziehende Kraft)*, this Potency had already appropriated the Center of concrete reality to itself. Any attempt to liberate the world from the totalitarian grip of his power would accordingly be experienced by early human beings as a denigration of the deity's rightful supremacy. This prospect was enough to arouse uneasy feelings. But what seemed to the religious mind of that era as blasphemy and godlessness was in fact, according to Schelling, a necessary "peripheralization" of the first Potency. God B would eventually have to yield the spiritual Center of the universe in order to make way for the arrival of a more complex and humane deity.[42]

This process could hardly have been instantaneous. Schelling maintains that a long period of time was required during which god B resisted subordination, struggling either to remain in the Center, or failing that, to reassert himself at the spiritual "periphery." Either way, the goal of B would be to remain a *self* and an exclusive unity in his own right. Tenaciously, the first Potency would resist the threatened loss of self *(Entselbstung);* yet on the other hand, the religious devotee must have half-sensed that this transformation could be the call of destiny.[43] The restless sensation that this realization produced gradually came to be identified with the character of god B.

The mythological mind, in wrestling with this inner conflict, unconsciously sought to project its principal preoccupations onto the natural world. Such projection was not consciously intended as allegorical symbolism, but rather was experienced as the outward manifestation of a very real process. (Only in retrospect would it be possible for modern analysis, with the aid of suitable dialectical tools, to see how the projections made use of available natural elements in order to represent the worshipper's inner condition.) Schelling suggests that in the present instance these elements had to possess the following features: (a) a retention, in some manner, of exclusive unity, i.e., of "being-for-self"; (b) a maintenance of strict uniformity and an absence of significant differentiation; (c) restless motion without, however, involving any essential change of place; and (d) location at the "periphery" of the visible universe.[44] This set of desiderata, according to Schelling, came from the conjuncture of the centripetal principle of "selfhood" *(Selbstheit)* with the centrifugal force of "self-abandonment" *(Entselbstung)*. What emerged was another form of god B, now appearing as the revolving sphere of the starry heavens.

Adapting Hebrew and Arabic names for the cult of "star-worship," Schelling designates this type of religion as "Zabism."[45] This name must not mislead, however. Schelling insists that the sense of reverence felt toward the sky and heavenly bodies arose in response to purely inner, spiritual needs. He argues against the style of interpretation favored by the naturalist school.[46] It was not the case, he thinks, that the sky qua physical entity directly inspired worship. On the contrary, it was the inner yearning for an existential power residing at the "periphery" of the universe that found expression in the worship of heaven. He cautions, moreover, that it was not the stars themselves which were idolized, but rather the universal Lord who commanded them, as a general commands his armies.

Initially, Zabism made no specific distinctions among the various heavenly bodies in the sky. They were all seen as manifestations of a single, undifferentiated power—the one god, whom the Greeks would later call "Uranus." Moreover, because the first Potency at this stage continued to reign alone and without any express rivals, Zabism remained essentially pantheistic. Such tentative differentiation as did emerge still treated the stars and related phenomena as secondary manifestations of a single, monolithic power. Thus, although the astral religion did introduce slight tendencies toward incipient polytheism, on the whole it remained "relatively monotheistic."[47] Schelling cites the religions of the early Persians, Arabs, and Jews as instances of Zabism.

At this juncture, it is appropriate to pause briefly and take stock of the ground covered so far in this chapter. One naturally wishes to ask, What is of primary importance in Schelling's conception of relative monotheism? Is there anything of lasting significance in his theories about the original conditions of humanity, about their undifferentiated worldview, and about the kind of quasi-pantheistic *Urreligion* that resulted from it?

On a strictly empirical level, many of Schelling's theses appear questionable today. The prevailing methods and data in anthropology, archaeology, history, philology, and related disciplines were not yet sufficiently reliable in the first half of the nineteenth century to serve as the basis for sound historiography. It must also be admitted that what Schelling and his contemporaries lacked in factual knowledge they sometimes made up for in imaginative speculation. This point is too obvious to require belaboring.

Nevertheless, a number of Schelling's ideas remain pertinent and suggestive. Several twentieth-century scholars, for example, have found fresh evidence suggesting that belief in a single Supreme Being, often associated with the sky, is fairly typical of hunter-gatherer and pastoral nomad societies.[48] Despite the paucity of concrete information available to Schelling, it is remarkable how well his theory in this instance fits. Could it be that he is right in suggesting a causal relationship between the maintenance of a nomadic life-style and the belief in a pantheistic nature god? Could he also be correct about a relationship between the invention of agriculture and the rise of systematically differentiated, polytheistic cosmologies?[49] Supposing for the moment that there are such connections, what should one think of his arguments to the effect that the causal direction is generally from the realm of myth and ideology to the material realm, instead of its being (as is more often assumed currently) the other way around?[50] These are certainly challenging issues, worth following up. Yet the theoretical arguments are still a bit too tenuous, in my opinion, and the empirical evidence too fragmentary, to permit the drawing of definite conclusions.

Another of Schelling's insights involves what is perhaps his most important contribution to the study of religious psychology: the theory of the irrational unconscious in its relation to symbols and myths. Previous thinkers, to be sure, already suspected that religious representations might involve hidden assumptions or concealed ideas that could conflict with the ostensible doctrines of the faith. Hegel, in particular, explored some of the cognitive dissonances that could result from the collision between overt and covert beliefs. But Schelling has gone a step farther. According to his theory, the unconscious is more than just a repository for suppressed ideas, more even than a cache of dissimulated motives: it also contains, he thinks, fundamental urges and powers that directly oppose reason—not because their conceptual content is so well hidden, but because they are not, in fact, ideas at all.

The implication of this theory is to alter the model of those mysterious impulses and desires that sometimes irrupt from the deepest regions of the unconscious to affect religious experience. The sources of this irruption, Schelling suggests, may consist not so much in logical misconceptions or cognitive dissonances (as the Hegelians argued), but rather in the tenacious power of a willful self-centeredness, a power that allegedly could break outside the very bounds of rationality. It was because of this blind will, he thinks, and only secondarily for ideological reasons, that there has emerged into human history a force that can actually resist and put a brake on the otherwise inexorable flow of dialectical processes.

In the jargon of Schelling's metaphysics, as seen above, the development of this capacity originated in a spiritual "inversion" of the first Potency, which then led to a turn away from the eternal truths of the "Idea-world" in favor of an unprincipled, "inward-drawing power." It is not necessary, however, to adopt this esoteric terminology in order to appreciate the phenomena to which it is addressed. The main point is to see how Schelling uses this language in order to cast light on an invisible conflict going on between the conscious and unconscious forces acting within the religious mind. This is what underlies the paradoxical notion that the existential "Basis" of universal selfhood was actively engaged in resisting the dictates of a higher Providence.

Nor is this all. For even in promoting this emotional resistance, even in raising the impulses of self-centeredness to their strongest pitch, the spirit of god B would still, according to this theory, have retained some vague intimations of another possible destiny transcending the self, a destiny that would be at once humbler and more profound. These intimations must have been present, thinks Schelling, because the "inverted" nature of B always presupposed a prior condition of harmony with, rather than opposition to, the broader interests of the cosmic order.[51]

The religious consciousness therefore found itself pulled in different directions by the dimly perceived impulses of its own spiritual desires. The result was a peculiar kind of ambivalence, an indecisive oscillation which eventually spelled the end of B's hegemony and ushered in the Second World Age. But this is to anticipate the next stage of Schelling's extended hermeneutical exegesis.

The Rise of Cronus

Despite the peripheralization of Uranus, this deity still remained an utterly exclusive nature god, who refused to acknowledge any higher principle than the selfhood of immediate existence. The processes of rationalization and self-subordination, however, had to continue in order for the religious mind to realize its true destiny. Very dimly and tentatively, the second Potency, god A^2, began to make its influence felt.

Initially, as was already mentioned above, A^2 appeared as the Nameless God. According to Schelling, this condition was symptomatic of a general uneasiness occasioned by the barely perceptible stirrings of the coming revolution. Still locked in the compact worldview associated with their originally nomadic way of life, people were apprehensive about the implications of spiritual differentiation and personal individuation: What would be the expected consequence, for example, if the divine attribute of goodness were to be distinguished from that of power, if the nurturing spirit of fecundity were separated from that of creative inventiveness, or if the custody of the dead were divided from the care of the living? Similarly, what would happen if the rights and responsibilities of a celibate priestess were to be detached from those of a wife and mother, or if the duties of a soldier were sharply differentiated from those of a farmer? Surely disaster would follow, as the previously unified domain of god B disintegrated into a multiplicity of discrete functions. Faced with this prospect, early humanity experienced sorrow and dread.[52] Basically, consciousness was not yet ready to assimilate the notion of an informing spirit as opposed to that of formless being.

Nevertheless, a vague dissatisfaction set in with the blind religion of merely worshipping the ground of existence. People increasingly desired to acknowledge, somehow, the multiplicities of structure, the logical interrelations and articulations among all the differentia of things, the great wonder of being able to control these various differentia. But this would require recognizing the rational spirit in its role as subordinator of material being, mind as the harbinger of civilization. At first this idea was still too difficult to bear. The religious mind clung to the miracle of being and turned apprehensively away from the miracle of intelligibility. Yet in the end, this crucial dialectical move was inevitable, according to Schelling: "The entire process that follows," he claims, "thus involves for the blind principle, B, a transition from blindness and unintelligence to understanding."[53]

Ironically, even as it turned first away from god A^2, the religious consciousness implicitly was induced to recognize its reality. For in order to reject the claims of the formal intelligence, in order to repudiate the worth of a precisely articulated worldview, it was first necessary to admit that these allegedly false values did at least have some purchase on being. Thus, the mythological consciousness was forced to acknowledge the existence of A^2, even while steadfastly rejecting its claims to divinity.[54] For this reason, the revised strategy of the inverted first Potency could no longer simply be to ignore the approaching second Potency. Instead, the goal was to oppose and, if possible, to *destroy* the antagonist.

This dialectical twist constituted the defining characteristic of the first Potency in its next mode of appearance as "Cronus." Schelling believes that the worship of Cronus was actually not another cult different from that of Uranus, but was the same relative monotheism in another form.[55] The alteration in form consisted in this: Previously, it had been possible just to ignore the claims of the discriminating intelligence. That was the heyday of unfettered Zabism. But at this point, with the dawning of a more sophisticated consciousness, it seemed that the only feasible expedient for conservatism was to make use of the new intellectual resources precisely in order to subvert them—to sabotage the approaching revolution before it became irreversible. Ruthless determination and guile were now perceived as necessary in order to ward off the new and threatening world order. Hence, this stage of religious development was an extremely reactionary one, consisting in a stubborn attachment to the old god B and a fierce defense of his power and prerogatives.

The early religious mind, however, saw these qualities of its faith as attributes of god B himself. Thus, the chief difference between Cronus and his father Uranus was that, whereas Uranus had been impassively "blind" as the unchallenged lord of the universe, Cronus was wilfully and consciously resistive to the new god.[56] Whereas Uranus had been able to maintain his supremacy by simply keeping all his potential rivals locked inside their mother's womb, for Cronus that method was no longer sufficient. Now deceit was necessary, tortuous stratagems, and the bloody use of the curved "sickle." Cronus, in other words, was the nature god qua seeking to retain hegemony of the universe by holding the new god of civilization at bay.

Not content to be a principle of placid undifferentiation (as Uranus was), Cronus was the principle in active opposition to all intelligible order and differentiation. Even the very idea of change, insofar as it presupposes an implicit order of temporal succession, was anathema to the spirit of Cronus. Schelling concludes that, contrary to familiar allegorical readings (dating back as far as Aristotle) of Cronus as "Father Time," etc., he is rather the exact opposite. Far from symbolizing actual time, which consumes all things, Cronus is rather the chaotic spirit of a present that resists being relegated to the past and accordingly seeks to consume time itself.

> When Cronus swallows his own offspring, this is not in the same sense that time takes back what it had once begotten. For Cronus begets nothing, swallows his children already at birth before they have glimpsed the light of day; not like time, which gives birth to its children, allows them to exist, and then swallows them up again.[57]

The role of Cronus was marked by a peculiar dissemblance, both with regard to his predecessor and his coming antagonist. On the one hand, as the principle of insistent unity, Cronus was committed to resisting differentiation; yet on the other hand, in setting himself against both the new spirit of change and the former spirit of unopposed uniformity, he was already covertly positing his own distinction from each. To maintain such a stance required cleverness and duplicity. Thus, because Cronus struggled to maintain supremacy by hook or by crook, he was pictured as the sly, "crooked" god—the god who used his intimations of a higher spirituality in order to block it, to grasp power for himself and to keep the controlling position.[58] This dual purpose required turning against the old quasi-pantheistic star-worship no less than against a well-articulated polytheism. Cronus therefore used guile in order to "emasculate" Uranus and usurp his throne. This represents the power of egotism screwed to its most intense pitch for the sake of avoiding submission to a higher universal order.

Schelling's account of the succession from Uranus to Cronus relies primarily on a free interpretation of Hesiod's *Theogony*. But he also finds similar motifs in the Canaanite and Phoenician cults of Moloch, El, and Baal.[59] In all of these mythologies, god B assumed the role of a relentlessly savage deity intent on retaining absolute power. Any sign that the people were straying from the "one true god," or any hint that they might be receptive to the lures of the new deity, would have to be punished with iron-fisted determination. This attitude was, thinks Schelling, the origin of human sacrifice, a ritual that reenacted the destruction of A^2, while also terrorizing the faithful into continued spiritual obeisance:

For anxiously, jealously, yes with deadly weapons does consciousness protect the treasure immersed in being, and it also fills with terror the sensibility that is on the verge of opening up to the liberating god; in such a way, that the first intimation of freedom from the oppressive real god, this first transformation, I say, consciousness experiences as guilt calling for blood. Therefore the first bloody expiatory offerings fall here. Yes, to this god who consumes like fire everything that threatens his uniqueness (Uranus had no other Potency beyond himself), to him first the free human being falls as a sacrifice, as if to rebuff that milder god who is a friend to humankind, and as a bloody expiation for the guilt which the human assumed in allowing place for the other god.[60]

Accordingly, just as Cronus had gained power by usurping the throne of his "father" Uranus, so he now sought to retain it by blocking his potential successor. It was for this reason that the approaching A^2 was so often represented in mythology as only a demigod, born of a mortal woman, and as having to endure the most difficult and at times horrible ordeals. This requirement reflected an implicit accommodation of the new world spirit to the obsessive compulsions of the old. In Greek myth, for example, this semidivine being was partially represented by Herakles, in Phoenician myth by Melkart, and in Jewish myth by Isaac.[61] In all these instances, a "jealous god" was pictured as seeking to retain hegemony by demanding the sacrifice of a perceived interloper.

At this point, however, a curious psychic transformation occurred in the mind of Cronus's devotees. For precisely in the act of destroying his antagonist, Cronus became intimately identified with him. Schelling give three basic reasons for this identification. (1) In the first place, Cronus was already the god of a divided consciousness, as being both the chaotic lord of existence and at the same time the reluctant herald of the new age of civilization and coherent intelligibility.[62] To the extent that the worshipper of god B had already been affected by the spirit of A^2, and perhaps had even begun using that Potency's methods and skills, any provisional "victory" of the former Potency would implicitly also redound to the credit of the latter. The "wily" quality of Cronus, in other words, already signaled his dependency upon the higher spiritual values of his opponent. (2) Secondly, in witnessing the violent encounter between god B and god A^2, consciousness experienced an overwhelming sense of confusion. The sacrificer and the victim, the slayer and the slain, became inseparably merged in the experience of a single, transpersonal event.[63] (3) Finally, the martyrdom of god A^2 constituted an eloquent and persuasive testimony to the inner power of the new religious principle. Insofar as the victim submitted to the wrath of the tyrannical nature god, that wrath was appeased. By the same token, the appeasement legitimized the demigod's sufferings as having been necessary in order for him to "earn" the status and privileges of full-fledged divinity.[64]

Later on, this identification of Cronus with his semidivine victim found expression in representations of the latter as the former's "son," "brother," or "nephew." (Thus, for example, Isaac was Abraham's son, Osiris was Set's brother, Herakles was Zeus's son, and Melkart was El's nephew.[65]) This implied, in turn, that god A^2 was actually an extension of god B's own self. In consequence of this identification, the being who had previously appeared as a vengeful persecutor now came to share somewhat in his victim's ordeal: the two deities were even seen as suffering together for the sake of a noble cause. That cause, however, could only have been for the betterment of the human condition. Hence the tragic death of god A^2 was credited with having ushered in the new age of spiritual enlightenment. According to Schelling, this explains how it was that the mythological consciousness could in the end ascribe to Cronus himself the supreme sacrifice of having given his own kin "for the sake of humankind."[66] And yet that "son" did not perish utterly, but was restored and allowed to continue in the role of humanity's benefactor. This, again, was apparently due to the magnanimity of Cronus. With a profound sense of gratitude, therefore, the people gave thanks to the great god whose mercy had saved the human race.[67] (Parallels with the Judeo-Christian concept of the Messiah should be obvious. For Schelling, pagan mythology is continuous with the doctrines of Christianity, and the Messiah is essentially a further development of the ancient prototypes.)[68]

It is interesting to observe, in this connection, the psychological dimensions of Schelling's conception of the identification of god B with god A^2. In certain respects, this idea anticipates modern psychoanalytic theories regarding the phenomenon of atonement via displacement, whereby an originally hostile agent assumes the qualities and behavior of his former antagonist. Thus, according to Sigmund Freud, the emotional energies motivating primitive ritual activities resulted from an inherent ambivalence toward the sacrificial victim. Moreover, Freud adds, this victim was himself (or herself, or itself) a symbolic representative of the deity. For just as the mythical Oedipus both loved and hated his father, Laius, in the same way the worshipper both revered and resented his god (the primordial father-figure). Like Schelling, Freud theorizes that the resulting emotional disequilibrium had to be discharged. Toward that end, the unconscious love-hate relationship was expressed by first ceremoniously killing, then mourning, and finally "exchanging places" with the slain god-substitute. In this manner, the guilt incurred by the aggressor could be symbolically resolved. In Freud's view, this process of dynamic displacement constituted the archetypal core of all religions.[69]

(It should be noted, however, that Schelling would reject Freud's attempts to reduce all religious phenomena to expressions of infantile fantasies, particularly the oedipal complex. This mode of explanation commits what Schelling would call the fallacy of psychologism.[70] He would also dispute the one-sided preoccupation with problems of male sexuality. Nevertheless, despite these differences, a remarkable agreement remains between the two thinkers with respect to the place of emotional ambivalence and displacement in religious experience.)

Yet if Schelling's idea anticipates to some degree the ideas of twentieth-century psychology and anthropology, his application of these insights to the phenomenology of religions is problematic. A primary deficiency, as we have seen, is the chronic lack of empirical evidence. Whereas Freud, Evans-Pritchard, and Eliade, for example, have been able to draw on extensive clinical and field experience to support their hypotheses (although this does not, of course, guarantee the accuracy of their findings), Schelling has little more to rely on than his knowledge of ancient classical texts, supplemented by a fertile imagination. In part, this situation reflects the undeveloped condition of the humanistic sciences in the nineteenth century. But in other respects it is symptomatic of a basic ambiguity in Schelling's approach (as discussed in the last two chapters). Unclear, perhaps even in his own mind, as to whether his aim is the empirical verification of *a posteriori* propositions or the graphic exemplification of *a priori* propositions, he tries to have it both ways. As a result, he often seems to undercut himself in either endeavor.

Schelling's proposition that the entire human race once maintained a quasi-pantheistic star cult is a case in point. This assertion is difficult enough, on the basis of the slim empirical evidence, to accept. Still more questionable is his claim that the formerly pacific deity of that earliest faith, on being confronted with competition from another religious principle, turned into a savage god of vengeance, punishing all who strayed from exclusive devotion to him. What makes these theories doubtful is not so much any impossibility in the proposed psychospiritual scenario as the sheer uniformity of it all—as if the very same religious drama must have replayed itself again and again, without exception, in the most diverse corners of the globe. Schelling has discovered a motif which may indeed have occurred in different parts of the world, but to generalize it across the board is an exaggeration. In light of what is known today about the tremendous disparity of culturally formative conditions in which the peoples of the world have lived, it seems more plausible to suppose that the characters and histories of their gods must have been equally various. Schelling's overgeneralization, however, is doubtless a consequence of the hidden apriorism in the philosopher's agenda.

Nevertheless, once having made allowances for the misguided notion of uniformity imposed by Schelling's schematism, it must be acknowledged that his ideas concerning the developmental patterns in religion provide much that is worth thinking about. Most fruitful is his suggestion that an important aspect of religious life—particularly in the more "primitive" religions—may involve attempts to resolve deep existential anxieties by means of fusing highly valued spiritual qualities that are perceived as vulnerable with precisely those forces that appear to threaten them.

Schelling's ideas raise, by implication, a number of important corollary issues. Could it be that the practice of human sacrifice was in fact a ritualized version of reconciliation with a hated spiritual antagonist through displaced identification with the enemy? Is it even possible that the Christian cross—that instrument of torture transformed into a symbol of redemption—is really just another manifestation of the same phenomenon? More generally, is religion by its very nature a neurotic response pattern to unconscious desires, fears, and aggressions in the worshipper? Or can it be a wholesome and effective means of resolving psychic conflicts? Is the presence of ambivalent motives in the believer's unconscious a necessary component of all religious experience?

In order to decide these and related questions from a Schellingian perspective, one must first see how he treats subsequent phases in his taxonomy of religious types. The next chapter will accordingly take up the development of the second Potency, A^2, in order to see how it changed internally as it worked to overcome the opposition of the first Potency. The theme of a mysterious identification between the two principles will come up again in that context.

For the present, the important thing to emphasize is that the mythological mind found itself caught in the pincers of a seemingly irresoluble double-bind between the forces of the conscious and the unconscious. On the one hand, it was unbearable to think of forgoing the promise offered by the vast new world of culture and civilization; on the other hand, it was agonizing to contemplate forsaking the undifferentiated unity of being to which the mind's very sense of self-identity had previously always been attached.[71] According to Schelling, this painful conflict was often reenacted through ritual self-degradations, self-mutilations, and so on. Examples of this phenomenon were the temple prostitution practiced by devotees of the Babylonian goddess Mylitta, the limping gait cultivated by the priests of the Phoenician god Baal, and the self-emasculations inflicted by votaries of the Phrygian demigod Attis.[72] In all such cases, Schelling contends, the worshipper was giving expression to irresistible psychic compulsions over which the rational intellect had no control. Whatever direction it turned, the mind experienced agonies of doubt. Schelling notes that the Greeks expressed this internal religious conflict through the telling word *Deisidaemonia*, which he interprets to mean "fear at the prospect of losing one's god."[73]

– 11 –

From Dionysus to Iakchos

The preceding chapter traced the sequence of stages by which the worship of god B gradually changed from an artless "relative monotheism" to an increasingly anxious, almost schizophrenic cult of the "jealous god." This development was reflected in the different manifestations of god B, first as the quasi-pantheistic one god, then as the partly peripheralized sky-god Uranus, and then again as the fiercely defensive Cronus. Despite these variations, however, in each case the dominant characteristics of the religion included the attachment to the basis of natural existence in all things, the demand of total exclusiveness in worship, and the sense of undifferentiated unity with, and in, the universal lord.

Yet these religions and their associated mythologies remained incomplete for Schelling insofar as they failed to do justice to the higher Potencies of spirit. In order for the latter Potencies to come into play, consciousness would have to commit itself to the process of maturation through "peripheralization." This crucial step was not possible from within the context of the Cronus cult itself. There the worshipper was still only able to recognize god A^2 while engaged in the effort to repudiate him and thereby to undercut the very basis of any recognition. The religious dialectic required a more receptive mode of awareness, so as to be capable of internalizing the insights already provisionally arrived at. By the same token, it was also imperative to assume a more flexible stance with respect to the possibilities of the future. None of these qualities was accessible to god B in his elemental, masculine form. To make the needed adaptations, a feminine spirit was indispensable. The next major step in the development of religious consciousness, therefore, would require the help of female divinities.

The Significance of Goddesses in Mythology

According to Schelling, feminine deities traditionally assumed the role of being the harbingers, bearers, and chief sustainers of their masculine counterparts. It was they who maintained the gods in their positions of power and authority; and it was also they who, in times of historical transition, would introduce the new religious principles of the succeeding World Age. The fact that these kinds of supportive functions were allocated to goddesses more often than to gods could not have been arbitrary. On the contrary, it showed that the mythological consciousness was expressing its religious intuitions artlessly by assigning to the feminine deities analogous functions, *mutatis mutandis,* to those assumed by actual women in ordinary life.[1]

Two cardinal features of feminine nature determined the main functions of goddesses in ancient religions: (1) their capacity for motherhood, and (2) their perceptive consciousness. How, then, did these qualities manifest themselves in the formation of world mythologies? And what dialectical processes determined their appearance at certain critical stages in the evolution of religion?

Motherhood

The demand for a spiritual principle analogous to that of physical motherhood derived from the need to bring forth the still dormant powers of the religious universe into full activity. In order to make place for these dormant powers, however, it was first necessary to transform the existing status quo from a condition of preemptive activity into one of receptive potentiality, i.e., into the supplying of material for use by other beings still "unborn." Consequently, the regnant masculine divinity would have to undergo a process of simultaneous "materialization" and "feminization." Both of these terms point to a diminution of the deity's direct authority for the sake of an enhanced creativity. (We might say, making a pun in English that is not available in German, that the regnant deity had to be transformed into a pregnant deity.)[2]

Schelling employs a conception of "material cause" which is Aristotelian. It is basically the complementary opposite of "formal cause," the latter functioning by means of imprinting a defining essence upon its appropriate matrix. Such a process would only be feasible, however, to the extent that the material cause yielded itself to the influence of the seminal forms. In the present instance, this meant that the formerly exclusive god B would have to make way for the coming of god A^2 by serving as his "mother." Schelling regards as highly significant the etymological connection between the Latin terms *materia* and *mater*. This linguistic relation indicates the direction that B would have to take in order to fulfill the exigencies of dialectical progress.[3]

Table 3 Two Mythological Kataboles Leading to the Development of Polytheism.

| Original Sky God "Uranus," etc. | First Katabole | → | First Mother Goddess "Urania," etc. ↓ **Conception** of An Unnamed God | Jealous Sky God "Cronus," etc. | Second Katabole | → | Second Mother Goddess "Cybele," etc. ↓ **Birth** of The God(s) to Come |

(Compare with table 2, p. 180, above.)

This was the implicit origin of the Great Mother Goddess, an almost universal figure in ancient religions. For Schelling she was not so much the mother of plant and animal life as she was the genetrix of the polytheistic pantheon. Depending upon the stage of development involved, the Great Mother would possess correspondingly articulated features. During the reign of Uranus, she assumed the form of "Urania," the Queen of Heaven who first "conceived" of the coming new god.[4] Later, when Cronus had the dominion, a similar process of "feminization" gave rise to the Phrygian Cybele, who combined the stridently self-assertive qualities of her masculine counterpart with an explicit recognition of A^2's divinity. In this sense, it was Cybele that finally "gave birth" to the god whom Urania had conceived.[5] Schelling designates the "conception" and "giving birth" of A^2 respectively as the first and second spiritual *kataboles* or "ground-layings," for the era of full-fledged polytheism.[6] (See table 3.) These two goddesses were really just variant forms of B, as indeed Uranus and Cronus themselves also were.

The essential attribute of motherhood did not end with the first Potency, however. According to Schelling's interpretation, it would recur wherever a radical revolution in religion was about to take place. Always it was the feminine divinity, the goddess, who anticipated and furthered new developments, whereas the masculine divinity struggled to protect the status quo. For example, it was the Egyptian goddess Isis who, as the feminine counterpart of god A^2, brought forth the triumphant Horus (a form of A^3). Thus, motherhood represented the progressive quality which would be a hallmark of the central goddesses in mythology until the final stages of mythological evolution had been reached.[7]

Consciousness

Just as in the human world women are traditionally credited with deeper empathetic insight than men, so in the divine world goddesses have been endowed with penetrating consciousness. This again is another reflection of the female's allegedly greater sensitivity. Insofar as the receptive feminine soul constitutes the underlying psychic foundation on which the activities of the masculine are erected, she would naturally appear as the interior aspect of that to which he is the corresponding exterior aspect.

In Schelling's formulation of this interpretive hypothesis, his reliance on the principles of philosophical idealism is evident. For him, all experience, and indeed all reality, requires both a subjective and an objective moment. Since the former pole involves the fluid potentiality to accommodate itself and absorb the determinations of the latter,[8] it seems to him appropriate to identify consciousness with the feminine character. The structural solidity of the objective moment, on the other hand, he associates with masculinity. These two together, the god-positing subject and the god posited as object, are equally necessary aspects, both expressing the same truths from different perspectives.[9]

Because of the goddess's position as the representative of religious consciousness, she was the natural mediator between the human and divine worlds. In worshipping her, the devotee would become aware as never before of the highest potentials within himself. Indeed, the self-transformative powers capable of being released in this manner were enormous, for they opened the possibilities of spiritual revival and rebirth. The festivals in honor of Demeter, for example, were a case in point. In their purest form as the Eleusinian Mysteries, they enabled initiates to transcend the very limits of the Greek mythological system and catch glimpses of the religion's ultimate significance.[10]

Despite Schelling's evident appreciation of the role of goddesses in world mythologies, he nevertheless devotes far more attention to the critical exegesis of the male gods. There are several reasons for this imbalance. As a product of his times, Schelling is undeniably what one would characterize today as a male chauvinist, and he does not blush to assert that the feminine principle must be "subordinate" to the masculine.[11] Schelling reads the feminine deities as primarily representing meekness, yielding and submissiveness in relation to the masculine principles. This interpretation can lead to some rather implausible conclusions—as for example, when he treats a male deity's loss of power and prestige as if this were the symbolic equivalent to becoming "female."[12] In general, Schelling overlooks the possibility that a goddess could be a formidable power in her own right, not merely figuring as the subordinate counterpart or harbinger of a god. This typically nineteenth-century bias may offend our late-twentieth-century sensibilities. Moreover, it sometimes compromises the validity of Schelling's interpretations of myths.

It is worth bearing in mind, however, that the preponderance of mythological materials available were in fact heavily male-oriented. Throughout human history, the exploits of the gods have tended to receive a disproportionate share of attention and space in sacred narratives and scriptures. Consequently, the prejudices of the ancients themselves provided the occasion for continued partiality in the scholarship applied to them, and to some degree perhaps even made this inevitable.

Having noted these qualifications and cautionary provisos, the present investigation now turns to the analysis of another spiritual power, the one who in Schelling's view was undoubtedly the most significant in all mythology: the god A^2.

The Coming of Dionysus

Dionysus, as Schelling has explained, could not effectively enter the stage of world history except in the company of a female divinity. In fact, it is argued that the first appearance of A^2 must have occurred in a merged form, as inseparably linked with a feminized version of B. The religious consciousness, in struggling to accommodate the stirrings of the new spiritual principle, could only conceive of doing so through the gentle mediation of what was old and familiar. The goddess Urania could satisfy this need by assuming the role of god A^2's mother and constant companion.[13]

Schelling finds empirical verification of his theory in the reports of Herodotus concerning the religion of the coastal "Arabians."[14] According to him, these people worshipped a lunar goddess by the name of Alilat and a solar god by the name of Orotal. Herodotus had no difficulty in identifying these as Urania and Dionysus, and Schelling fully accepts his authority. Especially telling, to the philosopher's mind, was one pregnant sentence in the historian's account: "They hold," Schelling translates, "Dionysus and Urania alone to be god"—using the singular form here instead of the plural form that one might rather have expected, i.e, "to be *gods*."[15]

Based on this slender evidence, together with some etymological speculations regarding the verbal connections between "Alilat" and "Orotal," Schelling draws the conclusion that the two divinities were merged in the consciousness of the Arabians. Here then, he thinks, is a concrete example of god A^2 in a condition of inseparable fusion with the feminized B. Moreover, she being associated with the moon as he with the sun, their connection with the sky-worship characteristic of Zabism was clearly established. Yet the seeds of the revolution were already implicitly present, insofar as the "sun" in this context symbolized the differentiated multiplicity of organic life to which A^2 would give rise. Hence the synthetic union of the solar and lunar deities was intrinsically unstable. Sooner or later it was bound to break apart, and then the state of war between B and A^2 would return in full force.

Schelling discovers further confirmation of his theory in a myth of Herakles, considered as allegedly another manifestation of A^2. In Lydia, so the story goes, Herakles was obliged to do penance for a previous misdeed by serving for one year's time as the indentured slave of Omphale, the country's queen. It amused that regent to dress her mighty vassal, whose true identity she did not know, in the dress of a woman and to set him about housewifely chores, an episode in enforced transvestism that has been a favorite subject in art through the centuries. Subsequently, the myth continues, Omphale became the mistress of Herakles and bore him several sons.

On Schelling's interpretation, this tale of Herakles and Omphale is highly significant, though overlaid and corrupted by many later accretions. Putting aside all the peripheral details, such as the notion that Herakles was doing mandatory penance, Schelling concentrates on the one essential image—that of the great hero and future savior of humankind appearing as a woman.[16] By this stratagem, a revolutionary innovation was able to seem less threatening to the old order than it actually was and thereby gain a first tentative entry into the mythological mind.

Again, however, the unconscious strategy of feminization as a means of introducing the rebel god A^2 was a temporary expedient at best. The new religious principle represented by this deity could not masquerade indefinitely as a harmless extension of the old. For in A^2 an essentially different worldview, with an alien system of values, was about to make its fateful entrance. Whereas previous divinities, under all their various names and forms, had been so many manifestations of the one god B, this god A^2 was something else again. Schelling gives him a distinctive epithet: "the relatively spiritual god."

Unlike the monolithic "real god," Cronus, who was indifferent to organized structures and valued only bare existence, Dionysus appeared as the "relatively spiritual god . . . lord and friend of all that was human . . . creator of genuinely human life, gracious to the individual and to humanity."[17] As the bringer of sophisticated agricultural methods, indicated by his traditional association with the grape, Dionysus was simultaneously the originator of urban life and the founder of civilization.[18] In general, as the source of an unconfined multiplicity, in contrast to the previously stifling conditions of existential uniformity, he was the "liberating god," who first introduced humanity to the possibilities of a higher spiritual life.[19] In different cultures he was variously worshipped as Melkart, Orotal, Axiokersos, Osiris, Shiva, Prometheus, or Herakles; but these differences in nomenclature hardly matter to Schelling. Hence, the philosopher generally uses one Greek name, "Dionysus," to refer to all the embodiments of the new god. Furthermore, he finds that every complete mythological tradition has preserved in connection with this deity the same basic motifs.

Born of a mortal woman (symbolizing his initially subordinate position), the youthful "Dionysus" progressively gained recognition and power. Initially only a demigod or daemon, he had to become a full-fledged god through his own activities.[20] This required overcoming innumerable obstacles put in his path by Cronus or his confederates. Dionysus would also repeatedly perform miraculous feats in order to remove some threat to humanity or enhance the quality of civilized life.[21] Throughout the mythological sequences, Dionysus always emerged as the coming deity, whose concluding victory was seen as the immanent goal and end of the entire process.[22]

(It is worth noting, by way of anticipation, that the ultimate manifestation of this divine power would be none other than Christ himself—who, like his prototypes in mythology, would be born of a mortal woman, struggle against regressive religious values, sacrifice his life for the sake of humanity, and in the end be resurrected in his triumphant divinity. But, of course, the full significance of these events could only emerge in and through the *revealed* religion.)

In the pagan faiths, the contest between the conservative and the radical religious principles was all the more violent and extreme precisely because they did not (as in Christianity) already implicitly recognize and include one another. On the contrary, the myths represent the older god as desperately struggling to maintain his supremacy and to prevent Dionysus from overthrowing him. Cronus punished all disloyalty to himself with ruthless savagery, and he especially directed his rage at this bold usurper.[23] But in the end, he was forced to yield to the innovative stranger, and thus a new world order came into being.

According to Schelling, the entire history of religions among virtually all the ancient peoples and cultures is to be interpreted in terms of the conflict between the first and second Potencies. This is why he attaches supreme importance to the proper understanding of this particular theme, as holding the indispensable key to unlocking the true meaning of myths.[24] For he thinks it was this life-and-death struggle between Cronus and Dionysus that was responsible for generating the "complete" world mythologies. Schelling writes:

> Out of this battle between the one deity (now posited for the first time as vanquishable) and the higher, relatively spiritual god who overcomes the material god—out of this battle there develop . . . the later stages of mythology, e.g., the pantheon of the Phoenicians, of the Carthaginians, of the Egyptians, of the Indians, and even of the Greeks.[25]

Divine Madness and the Strange Paradox of the "Dionysian" Motif

At this point, however, the reader may wish to raise an objection to the interpretation of Dionysus outlined above. It has just been suggested that the role of that deity in mythology was to serve as the bringer of differentiated consciousness, form, harmony, and order to a world where these had previously been lacking. Characterized as the patron of agriculture and civilization, Dionysus was allegedly the one who first introduced the benefits of a higher spiritual culture by means of tempering the baser instincts of human beings.

Yet how well does this description correspond to the more common understanding of Dionysus's nature? Can it really be true that this deity was, as Schelling claims, the paradigm of humane values, refinement and self-restraint? Is it plausible to suppose that just this god should be credited with taming the barbarism of an earlier, primitive age and with instituting the reflective mental attitudes appropriate to life in civilized society? Or was he not really just the reverse? Granting that a transition might well have occurred in the development of human consciousness from the monolithically compact worldview of prehistory to the discriminating intelligence of historical times, was Dionysus himself the catalyst of all these changes, or was he not rather the spirit of a defiant counterreaction? It seems *prima facie* more logical to believe that the great Loosener of social inhibitions and celebrant of the instinctual life would have been an advocate of returning to the "state of nature," indeed an archetype of what another nostalgic age would call "the noble savage."

In modern usage, the word "Dionysian" is generally associated with the frenzied, orgiastic revelries of the Bacchanalia, whose participants would lose their sense of individuality and merge in the undifferentiated unity of existence as such. During these wild festivals, it would appear, a person's ego and sense of separation from the objective world, as well as the intellect's discriminating faculty, would temporarily be suspended in favor of a liberating monism and embracement of the irrational ground at the root of all being. Surely this sort of experience would be the polar opposite of the form-giving, rationalizing activity which might rather be associated with an Athena or an Apollo. (One is reminded, in this connection, of Nietzsche's much later distinction in *Die Geburt der Tragödie*, between the Dionysian and the Apollonian moments of consciousness.)[26]

As if these perplexities were not enough, there is also the problem of the close association between Dionysus and the cultivation of the grape. In some traditions, notably the Greek and Egyptian, Dionysus (or Osiris) was specially associated with this plant as one of his symbolic attributes. This fact, together with the circumstance that wine was the main intoxicating beverage, would appear to be more supportive of a Nietzschean than a Schellingian interpretation of Dionysus's significance. The madness of intoxication could arguably lead to a sense of undifferentiated unity with the All, whereas cool sobriety would seem more appropriate for the rational activities of civilized life.

Schelling would caution, however, against a too naturalistic interpretation of the worship of Dionysus—an interpretation that would see in it nothing more than an elaborate celebration of the grape harvest. Such theories, as he has argued on other occasions, invert the true relationship.

Actually, the yearly harvest festivals served the function of infusing ordinary life with a higher religious significance. They gave concrete expression to the innermost longings of the human spirit. It was not the other way around, as if the rituals themselves were nothing but schematic reenactments of farming practices.[27] In Schelling's view, the real purpose of these sacred rites must have been to activate and commune with the second Potency itself. Thus, although grapes and wine could indeed symbolize Dionysus, it does not follow that Dionysus was understood literally as just the god of the grape.

The possibilities for seeing deeper meanings in the processes of wine production are not difficult to discover. The technique of fermentation through aging was not only an important invention in its own right, but it could also provide an evocative image of psychic renewal. Schelling elaborates on this. The juice of the grape in its original, chthonic condition (as the "blood of the Titans")[28] would be pressed ("conquered") and, in death, transmuted through the fermentation process into the drink of the gods. In the same way, then, the intoxicating propensities of alcohol could be transformed through moderation into a spiritually liberating experience. On the other hand, the drunken behavior of the Maenads and Bacchantes, etc., may have been merely a vulgar manifestation, an exoteric version for popular consumption, of the true and secret Dionysian rituals.[29] In any case, thinks Schelling, when properly understood the fruit of the vine could very well have served as an emblem of higher civilization.

Nevertheless, even if one concedes Schelling all these points, the fact remains that the worship of Dionysus as practiced in ancient Greece, like the parallel worship of Osiris in Egypt and Shiva in India, did involve elements of wildly ecstatic abandonment and at times even savagery. These features of the Dionysian cult cannot be explained away. The chief problem facing the interpreter, therefore, is how to account for the destructive, patently uncivilized dimensions of a religious movement whose essential message allegedly was the annunciation of a higher and more humane culture. What arguments or evidence, if any, might resolve this paradox?

By way of approaching an answer, Schelling observes that the consciousness still wedded to god B must have experienced bewilderment, if not total confusion, when first confronted with god A^2. All that had once seemed secure, all that had been definite and clear, was now thrown into turmoil.[30] The benefits that the new Potency might be able to confer hardly seemed worth the price in emotional strain. In this situation, therefore, disappointment blended with tremulous excitement to produce a kind of hysteria, so that excessive modes of behavior and even perverse actions would have been a natural result. Moreover, because all these effects were elicited by the unwelcome arrival of Dionysus, he was held responsible as their proximate cause:

> The first natural movement of consciousness is, then, to put itself against him, to deny him recognition as god. In any case, he is the god whom consciousness merely *endures,* to whom it has no free relationship, who enters into the peace of the first consciousness only as a judgment, as a destiny, and not as the liberating being that he is, but rather appears only as the *disorienting,* pitilessly provocative one and therefore as inducing madness *(Wahnsinn).* . . . Who is not familiar with that image of Dionysus as the god that causes madness, an image which has lasted from the earliest times all the way down to those later resonances among Roman poets, as, e.g., Horace's *Quo me rapis Bacche?* The effect of the god is a fateful one for consciousness, which it cannot escape.[31]

This temporary bout of madness might, however, prove ultimately beneficial if channeled in the right directions. Schelling, as a true romantic, is convinced that under optimal circumstances the energy mobilized by such an experience could provide the inspiration leading to a breakthrough out of a mental impasse. Original insights, fresh possibilities for change and development could occur to the mind thus thrown off its normal pathways. Indeed, Schelling already argued as early as 1810 that a certain degree of "controlled madness" was necessary for all genuinely creative thinking.[32] In taking this position, Schelling is following a tradition at least as old as Plato, who distinguished between a lower order of madness and a higher, divine madness of lovers, poets, and philosophers.[33]

These reflections will perhaps suffice to explain how a god whose true mission was the establishment of culture and higher civilization might first have manifested his influence in the form of incitement to lunacy and deranged forms of behavior. What remains so far unclear, however, is how the worship of Dionysus could have come to be associated with the experience of losing one's sense of personal identity and merging with an undifferentiated cosmic unity.

On closer consideration, it becomes evident that the required principle of undifferentiated unity already has an assigned place in the system of the Potencies: it is nothing else than the inverted first Potency, B. As explained in the previous chapter, however, the power of god B characteristically belongs not to Dionysus but to that deity's chief rival and antagonist, Cronus. This proposition is central to Schelling's whole interpretive framework for mythology. According to the theory, it was in fact the spirit of Cronus that was the underlying ground (as opposed to the merely proximate cause) of all the wild, orgiastic revelries.[34] Moreover, it was the influence of Cronus that, as the "inward-drawing power" opposed to multiplicity, must have been ultimately responsible for moving people to attempt the abandonment of their separate identities so as to merge in the undifferentiated experience of immediate Oneness.[35] In contrast, Dionysus was the principle of formal differentiation and order who, as god A^2, sought to restrain the blind power of B. Again, it was Dionysus who worked to introduce the spirit of organic harmony into existence, without which a developed human culture would have been impossible. Surprisingly, therefore, Schelling's Dionysus must have been precisely that mythological agency whose mission it was to oppose and subordinate the so-called "Dionysian" element of experience.[36] But how is this to be understood?

Now, according to Schelling, god A^2 could come into his own and establish a new world order only by means of first appeasing the old god B. This meant that the primordial ground of existence, the boundless and undifferentiated first Potency, had to receive its due, precisely in order to usher in the distinction-making and form-giving capacities of a higher rationality. In other words, god A^2 had to identify himself provisionally with the same style of religious motivation and activity as used by his old antagonist, god B, imitating him for the sake of symbolically appropriating him.[37] At this still rather primitive level of spiritual evolution, the only model available for assimilating the religious values of another Potency was by means of violent conquest. It was expected that either B would destroy A^2, or else A^2 would destroy B. So there was no alternative at hand except to imitate the aggressive behavior of the exclusive first Potency. And yet the unconscious goal of all A^2's actions was just to surmount that very mode of relationship among the Potencies.

Just as B had originally been the all-consuming fire that prevented the principles of multiplicity and individuality from developing, so now B itself must in turn be dismembered and torn to shreds *(zerissen)* in order for multiplicity to be capable of unfolding freely.[38] This could not happen directly, however; for god B would refuse to yield the Center unless and until the principle of his own being were granted some satisfaction. Hence, god A^2 first had to present a version of himself as a sacrificial victim to the old titanic power of B, had to allow himself to be torn to shreds, in order to demonstrate through example how the loss of undifferentiated being could yet be transcended and overcome.

The aspect of A^2 which undertook this role of the conquering victim was, according to Schelling, "Zagreus." This was the lowest dimension of Dionysus's being, appearing here in a guise which reduplicated the character of Cronus himself. Zagreus was the "wild Dionysus," the one who would on occasion even demand blood sacrifice, in clear emulation of the methods used by the formerly unrivaled, still wishfully exclusive god of Zabism.[39] This explained how it was that Zagreus could be described as "pitiless," even though that quality properly belonged to his ancient antagonist, Cronus.[40] In consequence of such an identification, the eventual death-through-dismemberment of Zagreus could be symbolically resolved into the overcoming and transfiguration of Cronus himself. And yet it was none other than Cronus (or his representatives, the Titans) who demanded the sacrifice of Zagreus. Religious poets treated this paradoxical theme in a manner which frequently resonated with the deep tensions and ambivalences involved. Schelling writes:

> When they represented these sufferings as a dismemberment at the hands of the Titans, then the underlying thought could have been that the god had to suffer that which was Titanic within his own nature. For the word "Titan" comes . . . from τείνω, τιταίνω, meaning "to tense." Now the first Dionysus is, however, the cause of all tension, and so he is the cause and the principle of all that is titanic. It is to that extent not unthinkable that titanic powers, and Cronus in particular, were represented in the Mysteries themselves as taking part in the suffering and death of Dionysus. In this manner, Cronus is abstractly conceived as that which holds back the god who was material (or already inclined toward materialization), and which thereby brings about his dismemberment. Zagreus acts as this god qua being at the point of yielding himself, or Cronus: Zagreus = Typhon: (the dismembered) Osiris.[41]

This quote clearly indicates that the divine antagonist, originally external to Dionysus-Zagreus, was now to be understood as internal to him. This process of internalization was, for Schelling, a secret of the mythological system—it was the reason why the satisfactions through appeasement, etc., could work. This certainly was not a scheme of divine justice, in the sense of propitiating a presumably higher, external authority. It was, rather, an expression of inner catharsis, in the sense of conciliating a lower principle within the god (and, by extension, the worshipper) himself. Ultimately, the purging action of the cathartic reenactment would bring about an acceptance of limitation and thereby an overcoming of the religious consciousness's own lower nature. Cronus would realize the necessity of his "materialization" (i.e., his subordination) and submit to the loss of his former supremacy.

The hinge point of this internal catharsis therefore depended for its efficacy upon god A^2's prior success at appropriating the nature and attributes of god B. Initially, to be sure, this move resulted in a brutalization of A^2, a return to the chthonic worldview of an earlier age. Yet precisely by means of this retrogressive appropriation, on Schelling's interpretation, the civilizing spirit of A^2 was able to penetrate the character of B and thus begin the work of rendering it harmless. The final aim was the complete subordination of B under the power of A^2, in the process of which B would cease to be an "actuality" in his own right, and become instead a "potentiality" for the sake of A^2 and A^3. The intuitive goal was that B would return to the condition of being A^1, bequeathing its power and serving as the throne and support for the two higher Potencies.[42] This model of transformation—proceeding by the four stages of appeasement, identification, appropriation, and subordination—lies at the heart of Schelling's theory.

It is interesting to consider, in this connection, how psychologically daring some of this nineteenth-century philosopher's ideas really are, concerning especially the instinctive relations of god A^2 with god B. His claim is that A^2 (and by implication the consciousness committed to him), having been originally victimized by B's hostility (and that of the consciousness loyal to *him*), would partially assimilate the values of the antagonist and thus seek to overcome him. This theory partly anticipates modern conceptions regarding the phenomenon of "identification with the aggressor," whereby individuals who feel menaced are said to assume the qualities and behavior of the figures that threaten them. According to many psychologists, the unconscious hope in such cases is to reduce a perceived danger by means of imitating the frightening behavior and thereby vicariously "exchanging places" with the aggressors. If this is true, then perhaps a similar implicit psychic strategy could also underlie certain religious experiences and practices. Indeed, a *locus classicus* in psychoanalytic literature describing the syndrome of identification with the aggressor, Anna Freud's *Das Ich und die Abwehrmechanismen*, notes specifically that this kind of defense mechanism played an important role in the "religious ceremonies of primitive times."[43]

Yet despite a striking similarity on this point between Schelling and the Freudians, their disagreement with respect to the ultimate prognosis is even more significant. For the psychoanalysts, the experience of identification with the aggressor is purely delusory: it leads the victim to misread his true situation and so act in totally inappropriate ways. In that case, the only cure would be to disabuse him of the delusion. To Schelling, by contrast, the identification of Dionysus-Zagreus, as the sacrificial victim, with Cronus, as the hostile destroyer, was in fact the first step in a salutary process of spiritual restoration. According to the philosopher's theory, these identifications were not delusionary but authentic, not one-sided but reciprocal.

This mutual rapprochement of the two divine principles complements the movement, originating from the other side, that was discussed in the previous chapter. Together, the two movements of spiritual assimilation would bear a common fruit. For just insofar as the wrath of the "real god" was accepted as legitimate and appeased at great cost by the "relatively spiritual god," to that same extent the more primitive deity was induced, in turn, to identify himself with the interests of the higher. Moreover, just insofar as A^2 could demonstrate to B the route to psychic recovery ("resurrection") after being most cruelly sacrificed, by the same token, B learned to acknowledge the inherent superiority of A^2. Gradually, but inevitably, the moment of religious experience embodied in Cronus (viz., Zabistic pantheism) came to recognize that its own deepest interest and destiny consisted in subordination to the ordering principle of A^2 (systematic polytheism).

In Schelling's view, this alone explains how it was possible for the symbolically and ritually enacted synthesis of the two opposed divinities to bring about a lasting regeneration. For the mythological consciousness the intuitive hope was that the vanquished Cronus would become miraculously transformed into the triumphant Dionysus. Simultaneously, the formless unity of spiritual indeterminacy would give way to the differentiated unity of organic harmony. It was, then, this transformation—not the orgiastic experience per se of entering into an all-consuming, impersonal Oneness—that constituted the true secret underlying the worship of Dionysus.[44]

Schelling's interpretation of the mythological significance of Dionysus is nothing if not ingenious. He successfully brings out new hermeneutical possibilities and problems which previously occurred to no one. Whether or not all—or even most—features of his theories are historically accurate may well be doubted. Certainly there is an abundance of recently discovered archeological and philological evidence which was not available in the mid-nineteenth century, and which may require substantial modifications of his views. Yet these limitations in specifics are less important than the general design and methodology of Schelling's approach. His theory of spiritual/psychological Potencies, with a capacity for misalignment or displacement from their proper spheres of influence, and his explorations into the ways such a displacement could then penetrate all aspects of human existence, have been ground-breaking. Schelling is the first modern thinker to suggest that the forms of life associated with a religion might inwardly possess a quite different purport from what their surface appearances would seem to indicate. This idea has been extremely influential among twentieth-century students of religion.

Iakchos: The Archetype of Spiritual Balance

The progressive conquest and subordination of god B by god A^2 involved a profound metamorphosis in religious consciousness. In abandoning primitive Zabism and the undifferentiated unity that was its sole previous object of worship, human culture made a tremendous step forward. Loosened from the grip of an inflexible unity, which had been all the more powerful and tenacious because of its origins in the unconscious, the minds of the ancients opened up to the claims of multiplicity. According to Schelling, it was this fundamental change in ways of thinking that ushered in the transition to higher civilization. People became increasingly aware of the differentiated structures that gave order to the physical universe, and they learned to apply similar principles to organizing their own societies. Thus, fields were measured, plants cultivated, animals domesticated, cities built. Most significant of all, a rich pantheon of polyvalent deities came to populate the spiritual universe.

None of these developments would have been possible if the Great Crisis, heralding the end of the cognitive and affective uniformity characteristic of the First World Age, had not occurred. Gradually, the regnant model of truth shifted from a preoccupation with the one pantheistic reality underlying all things to a more discriminating concern with the formal principles by which they were arranged and structurally ordered.

Yet, despite the importance of these historical changes, Schelling insists that what was of positive value in the earlier worldview could not altogether disappear. Specifically, the conquest of Cronus at the hands of Dionysus could not mean an end to all feeling for the pervading unity in things, but instead the basic conception of unity itself would have to undergo a radical revision. Schelling distinguishes between a lower-order unity, which as a monochromatic uniformity is incompatible with multiplicity, and a higher-order unity, which, as the unifying term of an organized whole, in fact presupposes multiplicity.[45] The latter principle, he maintains, could only emerge into consciousness after the former had been completely sublimated. Ultimately it would prove to be the basis of absolute, as opposed to merely relative, monotheism.

This revision was no easy matter, however. The differentiating activity of Dionysus, in shattering the original unity of Cronus, did not *ipso facto* bring into being the higher-order unity needed to replace it. In order to realize that next crucial achievement in the dialectic of religion, it was necessary for the third Potency, A^3, to become operative and complete the process which A^2 by itself could only begin.

There was, moreover, another critical reason why the religious dialectic could not end with the worship of Dionysus. This concerned the involuntary character of the second Potency's activity over the first. According to Schelling, A^2 was compelled by its own internal nature, by its own irresistible drive, to work upon B and move it in the direction of self-subordination and openness to rational differentiation. Consequently, Dionysus was not free to decide whether to seek the overcoming of Cronus; he was forced to do this, just as Cronus, in turn, was constrained to follow the bent of his essential nature. Out of the dialectical consequences of the necessary collision of A^2 with B there arose the need for a third Potency, in order to achieve the logical balance between the first and second Potencies. Until A^3 supervened on the scene, there was and could be no rational balance, no genuine freedom of thought.

Schelling explains Dionysus's involuntary psychological effect on Cronus in the following terms:

> We must recall, in order to understand this feeling, that the god [Dionysus] is not by any means free to act, but he is rather by his very *nature* an active principle, which is *only* active, and for that reason is the blindly active principle.[46]

In a related passage, Schelling adds that the second Potency had no other purpose in existence than that of overcoming the first Potency, reducing it to its proper position as ground and support of the true deity. But precisely because the second Potency had no other telos than this, it became "exhausted" *(erschöpft)* in the execution of that aim.[47] In short, Dionysus had to give up his own life for the sake of subduing Cronus.

Yet in order for a true spiritual harmony to develop between the respective claims of "real" unity and "relatively spiritual" multiplicity—or, otherwise expressed, between the claims of existence and intelligibility—it was necessary for a third Potency to arise and bring the first two into equilibrium. Schelling is convinced that the teleological goal of all processes must be to retain or regain the central nerve of pervasive cohesion, the synthesizing unit, which would coordinate and synthesize the elements of multiplicity into an organic system. In the sphere of religion, the principle that could achieve this apperceptive unity was none other than "spirit" *(Geist),* the dialectical archetype of inner balance. For the Greeks, Schelling maintains, this was the function represented by the boy-god,

"Iakchos." His presence was essential; for, again, the activity of Dionysus was by itself insufficient to achieve the desired goal:

> But *precisely because* this second Potency as it were exhausts itself in the suppression and overcoming of the first, for just that very reason consciousness demands *(verlangt)* a third Potency, which in a sense has nothing to do; it demands a god who is, so to speak, inactive, i.e. a free god, a god who is there merely in order to put the *seal* on the relationship of subordination, and in order thereby to transform this very relationship into a stable and enduring one. . . . Consciousness, I say, demands a third Potency, which has nothing more to do, which does not work (like the second) necessarily, does not have to work, but which is thus free to work, is confident of its being and with it can undertake and do whatever it will.[48]

God A^3 would thus appear on the surface to be "inactive"; yet on a deeper level it would be the compelling drive which, as the final cause, motivated the entire dialectical process. "Active" in the same equivocal sense that Aristotle's Unmoved Mover was "active," the third Potency would not directly participate in the stresses and strains of religious upheavals. Instead, it would transcend the contest between A^2 and B, at the same time providing the teleological framework within which subsidiary causes would discharge their respective functions. Hovering above the fray of the mythological battlefield, god A^3 would supply the ideal toward which all the participants, knowingly or unknowingly, were striving.

Yet how convincing is Schelling's justification for introducing this supervenient phase in the evolution of religions? It must be admitted, not very convincing. The structure of his argument moves rather arbitrarily from (1) the determination that there existed a "demand of consciousness," to (2) the conclusion that the "demand" must have been fulfilled. This line of reasoning may even look ad hoc initially, but in fact it is a typical example of the production-dialectic described in earlier chapters.[49] In the present instance, the method has been employed in order to deduce the necessary emergence of the third Potency into world history. But once again, Schelling's reasoning follows a standard pattern: first he establishes the preliminary *lack* of a sustaining principle to integrate the conflicting interests of B and A^2; then he goes on to show the fundamental *need* for such a principle; and finally, as will be seen momentarily, he elicits the putative process that would bring the requisite principle into concrete actuality.

Yet although this derivation appears dubious from a purely logical standpoint, it may nevertheless be useful as a guide to understanding the speculative thought processes of ancient religious thinkers. To the mythological consciousness, caught in a double-bind of *Deisidæmonia,* the transition from a perceived ontological need to its positive fulfillment would probably have seemed quite legitimate. Such a move was, in any case, unlikely to raise too many critical scruples. Thus, it may be that what Schelling's argument lacks in rigor it makes up for in a different kind of verisimilitude.

According to this argument, then, the role of god A^3 in human history was inversely related to that of god B. To the extent that the latter occupied a dominant position in religious life, the former had to remain unmanifest as a merely implicit potentiality. Hence, during the First World Age, consciousness was insufficiently clarified to experience the enlightening presence of a fully spiritual deity. By the same token, conversely, the pantheon of gods in the throes of *Deisidæmonia* was unable to free itself from turbulence until such time as the third Potency finally deigned to reveal itself. The two movements were opposite sides of the same coin: god B could only retire fully from actuality and return to his rightful condition of subordinate potentiality if and when god A^3 simultaneously asserted his rightful place in religious consciousness.

At this point, however, a remarkable spiritual transformation occurred. As the first Potency withdrew from its previous condition of assertive actuality and took up a properly subservient role, it thereby ceased to be the "inverted" B and became instead the reconstituted A^1. In other words, the first Potency refrained from being any longer "that which ought not be," i.e., the relentless antagonist of religious progress, and found its vocation as the foundation of continuing advancement. This new function assumed by the first Potency was, to Schelling's mind, the true calling for which it had been predestined.[50]

The result was that this god B came to be posited as already-past: this was a creative, cosmogonic deity whose era had passed into obsolescence. Thus, B now appeared as the once powerful but now dethroned god, whether as "Uranus" (pure pantheism) or as "Cronus" (Zabism qua resisting polytheism). In his role as the fully overcome and subordinated first Potency (A^1 = B), this god rematerialized eventually as Hades, lord of the underworld. All of these various deities were images of the formerly supreme deity, now retired and essentially otiose.[51]

The great mystery here is that this subordinated god A^1 then became assimilated to god A^2 and even, by extension, to god A^3. Once the three Potencies emerged out of their previous condition of irreconcilable opposition, once they began to cooperate in sustaining a single, harmoniously organized universe, it became feasible for the mythological consciousness to identify them with each other as aspects of a single, more fundamental Power.[52] Moreover, because the transition of the first Potency from B to A^1 was essential in order for A^3 to manifest itself, the latter appeared as the restored version of the former. Thus, Zagreus would be able to "resurrect" *(auferstehen)* as Iakchos.[53]

With the actualization of god A^3, all of the essential principles determinative of myths were now manifest, and thus the age of the "complete mythological systems" was finally established. According to Schelling, the incomplete religions were those that included just one, or at most two, of the divine Potencies. Examples included the Zabism of early Persia as well as Buddhism—both of which, in Schelling's opinion, were undeveloped systems featuring only the inverted first Potency. When the second Potency became active, as in the religions of ancient Syria and Mesopotamia, this represented an important step forward; but even these systems were still incomplete. Only when the third Potency emerged into full consciousness, combining and harmonizing the activities of the other two, did the authentically "complete" religions finally come into being[54] (see table 2, p. 180 above). Then at last the undifferentiated unity of the first Potency, reduced to its appropriately subordinate position, became capable of assuming a definite and positive relation to the differentiated multiplicity of the second Potency, so that both of them together could be mediated through the self-differentiating unity of the third Potency. Prime examples of complete mythological systems, in Schelling's interpretation, were those of Egypt, India, and Greece.

Some Empirical Evidence, Ancient and Modern

Schelling gathers historical, philological and archeological evidence in favor of his interpretation. To show that Zagreus, Bacchus and Iakchos were, in the first instance, distinguished from each other, he cites a number of classical sources.[55] Yet the Greek writers frequently identified Zagreus with Iakchos, in precisely the same way as they sometimes also did Zeus with Dionysus, and as the Egyptians synthesized Set with Osiris.[56] This identification, Schelling thinks, was no accident.

Another piece of evidence Schelling finds particularly significant was a statue attributed to Polycleitos (now lost, but described in Pausanias's *Description of Greece*) representing a symbolic, almost surrealistic fusion of Zeus and Dionysus into a single deity. In one hand the god held a chalice of wine and in the other a thyrsus (symbolizing Dionysus), while on top there perched an eagle (emblem of Zeus).[57] Because Schelling has already concluded on other grounds that Zeus was a sublimated form of Cronus[58]—namely that form in which B has become completely clarified and respiritualized as an *existent* A^1—he regards this statue as a remarkable empirical confirmation of his thesis.

One difficulty standing in the way to any claims of universality for the above theoretical schemata would be the possibility that some of these myths might have influenced others from different traditions, mingling with them through contingent historical circumstances. In that case, the similarities between the Set/Osiris motif in Egypt, for example, and the Cronus/Dionysus or Zagreus/Iakchos motifs in Greece, might not indicate anything much one way or the other about the necessity of their successive manifestations. Schelling briefly worries about the possibility of such intercultural influences, but he soon returns to his favored mode of interpretation in terms of the *Potenzenlehre*. The other approach, he argues, treats essential thematic parallels as circumstantial rather than recognizing them as dialectically necessary.[59]

Despite the inconclusiveness of Schelling's empirical evidence, his theories do find partial corroboration in modern times from unexpected quarters. In Africa, for example, Geoffrey Parrinder notes that among traditional indigenous cultures there is a widespread belief in a formerly active supreme deity who now has become remote and detached from worldly concerns. This deity receives little attention or worship from the people, who instead cultivate the favor of his successors—more accessible, friendly, and humanely oriented gods or semidivine ancestors.[60] This feature of many African religions tallies quite well with Schelling's thesis concerning the aboriginal sky-god whose subordination or retirement ushered in the subsequent mythological age.

Mircea Eliade provides further evidence tending in the same basic direction. He discusses the conception of a *deus otiosus* and brings out the fact that the essential attributes of this displaced, once supreme god frequently became amalgamated with the natures of the more complex and differentiated deities that superseded him.[61] On this point, the correspondence of Eliade's ideas to those of Schelling is striking.

Especially significant, in Eliade's view, is the theme of a murdered creator-god, who thus became otiose and vanished from active participation in the people's religious life. Uranus was a typical case in point. His castration was the symbolic analogue of a violent death.[62] Yet even in this "death" and removal from the manifest regions of ritual and mythology, the *deus otiosus* continued to play a vital role, according to Eliade. The dead god's body made up the material substance, just as his spirit provided the intellectual sanction, for what came after him: "The new thing thus shares in the substance of the slain divinity and hence in some sort continues his existence."[63] Indeed, Eliade even goes so far as to suggest that the "genuine religions" in human history first appeared after the conquest or departure of this formerly supreme being.[64] This event signaled humanity's entrance into a fuller spiritual maturity. Eliade's implied contrast between "genuine" and "nongenuine religions" parallels Schelling's distinction between the "complete" and "incomplete" mythological systems.

Secrets of the "Uncanny" Lurking beneath the Surfaces of Mythology

With the development of complete mythological systems, it gradually became possible for the poetic imagination to take hold of the symbolic materials and mold them into ever more satisfying expressions of spiritual, and at times even profound philosophical, insight. This was because the unconscious constraints of dialectical necessity eased, so that the conscious mind could assume a correspondingly greater role in the creation of myths. Herein consisted the freedom which emerged as a product (especially of Greek culture). What previously had occurred via internal compulsion in the religious lives of the people now became accessible to their own deliberate control and manipulation.[65]

This did not entail, however, that the new poetic "freedom" involved abandonment of the underlying Potencies or escape from dialectical necessity. (The erroneous belief that this sort of "existential freedom" would be the outcome of Schelling's philosophy has constituted one of the greatest stumbling blocks to understanding his true position.) On the contrary, instead of freedom from the dialectical process, the true outcome had to be a freedom within that process, i.e. consciously willing it and thereby making it one's own.

It is important to appreciate this central feature of Schelling's philosophy. Freedom, for him, consists neither in the necessity of the dialectical process per se, nor in the contingency that permits individuals or even whole communities to assume different, partially undetermined stances in relation to the dialectic. The latter sort of contingency is trivial, in Schelling's view, and when not directed by a recognition of, and self-subordination to, that which is necessary, it results in a blindness which is the opposite of freedom. If, however, one does recognize what is necessary and essential and willingly subordinates oneself to it, if one orients the contingent aspects of life in harmony with the exigencies of the dialectical framework, then Schelling thinks it is possible to realize a genuine and creative freedom.

The distinction of Greek culture derived from the fact that it was able to achieve just this kind of liberation within the framework of dialectical necessity. This was why Greek mythology possessed a plasticity of expression and a human quality such as no previous culture had ever before attained. The epics of Homer especially displayed this new quality in portrayals of mortals and immortals relating almost on a basis of equality. The secular, almost irreligious, tone of these works reflected a fundamental change in the Greek consciousness. These narratives, Schelling observes, dwell neither on the theogony of the gods nor on their essential, world-generative functions.[66] Instead, the poet's imagination was free to play with the mythological materials in order to create his own themes and express preeminently human concerns. This creative freedom, which implicitly presupposed the presence and harmonious interaction of the divine Potencies, was the true source of the Greek genius.

Yet even though the calm and bright exteriors of the Greek worldview reflected the culmination of mythological development and the triumph of the harmonizing third Potency, this did not mean that the primordial struggles and tensions among the first two Potencies had totally disappeared. Far from it. Those fierce and monstrous forces remained hidden just underneath the surfaces of things, and hermeneutical analysis would overlook them at its peril. Only by means of realizing their continuing presence, albeit in a sublimated or repressed *(verdrungen)* state, would it be possible to account for the great psychological power and universality of the Greek myths.[67]

Twentieth-century Schelling scholars have been slow to appreciate the importance of this discovery of repressed ambivalences in the representations of Dionysus. Indeed, even as insightful a scholar as Xavier Tilliette seems to have missed this crucial feature of Schelling's interpretation of the Dionysian motif. Tilliette writes as if the tumult, intoxication, and orgies of self-abandonment associated with this god were, for Schelling, simply "the expression of the explosive joy evoked by the second god, the liberator."[68] Tilliette recognizes, to be sure, that these popular manifestations played no part in the celebrations of the esoteric Dionysian Mysteries themselves. But he gives no hint of Schelling's insistence on the deeper significance of these popular rites as reflections, not of Dionysus proper, but of Dionysus qua ambivalently identified with his opposite, Cronus. The closest that Tilliette comes to seeing the point of Schelling's novel hypothesis is his acknowledgment that Bacchus (the exoteric aspect of Dionysus) "has passed through a crisis of madness and folly." But on

Tilliette's reading this "folly" appears to signify only the venial faults of overindulgence. "Schelling knows nothing," Tilliette mistakenly adds, "of the artifices of that roguish and scintillating demon of Nietzsche."[69]

Quite the contrary, Schelling continually emphasizes that mythical representations may be associated symbolically with their exact opposites in terms of the latent affective or conative drives. Early in his career, for example, he pointed to the ambivalent significance of tigers and panthers as the boon companions to the god Dionysus. These creatures, at once so playful and charming and yet potentially so sadistic, reflect the condition of a mind that is suspended in "the last battle between division and unification, between consciousness and unconsciousness."[70] Likewise, in another early work, Schelling speculated on the necessary fusion of wrath and love as coterminous aspects of a single creative power. The aspect of wrath was of course that which ought to be subordinated, and yet as the indispensable foundation of love it must never wholly disappear, either.[71] This doctrine of the ambivalent forces implicit in all things would remain a dominant motif throughout Schelling's career. His *Philosophie der Mythologie* applies it to the Homeric age in terms that would later find a resonance in psychoanalytical theories of the twentieth century:

> The Homeric pantheon tacitly contains a Mystery within it, and is as it were built up over an abyss, which it bedecks as with flowers. The Homeric polytheism is itself a unity transformed into a multiplicity. Greece has a Homer precisely because it has Mysteries, i.e., because it has succeeded in completely conquering that principle of the past, which in the Oriental systems was still dominant and on the surface. It has succeeded in putting that principle back into the interior, i.e., into secrecy, into the Mystery (out of which, after all, it had emerged in the first place). The pure sky that hovers above the Homeric poetry was first able to extend over Greece after the dark and darkening power of that uncanny *(unheimliches)* principle (for one calls "uncanny" all that which should have remained in secret [*im Geheimnis*], in concealment and latency, but which has nonetheless stepped forward)—that æther which forms a dome over the Homeric world was first able to spread itself out after the power of that uncanny principle, which dominated in earlier religions, was precipitated down in the Mystery. The Homeric age was first able to conceive of that purely poetic narrative of the gods after the actually religious principle had been hidden in the interior and thus allowed the spirit to turn freely toward the outside.[72]

Note in this passage the significant play on words between *das Unheimliche* and *das Geheimnis*. It suggests that the act of bringing unconscious motivations into the light of full consciousness produced an acute shock in the mythological mind. According to Schelling, the early Greek worldview (as mirrored in Homer) was based on powerful repressed emotions whose inner significance was preserved only in the Mysteries. Moreover, it was only because of this successful repression that the Greeks were able to achieve the fulfillment of culture and reason that later blossomed in their golden age.[73]

Schelling's idea of a psycholinguistic connection between (a) the feeling of horror evoked by the "uncanny," and (b) the condition of secrecy in which a dreaded principle was to have been concealed, later struck Sigmund Freud as particularly acute. He commented on it in an essay on the same subject and made use of Schelling's discovery in formulating his own theories about the hidden content that often lurks behind the surface experiences of conscious life.[74]

In exploring the systematic ambivalences that underlie mythical narratives and symbols, Schelling's philosophy has opened the way for modern developments in the theory of interpretation. Indeed, it is not too much to say that his work anticipates the most significant aspect of the approach that Paul Ricoeur would later characterize as a "hermeneutics of suspicion." Although Ricoeur applies this phrase primarily to Marx, Nietzsche, and Freud, with whose general orientations Schelling would not at all have been in sympathy, yet the similarity in approach with respect to this one methodological principle—viz., the principle of unmasking dissimulated meanings—is striking. For Schelling, just as for those later hermeneuts of suspicion, one of the primary tasks of interpretation is to expose the false consciousness and self-deception that typically permeate much religious symbolism. A "master of suspicion," says Ricoeur, never takes for granted the ostensible meanings that such symbols possess.[75]

Exactly the same strategy motivates the work of Schelling. Always distrustful of the apparent meanings that mythological materials evidently purport to convey, he turns these on their head in order to show that their true import was exactly the opposite of what they seemed. He refuses, moreover, to accept at face value the self-interpretation of the mythological consciousness itself, taking instead as a working hypothesis the ever-present possibility of unconscious duplicity on the part of the believer.

Unlike the modern practitioners of the heremeneutics of suspicion, however, Schelling would sharply disagree with the intention to destroy faith by means of a reductive interpretation. On the contrary, he contends that genuine understanding must begin with a faith in the reality of its object. In this conviction, Schelling stands with Ricoeur in opposition to the attitude of unbounded suspicion.[76] For Schelling, hermeneutics must engage in a listening involvement with the religious object, taking seriously its claims, responding to the spirit of its word. Nevertheless, even while keeping open to the essence of the object, Schelling's analysis emphasizes the ambiguity and radical capacity for self-deceit that often conceal the true character of religious experience. In this sense, Schelling may be said to have prepared the way for the development of a "postcritical hermeneutics," one that would assimilate, even while moving beyond, the one-dimensional reductionism practiced by the masters of suspicion.

– 12 –

The Self-Overcoming of Mythology

Looking back over the territory covered in the previous chapters, two insights stand out as key for Schelling's interpretation of mythology. The first of these is his recognition that the significance of religions derives not so much from their doctrinal content as from their provision of concrete experiences in the worshippers' lives. The phenomena of faith, on this view, primarily comprise intense, experiential motifs—motifs whose underlying values may even contain elements of the irrational and self-destructive. True myths, according to Schelling, are never parables constructed for the communication of religious ideas. Like the scripts of plays or the scores of symphonies, they present something to be lived through and inwardly reenacted.[1] Only in that way can the believers face deeper-lying spiritual issues of which they often were not even conscious.

This brings up a second major insight of Schelling's: his discovery of the ambivalent attitudes and unconscious conflicts that lurk under the surfaces of much religious experience. These ambivalences include more than just inconsistent concepts or colliding ideologies; they are emotional struggles involving inchoate levels of the psyche that often lie beneath the level of consciousness. It was in fact because of these irrational strata in the old pagan religions that many of their most primitive practices and beliefs could persist for centuries after their ostensible justifications had long since disappeared.

These two insights of Schelling's, along with the nexus of interpretive strategies that develop out of them, typify what is characteristic of his hermeneutical approach, especially as contrasted with that of other idealists like Hegel. For the latter thinker, as noted above, the "truth" of mythology consisted exclusively in its conceptual content. Although Hegel would deny that the "concept," properly understood, is anything like an abstract formula, separable from its concrete manifestations, yet the fact remains that for him the real significance of myths is revealed, and can only be revealed, in thought. Schelling, by contrast, maintains that beyond rational comprehension there must also be a direct experience of religious truths, and he also makes the related claim that such experience would partly involve an encounter with the forces of chaos, both human and divine.

In this concluding chapter of our study of Schelling, it is appropriate to reflect on the ontological presuppositions that have prescribed such a plunge into the extralogical dimensions of experience. (1) One must ask, first of all, what fundamental dynamic of the human spirit is responsible for the systematic ambivalences in mythology that Schelling claims to have discovered. Are these ambivalences contingent by-products of the forces operative in religion, or are they somehow essential to this entire realm of experience? (2) Moreover, supposing that experiential ambivalences in religion are found to be essential, there would remain the question as to what transcendent implications, if any, follow from this peculiarly human phenomenon. In other words, is religious psychology merely a branch of the human sciences, or does it point beyond nature toward a supernatural reality? To formulate the same question in Schellingian terms, how is a mediated relationship through the Potencies with a transcendent God thinkable? (And if thinkable, is it also demonstrable?) (3) Thirdly, it is necessary to inquire into the final outcome of the mythological process. If there is much in religion that is false and even at times morally reprehensible, one wishes to know what dialectical processes would provide for the purging of accumulated errors and lead to a presumably higher perspective. Assuming, as Schelling does, that "absolute monotheism," and Christianity in particular, are ultimate religious truths, how would the development of historical polytheisms have contributed to the apprehension of such truths? And by what internal dynamic could the pagan religions have come to recognize what was wrong and delusory within themselves?

All of these questions raise similar concerns. They inquire into the character of the fundamental interface between appearance and reality, between psychology and "pneumatology," between the relative and the Absolute. In probing these dimensions, such questions actually burst the confines of mythology proper and by implication confront the ultimate significance of God and human existence. Consequently, Schelling treats these issues primarily in his philosophy of revelation, following upon the completion of his philosophy of mythology. They point beyond the scope of the present study and can only receive the briefest treatment here. Nevertheless, a few pages devoted to these crucial issues will help give a sense of where Schelling's philosophy of mythology is leading and what role it plays within his final system as a whole.

The Origins of Ontological Ambivalence in a Displacement of the Potencies

Let us briefly recapitulate the ontological theory underlying Schelling's interpretations of mythology. He argues that the original source of the recurrent ambivalences observable in all spheres of human and natural life, but especially prominent in the pagan religions, was the inversion of the Potencies which first brought into being the visible universe. Prior to that event, it will be recalled, the pure Potencies subsisted in ideal interrelations to one another as the formal principles constitutive of every possible reality. But with the existentializing *Daß* of God's creative will and the simultaneous empowerment of a subsidiary *Daß* which he conferred upon finite spirits, an actual, material universe came into being. The finite spirits, no longer bound by the limitations of the ideal world, were now free to turn away from the divine order and deliberately to alienate themselves from "that which ought to be."

The possibility of such an alienating act, Schelling maintains, was not evil in itself. It was necessary as the basis of individual freedom in finite creatures; otherwise, there would have been no independent foundation, no ontological selfhood, such as would permit a free and uncoerced relation between the individual spirit and God.[2] The creation's act of turning away from God, therefore—that primordial Fall reflected in the myths of so many peoples—actually was a necessary means to a higher end, making possible an ultimate return in freedom to the divine order once again. Thus, Schelling endorses a modified version of the doctrine of the *felix culpa*, or fortunate fault, which provided the original stimulus for spiritual regeneration and final reconciliation with God. Schelling boldly draws his conclusion: God had to permit "that which ought not to be" in order by means of it to produce in the end "that which ought to be."[3] But because this negative power of the antidivine is only a *conditio sine qua non*, or necessary condition, for the existence of free and independent spirits separate from God, he did not will the inversion of the Potencies for its own sake, but only indirectly as a means to a higher end.

Whatever the final justification for the original inversion of the Potencies, it is clear what the consequences were for the natural world. The "displacement" *(Verstellung)* of the Potencies was the source of everything that went wrong with it.[4] The sensible universe, for Schelling, is and always has been out of kilter with its own essential principles. That is why it is corrupt, riddled with sickness, death, and evil.[5] Moreover, an exactly analogous condition of original perversity applies to human nature as well.

The Potencies of the human personality are arranged in an inverted relationship to one another. That aspect which in principle should be subordinate—the instinctual egotism of the lower self—has assumed the upper hand, while that which should by rights be dominant—the rational and moral will—has been humbled and provisionally laid low.

When this "displacement" is applied to the religious universe, the result is a series of deities whose outward aspects, activities, and manifestations are often quite different from their true characters. The role-reversals of Cronus and Dionysus, reviewed in the previous chapters, are prime examples of this phenomenon. Schelling adds that all of mythology's "material gods"—i.e., deities representative of the inverted first Potency, B—have a double nature, and generally appear as "disguised" (*verkleidet*), as a result of being both blindly resistive and yet inwardly yielding to the harmonizing influence of the higher Potencies.[6] Schelling also points out that these tensions and conflicts are actually reflections of the internal events occurring in the minds of the worshippers themselves. To that extent, then, their origins are indeed subjective. What makes them no less objective is the dialectical necessity and universality of the religious paradigms themselves.[7]

In a certain qualified sense, Schelling can be said to anticipate the development of modern "projection theories" of religion, although he never uses that expression. But he does concur in three basic observations that modern projection theories like Nietzsche's and Freud's have emphasized: (1) the internal origins of the religious representations in the minds of the worshippers themselves; (2) the imposition of these "divine" qualities and characteristics onto the externally observed world of nature; and (3) the progressive inwardization of such externalized models by means of reappropriating the divinized natural world as a sacred ideal for directing the lives of human beings.

One particularly striking passage from the introduction to the *Philosophie der Offenbarung* illustrates these features. Here, Schelling is again discussing Zabism:

> The same necessity which turned the spirit of the people toward the sidereal regions, and which to that extent was the law of their *consciousness*, was at the same time the law of their *lives*. Conversely one can also say: What humanity saw in the stars, in those nomads of heaven with their uniform and barely variable movement through the "deserts of the aether" (to speak with Pindar)—humanity saw in these just the highest prototypes for its own life. In the place of the true God there stood for this consciousness that *king of heaven,* in whom it possessed only the One aspect of the true God, and even this not in its essence, in its truth,

but to which it clung so much the more in order not to lose the God completely.[8]

This passage shows that in some degree Schelling does recognize important features of modern projection theory. Where he differs, however, is in his attitude toward the internal mechanisms of the projections. For him, these are neither socially conditioned stereotypes nor neurotically induced illusions. Rather, they are dialectically generated archetypes springing from the deep structure of the psyche, constituting "one aspect" of God. From there derives the portion of truth that Schelling thinks always resides within them.

A Progressive Discharging of Religious Projections

In order to understand Schelling's theory of how the mechanisms of psychic superimposition function, it is necessary to recall his ontological distinction between the *Was*, or "whatness" of things, and the *Daß*, or "thatness" of them. The former refers to an entity's essential nature and the latter to its modal status as either existing or not existing. In the case of God, this distinction is especially important. The *Was*, of which the Potencies are the primary constituents, defines his divine characteristics and manifestations, whereas the *Daß* is his pure, existentializing fiat which creates and sustains the universe in actual being.[9] On this account, the source of many theological controversies concerning the existence of God has been a fundamental confusion of the *Was* with the *Daß*, leading to an uncritical projection of the former onto the latter. When this happens, the result is that one or more aspects or features of God's nature are selected out and treated as if identical with him, whereas in fact no one of them, or even their total aggregate, *is* God in truth. Instead, the Godhead of God consists in the unity running through and connecting all the diverse moments of his *Was*.[10]

Yet if it is in one sense a "mistake" to have projected the qualities of the *Was* onto the *Daß*, this error was historically unavoidable and ultimately derived from God's own creative will. For in order to bring an actual (as opposed to merely possible) universe into existence, God has freely assumed the features of the *Was* and "clothed himself" *(sich bekleidet)* with them.[11] This self-investiture with the divine essence transpired on two different levels—one in eternity and the other in space and time. The eternal self-investiture is always perfect and complete, revealing the true interrelations of the Potencies to each other and to the *Daß* that unifies and sustains them. The temporal self-investiture, on the other hand, is progressive and hence liable to various distortions *(Verstellungen),* depending on the degree of clarity achieved by the Potencies at each stage in world history. Schelling characterizes this latter aspect of God's self-manifestation as the "divine irony," which has determined that he should appear as being other than what he actually is.[12] Indeed, Paul Tillich, in his exegesis of Schelling, goes so far as to suggest that in a sense God acted "deceptively" in assuming the initially undeveloped Potencies as "masks" to conceal his true person.[13]

Now, as long as the exclusive first Potency, B, dominated the other two and refused to let them unfold according to their nature, as long as the condition of tension among the three inverted Potencies prevailed, the transcending unity of the pure *Daß* could not stand forth as free and immaterial.[14] Instead, the discordant and misaligned Potencies struggled with each other for supremacy in the material universe, and in that process they obscured the true character of divinity. Schelling insists that the personality of God, as it is in itself, transcends essence (the *Was*) altogether.[15] But the Potencies, because of their displacement, superimposed their own essential attributes indiscriminately upon the transcendent *Daß* no less than upon one another. This was the source of all the errors implicit in human religions, since the divine presence which people felt and sought to express was reflected through distorted images.

According to Schelling, this distortion was the cause of those tensions and internal conflicts among the devotees of ancient religions that resulted in psychic ambivalences. For if this were not the case, if mythological representations had been the products merely of one-dimensional image making among self-deluded believers, and if straightforward human urges were alone responsible for the gods and goddesses worshipped so zealously in the past, then why should people's feelings toward these divinities have been characterized, as they almost invariably were, with deeply inconsistent attitudes? Did not the very existence of these conflicts testify to the presence of a higher spiritual power that was seeking to penetrate through the veil of human illusions?

Schelling further hypothesizes that the discovery by the ancient pagans of their own ambivalences toward their deities could have served as a necessary first step to the transmutation of these gods into something far greater. Had it not been for the experience of such ambivalence, the mythological mind would have been satisfied indefinitely with its inadequate forms of worship. But the ambivalences produced tensions, which in turn led to the disclosure of richer and deeper patterns of meaning. From behind the alluring forms and mysterious powers of the old gods, there emerged the dawning sense of a Presence that was seeking to break through the outer appearances—the sense of a sublime Will that was using them as the means to express and reveal its inmost self.

Table 4

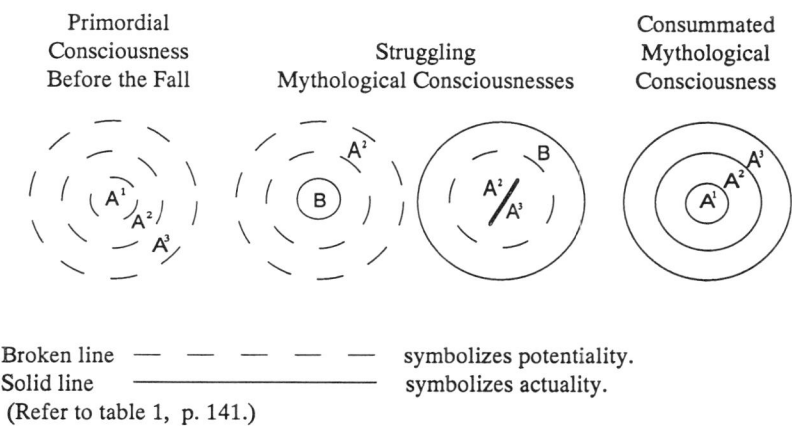

Broken line — — — — — symbolizes potentiality.
Solid line ——————— symbolizes actuality.
(Refer to table 1, p. 141.)

In order for God to reveal his true nature, Schelling continues, it was necessary to remove the distorting cover by means of a progressive "ejection" *(Ausscheidung)* of the Potencies, one by one, from his transcendent personality. God accomplished this by first positing them in the condition of tension and then allowing them to work out their own realignments in and through the historical process.[16] The inner nisus of the Potencies led instinctively toward the ideal of subordination and service to God, even though the inverted first Potency initially fought against this. The eventual conquest of B and corresponding realignments of A^2 and A^3 in relation to it was actually foreseen from the beginning. Thus, Schelling regards the unitary, though generally hidden, goal of all mythologies to have been the gradual divestment from God's personality of the outer garments and disguises by which he originally was concealed.

How convincing one finds this speculative history of religions will depend, of course, on the extent to which one accepts the metaphysical theory on which it is based. Although that theory is appealing in certain respects, it does not appear to be provable. Certainly Schelling has not proven it. Since other parts of this study have already provided critical evaluations of Schelling's ontology, it is unnecessary to repeat all of them here. But one criticism that was made earlier is especially relevant: namely, that the absolute distinction between the *Was* and the *Daß*, on which so much of Schelling's theology depends, seems to imperil the theory of a progressive "ejection" *(Ausscheidung)* of the Potencies from the inward, transcendent spirit of the Deity. God's very personality, indeed, seems in danger of dissolving into an abstract nothingness. Devoid of either universal or particular attributes, it is indescribable and even unthinkable. Yet Schelling insists that it is fully individual and concrete. This is the core of religion toward which, according to his theory, all the particular religions of history have inevitably tended. It can be seen via "metaphysical empiricism," even though it cannot be grasped through concepts.[17] Clearly, this doctrine represents a kind of mysticism (despite Schelling's own denials), and as such it resists rational analysis. In the end, the only guarantee one can have of this pure *Daß* would be that provided in the inwardness of a divine revelation. And that, of course, lies outside the domain of academic scholarship.

Several important questions remain. Granted that Schelling's theory of a progressive *Ausscheidung* of the Potencies is not provable by the canons of ordinary scholarship, can the hermeneutical model constructed on the basis of this theory still be viable? Can a case be made, that is, for interpreting the history of religions and their mythologies *as if* these were the results of a Providential process, even though one perhaps cannot demonstrate the logical coerciveness of such an interpretation? Would it be feasible for Schelling's reading of myths to provide at least a fruitful source of speculative insights, even as an avowedly religious reading of religions? Might his vision of the development of faith be arguably plausible, even if not completely demonstrable? In order to answer these questions, it is necessary to examine Schelling's final exhibit: the culminating stage in his system of world mythologies.

The Eleusinian Mysteries

Like other thinkers of the period, Schelling is fascinated by the enigma presented by the Greek Mysteries, especially the Eleusinian Mysteries celebrated in honor of Demeter. What great "secret" did these rituals conceal, and why was silence concerning them so strictly enjoined that its infraction was punishable by death? Some scholars, typical of the Enlightenment, theorized that the Mysteries taught merely the nullity of the official religion and the vanity of belief in supernatural beings or powers. Johann Heinrich Voß and Christian August Lobeck were representatives of this school. For them, the purpose of the secret gatherings was to disabuse people of their superstitions and induct them into a new age of rationalism, with purportedly naturalistic or Euhemeristic reinterpretations of the old religious beliefs.[18] Other investigators, however, took more seriously the esoteric wisdom and spiritual illumination attributed to the initiates, taking the contemporary or nearly contemporary reports of such witnesses as Plato, Plutarch, and Pausanias as evidence. Creuzer and Sainte-Croix, for example, surmised that participants in the Mysteries must have learned the doctrine of an absolute distinction between matter and spirit, as well as the higher ethical values that this knowledge entailed.[19] Still a third group of scholars contended that the true message of the Mysteries was a denial of polytheism and the elaboration in its place of an abstract form of monotheism. William Warburton was apparently the originator of this influential hypothesis.[20] Yet in Schelling's judgment, all of these conjectures were, to a greater or lesser degree, lacking in insight.

Schelling argues against these theories, claiming they fail to pay sufficient attention to the intimate connection between the Mysteries and the exoteric religious system that preceded them. Even Creuzer fell into this error insofar as he overintellectualized the Mysteries, seeing in them a universal and philosophical set of doctrines. But Schelling insists that the contents of the Mysteries cannot have been so incongruent with the religious consciousness from which they arose. Instead, they must have represented the highest fulfillment and completion of the entire mythological process.[21] Furthermore, he thinks it is also a misconception to suppose that the primary contents of the Mysteries would have been doctrinal at all. Not only would such a "secret" have been impossible to keep, but the evidence indicates that it was possible to state openly and with impunity various excerpts from the ritual ceremonies.[22] Schelling concludes, therefore, that the essence of the Mysteries must have consisted in their being a highly dramatized and intensely personal experience, one which somehow consummated the spiritual meanings implicit in the popular religion. What, then, could this experience have been?

Schelling's answer is that it must have involved a schematized recapitulation of the chief episodes in the history of the mythological consciousness itself.[23] Just as a living embryo in its mother's womb undergoes a series of stages that recapitulate the evolution of the species, in the same way the initiation ceremonies in the Mysteries conducted the aspirants through a succession of spiritual attitudes and emotions, culminating in the Final Crisis of the entire developmental process. Thus, there would have been representations of the loss (secession) of Persephone and her eventual recovery (reintegration) by Demeter, leading to the salvific emergence of Kore. There would also have been depictions of the frenzy (rebellion) of Zagreus, his subsequent overcoming (subordination) by Bacchus, heralding the triumphant entrance of Iakchos. By means of such artfully contrived reenactments, thinks Schelling, the candidates' consciousness would have been cleansed and purified, passing symbolically through the stages of Zabism, "incomplete" polytheism, and finally the various levels of the "complete" mythological systems. The result would have been a regenerative catharsis similar to that which Aristotle found characteristic of drama in general.[24] In this case, however, the significance would have been unequivocally spiritual and its goal the most sublime form of spiritual regeneration.

The previous two chapters of this study have already noted Schelling's theory concerning the remarkable assimilation of identities that took place among the three Potencies and the gods associated with them. Thus, the subordinated Cronus became fused with the triumphant Dionysus, just as the latter, in turn, willingly subordinated and attached himself to the crowning glory of Iakchos. In the Mysteries, this half-conscious, implicit awareness of identity must have been raised to the level of explicit experience. Schelling accordingly maintains that the chief secret of the Mysteries must have involved a direct, intuitive seeing of that supreme truth. This transpired when the three chief gods celebrated in the Mysteries—Zagreus, Bacchus, and Iakchos—became recognized in conjunction as simply different manifestations of one and the same Dionysus. For it was not only the essential interdependency of these gods that the Mysteries celebrated,

> not only in their indissoluble concatenation, but [it was] finally also as one and the same God, or as successive personalities of one and the same God, that these causal gods were the contents of the Mysteries. In other words: *this* was the highest among the teachings of the Mysteries, that those causal gods (*verursachende Götter*) were not only indissolubly unified, but that they were just one and the same God—we can say, going out of himself, through himself, into himself—just different forms or rather, moments, of this One.[25]

Nor was this all. Following the principle of parallelism between the objective moment and the subjective moment, Schelling adds that both sets of three-in-one relationship among the gods and corresponding goddesses must have been mystically identified as well. For they were all aspects of

Table 5

Consciousnesses	Potencies	
Persephone	Zagreus (A^1)	
Demeter (Demeter proper)	Bacchus (A^2) (Dionysus proper)	The One True God "Lord of Being"
Kore	Iakchos (A^3)	

one and the same transformative spiritual process: Demeter was the spiritual counterpart of Dionysus. In the language of myth, the consciousness is the "wife" and the object of consciousness is the "husband." Thus, for example, just as Persephone, as the queen of the underworld, ruled in the myths with the king of the underworld, Hades, in the same way she now appeared in the Mysteries as the spouse of the Dionysus-figure that corresponded to Hades (god B): Zagreus. In completely analogous fashion, Demeter (proper) was the spouse (consciousness) of Bacchus (Dionysus proper = god A^2); and likewise Kore was the Mystical Spouse of Iakchos (a resurrected version of Zagreus). Schelling also finds it significant that Demeter was in most traditional accounts the mother of Iakchos as well as of Kore (a restored version of Persephone), and it was in their birth and anticipated union that Demeter found her happiness and peace.[26] These Mystery-relationships are represented schematically in table 5.

As one can easily see, Schelling's interpretation of the Mysteries is based upon the positing of a close symbolical and ritual association between the Dionysia and the Eleusinian Mysteries of Demeter. For him, they are in fact different aspects of one and the same fundamental mystery, which cut across all sectarian divisions:

> We have now fully developed the mystical triad from both the masculine and the feminine sides. The self-same moments which there are presented as Zagreus, Bacchus, and Iakchos are here represented in just so many feminine forms as Persephone, Demeter and Kore.
>
> This triune in its unity was the highest object of the blessed contemplation and comprehension in the holiest Mysteries of Greece.[27]

Schelling's theory of the mystical associations connecting the Eleusinian Mysteries with the Dionysia is fascinating, but it rests on rather scant empirical evidence. Twentieth-century scholars of the classical period tend to call these ideas into question. There is apparently no positive proof that either Dionysus or Iakchos was celebrated in the Eleusinian Mysteries, which were dedicated to Demeter.[28] Nevertheless, it still seems possible, indeed rather likely, that the more reflective Greeks might have found productive analogies and made thematic comparisons between the various Mystery cults. All this is purely speculative, however. The suggestion that there might have been a secret teaching of One Supreme God behind all the multiform, polytheistic manifestations is intriguing, even though it is also a typical specimen of creative theorizing among the romantics.

With the attainment of a three-in-one Supreme God, on this account, the Greeks stood right on the threshold of an explicit formulation of absolute monotheism. This explained, in Schelling's view, how it was that Plato and Aristotle could develop such refined monotheistic theologies. It also explained the classical world's receptivity, at the beginning of the present era, to the deeper teachings of Christianity.

Then at last the full significance of the parallelism between the son of Semele and the son of Mary would stand revealed—how the one's sacrificial death and return to life exactly presaged and in a sense precipitated the other's atoning death and resurrection. Melkart, Osiris, Shiva, Dionysus, etc., were none other than pagan manifestations of the same divine principle that would finally emerge in his true form as Jesus Christ.[29] Schelling even goes so far as to suggest that, from a suprahistorical perspective, the "passion" of Christ began not with the events in Galilee, but with the first appearance of the second Potency in prehistoric times:

> The passion of the Messiah does not begin, as one assumes according to a limited Christian perspective, with his becoming human. The Messiah suffers from the very beginning: He is posited in a negated, *suffering* condition from the moment when he is [negatively] restored to human consciousness—for only therein could he have actualized himself—that is, from the moment when he is posited as mere Potency, as being outside of actuality. The second Potency was only actualized and glorified through the overcoming of B . . .[30]

The process of overcoming the inverted first Potency, in turn, would only reach its consummation at the moment when the age of mythology at last yielded to the age of revealed religion. Thus, the explicit appearance of Christianity in human history really marked the penultimate stage of the implicit activity of Christ—who had already assumed, as it were, the masks or personae of the pagan savior-gods in order to set his redemptive work in motion.

But first the old mythological consciousness had to put itself finally to rest. This it accomplished by means of carrying out the subordination and repotentialization of the first Potency ($A^1 = B$) to its furthest development. Once that Potency, the so-called "real principle," had been completely overcome, the ancient myths no longer seemed to be literal truths in themselves, but were now taken as figurative images of that One God who remains eternally the same throughout the flux of time. Schelling characterizes this transformation of religious consciousness as "the gentle death, the true euthanasia of the real principle, which in its passing and going under leaves behind in its place a lovely and enchanting world of appearances."[31] This world of appearances was now perceived as the sheerest of veils, no long capable of actually deceiving, which was cast—more as an ornament than as a covering—over the ultimate Truth.

This realization constituted, in effect, the self-overcoming of the mythological consciousness. Afterward there would be no further need to superimpose material images any longer onto the immaterial *Daß* of the Godhead. The Greek mind, to be sure, still lingered lovingly among the enchanting projections of its mythological creations, but at the same time, in its Mysteries, it apprehended the heralds of a higher, new religion that was yet to come. The mystical marriage of Kore and Iakchos, which according to Schelling was the crowning event of the secret rites, simultaneously celebrated the culmination and conclusion of the age of mythology:

> This image of the wedding with the god derives from the most ancient times, it goes through the O.T., and if one may be allowed to compare the holiest with the profane, the Church itself is after all called the bride of Christ. This ceremony in the Mysteries was named ἱερὸς γάμος, the holiest wedding, through which all now comes to an end, consciousness is wholly released from the necessity of the mythological process and a new world—but only represented in the deepest secrets of the Mysteries as just a future world—begins for consciousness.[32]

Thus, the inmost secret of the Mysteries represented the longing for a new religion that would surpass and replace the old religion. This idea, in Schelling's opinion, constituted the deepest insight and wisdom of which natural human consciousness was capable. Beyond that stage, the only possible progress would have had to depend upon the special dispensation of divine revelation. But that possibility would be the theme of another work. Having reached this conclusion, the philosophy of mythology, like its object, comes to its appropriate end.

Toward a "Sublimated Projection Theory" of Religions

It is interesting and instructive, in closing, to reconsider the general type of hermeneutical orientation that Schelling has developed for interpreting myths. One the one hand, he evidently shares many of the same skeptical doubts and suspicions about the underlying nature of religion as the projection theorists do—thinkers like Strauß, Feuerbach, Nietzsche, Freud, and others. Like them, Schelling sees that the ostensible meanings of religious motifs and practices are often quite divergent from their true psychological significance, which may lurk hidden behind the surface facades. On the other hand, however, Schelling refuses to jump to the conclusion that most projection theorists have drawn—namely, that religion is "nothing but" the imaginative picturing of human wishes, fantasies, hopes, and fears. To deflate religious symbols and myths in this way without further ado would seem premature and even, ironically, insufficiently critical. For should one not be equally suspicious of the motives driving the "hermeneuts of suspicion" as they have been of those determining religious traditionalists?

Let us review briefly some general points on which Schelling would agree with the projection theorists.

(1) In the first place, Schelling brings out the subtle interplay of objective and subjective elements, whereby the "external object" is structured in conformity with internal presuppositions and in turn then serves, by a circular inversion, to reinforce those same presuppositions in the experience of the subject. Like Feuerbach and Strauß, he recognizes that what appear in religious representations as separate agencies over against humanity are, more often than not, expressions of the religious mind's own inner workings, forces of the psychic microcosm "writ large" and thrust outward onto the receptive medium of the macrocosm. Thus, even purportedly historical "facts," such as the founding of Rome by Romulus and Remus, or the escape from the Flood by Noah, Schelling sees as originally archetypal figures mistakenly "historicized" by a later age. Yet, he asks, does this acknowledgment suffice to prove that such narratives are devoid of a true content, that these momentous events never "happened" in any sense at all? Might it not be the case that genuinely divine powers once dwelt within these psychic agencies of the human mind?

(2) In the second place, Schelling perceives the ambivalent motives and even irrational drives underlying many religious beliefs. Anticipating Freud, he detects the feelings of secret envy and hostility which have often underlain the rituals of sacrifice, the sacred symbols of spiritual rebirth, and so on. Themes such as the martyrdom of Osiris, the ordeals of Dionysus, and even the passion of Christ, often involved, according the Schelling's interpretation, hidden aggressive impulses projected onto the divine savior, whose role it was to "purify" them. But granted that some of the baser human instincts might have been present in these religious motifs, does it follow that they were therefore empty of a deeper significance as well? Or is it not at least possible that a cathartic release of the lower spiritual energies might have been preliminary to their taming and subsequent reintegration into a higher unity?

A sure sign, according to Schelling, of the deeper significance inherent in most religious phenomena, and of the necessary struggle to break through the outward trappings in order to reach the transcendental core within, was precisely the pain experienced as a result of the ambivalence toward the ancient deities. We have already seen that the discovery of this ambivalence was among Schelling's most significant contributions to the study of religions. At this juncture, it is appropriate to reflect more generally on the possible role of ambivalence as indicative that a higher spiritual consciousness was emerging. Could it be that Schelling is right—that the experience of ambivalence in religions is the sign not of a psychological cancer undermining all claims to religious legitimacy, but rather of a vital truth waiting to break out of the chrysalis stage in which it as been temporarily encased?

(3) Schelling would agree with the projection theorists that these various components became superimposed and fused onto the objects of worship, whose real character could be quite different from what the devotees themselves believed. Hence it is indeed possible, as the skeptical "hermeneuts of suspicion" have maintained, that religious representations involve elements partly derived from human desires, from the need for social legitimation, or from the cultural schemata by which people interpret their experience. Yet as Schelling has pointed out, this recognition does not prove that such factors are merely contingent phenomena, nor does it preclude the possibility of a genuine spiritual presence residing within and behind the religious representations.

What makes Schelling's approach strikingly different from standard projection theories is the way that he conceives of the underlying causes and directions of change in the history of religions. Whereas the projection theorists have tended to treat the discovery of unconscious meanings or covert ulterior motives as sufficient grounds for the dismissal or explaining away of religious motifs, Schelling's purpose is to demonstrate that these very projections themselves and the processes by which they unfold in human experience may be factors in the revelation of a divine providence. This paradoxical hypothesis provides new possibilities for the interpretation of religion.

Unlike Hegel, Schelling denies that the true dynamics of religious development could consist just in the progression from a more primitive to a more complete and intellectually self-conscious *comprehension* of the Whole. No comprehension of anything—even of the entire universe or of God himself—could qualify as that supreme state of blessedness which is the goal of all religions. For to comprehend something in concepts, Schelling would argue, is still to remain on the level of idealized projections. To the extent that dialectical progress moves in the direction of increasingly adequate comprehension (and Schelling allows that it does), this growth would be a necessary but not sufficient condition for a redemptive spiritual transformation. Although scholars of religion might be justified in suspending belief in the reality of such a spiritual transformation, they are hardly justified in ruling out the possibility *a priori.*

Viewed in this light, then, what could the true goal of religions be? Or, to put the question another way, what is the ultimate meaning of "revelation"? Schelling's answer depends upon a radical rethinking of both the origin and the final hope of religious evolution.

According to his argument, as we saw, the world-historical religions and mythologies came into being in the first place because the human spirit is fundamentally "God-positing" *(Gott-setzend).* By this Schelling means that the very nature of human consciousness involves an awareness, ever-present even when concealed or perverted, of the divine spark *within* consciousness.[33] This indwelling presence of the divine need not, however, be objectively present or clearly apprehended. The point is that it implicitly informs and directs the path of the successive religious conceptions, in that way conferring on them a definite reality they otherwise would lack.

Schelling's thesis concerning the inherently God-positing nature of the human spirit invites comparison with a hotly debated topic in twentieth-century theology: namely, the question whether even a fallen human nature bears within itself the capacity to open up to God. Emil Brunner, for example, has argued that one must posit an innate "point of contact" *(Anknüpfungspunkt)* between the human and divine within all people, even those who have not benefited yet from the grace of God's final revelation. It is due to such an *Anknüpfungspunkt,* Brunner maintains, that humans have the ability to be addressed *(Ansprechbarkeit)* by God. Only on this basis can one explain the continuity between other religions and Christian faith.[34] Karl Barth, on the other hand, follows Kierkegaard in vehemently rejecting the idea that sinful human nature would be capable on its own of turning to God.[35] For Barth, this would be tantamount to denying the necessity of grace to transform and redeem a corrupt humanity.

In this debate, Schelling would have been much more sympathetic to Brunner's position than to Barth's. But Schelling would have admitted that the human spirit's original "God-positing" character also requires additional grace in order to become fully actualized. The root issue is whether the grace given in Christian revelation is radically discontinuous with the experience of the divine in other religions (as Kierkegaard and Barth would insist), or continuous with them (as Schelling and Brunner would maintain).

However, if it should be asked whether Schelling has provided a coercive logical proof that a God-positing awareness is an essential attribute of the human spirit, the answer is that he has not. Indeed, according to him, such a "proof" would miss the point, because one of the main theses of his theory is that the bonds of relation between God and creature constitute the very foundation of individuality, touching a deeper level of intimacy even than essence itself.

To be able to make such an affirmation, of course, requires a suspension of normal philosophical procedure, which takes provability as a touchstone of rational discourse. On the other hand, this suspension does not itself "prove" that Schelling's position is necessarily false. He has, after all, taken pains to show the *compatibility* of his principles with rational philosophy, even while eschewing any claims to establish an indubitable link between them. In the end, the feasibility of Schelling's endeavor depends on the notion of a higher criterion of evaluation than reason alone can provide. Conversely, to recognize this suggests the need—and the right—to examine the alternative criterion to see if a viable case can be made to justify it philosophically.

Schelling proposes as the final outcome of religious evolution a direct, personal experience of God—an experience which, if it is to be fully satisfying, must be unmediated by concepts. This experience of the *Überseiende* is no easy matter, however, especially in view of the mind's inveterate tendency to clothe its objects in unconsciously derived interpretive schemata and values. The latter may in the end prove to be tools and means to God's inherent purposes (assuming there is a God), but their *prima facie* effect is to mask God's true nature. How, then, is the initial concealment of God behind his Potencies to play a role in his eventual final revelation? How could their initially "inverted" condition serve as the preliminary framework for God's emergence into full presence?

Schelling's answer hinges on the fundamental distinction between the *Was* and the *Daß*. He suggests that all the world's faiths have tended, in sundry degrees and through innumerable detours, toward a progressive opening of God's *Was,* whereby the mind's projections become less and less of a barrier to the living Truth that confronts us. The consummate goal of this development, if it continues as hoped, would be nothing less than the apprehension of God's supreme *Daß*—without any obscuration by the Potencies, without even the interposition of rational thought itself. Such an apprehension could only occur through a direct communion between the Person of God and that of the worshipper. However difficult and convoluted the path of religious development might be, this goal is indispensable, "for person seeks person."[36]

Yet, even in pursuing this aim, reason must never be discarded, nor the Potencies forsaken. To have attempted this was, in Schelling's opinion, the chief defect of Indian religions and other, similar forms of world-denying mysticism.[37] This kind of error stemmed from supposing that to transcend the *Was* it was necessary to repudiate it, or that to go beyond the rational one must sink into irrationalism. The error was compounded if one imagined that by intuitively apprehending the *Daß* one could acquire an indubitable knowledge and possession of it.[38] On the contrary, Schelling insists, intuitive insight can only make a new beginning, for the true ideal of the spirit is not to do away with reason or to annihilate the forms of essence, but to subordinate them to a higher end.

This was the great virtue of the Greek religion—not that the people ceased to make use of divine images and representations, but that they saw through them *as* representations, as the vessels of truths that went far beyond their immediate apparent contents.[39] Such wisdom was only possible, however, to the extent that one first had completely realigned the Potencies, ejected them from confused misidentification with the *Daß,* and finally reintegrated them as the outward manifestations of an inherently incomprehensible Deity.

This achievement, in turn, prepared the way for the final revelation of God in Christianity. According to Schelling, the God-positing character of the human soul has at last become ready for that ultimate transformation which one may legitimately hope for but can never claim as a certainty—the experience of redemption.

Is this account plausible? Has Schelling provided a way of viewing religious developments in a manner that is intellectually satisfying even if not directly provable, persuasive even if not compelling belief? As already indicated, the detail of this theory is not wholly convincing. But the more crucial issue is whether the overall interpretive approach he has developed can suggest possibilities and teach important lessons about a new hermeneutical model. If so, then perhaps one should be willing to look beyond any inadequacies of his particular philosophy of mythology in order to focus on the general orientation it represents.

Schelling's conception of the originative principles of myths and the methodological strategy he proposes for interpreting them constitute a distinct alternative to modern projection theories. His strategy of detecting psychic ambivalences, realigning the priorities, ejecting what should be subordinate, and reintegrating the resulting paradigm suggests new ways of treating the phenomena of religion. While pursuing a hardheaded and critical hermeneutics, Schelling simultaneously retains a transcendent reference point.

Moreover, it is quite possible that the model he has developed could be generalized and extended beyond its specific association with the doctrine of Potencies. Such generalization would be all the more desirable if one has doubts about the details of the *Potenzenlehre*.

In order to pinpoint the features of Schelling's interpretive model that are susceptible to creative adaptation, it is perhaps most useful to characterize it as a "sublimated projection theory" of religion. This type of theory would embrace three distinct phases.

(1) First, it would recognize that diverse and even inconsistent paradigms can be confusedly superimposed on religious motifs, resulting in ambivalences toward the objects of worship. This might be called the "deconstructive" phase of interpretation, since it would share the aim of the modern hermeneutics of suspicion to expose the false facades and bad faith that so often overlay religious representations. The discovery of ambivalences, however, could serve as an indication that the locus of the mind's God-positing character may be in a state of disequilibrium preparatory to some kind of conversion experience.

(2) The second stage would involve reordering the paradigms by means of reintegrating and aligning their component parts. This would be the "mystical" phase, because it would be predicated on the possibility of a profound but rationally unprovable experience of spiritual illumination, or "ecstasy." To the religious mind, such "ecstasy" could be seen as verifying a transcendent dimension beyond the immediate objects of worship; but it need not be so interpreted. The mystical component of religion neither can nor should look for confirmation from an irreligious perspective.

(3) The third stage would consist in experiencing this very succession—from ambivalence through reintegration to illumination—as the result and ultimate telos of God's plan. This could be characterized as the "theodicean" phase. Here, the religious mind would sublimate the outer forms and appearances of its faith by recognizing them *as* representations (projections). But at the same time it would find reinforcement and a manner of "confirmation" for its representations by regarding them as the signs and symbols whereby a higher Spirit appears to be communicating, gradually and by a series of progressive accommodations, with our own. This "confirmation," to be sure, could only be convincing to those who already accept the possibility of such a transcendent dimension.

Schelling himself definitely envisioned this possibility. His entire effort in the *Philosophie der Mythologie* was dedicated to demonstrating the presence of divine Providence at every stage and juncture of world history. For him it was the one true God who first projected the obscuring shroud of primitive Zabism; it was also God who then initiated the Great Spiritual Crisis responsible for the rise of polytheisms; and it was still none other than God who finally lifted the canopy of polytheism from the world's temples so as to unveil the deeper truth within: the Personality of absolute monotheism.

Although one may reject many of the specifics comprising Schelling's philosophy of mythology, he deserves credit for having pioneered the development of a provocative alternative to modern reductive theories—a sublimated projection theory of religions.

Notes

Preliminary Note

In the following notes, as well as throughout this book, all renderings from the German are my own. For the convenience of readers, however, I also refer where feasible to the corresponding passages in published English translations. The wording of these published translations naturally diverges in places from what readers will find here, but the differences in most cases are minor.

The general format used for book citations is that recommended by the *Chicago Manual of Style,* with one notable exception. For the sake of brevity, ease of reference and unambiguity, uppercase Roman numerals are used exclusively for the volumes in Schelling's collected works: *Sämtliche Werke,* 14 vols., edited by K. F. A. Schelling (Stuttgart & Augsburg: J. G. Cotta'scher Verlag, 1856–61). Wherever uppercase Roman numerals occur in the following pages, they always refer to this standard edition. Those of Schelling's works for which published English translations exist (a minority) are identified by name in these notes; the rest are generally cited by volume and page number only. For full titles of individual works within the *Sämtliche Werke,* the reader is referred to the Bibliography.

It is perhaps worth mentioning that the terms "above" and "below" as used in these notes are conventional cross-references indicating page numbers within this, my present work.

Introduction

1. See, for example, Werner Hartkopf, *Studien zur Entwicklung der modernen Dialektik,* 3 vols. (Meisenheim am Glan: Anton Hain, 1972–76); Panajotis Kondylis, *Die Entstehung der Dialektik: Eine Analyse der geistigen Entwicklung von Hölderlin, Schelling und Hegel bis 1802* (Stuttgart: Klett-Cotta, 1979).

2. Schelling subsequently explained his silence as having been in order to give the "negative philosophy" of Hegel and his school a chance to develop fully. One wonders, however, whether this explanation was quite candid. See his *Sämmtliche Werke,* 14 vols., K. F. A. Schelling, ed. (Stuttgart & Augsburg: J. G. Cotta'scher

Verlag, 1856–61), XIII:86. (All subsequent citations of Schelling, unless otherwise indicated, will be to this edition.)

In any case, the texts of Schelling's *Philosophie der Mythologie* and his *Philosophie der Offenbarung* are based on his lecture series given in Berlin between 1841 and 1847. According to his son and editor, the essential content of the lectures on mythology was already complete as early as 1828 (XI:v). Gerbrand Dekker has reported on the discovery of a manuscript quite similar to that contained in *SW*, which on the basis of external and internal evidence he dates at 1830; see *Die Rückwendung zum Mythos. Schellings letzte Wandlung* (Munich/ Berlin: R. Oldenbourg, 1930), 14–18. Schelling himself asserted (XIV:231) that his lectures on the philosophy of revelation had remained virtually unchanged since 1831.

3. *Historisch-kritische Einleitung in die Philosophie der Mythologie* XI:3–10, 192–94. Later chapters of the present study will examine what the "independence" of these "actualities" involved.

4. XI:4, 220–22; XII:128.

5. XI:202.

6. Ibid., 199; cf. also 5ff., 219, 251.

7. Ibid., 12ff.

8. Cf. Ibid., 59–63, 199ff., 238ff.

9. Ibid., 20.

10. Ernst Cassirer, *Von Hegels's Tod bis zur Gegenwart (1832–1932)*, vol. 4 of *Das Erkenntnisproblem in der Philosophie und Wissenschaft der neueren Zeit* (Darmstadt: Wissenschaftliche Buchgesellschaft, 1973), 301; cf. W. H. Woglam and C. W. Hende, trans., *The Problem of Knowledge: Philosophy, Science, and History since Hegel* (New Haven: Yale University Press, 1950), 297–98. See also Cassirer's *Philosophie der symbolischen Formen* (Darmstadt: Wissenschaftliche Buchgesellschaft, 1977), 2:6–22; cf. R. Manheim, trans., *The Philosophy of Symbolic Forms* (New Haven: Yale University Press, 1953–57), 2:3–16.

11. Gordon D. Kaufman, *The Theological Imagination* (Philadelphia: Westminster Press, 1981); Garrett Green, *Imagining God* (New York: Harper & Row, 1989).

12. XII:182.

13. XI:168; XII:182, 637.

14. Bronislaw Malinowski, *Science, Religion and Reality* (Garden City, N.Y.: Doubleday, 1954); Peter L. Berger, *The Sacred Canopy: Elements of a Sociological Theory of Religion* (Garden City, N.Y.: Doubleday, 1969).

15. Robert N. Bellah, "Religious Evolution," *American Sociological Review* 29 (1964): 358–74.

16. XI:390; XII:126.

17. XII:208.

18. Claude Lévi-Strauss, *Mythologiques*, 4 vols. (Paris: Plon, 1964–71); cf. J. Weightman and D. Weightman, trans., *Introduction to the Science of Mythology*, vols. 1 & 2 (New York: Harper & Row, 1969–); also by Lévi-Strauss, "The

Structural Study of Myth," *Journal of American Folklore* 67 (1955): 428–44. See Edmund Leach, "Lévi-Strauss in the Garden of Eden: An Examination of Some Recent Developments in the Analysis of Myth," *Transactions of the New York Academy of Sciences,* ser. 2, vol. 23 (1961): 386–96.

19. XII:241.
20. XI:124; XII:184.
21. Cf. *Bibliographie zur Symbolik, Ikonographie und Mythologie* (Baden-Baden: Verlag V. Koerner, 1968–present); also Donald Capps, Lewis Rambo and Paul Ransohoff, *Psychology of Religion: A Guide to Information Sources,* sec. B: The Mythological Dimension of Religion (Detroit: Gale Research Co., 1976).
22. Cf. Carl Gustav Jung and Károly Kerényi, *Einführung in das Wesen der Mythologie. Das göttliche Kind, das göttliche Mädchen* (Zurich: Rascher, 1942); cf. R. F. C. Hull, trans., *Essays on a Science of Mythology: The Myth of the Divine Child and the Mysteries of Eleusis* (New York: Pantheon Books, 1949). Also Bruno Bettelheim, *Symbolic Wounds, Puberty Rites and the Envious Male* (Glencoe, Ill.: Free Press, 1954).
23. XI:300; XII:123–31.
24. *System der transzendentalen Idealismus (1800)* III:368–72, 624–29; cf. P. Heath, trans., *System of Transcendental Idealism (1800)* (Charlottesville: University Press of Virginia, 1978), 27–29. In suggesting the possibility of an "intellectual intuition," Schelling was, of course, deliberately flouting the Kantian stricture against seeking to overstep the limits of phenomenal experience. Cf. *Kritik der reinen Vernunft* (1787), vol. 3 of *Gesammelte Schriften,* ed. Preussische Akademie der Wissenschaften, 20 vols. (Berlin: G. Reimer, 1900–1942), 200ff. (B 294ff.); cf. Norman Kemp Smith, trans., *Critique of Pure Reason* (Toronto: Macmillan, 1929), 257ff.
25. XI:315f., 402.
26. Ibid., 563; XII:44, 58; XIII:150, 160.
27. XII:123–31.
28. Cf. Rudolf Bultmann, *Das Verhältnis der urchristlichen Christusbotschaft zum historischen Jesus* (Heidelberg: C. Winter's Universitätsverlag, 1960). Bultmann distinguishes carefully between the inner, spiritual content of the Christian kerygma and its external trappings. In the end, he concludes that the kerygma, properly understood, "has taken the place of the historical Jesus" (26). Consequently, "all speculations about the kind of being attributable to the resurrected one, all stories about the empty grave, and all Easter legends, whatever aspects of historical fact they may contain, become irrelevant" (27).

Paul Ricoeur has expressed much the same idea in terms of the "polarity between myth and kerygma," the goal being to attain the latter by means of penetrating through the former. See Paul Ricoeur, "From Existentialism to the Philosophy of Language," *Criterion* (University of Chicago Divinity School) 10 (Spring 1971): 14–18; reprinted in *The Philosophy of Paul Ricoeur,* ed. Charles E. Reagan and David Stewart (Boston: Beacon Press, 1978), 86–93. Cf. 91.

29. For a late nineteenth-century exegesis and appraisal of Schelling's thought, published a quarter-century after his death, see Gustav Adolph Constantin Frantz,

Schellings positive Philosophie. Nach ihrem Inhalt wie nach ihrer Bedeutung für den allgemeinen Umschwung der bis jetzt noch herrschenden Denkweise dargestellt, in 3 parts (Köthen: P. Schettler, 1879; reprinted in Aalen: Scientia, 1968). While acknowledging that Schelling's theories would require some revision in the light of subsequent scholarship, Frantz compares him favorably with Fichte, Hegel, Schopenhauer, and other philosophers of the day. Frantz also defends Schelling's work on mythology against the harsh judgment of Max Müller and cites the researches of Michael Strodl to corroborate some of Schelling's more daring conclusions.

Chapter 1. The Origins of Pagan Religions

1. St. Martin of Braga, *De correctione rusticorum,* trans. C. W. Barlow, in *The Fathers of the Church: Iberian Fathers,* vol. 1 (Washington, D.C.: Catholic University of America Press, 1969), 71–85. See especially chaps. 7–9, 74–76. Cf. Jan de Vries, *Forschungsgeschichte der Mythologie* (Freiburg/Munich: Karl Alber, 1961), 54–55. Also by the same author, *Perspectives in the History of Religions* (Berkeley: University of California Press, 1977), 17.

2. John Milton, *Paradise Lost,* bk. 1, lines 381–85. The following hundred verses contain detailed descriptions of these "abominations"—chiefly ancient deities of the Canaanite and Phoenician religions.

3. Cf. Gerhard Voß, *De theologias gentili, sive de origine ac progressu idolatriae* (Amsterdam: J. Blaev, 1668; c. 1641). Also see Hugo Grotius, *De veritate religionis christianae* (Oxford: Clarendon Press, 1827, c. 1627). For a succinct summary of their views, see de Vries, *Forschungsgeschichte,* 70–75 and 75–76, respectively. Schelling discusses Voß's ideas at XI:86, 179, 214; XII:181. Grotius is mentioned briefly at XII:26.

4. XI:178–80.

5. Charles de Brosses, *Du culte des dieux fetiches* (n.p., [1760]), see esp. 10ff., 76f., 158ff. Cf. de Vries, *Forschungsgeschichte,* 91–95. See also the excerpts from de Brosses' work in the anthology compiled by Burton Feldman and Robert D. Richardson, *The Rise of Modern Mythology, 1680–1860* (Bloomington: Indiana University Press, 1972), 168–76. For Schelling's critique of de Brosses' hypothesis of fetishism, see XII:294f. Other proponents of this hypothesis will be discussed in the next chapter, in connection with "naturalism," pp. 31–40.

6. XI:73–74. Even Hume, notes Schelling, admitted that the practices of simple animists and fetishists do not constitute genuine religions. Schelling quotes from Hume's *The Natural History of Religion* (1757): "To any one, who considers justly the matter, it will appear, that . . . these pretended religionists are really a kind of superstitious atheists, and acknowledge no being, that corresponds to our idea of a deity" (Stanford, Calif: Stanford University Press, 1957), 33. Schelling's slightly different rendering comes from a French translation of the work.

7. Publication by Gotthold Ephraim Lessing between 1774 and 1778 of the so-called *Wolfenbütteler Fragmente,* written by Hermann Samuel Reimarus but withheld from publication during his lifetime, raised troubling questions as to how much even of the Gospel narratives was mythological in character; cf. R. S. Fraser, trans., *Reimarus: Fragments* (Philadelphia: Fortress Press, 1970).

8. Gotthold Ephraim Lessing, *Die Erziehung des Menschengeschlechts,* in vol. 8 of *Gesammelte Werke in Zehn Bänden* (Berlin: Aufbau Verlag, 1956), 590–615; cf. H. Chadwick, trans., *The Education of the Human Race,* in *Lessing's Theological Writings* (Stanford, Calif.: Stanford University Press, 1956), 82–98.

9. Lessing, *Erziehung,* par. 76, p. 610: "When these truths were first revealed, they were, to be sure, not yet truths of reason; but they were revealed in order to become truths of reason"; cf. trans., 95.

10. XI:84.

11. Ibid. In a footnote, Schelling suggests that Lessing's reluctance to identify himself as the work's author was proof that he himself was dissatisfied with its execution.

12. Ibid., 175, 196–98. Without specifically mentioning Hegel in this connection, Schelling evidently intended the same critique to apply to him.

13. Sir William Jones, "On the Gods of Greece, Italy and India, written in 1784 and since revised by the President," *Asiatic Researches* (London: Vernor and Hood, 1798), 1:221–75. Cf. esp. 221–22 and 271. For excerpts from Jones's work, cf. Feldman and Richardson, *The Rise of Modern Mythology,* 267–75. See also de Vries, *Perspectives,* 41.

14. Jones, *The Works, in Six Volumes* (London: G. G. Robinson, J. Robinson, and R. H. Evans, 1799), 6:423–26. Included are two short translations from the *Yajur Veda:* "Isavasyam" (Isa Upanishad), followed by an additional page, "From the Yajur Veda." Schelling refers to these passages in XII:475. For other references to Jones, cf. XII:465, 468, 508, 556.

15. Abraham Hyacinth Anquetil-Duperron, *Oupnek'hat, id est, secretum tegendum: Opus ipsa in India rarissimum, continens antiquam et arcanam, seu theologicam et philosophicam, doctrinam,* 2 vols. (Argentorati [Strassbourg]: 1801–2). Schelling refers to Anquetil's work at XII:476–77.

16. Friedrich Schlegel, *Über die Sprache und Weisheit der Indier. Ein Beitrag zu Begründung der Alterthumskunde. Nebst metrishcen Übersetzungen indischer Gedichte* (Heidelberg: Mohr und Zimmer, 1808; reprinted in Amsterdam: John Benjamins B.V., 1977). Schlegel emphasized and clearly preferred a dualistic, as opposed to pantheistic, interpretation of the Hindu scriptures (127ff.), a preference for which he later was criticized by Schelling (XII:19).

17. Marie Elisabeth de Polier, *Mythologie des Indous, travaillée par m^{dme} de la ch^{nsse} de Polier, sur des manuscripts authentiques apportés de l'Inde par feu mr. le colonel de Polier,* 2 vols. (Roudostadt. La librairie de la cour: Paris: F. Schoell, 1809). De Vries characterizes the extensive influence of this book as in part harmful, because of its one-sided and often ill-informed presentations. Yet for a

time it provided one of the few sources of original materials, and Friedrich Creuzer, among others, relied heavily on it. See de Vries, *Forschungsgeschichte*, 150; cf. *Perspectives*, 41.

18. Cf. *The English Works of Raja Rammohun Roy* (Allahabad: Panini Office, 1906), 19–77. Featured are translations from the *Kena* and *Isa Upanishads* (both 1816), as well as the *Mundaka* and *Katha Upanishads* (both 1819). Schelling himself never saw Roy's work, but based his somewhat negative judgment of it (XII:475–76) on a review in the *Journal Asiatique*. Yet, that review to the contrary, Roy's translation is in fact fuller and more detailed than that of Jones. There is little plausibility to Schelling's inference that Roy must have suppressed polytheistic elements in order to support a bland, deistic interpretation.

19. Henry Thomas Colebrooke, "On the Vedas, or Sacred Writings of the Hindus," *Asiatic Researches* (London: Vernor and Hood, 1798), 8:369–476. This essay includes translations of selected passages from the *Aitareya, Brihadaranyaka*, and other Upanishads. See also Colebrooke's *Essays on the Religion and Philosophy of the Hindus*, new ed. (London and Edinburgh: Williams and Norgate, 1858), reprinted from *Asiatic Researches* and from the *Transactions of the Royal Asiatic Society*. (Schelling refers to Colebrooke at XII:467 as "the greatest expert on Indian literature.")

20. XI:88. For more on Schelling's knowledge of, and attitudes toward, the recent blossoming of Indological studies in Europe, see Jean W. Sedlar, *India in the Mind of Germany: Schelling, Schopenhauer, and their Times* (Washington, D.C.: University Press of America, 1982).

21. (Georg) Friedrich Creuzer, *Symbolik und Mythologie der alten Völker, besonders der Griechen* (New York: Arno Press, 1978; a facsimile reprint of the 2d ed., Leipzig: Heyer and Leske, 1819–23). Schelling also specifically recommends (XI:89) an abridged version of this work, which "contains in one volume all that is essential": *Symbolik und Mythologie . . . im Auszüge von Dr. Georg Heinrich Moser* (Leipzig: Carl Wilhelm Leske, 1822). For a useful discussion of Creuzer's work, see Alfred Bäumler, *Das mythische Weltalter* (Munich: C. H. Beck, 1965, c. 1926), 103–14. For Creuzer's influence on Hegel, see Martin Donougho, "Hegel and Friedrich Creuzer; or, Did Hegel Believe in Myth?" In *New Perspectives on Hegel's Philosophy of Religion*, edited by David Kolb (Albany: State University of New York Press, 1992), pp. 59–80.

22. Because of Creuzer's tremendous importance for Schelling, I provide here a virtually complete listing of Schelling's references to him in the *Philosophie der Mythologie* and in relevant parts of the *Philosophie der Offenbarung*: XI:89–90, 126, 137, 226; and XII:146, 148, 157, 161, 207, 213–14, 220, 245, 249, 251, 255, 277, 288–90, 334, 386, 391, 397, 409–10, 416–17, 442–43, 460, 465, 469, 558, 614, 622, 643, 651, 662, 667; and finally XIII: 433, 438, 444, 453, 460, 475, 488, 498–99, 503, 509, 516. It is worth noting that Creuzer himself was also, in turn, considerably influenced by Schelling. See *Symbolik* 1:x, 4:vii, as well as Creuzer's review essay, *Über einige mythologische und artistische Schriften Schellings*,

Ouwaroffs, Millins und Welckers (Heidelberg: Mohr and Winter, 1817). Cf. also de Vries, *Perspectives*, 51.

23. *Symbolik* 1:6ff., 36, 57f. and passim. Compare Herodotus, *Histories*, bk. 2, chaps. 49–57. Excerpts from Creuzer's work may be found in Burton Feldman and Robert D. Richardson, *The Rise of Modern Mythology, 1680–1860* (Bloomington: Indiana University Press, 1972), 387–96; also Károly Kerényi, *Die Eröffnung des Zugangs zum Mythos* (Darmstadt: Wissenschaftliche Buchgesellschaft, 1967), 35–58. See also de Vries, *Forschungsgeschichte*, 150ff., and *Perspectives*, 50f.

24. *Symbolik* 1:xi–xii. An illustrative example of Creuzer's hermeneutical style occurs in 2:484ff., where he compares the original "triadic form" of Zeus to the Trimurti concept of ancient Hinduism. Creuzer adds that this "intimation . . . of the one, almighty power which unites all that exists" disappeared as Greek civilization approached its zenith.

For Schelling's summary and assessment of Creuzer's theory of an original monotheism, see XI:89–90, 137; also cf. XII:220 (for Schelling's view of Creuzer on Persian monotheism), 391 (Egyptian), 460 (Indian), and 643 (Greek).

25. Colebrooke concluded from his philological studies that the earliest Indian and Persian religions were closely related ("On the Vedas," 474). He went still further, arguing for an original monotheism as taught in the Hindu scripture, and minimizing the elements of apparent polytheism: "The real doctrine of the whole Indian scripture is the unity of the deity, in whom the universe is comprehended: and the seeming polytheism, which it exhibits, offers the elements, and the stars and planets, as gods." For Schelling's critique, see XII:470–71.

26. Strangely, Schelling almost never referred to the writings of this important thinker. See, for example, Görres' influential *Mythengeschichte der asiatischen Welt*, 2 vols. (Heidelberg: Mohr and Zimmer, 1810), and also his *Über die Grundlage, Gliederung und Zeitenfolge der Weltgeschichte. Drei Vorträge, gehalten an der Ludwig-Maximilians-Universität in München* (Breslau: Max and Komp, 1830). Schelling's silence seems all the more remarkable since, as de Vries observes, Görres' thoughts on the nature and transformations of the *Urreligion* were in some respects closely similar to those of Schelling's primary source, Creuzer himself. Cf. de Vries, *Forschungsgeschichte*, 157–59; *Perspectives*, 47–48. Also, cf. Tilliette, *La mythologie comprise* (Naples: Instituto Italiano per gli studi filosofici, 1984), 54–57.

The most probable explanation for Schelling's virtual silence about Görres is that it stemmed from concern over the latter's completely unscholarly method, his fanciful speculations, and perhaps his outspoken ultramontanism. To have used Görres as intellectual support would therefore have seemed unacceptable to Schelling. (Consider, for example, Hegel's condescending 1831 review of Görres' Munich lectures, reprinted in G. W. F. Hegel, *Berliner Schriften 1818–1831*, vol. 11 of *Werke: Theorie Werkausgabe*, 20 vols., ed. E. Moldenhauer and K. M. Michel [Frankfurt am Main: Suhrkamp, 1970], 487–513; see esp. 493.) Yet some scholars believe that Schelling probably maintained a cool respect for Görres, in whom he would have recognized an ally in the cause of integrating mythology with Christianity. See Thomas Franklin O'Meara, *Romantic Idealism and Roman Catholicism* (Notre Dame, Ind., and London: University of Notre Dame Press, 1982), 133.

In any case, rather than apologize for, or combat, Görres's theories, which perhaps seemed to Schelling no less politically explosive than intellectually frivolous, he apparently chose to ignore them.

27. Schelling was, however, very critical of the attempts which had been made to interpret Indian culture as a direct, primary source of the Hebraic, Greek, or other Western traditions. Cf. XI:21, 87; XII:431, 465.

28. For a summary outline closely conforming to Schelling's *Historischkritische Einleitung in die Philosophie der Mythologie* (1842; vol. XI of Schelling's *SW*), including his critiques of earlier treatments of mythology, see Jochem Hennigfeld, *Mythos und Poesie. Interpretationen zu Schellings "Philosophie der Kunst" und "Philosophie der Mythologie"* (Meisenheim am Glan: Hain, 1973), esp. 91–133. In the following chapter I have adopted a different approach, less summary and more analytical than Hennigfeld's, both in order to avoid duplicating previous work as well as to highlight those issues and controversies that are particularly relevant for our purposes.

Chapter 2. Allegory, Symbol, or Reality?

1. Jan de Vries, *Forschungsgeschichte der Mythologie* (Freiburg/Munich: Karl Alber, 1961), 4–5; cf. by the same author, *Perspectives in the History of Religions* (Berkeley: University of California Press, 1977), 5–6.

2. Naturalistic interpretations were further developed by Metrodorus of Lampsacus, a disciple of Anaxagoras, who credited his teacher with having originated the idea. Cf. Robert S. Brumbaugh, *The Philosophers of Greece* (Albany: State University of New York Press, 1981), 107.

3. See Plutarch, *De Isidi et Osiridi* (c. 100 C.E.), trans. and ed. J. Gwynn Griffths (Cambridge: University of Wales Press, 1970), chaps. 33–40, esp. 372a. Plutarch espoused a spiritual, Platonic style of allegory.

4. Cf. Christian Gottlob Heyne, *Questio de causis fabularum seu mythorum veterum physicis*, in vol. 1 of *Opuscula academica collecta et animadversionibus locupletata*, 6 vols. (Göttingen: H. Dieterich, 1785); also Gottfried Hermann, *De mythologiae Graecorum antiquissima dissertatio* (Lipsiae: G. Fleischerum, 1817). For Schelling's critique of Heyne, see XI:30ff. For his parallel critique of Hermann, see XI:34ff. Compare de Vries, *Forschungsgeschichte*, 143–49 and 178–83.

5. Gottfried Hermann, *Dissertatio de historiae Graecae primordia*, in vol. 2 of *Opuscula*, 8 vols. (Lipsiae: G. Fleischerum, 1827–77), 121. Cf. de Vries, *Forschungsgeschichte*, 180. Schelling scathingly criticized this interpretation, XI:58f. For other references in Schelling to Hermann, cf. XI:40, 214, 236; also cf. XII:15, 128, 136, 290, 296.

6. See Frank Byron Jevons, *An Introduction to the History of Religions* (London: Methuen, 1902, c. 1896), 263. Cf. de Vries, *Forschungsgeschichte,* 279–81. See also Paul Ehrenreich, *Die allgemeine Mythologie und ihre ethnologischen Grundlagen* (New York: Arno Press, 1978, c. 1910), 109, 118–21. (Cf. *Forschungsgeschichte,* 274–78.) Compare Robin Horton, "African Traditional Thought and Western Science," in *Rationality,* ed. Bryan R. Wilson (Oxford: Basil Blackwell, 1979), 131–71.

7. Fragments of Euhemerus's writings have been preserved in the works of Diodorus of Sicily, vol. 3, bk. 6, chap. 1. Cf. Franz Susemihl, *Geschichte der griechischen Literatur in der Alexandrinerzeit* (Leipzig: B. G. Teubner, 1891), 1:316–22; Baron Friedrich von Hügel, *The Reality of God* and *Religion and Agnosticism,* two titles bound in one volume (London: J. M. Dent & Sons, 1931), 224–32.

8. Snorri Sturlason, *The Prose Edda* (c. 1230), trans. A. G. Brodeur (New York: American-Scandinavian Foundation, 1916). See especially the prologue, chaps. 3–5, pp. 6–9. Snorri relates that Thor and Odin were powerful lords in Asia (whence they were called "Aesir"), descendents of the Trojan king Priam. Odin allegedly brought a large group of followers to the north and eventually settled with them in Sigtuna, Sweden. Later generations venerated him as a god.

9. Samuel Bochart, *Geographiae sacra* (Cadomi: P. Caronelli, 1946), pt. 2, p. 487. Cf. de Vries, *Forschungsgeschichte,* 70.

10. Pierre Daniel Huet, *Demonstratio evangelica ad serenissimum Delphinum,* 3d ed. (Paris: Daniel Hortemel, 1690; 1st ed., 1679), 149–50. Cf. de Vries, *Forschungsgeschichte,* 78–79.

11. Huet, *Demonstratio,* 68–153. See esp. 140–41, where Huet writes that "all the gods of fable are one and the same—most assuredly Moses." Huet adds that the goddesses are all either Sephora, Moses' wife, or Maria, his sister. Cf. de Vries, *Forschungsgeschichte,* 78, and Schelling, XI:86.

12. Thomas Carlyle, *On Heroes, Hero-Worship and the Heroic in History,* in vol. 3 of *Thomas Carlyle's Works,* 17 vols. (London: Chapman and Hall, 1885–88), pt. 2, p. 11; see also 6f., 9ff., 14ff.

13. Ernst Cassirer, *Sprache und Mythos. Ein Beitrag zum Problem der Götternamen* (Leipzig and Berlin: G. B. Teubner, 1925), 6ff., esp. 8; cf. trans. S. K. Langer, *Language and Myth* (New York: Dover, 1953), 8ff., esp. 10f. Also Paul Ricoeur, "The Hermeneutics of Symbols and Philosophical Reflection," *International Philosophical Quarterly* 2 (1962): 191–218; reprinted in *The Philosophy of Paul Ricoeur: An Anthology of his Work,* ed. Charles E. Reagan and David Stewart (Boston: Beacon Press, 1978), 36–58. See esp. 46. Cf. de Vries, *Forschungsgeschichte,* 360–63.

14. I:43–83.

15. Cf. ibid., 52, 68f., 74ff., 80, 83.

16. Ibid., 64f. and note 2.

17. Cf. *Vorlesungen über die Methode des akademischen Studiums* (1802), V:288; cf. E. S. Morgan, trans., *On University Studies* (Athens: Ohio University Press, 1966), 84.

18. V:353–736; cf. D. W. Stott, trans., *The Philosophy of Art* (Minneapolis: University of Minnesota Press, 1989).

19. According to Gerbrand Dekker, Schelling's first tentative employment of the term "Potency" occurred in his *Naturphilosophie* of 1798, but still in a very undeveloped form. Cf. *Die Rückwendung zum Mythos. Schellings letzte Wandlung* (Munich/Berlin: R. Oldenbourg, 1930), 34–35.

20. V:366; cf. trans., 14.

21. V:465; cf. trans., 88.

22. Most scholars date Schelling's discovery of Böhme from the time of his close collaboration with Franz von Baader in Munich, beginning in 1806. Wilhelm A. Schulze, however, claims that Schelling was ordering books by Böhme as early as 1802; cf. "Zum Verständnis der Stuttgarter Privatvorlesungen Schellings," *Zeitschrift für philosophische Forschung* 11 (1957): 575, note 10. Yet it was not until 1809, the year he published his *Philosophische Untersuchungen über das Wesen der menschlichen Freiheit und die damit zusummenhängenden Gegenstände*, that the influence of Böhme on Schelling's thought became evident in his writings.

23. V:390; cf. trans., 35.

24. Plutarch, *De Isidi et Osiridi* (c. 100 C.E.). See chaps. 45–46, esp. 373b; and chaps. 64–65.

25. Cf. Bengt Algot Sørensen, *Symbol und Symbolismus in den ästhetischen Theorien des 18. Jahrhunderts und der deutschen Romantik* (Copenhagen: Münksgrad, 1963).

26. Friedrich von Schlegel, *Prosaische Jugendschriften*, ed. Jakob Minor (Vienna: Carl Konegen, 1906, c. 1882), 2:364.

27. V:412; cf. trans., 49. Cf. Karl Philipp Moritz, *Götterlehre oder mythologische Dichtungen der Alten* (Berlin: Unger, 1795), 2–3. For more on Moritz's influence, see Tilliette, *La mythologie comprise* (Naples: Instituto Italiano per gli studi filosofici, 1984), 36–37. Tilliette includes an appendix, "Annexe I" (129–30), which lists extensive parallel passages between this early text by Schelling and that of Moritz.

28. V:414; cf. trans., 51.

29. See pp. 7–8 in the "Introduction," above.

30. Already in 1800, the *System des transzendentalen Idealismus* had discussed symbolism as a central facet of artistic and spiritual life. In that work, he had explained the symbol as an "unconscious infinity," incorporating the secret intimations of nature and feeling with the conscious deliberations of thought. Cf. III:619f.; cf. P. Heath, trans., *System of Transcendental Idealism (1800)* (Charlottesville: University Press of Virginia, 1978), 225f. In the *Philosophie der Kunst*, however, Schelling sought to present a more precise theory, free of the subjecitvist tendencies that still clung to the earlier, Fichtean work.

31. V:406; cf. trans., 45.

32. For English translations of these two works, cf. *The Ages of the World*, trans. and ed. F. de Wolfe Bolman, Jr. (New York: AMS Press, 1967, c. 1942); also, *Schelling's Treatise on "The Deities of Samothrace,"* trans. and ed. R. Brown

(Missoula, Mont.: Scholars Press for the American Academy of Religion, 1976). Both books include fine critical analyses by the translators.

33. *Weltalter* VIII:199; cf. trans., 83. See the discussion of this passage in Peter Loth Oesterreich's study *Philosophie, Mythos und Lebenswelt. Schellings universalhistorischer Weltalter-Idealismus und die Idee eines neuen Mythos* (Frankfurt am Main: Peter Lang, 1984), 32–38. The conception of the religious symbol as a veiled truth that simultaneously conceals what it reveals and reveals what it conceals was one of Creuzer's key ideas. Cf. *Symbolik und Mythologie der alten Völker, besonders der Griechen,* 2d ed. (Leipzig: Heyer and Leske, 1819–23; facsimile reprint, New York: Arno Press, 1978), 1:57–58.

34. *Über die Gottheiten von Samothrake* VIII:352; cf. trans., 18 and 50f. (notes).

35. *Weltalter* VIII:396f., note 80; cf. trans., 35. Compare XII:161, where Schelling again praises Creuzer for this discovery.

36. See below, chapter 5, p. 72 (note 15) and chapter 7, p. 133 (note 58).

37. XI:28ff.

38. Ibid., 195f.; cf. XII:139f. Schelling cautions in a footnote (XI:196), however, that he does not understand the term "tautegorical" in the same sense as Coleridge—that is, in the equivalent of a philosopheme—but rather as a lived reality. (Coleridge was actually not the originator of the concept of the "tautegorical." Tilliette points out in *La mythologie comprise* [Naples: Instituto Italiano per gli studi filosofici, 1984], 36, 70, that the credit for this idea should go to Karl Philipp Moritz. Cf. the latter's *Götterlehre oder mythologische Dichtungen der Alten* (Berlin: Unger, 1795), 2–3.

Schelling's footnote at XI:196 will be interesting to English-speaking readers, because it documents the great respect and appreciation that Coleridge earned from the German philosopher for his efforts to introduce Continental ideas and texts, including Schelling's own *Gottheiten von Samothrake,* into England. With uncharacteristic generosity, and a touch of humor, Schelling adds, "In return for the above-mentioned fitting expression, I willingly grant to him the borrowings which he has made, without attribution, from my writings, and for which he has been sharply—indeed, too sharply—censured by his own countrymen." For other references to Coleridge, see XI:277, 294. In the latter passage, Schelling lauds Coleridge as having been among the few who really understood him.

39. XI:33; cf. XII:621.

40. XI:56.

41. Ibid., 207.

42. Schelling's arguments against the *Erfindungs*-hypothesis were of central importance to his entire approach; hence they were carefully elaborated and often reiterated. See XI:47, 56ff., 125, 193, 200, 222; XII:3, 130, 669; XIII:500.

43. XII:638. Similar arguments for a reversal of the naturalistic analyses can be found at XII:174, 214, 385ff.

44. Ibid., 609.

45. Ibid., and cf. XIII:499. For the term "reverse Euhemerism" *(umgekehrter Euemerismus),* see XI:233.

46. Ernst Howald, editor of an anthology of polemical essays from the period, was moved to preface his study of the century-old controversy with the wistful observation that the "victory" of J. H. Voß, G. Hermann, C. G. Heyne, and others had led to the virtual "disappearance . . . from religious studies of a sense for the religious mentality," with the result that scholarship in this area had advanced little over the last hundred years. Cf. *Der Kampf um Creuzers Symbolik. Eine Auswahl von Dokumenten* (Tübingen: Mohr-Siebeck, 1926), 3. The questionable accuracy of Howald's assessment does not prevent it from being revealing about the perceptions of many students of mythology.

47. XII:639.

48. XI:28f.

49. G. W. F. Hegel, *Vorlesungen über die Ästhetik*, vol. 13 of *Werke: Theorie Werkausgabe*, 20 vols., ed. E. Moldenhauer and K. M. Michel (Frankfurt am Main: Suhrkamp, 1970), 511–16. See esp. 513: "Herr Friedrich von Schlegel has, indeed, . . . expressed the opinion: Every true work of art must be an allegory. This statement is only true, however, if it means nothing other than that every work of art must contain a universal Idea and a meaning which is true in itself." Cf. the English translation by T. M. Knox, *Aesthetics: Lectures on Fine Art* (Oxford: At the Clarendon Press, 1975), 400.

50. *Phänomenologie des Geistes* (1807), vol. 3 of *Werke*, 556ff.; cf. A. V. Miller, trans., *Phenomenology of Spirit* (Oxford: Clarendon Press, 1977), paras. 764–67, pp. 462ff.

51. *Vorlesunger über die Geschichte der Philosophie*, vol. 16 of *Werke*, 108; cf. trans. E. S. Haldane and F. M. Simson, *Lectures on the History of Philosophy* (London: Routledge & Kegan Paul, 1968), 87.

52. *Vorlesungen über die Philosophie der Religion*, vol. 16 of *Werke*, 139–51; cf. P. C. Hodgson, ed., *Lectures on the Philosophy of Religion*, trans. R. F. Brown, P. C. Hodgson, and J. M. Stewart (Berkeley, Los Angeles, and London: University of California Press, 1984), 1:238–50.

53. XI:247; cf. XII:315.

54. XIII:173.

55. XI:77, 245; XII:126.

56. XI:74ff., 198, 249; XII:126ff.

57. XIV:28f. Cf. Søren Kierkegaard, *Philosophical Fragments*.

58. XI:185.

Chapter 3. The Unconscious and the Irrational

1. Recall Hegel's famous dictum: "Whatever is rational is actual; and whatever is actual is rational." *Rechtsphilosophie*, vol. 7 of *Werke: Theorie Werkausgabe*, 20 vols., ed. E. Moldenhauer and K. M. Michel (Frankfurt am Main: Suhrkamp, 1970), 24; cf. T. M. Knox, trans., *The Philosophy of Right* (Oxford: At

the Clarendon Press, 1942), 10. To this Schelling issued a sharp retort: "If reason is *all* of being (and hence, conversely, all being is reason), then there is no little difficulty in introducing unreason, which yet is necessary in order to explain the actual world" (XIV:23).

2. Jan de Vries, *Forschungsgeschichte der Mythologie* (Freiburg/Munich: Karl Alber, 1961), 362–63; cf. by the same author, *Perspectives in the History of Religions* (Berkeley: University of California Press, 1977), 39–40.

3. Gottfried Wilhelm Leibniz, *Nouveaux essais sur l'entendement human* (c. 1703), bk. 2, chap. 1, paras. 9–19, and chap. 20, par. 6; in his *Opera philosophica*, ed. E. Erdmann (Berlin: G. Eichler, 1840), 223–26, 247–48.; cf. P. Remnant and J. Bennet, trans., *New Essays on Human Understanding* (Cambridge: Cambridge University Press, 1981), 111–18, 163–66.

4. Immanuel Kant, *Anthropologie in pragmatischer Hinsicht* (1798), in vol. 7 of *Gesammelte Schriften*, ed. Preussische Akademie der Wissenschaften, 20 vols. (Berlin: G. Reimer, 1917), sec. 5, pp. 135–37; cf. V. L. Dowdell, trans., *Anthropology from a Pragmatical Point of View* (Carbondale: Southern Illinois University Press, 1978), 18–21.

5. *System des transzendentalen Idealismus* III:382–84; cf. P. Heath, trans., *System of Transcendental Idealism (1800)* (Charlottesville: University Press of Virginia, 1978), 38f. Compare Hegel's argument about the implicit self-overcoming of limits: *Enzyklopädie der philosophischen Wissenschaften*, vol. 8 of *Werke*, pt. 1, sec. 60, p. 144; cf. W. Wallace, trans., *The Logic of Hegel* (Oxford: Clarendon Press, 1874), 99.

6. III:600; cf. trans., 209.

7. III:380, par. (c); cf. trans., 36.

8. III:627f.; cf. trans., 231f. Cf. Michael Vater's useful discussion of the role of the unconscious in his introduction to the English translation, *System of Transcendental Idealismus (1800)*, trans. P. Heath (Charlottesville: University Press of Virginia, 1978), xxvii–xxxii. The "Odyssey" metaphor, incidentally, was one of Schelling's favorites, to which he returned at VI:57 and XI:494.

9. For further information about Schelling's influence on nineteenth- and twentieth-century psychology, the reader is referred to Johannes Orth, *Der psychologische Begriff des Unbewußten in der Schelling'schen Schule* (Ludwigshaven a. Rh.: Weiss and Hameier, 1914); Odo Marquard, "Über einige Beziehungen zwischen Ästhetik und Therapeutik in der Philosophie des neunzehnten Jahrhunderts," in *Materialien zu Schellings philosophischen Anfängen,"* ed. M. Frank and G. Kurz (Frankfurt am Main: Suhrkamp, 1975), 341–77; also by Marquard, "Schelling—Zeitgenosse incognito," in *Schelling. Einführung in seine Philosophie*, ed. H. M. Baumgartner (Freiburg/München: K. Alber, 1975), 21–22; Detlev von Uslar, "Die Aktualität Schellings für Tiefenpsychologie und Psychologie," in *Schelling. Seiner Bedeuting für eine Philosophie der Natur und der Geschichte*, ed. L. Hasler (Stuttgart/Bad Cannstatt: F. Frommann and G. Holzboog, 1979), 163–66; and Edward Beach, "The Schellingian School of Psychology and its Legacy," in "Schelling's Philosophy of Mythology" (Ph.D. diss., Stanford

University, 1988; Ann Arbor, Mich.: University Microfilms International, order no. 8826096), 240–49.

10. Cf. Dale Evarts Snow, "The Role of the Unconscious in Schelling's *System of Transcendental Idealism,*" *Idealistic Studies* 19, no. 3 (September 1989): 231–50.

11. Cf. XI:315f., 388, 587; XIII:67ff. This paradoxical project will be discussed at greater length in chapter 6, below. For a different critical assessment of Schelling's discovery of the irrational, see György Lukács, *Die Zerstörung der Vernunft,* 3 vols. (Darmstadt and Neuwied: Luchterhand, 1973, c. 1954), 1:138–72; cf. P. Palme, trans., *The Destruction of Reason* (Atlantic Highlands, N.J.: Humanities Press, 1981), 155–92. Lukács treats Schelling as developer of the "first form of the modern irrationalism," and finds its root cause in the reactionary tendencies of the postrevolutionary Restoration in Europe. However, this critique begs the question if it presupposes that the idea of an irrational power must *a priori* be false.

12. Cf. Kant's discussion of this dilemma in his *Kritik der praktischen Vernunft* (1788), vol. 5 of *Gesammelten Schriften,* ed. Preussische Akademie der Wissenschaften, 20 vols. (Berlin: G. Eimer, 1900–1942), 100ff.; cf. L. W. Beck, trans., *Critique of Practical Reason* (Indianapolis, Ind.: Bobbs-Merrill, 1956), 104ff. Spinoza's philosophy, which was experiencing a renaissance in the early nineteenth century, also had an influence: see his *Ethics,* trans. R. H. M. Elwes (New York: Dover, 1955, c. 1677), pt. 1, propositions 14–15, pp. 54–55, to which Schelling obliquely alluded at VII:359. Yet neither Spinoza's nor Kant's solution satisfied Schelling.

13. VII:359f.; cf. J. Gutmann, trans., *Philosophical Inquiries into the Nature of Human Freedom* (La Salle, Ill.: Open Court, 1986), 34.

14. VII:374; cf. trans., 51.

15. VII:469f. Cf. *Die Weltalter* VIII:337ff.; cf. F. de Wolfe Bolman, Jr., trans., *The Ages of the World* (New York: AMS Press, 1967, c. 1942), 227ff. Page 337 of the *Weltalter* manuscript is especially significant, in that it draws a connection between "creative madness" and the Greek cult of Dionysus. Schelling was later to make much of the Dionysian Mysteries in his *Philosophie der Mythologie.*

16. XI:185ff., 246; XII:126.

17. *Weltalter* VIII:225; cf. trans., 111f.

18. *Weltalter* VIII:309f.; cf. trans., 197ff. Cf. *Die Weltalter. Fragmente in den Urauffassungen von 1811 und 1813,* ed. Manfred Schröter (Munich: Biederstein and Leibniz, 1946), 25, 59 (top margin pagination has I:45f., 107f.). One is reminded here of Ernst Haeckel's famous dictum, "Ontology recapitulates phylogeny" (1868). Schelling, however appropriated and modified substantially the same idea from a much earlier source: Carl Friedrich Kielmeyer, *Über die Verhältnisse der organischen Kräfte unter einander in der Reihe der verschiedenen Organisationen, die Gesetze und Folgen dieser Verhältnisse, Eine Rede, den 11. February 1793 . . . gehalten* (Tübingen: C. F. Osiander, 1814), esp. 38ff. Kielmeyer also discussed the struggle among species for survival as holding the key to evolution,

44f. For his influence on Schelling, cf. Kuno Fischer, *Schellings Leben, Werke und Lehre* (Heidelberg: C. Winter's Universitätsverlag, 1899), 344f.

19. XII:649; XIII:428. Cf. Creuzer's *Symbolik* 1:111, 113, 121, 206, 208.

20. XIII:470. Cf. Euripides, *The Bacchae*, line 861.

21. *Weltalter Fragmente, Druck I* (1811), 42 (top margin pagination, I:76); also cf. *Weltalter* VIII:337; cf. trans., 227; and XII:427.

22. XII:649; XIII:471.

23. Gotthilf Heinrich Schubert, *Die Symbolik des Traumes* (Bamberg: C. F. Kunz, 1814), 39–40. Schubert was one of Schelling's most devoted disciples. He befriended Schelling in the Jena period (1798–1800), then moved to Würzburg and later to Munich at about the same times as his mentor.

Chapter 4. Toward a New Ontology of Eternity, Temporality and Freedom

1. X:57f.; XI:278f., 581ff. Cf. Gottfried Wilhelm Leibniz, *Leibniz-Arnauld Correspondence (1686–1687)*, in vol. 2 of *Die philosophischen Schriften*, ed. C. I. Gerhardt (Berlin: Weidmannsche Buchhandlung, 1875–90), 11–138; cf. G. H. R. Parkinson, trans. (Manchester: Manchester University Press; New York: Barnes and Noble, 1967).

2. XI:363.

3. Ibid., 249, 317; yet see also VII:432f.

4. For the distinction between "formal freedom" and real freedom, see his 1809 study, *Philosophische Untersuchungen über das Wesen der menschlichen Freiheit und die damit zusummenhängenden Gegenstände* (the so-called *Freiheitsschrift*) VII:352; cf. J. Gutmann, trans., *Philosophical Inquiries into the Nature of Human Freedom* (La Salle, Ill.: Open Court, 1986), 26.

5. Cf. XII:587, which appears on the surface to espouse determinism.

6. Ibid., 131.

7. XI:464. For other mentions of the Primordial Fall from the Idea-world into the sense-world, cf. XI:419 and 414, note. In the last-named passage, Schelling quotes from Kant's *Kritik der praktischen Vernunft* (1788), vol. 5 of *Gesammelte Schriften*, ed. Preussische Akademie der Wissenschaften, 20 vols. (Berlin: G. Reimer, 1908), 100ff. (See chapter 3, above, note 12, p. 264.)

8. *Die Weltalter* VIII:306; cf. F. de Wolfe Bolman, Jr., trans., *The Ages of the World* (New York: AMS Press, 1967, c. 1942), 194f.

9. *Die Weltalter* VIII:308ff.; cf. trans., 196ff. Cf. *Weltalter Fragmente, Druck I*, 74ff. (top margin pagination, I:135ff.).

10. Plato, *Timaeus*, 37d. Schelling (*Weltalter* VIII:307; cf. trans., 195) traces the origin of this saying back to Pindar.

11. The word "proto-temporal" is my own, but it accurately reflects Schelling's thinking on this subject.

12. *Weltalter* VIII:260, 306; cf. trans., 148, 195. Cf. XII:65.

13. *Stuttgarter Privatvorlesungen* VII:429f. Schelling obviously was echoing Kant here.
14. *Freiheitsschrift* VII:389; cf. trans., 67f. Compare *Weltalter* VIII:263; cf. trans., 151. Cf. XI:429.
15. Aristotle, *Metaphysics*, bk. 9, chap. 6. Schelling discussed at length Aristotle's theory of "Pure Act," e.g., at XI:314, 331f., 354, and passim.
16. Kant, *Kritik der reinen Vernunft* (1787), vol. 3 of *Gesammelte Schriften*, ed. Preussische Akademie der Wissenschaften, 20 vols. (Berlin: G. Reimer, 1900–1942), 365ff. (B566ff.); cf. Norman Kemp Smith, trans., *Critique of Pure Reason* (Toronto: Macmillan, 1929), 467ff.
17. Cf. *System des transzendentalen Idealismus* III:485f., 578f.; cf. P. Heath, trans., *System of Transcendental Idealism (1800)* (Charlottesville: University Press of Virginia, 1978), 118f., 191f. Cf. *Freiheitsschrift* VII:382ff.; cf. trans., 59ff.
18. XI:401, 417, 420.

Chapter 5. Three Influences on Schelling: Böhme, Baader, and Hegel

1. For Böhme's indebtedness to the Kabbala, see Will-Erich Peuckert, *Das Leben Jakob Böhmes* (Jena: E. Dieterichs, 1924), 101. Peuckert cites passages which he claims show kabbalistic influences.
2. Cf. Ingrid Merkel, "Aurora; or, The Rising Sun of Allegory: Hermetic Imagery in the Work of Jakob Böhme," in *Hermeticism and the Renaissance: Intellectual History and the Occult in Early Modern Europe*, ed. I. Merkel and A. G. Debus (Washington, D.C.: Folger Shakespeare Library, 1988), 302–10. Also cf. R. H. Hvolbel, "Was Jakob Böhme a Paracelsian?" *Hermetic Journal* 19 (Spring 1983): 6–17.
3. Cf. the preface to his first major work, *Morgenröte im Aufgang* (1612), in vol. 1 of *Sämtliche Schriften* ["*SS*"], ed. Will-Erich Peuckert (Stuttgart: Fr. Frommann, 1955–61: a facsimile reprint of the 1730 edition), "Vorrede," par. 89, p. 20; English translation edited by William Law, *Aurora*, in vol. 1 of *The Works of Jacob Behman* (London: Richardson, 1764), 4 vols., "Contents," par. 6, p. 20.
4. *Morgenröte*, "Vorrede," par. 87, p. 19; cf. trans., par. 4, p. 20.
5. Harald Holz, *Spekulation und Faktizität. Zum Freiheitsbegriff des mittleren und späten Schelling* (Bonn: Bouvier, 1970). Holz seeks to debunk the "legend" of Schelling's indebtedness to Böhme (p. 7). Instead, Holz claims that Neoplatonic and Patristic sources exercised the paramount influence on Schelling's later thought.
6. Frederick O. Kile, *Die theologischen Grundlagen von Schellings Philosophie der Freiheit* (Leiden: E. J. Brill, 1965); Robert F. Brown, *The Later Philosophy of Schelling: The Influence of Böhme on the Works of 1809–1815* (Lewisburg, Pa.: Bucknell University Press, 1977).

7. Cf. Werner Marx, *Schelling: Geschichte, System, Freiheit* (Freiburg im Br./ Munich: K. Alber, 1977), 107f., note 7; cf. T. Nenon, trans., *The Philosophy of F. W. J. Schelling: History, System, and Freedom* (Bloomington: Indiana University Press, 1984), 92, note 9. Marx observes that inasmuch as Böhme himself had been much influenced by Neoplatonism, the two theories as to Schelling's intellectual ancestry (i.e., Neoplatonic or Böhmean) are not mutually exclusive.

8. *Morgenröte,* chap. 23, par. 17; cf. trans., par. 18, p. 230.

9. Jakob Böhme, *Von der Gnaden-Wahl* (1623), in vol. 6 of *SS,* chap 1, par. 9; cf. trans., *On the Election to Grace,* in vol. 4 of *The Works,* Law edition, paras. 10–13, pp. 155–56.

10. *Weg zu Christo* (1620), in vol. 4 of *SS:* "Von Göttlicher Beschaulichkeit," chap. 1, par. 9, p. 167; cf. trans. W. Zeller, *The Way to Christ* (New York: Paulist Press, 1978), 196. Cf. *De signatura rerum* (1622), in vol. 6 of *SS,* chap. 2; cf. trans., *The Signature of All Things,* in vol. 4 of *The Works,* Law edition, 12–17.

11. "Von Göttlicher Beschaulichkeit," chap. 1, par. 10, p. 168; cf. trans. W. Zeller, *Thw Way to Christ,* 196.

12. *Signatura,* chap. 2, par. 7; cf. trans., par. 10, p. 13.

13. *Signatura,* chap. 2, par. 8; cf. trans., par. 11.

14. *Beschreibung der Drey Principien Göttliches Wesens* (1619), in vol. 2 of *SS,* chaps. 1–2; cf. trans., *The Three Principles of the Divine Essence,* in vol. 1 of *The Works,* Law edition, chaps. 1–2, pp. 9–16.

15. *Viertzig Fragen von der Seelen* (1620), in vol. 3 of *SS,* chap. 1, par. 66; cf. trans., *Forty Questions Concerning the Soul,* in vol. 2 of *The Works,* Law edition, par. 81, p. 16. Schelling would write frequently, especially in *Die Weltalter,* of his own first principle as "the power that draws together" *(die zusammenziehende Kraft).*

16. *Drey Princ.* chap. 2, par. 9; cf. trans., par. 9, p. 14.

17. *Theosophische Fragen* (1624), in vol. 9 of *SS,* chap. 3, par. 2.

18. *Gnaden-Wahl,* chap. 1, par. 24; cf. trans., par. 29, p. 156.

19. "Von Göttlicher Beschaulichkeit," chap. 1, par. 10, p. 168; cf. trans., *The Way of Christ,* 196.

20. After he published the *Morgenröte* in 1612, Böhme was prosecuted by the local pastor of Görlitz, Gregory Richter, and had to promise on pain of imprisonment to cease writing. This judgment he obeyed for five years, until, unable to restrain himself any longer, he began writing again in secret for private circulation among friends. The publication of his *Weg zu Christo* in 1623 by one of these friends led to renewed persecutions. Banished from Görlitz, Böhme lived for a time in Dresden and on the country estates of wealth supporters. Finally, stricken by illness in 1624, he returned home and died in the same year.

21. XIII:120–23; cf. XII:478, 597.

22. XIII:120. See also 115, where Schelling refers indirectly to Böhme and others as "mystical empiricists," and 125, where he comments on the fallacy of reification.

23. John Joseph Stoudt, *Sunrise to Eternity: A Study in Jacob Böhme's Life and Thought* (Philadelphia: University of Pennsylvania Press, 1957), 302.

24. Jürgen Habermas, "Das Absolute und die Geschichte: Von der Zwiespältigkeit in Schellings Denken" (Bonn: Ph.D. diss., Rheinische Friedrich Wilhelms Universität, 1954), 2. For a recent discussion of the similarities between Schelling's and Habermas's respective conceptions of history, see the first chapter of Werner Marx's *Schelling,* 13–62; cf. trans., 1–32. See also my comments, 164–69.

25. Cf. G. W. F. Hegel, "Vorrede zur zweiten Aufgabe" (1827), *Enzyklopädie der philosophischen Wissenschaften,* vol. 8 of *Werke: Theorie Werkausgabe,* 20 vols., ed. E. Moldenhauer and K. M. Michel (Frankfurt am Main: Suhrkamp, 1970), 27–28. See also Schelling, *Philosophische Untersuchungen über das Wesen der menschlichen Freiheit und die damit zusammenhängenden Gegenstände,* 1809 (the so-called *Freiheitsschrift*) VII:366f.; cf. trans. J. Gutmann, *Philosophical Inquiries into the Nature of Human Freedom* (La Salle, Ill.: Open Court, 1986), 41ff.

26. Thomas O'Meara, *Romantic Idealism and Roman Catholicism. Schelling and the Theologians* (Notre Dame, Ind.: University of Notre Dame Press, 1982), 79. For an account of Baader's volatile relationship with Schelling, see 79–89, 134ff.

27. Franz von Baader, *Fermenta Cognitionis* (1822–25), vol. 6 of *Sämtliche Werke* [*"SW"*], ed. Franz Hoffmann (Aalen: Scientia Verlag, 1963; reprint of Leipzig ed., 1852), 162.

28. Ibid., 166.

29. Ibid.

30. Ibid., 168, note.

31. Ibid., 178.

32. Schelling was, to be sure, already somewhat acquainted with Böhme as early as 1799, when Ludwig Tieck introduced the theosophist's work to the "Jena circle," of which Schelling was a part. It has even been suggested that Schelling's familiarity with Böhme may have gone back further, to his childhood as the son of a small-town Lutheran minister in Bebenhausen. See Wilhelm A. Schulze, "Zum Verständnis der Stuttgarter Privatvorlesungen Schellings," *Zeitschrift für philosophische Forschung* 11 (1957): 575–76, esp. note 10.

Yet Schelling's writings show few traces of Böhme's direct influence until the first Munich period (1806–9). Primarily for this reason, Franz von Baader is generally regarded as the man who focused Schelling's attention on Böhme. Indeed, Baader several times claimed credit for this himself.

For a fuller discussion of these biographical issues, see James Gutmann's introduction to his translation of the *Freiheitsschrift* under the title *Philosophical Inquiries into the Nature of Human Freedom* (La Salle, Ill.: Open Court, 1986), xlv–xlvi. Also, Robert Brown, *Later Philosophy of Schelling,* 114–15., note; O'Meara, *Romantic Idealism,* 84.

33. See Baader's essay, *Über den Begriff der dynamischen Bewegung* (1809), *SW* 3:285.

34. Hans Sedlmayr points out that this proposition regarding the deviant state of the existing universe was the core insight of Baader's theology. See "Über Wahrheit und Erkenntnis nach Franz von Baader," *Wahrheit und Verkündigung:*

Michael Schmaus zum 70. Geburtstag, ed. Leo Scheffczyck (Munich: F. Schoeningh, 1967), 1:109. Cf. Baader, *SW* 7:279 (*not,* as Sedlmayr has it, 268).

35. *Über den Paulinischen Begriff des Versehenseins des Menschen* (1837), *SW* 4:347.
36. VII:366; cf. trans., 42.
37. VII:365; cf. trans., 41.
38. *Weltalter* VIII:319; cf. trans. F. de Wolfe Bolman, Jr., *The Ages of the World* (New York: AMS Press, 1967, c. 1942), 208–9. For Schelling's versus Baader's differing positions on the doctrine of *felix culpa,* see Wilhelm A. Schulze, "Zum Verständnis der Stuttgarter Privatvorlesungen," 587–88.
39. XI:249, 317; XIII:292. For a critical analysis of Schelling's solution to this problem, see chapter 7, below.
40. *SW* 15:117.
41. Ibid., 118.
42. XIV:162; cf. 108.
43. See the final exchange of letters, in Baader's *Briefwechsel, SW* 15:420–21.
44. XIII:170.
45. G. W. F. Hegel, *Phänomenologie des Geistes,* vol. 3 of *Werke,* 15; cf. A. V. Miller, trans., *The Phenomenology of Spirit* (Oxford: Clarendon Press, 1977), par. 6, p. 4.
46. *Freiheitsschrift* VII:350; cf. trans., 24. Cf. also XI:388.
47. Cf. XI:289; XII:52, 55.
48. It is scarcely necessary to justify the name proposed for Hegel's method, since it is well known that *Aufhebung* is the key principle to his entire way of reasoning. See, for example, his *Enzyklopädie der philosophischen Wissenschaften,* vol. 8 of *Werke,* sec. 96, "Zusatz," pp. 204f.; cf. W. Wallace, trans., *The Logic of Hegel,* 2d ed. (London: Oxford University Press, 1892), 180.
49. Hegel, *Enzyklopädie,* vol. 8 of *Werke,* sec. 161, pp. 308ff.; cf. trans., 288ff.
50. The choice of the term *Erzeugungsdialektik* to describe Schelling's method is based on innumerable passages such as the following: "The dialectical method is, like the dialogical method, not demonstrative *(beweisend)* but productive *(erzeugend);* it is that in which truth becomes produced *(erzeugt wird)*" (XI:330). Similar statements occur in the *Weltalter* VIII:289f.; cf. trans., 178. Also XI:488, 522, 562.
51. An objection might be made at this juncture, however, that Schelling's texts, like Hegel's, not infrequently use the word *aufheben.* Why, then (it could be asked), was his dialectical method not just as much an *Aufhebungsdialektik?* The answer is that Schelling almost invariably used *aubheben* in a univocal sense, as meaning a "cancellation" or "annihilation," but not in Hegel's systematically equivocal sense as a simultaneous "preservation" and "making explicit" of the logical principles involved. On rare occasions, to be sure, Schelling did employ a bivalent sense of *aufheben* (e.g., at XI:389 and XII:178), but even in these cases the two senses are purely supplementary, as combining an extinction with a growth, rather than conveying that the cancellation itself *is* an elaboration and deepening

of the original content. In the overwhelming majority of cases, Schelling kept to a univocally negative meaning. A particularly illustrative example occurs at XII:438. See also VII:424f.; X:160; XI:485, 550, 556, 567; XII:364, 438; XIII:89, 453f., 507.

A further objection might be raised from the other side, viz., that Hegel, too, sometimes used the verb *erzeugen* to describe his own version of dialectic—for example, in a passage where he characterized the speculative movement of the syllogism as "diser sich selbst erzeugende, fortleitende und in sich zurückgehende Gang" *(Phänomenologie,* 61; *Phenomenology,* par. 65, p. 40). But this metaphor did not, as in Schelling's case, determine the entire cast of his thought.

We shall return to the distinction between Schelling's *Erzeugungsdialektik* and Hegel's *Aufhebungsdialektik* in Part Two of this study. See also my paper, "The Later Schelling's Conception of Dialectical Method, in Contradistinction to Hegel's," *Owl of Minerva* 22, no. 1 (Fall 1990): 35–54.

52. VII:424. Note how Schelling treats *aufheben* and *vertilgen* in this passage as virtually synonymous. For another passage where Schelling invokes the notion of a "self-duplicating" causal principle, cf. *Die Weltalter. Fragmente in den Urauffassungen von 1811 und 1813,* ed. Manfred Schröter (Munich: Biederstein and Leibniz, 1946), 68 (top margin pagination has I:124–25).

53. *Enzyklopädie,* vol. 8 of *Werke,* sec. 164, pp. 313ff.; cf. trans., 294f.

54. *Enzyklopädie,* vol. 10 of *Werke,* sec. 554, p. 366; cf. W. Wallace, trans., *The Philosophy of Mind* (Oxford: Clarendon Press, 1971), 292.

55. Edward A. Beach, "Absolute Knowledge and the Problem of Systematic Completeness in Hegel's Philosophy" (Ann Arbor, Mich.: Ph.D. diss., Northwestern University, 1980; Ann Arbor, Mich.: University Microfilms International, order no. 8104687).

56. *Phänomenologie,* 54ff.; cf. trans., par. 56, p. 34.

57. XIII:173 and passim, from the introductory volume to the *Philosophie der Offenbarung* (also known under the title *Begründung der positiven Philosophie*). Although this text dates from Schelling's Berlin lecture series given between 1841 and 1845, the same ideas and arguments had been delivered by Schelling in public lectures from the early 1820s on, reaching a fully developed form by the end of the twenties. See the foreword by his son and editor, XIII:vi–viii, and compare with note 2 in my Introduction, pp. 251–52 above. Much the same basic critique of Hegel can also be found in Schelling's *Grundlegung der positiven Philosophie: Münchner Vorlesung WS 1832/33 und SS 1833,* ed. Horst Fuhrmans (Turin: Bottega D'Erasmo, 1972); see esp. 216ff.

58. Feuerbach's essay, "Zur Kritik der Hegelschen Philosophie," first appeared in the *Hallische Jahrbücher für deutsche Wissenschaft und Kunst,* ed. A. Ruge and T. Echtermeyer, nos. 208–16 (30 Aug. to 9 Sept., 1839): 1657–1725, passim. (Reprinted in Glashütten im Taunus: D. Auvermann, 1972.) Marx picked up and continued the same objections in the fourth article of his "Ökonomisch-philosophische Manuskripte" (1844): "Kritik der Hegelschen Dialektik und Philosophie

überhaupt," in *Karl Marx, Friedrich Engels Gesamptausgabe (MEGA)*, (Berlin: Dietz Verlag, 1982), pt. 1, 2:399–418; English ed. R. C. Tucker, "Critique of the Hegelian Dialectic and Philosophy as a Whole," in *The Marx-Engels Reader*, 2d. ed. (New York and London: Norton, 1978), 106–25.

See Manfred Frank, *Der unendliche Mangel an Sein: Schellings Hegelkritik und die Anfänge der Marxschen Dialektik* (Frankfurt a. M.: Suhrkamp, 1975), 181–82; also by Frank, "Schelling's Critique of Hegel and the Beginnings of Marxian Dialectics," *Idealistic Studies* 19, no. 3 (September 1989): 251–68.

59. XII:114ff.

60. See the fine discussions of this point in Errol E. Harris's *An Interpretation of the Logic of Hegel* (Lanham, Md.: University Press of America, 1983), 187–88, 259–61.

61. This familiar Hegelian maxim is loosely paraphrased from the *Wissenschaft der Logik* (1812–16), vol. 6 of *Werke*, 13; cf. A. V. Miller, trans., *Hegel's Science of Logic* (London: George Allen & Unwin, 1969), 389. See also *Enzyklopädie*, vol. 8 of *Werke*, sec. 112, "Zusatz," p. 232; cf. trans., *The Logic of Hegel,* 209.

62. See, for example, Schelling's *System des transzendentalen Idealismus* (1800), III:603: "History as a whole is a continuous, gradually self-manifesting revelation of the Absolute"; cf. P. Heath, trans., *System of Transcendental Idealism (1800)* (Charlottesville: University Press of Virginia, 1978), 211.

63. *Enzyklopädie*, vol. 9 of *Werke*, sec. 258, "Zusatz," p. 50; cf. A. V. Miller, trans., *Hegel's Philosophy of Nature* (Oxford: Clarendon Press, 1970), 36.

64. *Enzyklopädie*, sec. 249, "Zusatz," p. 32; cf. trans., 20.

65. XIII:173.

66. Ibid., 89.

67. X:160.

68. XI:312.

Chapter 6. Schelling's New Philosophical Point of Departure

1. Schelling wrote, for example, in volume one of the *Philosophie der Mythologie,* that the "pure Potencies, [are] clear, and to that extent divine powers, which . . . are the subject of the present investigation, insofar as this has no other goal than the explanation of heathenism or of polytheism" (XII:99).

2. XIII:162.

3. G. W. F. Hegel, *Die Phänomenologie des Geistes,* vol. 3 of *Werke: Theorie Werkausgabe,* 20 vols. ed. E. Moldenhauer and K. M. Michel (Frankfurt am Main: Suhrkamp, 1970), 84ff.; cf. A . V. Miller, trans., *The Phenomenology of Spirit* (Oxford: Clarendon Press, 1977), paras. 90–110, pp. 58ff.

4. VI:36ff. At this stage in his development, Schelling waffled on the question as to the ultimate cause of this crucial "leap." Throughout most of this essay, he

tended to characterize the cause as a contingent act on the part of individual spirits, cf. 38, 41, 52; but toward the end of the piece he announced, in seeming self-contradiction, that the fall was necessitated by the Ideal Absolute itself. Cf. 57, 63.

5. *Philosophische Untersuchungen über das Wesen der menschlichen Freiheit und die damit zusammenhängenden Gegenstände,* 1809 (the so-called *Freiheitsschrift*) VII:359; cf. J. Gutmann, trans., *Philosophical Inquiries into the Nature of Human Freedom* (La Salle, Ill.: Open Court, 1986), 33.

6. Cf. *Freiheitsschrift* VII:362, 374ff.; cf. trans., 37, 50ff.

7. *Die Weltalter* VIII:210ff., 224, 328; cf. trans. F. de Wolfe Bolman, Jr., *The Ages of the World* (New York: AMS Press, 1967, c. 1942), 96ff., 110f., 217.

8. See chapter 5, above, pp. 72–75.

9. See chapter 4, above.

10. For an explanation of this term, see chapter 5, above, pp. 85–86, and chapter 7, below, pp. 113–14.

11. Walter Schulz, in his influential study, *Die Vollendung des deutschen Idealismus in der Spätphilosophie Schellings,* 2d ed. (Pfullingen: Neske, 1975), has called attention to the analogy between Schelling's theory of the radically "unthinkable" and Heidegger's doctrine of "thrownness" *(Geworfenheit).* See 314, note.

12. XI:363.

13. Martin Heidegger, *Schellings Abhandlung über das Wesen der menschlichen Freiheit* (Tübingen: Niemeyer, 1971); cf. J. Stambaugh, trans., *Schelling's Treatise on the Essence of Human Freedom* (Athens: Ohio University Press, 1985). Also Jürgen Habermas, "Das Absolute und die Geschichte. Von der Zwiespältigkeit in Schellings Denken" (Bonn: Ph.D. diss., Rheinische Friedrich Wilhelms Universität, 1954); and Walter Kasper, *Das Absolute in der Geschichte. Philosophie und Theologie der Geschichte in der Spätphilosophie Schellings* (Mainz: Matthias-Grünewald Verlag, 1965, c. 1954); Alan White, *Schelling: An Introduction to the System of Freedom* (New Haven and London: Yale University Press, 1983).

14. György Lukács, *Die Zerstörung der Vernunft* (Darmstadt and Neuwied: Luchterhand, 1973, c. 1962), 1:138–72; cf. P. Palme, trans., *The Destruction of Reason* (Atlantic Highlands, N.J.: Humanities Press, 1981), 155–92.

15. Cf. XIII:153.

16. See my "The Paradox of Cognitive Relativism Revisited: A Reply to Jack W. Meiland," *Metaphilosophy* 15, nos. 3 & 4 (July/October 1984): 157–71.

17. XIII:156; cf. XI:262. Schelling was also very critical of Hegel's attempts to reformulate the ontological argument. Cf. XII:115. For a useful summary of some of the interpretive controversies in recent scholarship concerning Schelling's rejection of the ontological argument, see Alan White, *Absolute Knowledge: Hegel and the Problem of Metaphysics* (Athens: Ohio University Press, 1983), 173–74, notes 5 and 6.

18. XIII:161. Note, however, that this critique ignores Hegel's careful distinction between "subjective thought" and "objective thought." Only the latter did he characterize as the concrete reality underling the phenomenal world. Cf.

Enzyklopädie, vol. 8 of *Werke*, sec. 24, esp. "Zusatz 1," pp. 80ff.; cf. W. Wallace, trans., *The Logic of Hegel*, 2d ed. (London: Oxford University Press, 1892), 143ff.

19. Cf. XI:303f., which quotes from Aristotle's *Posterior Analytics*, 100b, 7–11: "There is no knowledge of first principles except through intuition [Νοῦς]." Schelling was a close reader (in the original Greek) of Aristotle. Cf. also XI:265.

20. IX:229.

21. Cf. XI:262, 315f., 326, 359, 525.

22. Ibid., 124.

23. XIII:163. Schelling quotes from Kant's *Kritik der reinen Vernunft* (1787), vol. 3 of *Gesammelte Schriften*, ed. Preussische Akademie der Wissenschaften, 20 vols. (Berlin: G. Reimer, 1900–1942), 409 (B641); cf. Norman Kemp Smith, trans., *Critique of Pure Reason* (Toronto: Macmillan, 1929), 513.

24. XII:184.

25. XIII:126f., 154f.; cf. V:286f.

26. Friedrich H. Jacobi, *Von den göttlichen Dingen und ihrer Offenbarung* (Leipzig: G. Fleischer, 1811). Schelling replied the following year with an equally polemical counterblast, *Denkmal der Schrift von den göttlichen Dingen usw. des Herrn Friedrich Heinrich Jacobi und der ihm in derselben gemachten Beschuldigungen eines absichtlich täuschenden, Lüge redenden Atheismus* VIII:19–136. Schelling's antagonism toward Jacobi continued into his final period as well: cf. XI:280; XII:69; XIII:85. For an account of the *Pantheismusstreit* and its significance for German philosophy, see Frederick C. Beiser, *The Fate of Reason: German Philosophy from Kant to Fichte* (Cambridge, Mass., and London: Harvard University Press, 1987), 44–91. Also cf. Dale Evarts Snow, "F. H. Jacobi and the Development of German Idealism," *Journal of the History of Philosophy* 25, no. 3 (July 1987): 397–415.

27. XII:122f., 127.

28. IX:228ff.; XIII:127, 148f. This theory of the "ecstasy of reason" has provoked much controversy in twentieth-century scholarship. See, for example, Walter Schulz, *Vollendung*, 123f.; Joseph A. Bracken, *Freiheit und Kausalität bei Schelling* (Freiburg/Munich: K. Alber, 1972), 97ff.; Manfred Durner, *Wissen und Geschichte bei Schelling. Eine Interpretation der ersten Erlanger Vorlesung* (Munich: J. Berchmans, 1979), 74ff.

29. Paul Tillich, for example, has drawn upon this concept of the "ecstasy of reason," adapting it to his own theological principle involving the state of "ultimate concern." See his *Dynamics of Faith* (New York: Harper, 1957), 76–77.

30. XII:58; cf. *Die Weltalter* VIII:240, 256; cf. F. de Wolfe Bolman, Jr., trans., *The Ages of the World* (New York: AMS Press, 1967, c. 1942), 128, 144. See also XII:25. In other contexts, Schelling also used the term *Überexistierendes* to express much the same idea. See, for example, XI:563.

31. Martin Heidegger, *Schellings Abhandlung*, 4; cf. trans., 4. For a thoroughgoing attempt to interpret Schelling's philosophy of mythology along Heideggerian lines, see Karl-Heinz Volkmann-Schluck, *Mythos und Logos. Intepretationen zu Schellings Philosophie der Mythologie* (Berlin: de Gruyter, 1969).

32. Schelling resorted to this somewhat *ad hominem* argument in his *System des Transzendentalen Idealismus* (1800), cf. III:369; cf. P. Heath, trans., *System of Transcendental Idealism (1800)* (Charlottesville: University Press of Virginia, 1978), 28.

33. Ibid.

34. *Phänomenologie*, 22; cf. trans., par. 16, p. 9.

35. IV:403. This striking anticipation of Hegel's critique was brought to light by Karl Jaspers, in *Schelling. Größe und Verhängnis* (Munich: Piper, 1955), 302–3.

36. XIII:88.

37. Cf. Peter Suber, "Logical Rudeness," in *Self-Reference: Reflections on Reflexivity*, ed. S. J. Bartlett and P. Suber (The Hague: M. Nijhoff, 1987), 41–67. See also, by the same writer, "A Case Study in *Ad Hominem* Arguments: Fichte's *Science of Knowledge,*" *Philosophy and Rhetoric* (published by Pennsylvania State University Press) 23, no. 1 (1990): 12–42. Suber claims that a proposition is "logically rude" when *(inter alia)* it explains away criticism instead of answering it. He argues that, by setting out to diagnose the developmental limitations of his metaphysical opponents, Fichte legitimated a blanket dismissal of their objections to his own position. Suber provocatively adds, "What we are seeing . . . is not merely the rhetorical strategy of a rude idealist, but the rhetorical strategy of any dialectical thinker who believes that consciousness grows in stages of sophistication and access to truth" (27). If so, then the same judgment would presumably apply to Schelling (and many other thinkers) as well.

38. Joseph P. Lawrence makes an interesting attempt to defend Schelling along these lines in his *Schellings Philosophie des ewigen Anfangs* (Würzburg: Königshausen and Neumann, 1989), 14–18.

39. XIII:162.

40. Cf. XI:315f., 388, 587; XIII:67ff.

41. XIII:65f.

42. XII:115.

43. Manfred Schröter, "Vorwort" and "Einleitung des Herausgebers," introductory essays to Schelling's *Die Weltalter. Fragmente in den Urauffassungen von 1811 und 1813,* ed. M. Schröter (Munich: Biederstein Verlag and Leibniz Verlag, 1946), ii–lviii. Walter Kasper, *Das Absolute in der Geschichte. Philosophie und Theologie der Geschichte in der Spätphilosophie Schellings* (Mainz: Matthias-Grünewald Verlag, 1965). Walter Schulz, *Die Vollendung des Deutschen Idealismus in der Spätphilosophie Schellings,* 2d ed. (Pfullingen: Neske Verlag, 1975).

44. Horst Fuhrmans, *Schellings letzte Philosophie. Die negative und positive Philosophie im Einsatz des Spätidealismus* (Berlin: Junker & Dünnhaupt, 1940); and by the same author, "Der Ausgangspunkt der Schellingschen Spätphilosophie (Dokumente zur Schellingforschung)," *Kant-Studien* 48 (1956–57): 302–23. Xavier Tilliette, *Schelling. Une philosophie en devenir,* vol. 2 (Paris: Vrin, 1970); cf. also "Schelling contre Hegel," *Archives de Philosophie* 29 (Jan.-Mar. 1966): 89–108.

45. See, for example, the collection of critical articles on the Schelling/Hegel debate and related topics, published under the title *Ist systematische Philosophie*

Enzyklopädie, vol. 8 of *Werke,* sec. 24, esp. "Zusatz 1," pp. 80ff.; cf. W. Wallace, trans., *The Logic of Hegel,* 2d ed. (London: Oxford University Press, 1892), 143ff.

19. Cf. XI:303f., which quotes from Aristotle's *Posterior Analytics,* 100b, 7–11: "There is no knowledge of first principles except through intuition [Νοῦς]." Schelling was a close reader (in the original Greek) of Aristotle. Cf. also XI:265.

20. IX:229.

21. Cf. XI:262, 315f., 326, 359, 525.

22. Ibid., 124.

23. XIII:163. Schelling quotes from Kant's *Kritik der reinen Vernunft* (1787), vol. 3 of *Gesammelte Schriften,* ed. Preussische Akademie der Wissenschaften, 20 vols. (Berlin: G. Reimer, 1900–1942), 409 (B641); cf. Norman Kemp Smith, trans., *Critique of Pure Reason* (Toronto: Macmillan, 1929), 513.

24. XII:184.

25. XIII:126f., 154f.; cf. V:286f.

26. Friedrich H. Jacobi, *Von den göttlichen Dingen und ihrer Offenbarung* (Leipzig: G. Fleischer, 1811). Schelling replied the following year with an equally polemical counterblast, *Denkmal der Schrift von den göttlichen Dingen usw. des Herrn Friedrich Heinrich Jacobi und der ihm in derselben gemachten Beschuldigungen eines absichtlich täuschenden, Lüge redenden Atheismus* VIII:19–136. Schelling's antagonism toward Jacobi continued into his final period as well: cf. XI:280; XII:69; XIII:85. For an account of the *Pantheismusstreit* and its significance for German philosophy, see Frederick C. Beiser, *The Fate of Reason: German Philosophy from Kant to Fichte* (Cambridge, Mass., and London: Harvard University Press, 1987), 44–91. Also cf. Dale Evarts Snow, "F. H. Jacobi and the Development of German Idealism," *Journal of the History of Philosophy* 25, no. 3 (July 1987): 397–415.

27. XII:122f., 127.

28. IX:228ff.; XIII:127, 148f. This theory of the "ecstasy of reason" has provoked much controversy in twentieth-century scholarship. See, for example, Walter Schulz, *Vollendung,* 123f.; Joseph A. Bracken, *Freiheit und Kausalität bei Schelling* (Freiburg/Munich: K. Alber, 1972), 97ff.; Manfred Durner, *Wissen und Geschichte bei Schelling. Eine Interpretation der ersten Erlanger Vorlesung* (Munich: J. Berchmans, 1979), 74ff.

29. Paul Tillich, for example, has drawn upon this concept of the "ecstasy of reason," adapting it to his own theological principle involving the state of "ultimate concern." See his *Dynamics of Faith* (New York: Harper, 1957), 76–77.

30. XII:58; cf. *Die Weltalter* VIII:240, 256; cf. F. de Wolfe Bolman, Jr., trans., *The Ages of the World* (New York: AMS Press, 1967, c. 1942), 128, 144. See also XII:25. In other contexts, Schelling also used the term *Überexistierendes* to express much the same idea. See, for example, XI:563.

31. Martin Heidegger, *Schellings Abhandlung,* 4; cf. trans., 4. For a thoroughgoing attempt to interpret Schelling's philosophy of mythology along Heideggerian lines, see Karl-Heinz Volkmann-Schluck, *Mythos und Logos. Intepretationen zu Schellings Philosophie der Mythologie* (Berlin: de Gruyter, 1969).

32. Schelling resorted to this somewhat *ad hominem* argument in his *System des Transzendentalen Idealismus* (1800), cf. III:369; cf. P. Heath, trans., *System of Transcendental Idealism (1800)* (Charlottesville: University Press of Virginia, 1978), 28.
33. Ibid.
34. *Phänomenologie,* 22; cf. trans., par. 16, p. 9.
35. IV:403. This striking anticipation of Hegel's critique was brought to light by Karl Jaspers, in *Schelling. Größe und Verhängnis* (Munich: Piper, 1955), 302–3.
36. XIII:88.
37. Cf. Peter Suber, "Logical Rudeness," in *Self-Reference: Reflections on Reflexivity,* ed. S. J. Bartlett and P. Suber (The Hague: M. Nijhoff, 1987), 41–67. See also, by the same writer, "A Case Study in *Ad Hominem* Arguments: Fichte's *Science of Knowledge,*" *Philosophy and Rhetoric* (published by Pennsylvania State University Press) 23, no. 1 (1990): 12–42. Suber claims that a proposition is "logically rude" when *(inter alia)* it explains away criticism instead of answering it. He argues that, by setting out to diagnose the developmental limitations of his metaphysical opponents, Fichte legitimated a blanket dismissal of their objections to his own position. Suber provocatively adds, "What we are seeing . . . is not merely the rhetorical strategy of a rude idealist, but the rhetorical strategy of any dialectical thinker who believes that consciousness grows in stages of sophistication and access to truth" (27). If so, then the same judgment would presumably apply to Schelling (and many other thinkers) as well.
38. Joseph P. Lawrence makes an interesting attempt to defend Schelling along these lines in his *Schellings Philosophie des ewigen Anfangs* (Würzburg: Königshausen and Neumann, 1989), 14–18.
39. XIII:162.
40. Cf. XI:315f., 388, 587; XIII:67ff.
41. XIII:65f.
42. XII:115.
43. Manfred Schröter, "Vorwort" and "Einleitung des Herausgebers," introductory essays to Schelling's *Die Weltalter. Fragmente in den Urauffassungen von 1811 und 1813,* ed. M. Schröter (Munich: Biederstein Verlag and Leibniz Verlag, 1946), ii–lviii. Walter Kasper, *Das Absolute in der Geschichte. Philosophie und Theologie der Geschichte in der Spätphilosophie Schellings* (Mainz: Matthias-Grünewald Verlag, 1965). Walter Schulz, *Die Vollendung des Deutschen Idealismus in der Spätphilosophie Schellings,* 2d ed. (Pfullingen: Neske Verlag, 1975).
44. Horst Fuhrmans, *Schellings letzte Philosophie. Die negative und positive Philosophie im Einsatz des Spätidealismus* (Berlin: Junker & Dünnhaupt, 1940); and by the same author, "Der Ausgangspunkt der Schellingschen Spätphilosophie (Dokumente zur Schellingforschung)," *Kant-Studien* 48 (1956–57): 302–23. Xavier Tilliette, *Schelling. Une philosophie en devenir,* vol. 2 (Paris: Vrin, 1970); cf. also "Schelling contre Hegel," *Archives de Philosophie* 29 (Jan.-Mar. 1966): 89–108.
45. See, for example, the collection of critical articles on the Schelling/Hegel debate and related topics, published under the title *Ist systematische Philosophie*

möglich? ed. D. Henrich, *Hegel-Studien / Beiheft 17* (Bonn: Bouvier Verlag Herbert Grundmann, 1977).

46. For example, at XIII:92f., 128.

47. Tilliette, *Schelling. Une philosophie en devenir* 2:57.

48. For more discussion of some current issues in this interpretive and critical controversy, see chapter 9 of the present work.

Chapter 7. The Ontology

1. *Die Weltalter. Fragmente in den Urauffassungen von 1811 und 1813,* ed. Manfred Schröter (Munich: Biederstein and Leibniz, 1946), 74f. (top margin pagination: I:136f.); cf. also *Die Weltalter* VIII:225; cf. F. de Wolfe Bolman, Jr., trans., *The Ages of the World* (New York: AMS Press, 1967, c. 1942), 111f. Also cf. XI:497; XII:65.

2. Hegel, *Enzyklopädie der philosophischen Wissenschaften,* vol. 9 of *Werke: Theorie Werkausgabe,* 20 vols., ed. E. Moldenhauer and K. M. Michel (Frankfurt am Main: Suhrkamp, 1970), secs. 249 and 258, pp. 32f., 48ff.; cf. A. V. Miller, trans., *Hegel's Philosophy of Nature* (Oxford: Clarendon Press, 1970), 21f., 34ff. Regarding the succession of essential forms, Hegel wrote that "temporal difference has no interest for thought." See chapter 5, above, pp. 89–90, and note 63, p. 271.

3. *Weltalter* VIII:260; cf. trans., 147f.

4. XI:93.

5. Cf. VII:430; also *Weltalter* VIII:225, 260; cf. trans. 111f., 148; also *Weltalter Fragmente,* 79 (top margin pagination: I:144f.); also XI:312, 428f.; XII:42f.

6. For Schelling's attribution of causal efficacy to the principles of true dialectic, cf. XI:300, 346, 400, 403; XII:113. (Hegel, by contrast, would have argued for a dialectical *Aufhebung* of the principles of "causality" and "production" themselves.)

7. See, for an especially illustrative example of Schelling's method, XI:396f.

8. *Philosophische Untersuchungen über das Wesen der menschlichen Freiheit und die damit zusammenhängenden Gegenstände* (the so-called *Freiheitsschrift*) VII:350; cf. J. Gutmann, trans., *Philosophical Inquiries into the Nature of Human Freedom* (La Salle, Ill.: Open Court, 1986), 24. Schelling would explicitly reaffirm this view many years later. Cf. XI:388.

9. XI:388, 419, 463f.

10. Ibid., 464. How this should be possible is admittedly difficult to conceive. We shall come back to this topic in connection with the theory of the pure *Daß* at the conclusion of this chapter.

11. Ibid., 423ff.; XII:36, 87.

12. XI:422, 491, 499f. Schelling quotes the Latin motto *omnia ex homine suspensa* (all things are dependent upon man), 500.

13. Ibid., 289; XII:52, 55.

14. XI:289, 292, 395. Generally, Schelling employs the plus/minus form of notation for the Potencies in their state of rest, whereas he reserves the superscript notation for symbolizing them in their subsequent phases. For purposes of greater simplicity and uniformity, I shall use the superscript notation throughout.

15. Ibid., 302; XII:52, 55.

16. XI:302. Schelling also seems to use the term *in-sich-Seiende* interchangeably with *an-sich-Seiende*. Cf. 290, 303.

17. XII:49.

18. XI:306, 319, 325f.

19. Ibid., 387 (note), 488; XII:31, 142, 263; XIII:66f.

20. XI:273f., 296f., 360. In some contexts, Schelling distinguishes between *Sein*, in a generically unspecified sense of "being," and *das Seiende,* in the sense of "predicable being" or "determinate being." Such is the case here, where *das vollendet Seiende* refers to a universal which is fully determinate. See below, note 49, p. 277.

21. Compare XI:378 with XII:35ff.

22. Xavier Tilliette, *La mythologie comprise* (Naples: Instituto Italiano per gli studi filosofici, 1984), 92.

23. XII:51. Schelling further distinguishes the "wantless will" *(nicht wollender Wille)* of A^1 from the "will-less wanting" *(willenloses Wollen)* of A^2. See, in addition, XII:36, 58, 87.

24. XI:307f., 387 (note); XII:31. Cf. Plato's *Sophist,* 237a–259a.

25. XII:37, 51.

26. Ibid., 51. For the religious manifestations of this Potency, both as primitive pantheism and also as the spirit of primal illusion (*Maya* in ancient India, Απάτη in Greece), see ibid., 68, 148f., 153, 482.

27. Ibid., 44, 49f.

28. Ibid., 53f.

29. XI:389; XII:50.

30. XI:288, 290.

31. Ibid., 395; XII:111.

32. See, for example, *Freiheitsschrift* VII:337f.; cf. trans., 8f. In defending the priority of unity over plurality, Schelling is of course typical of the post-Kantians.

33. XII:51.

34. Ibid. Distant recollections of this Potency in its original condition are reflected in Greek myths of the blissful existence enjoyed by the earliest living creatures in their springtime of innocence. The same theme is also found in Old Testament narratives concerning the Garden of Eden. Cf. ibid., 156ff.

35. Ibid., 55.

36. XI:303.

37. Cf. ibid., 312, 492.

38. XII:55f.

39. XI:290, 303; XII:57. Perhaps significantly, this preposition *bei* (as opposed

to *mit*) is the same word used in connection with the Logos in Luther's translation of John 1:1, "und das Wort war bei Gott" (and the Word was *with* God).

40. XI:393; XII:113. Cf. Plato's *Philebus*, 23b–27d.
41. XI:317; XII:55f.; XIII:77.
42. XI:395; XII:111.
43. Schelling expressly denies that either A^1 or A^2 can be ultimately *aufgehoben* in A^3. At most, they might be temporarily "suspended" *(suspendiert)* by one another. Cf. XII:85ff.
44. XI:397.
45. XII:57f. Note, however, that A^3 is as yet just the *essence* of spirit, conceived as a possibility, not the actuality thereof. Elsewhere, Schelling emphasizes that actual spirit transcends all three Potencies together. Cf. XI:419ff.
46. XII:56; cf. *Weltalter* VIII:301; cf. trans., 189f.
47. Hegel, *Wissenschaft der Logik* (1812), vol. 5 of *Werke*. Remark appended to the conclusion of the section on Quantity, 385–86.; cf. A. V. Miller, trans., *Hegel's Science of Logic* (London: George Allen & Unwin, 1969), 324–25. Schelling takes note of this passage in a comment written in the margin of his lecture notes of 1845–46; cf. XII:60.
48. XI:291ff., 313ff.; XII:80ff. Even A^2, the principle of stable, objective being (as opposed to the dynamic potentialities of amorphous flux contained in A^1), is so far only a pure possibility. In other words, A^2 represents the possible objectivity that still needs to be actualized.
49. XI:293, 313. The reader is again reminded that the term *das Seiende* usually means "determinate being" or "predicable being" in Schelling's texts. *Sein*, on the other hand, is a somewhat looser term signifying being in general, whether determinate or indeterminate. See above, note 20, p. 276.
50. XI:324.
51. Ibid., 311; cf. XII:88.
52. *Weltalter* VIII:266f.; cf. trans. 154ff.; also XII:164.
53. XI:387, note; cf. XII:31.
54. We shall return to the theory of God as the ultimate source of actuality in the next section of this chapter. As for concrete applications and exemplifications of the theory, these must await Part Three.
55. XI:388; XII:38.
56. XI:388.
57. *Weltalter* VIII:215; cf. trans., 101; also XI:391; XII:87.
58. *Weltalter* VIII:216f., 336; cf. trans., 101ff., 226; also XI:390; XII:85. Some of these terms hark back to Jakob Böhme. See above, p. 72.
59. *Weltalter* VIII:211; cf. trans., 97; also XII:84, 87.
60. This theory of a provisionally "necessary evil" as the means to an ultimate good is one of Schelling's most controversial ideas. It would earn him, for example, the bitter hostility of his erstwhile colleague and friend, Franz von Baader. See chapter 5, above, pp. 80–81.

61. XII:84.
62. XI:390; XII:91, 93, 111.
63. XI:391.
65. Ibid., 389f.
66. Ibid., 390, 396f.; XII:85, 110f. Again, Schelling expressly denies that either B or A² can be logically *aufgehoben* by A³. Cf. XII:364. The overcoming of the antagonism, he insists, cannot be resolved conceptually, but only in the context of experience.
67. See above, p. 107.
68. Schelling uses the terms *überexistierende* and *das Überexistierende*, or in other contexts *überseiende* and *das Überseiende*, to indicate that which transcends existence and being altogether. Because the terms "over-being" and "over-existing" sound odd in English, the German words will be preferred and left untranslated when feasible. See chapter 6, above, p. 103, note 30.
69. XI:403.
70. XII:89; XIII:256.
71. Cf. XI:401, 417, 489; XII:61. Not all scholars would agree with the interpretation given here. Walter Schulz, for example, seems to believe that the *Daß* is only a provisional manifestation of God, one that needs to be "negated" in turn at a subsequent stage of development. See his *Die Vollendung des Deutschen Idealismus in der Spätphilosophie Schellings* (Pfullingen: Neske, 1975), 296. Compare also my critical analysis of Schulz in chapter 9 of the present work.
72. Schelling's reading of Aristotle is original and unconventional. He maintains that the "pure Act" (ἐνέργεια) in Aristotle is completely separate and distinct from the mere idea (εἶδος) and from the universal (καθόλου); cf. XI:314ff., 352. Instead of being itself universal form, Aristotle's substance (οὐσία) becomes in Schelling's hands the intrinsically formless cause of essence (αἰτία τοῦ εἶναι); cf. XI:313, 362. Hence, Schelling argues that the copula in the the crucial Aristotelian phrase το τί ἦν εἶναι (which Schelling renders as "that which IS *das Seiende*"), must not be understood predicatively, as if οὐσία were identical with essence-being *(das Seiende)*, but transitively: οὐσία, he says, is that which "IS," in the special sense of a making-to-be. It is the source and cause of essence, yet in itself it remains distinct from the latter; cf. XI:362, 403ff., and XII:53. Schelling's unusual interpretation is qualified, to be sure, by a passage at XIII:104ff., where he admits that Aristotle's trans-essential Cause of all (which therefore should be prior to every *Was*), nevertheless functions in his philosophy only as the end-point toward which the world system aims, not as the beginning-point from which it originates. Hence Aristotle's God tends to merge with pure *Was,* and οὐσία becomes conflated with εἶδος after all (XIII:105). According to Schelling, this was Aristotle's greatest mistake. See the useful discussion of these issues by Joseph P. Lawrence, *Schellings Philosophie des ewigen Angangs* (Würzburg: Königshausen and Neumann, 1989), 93–117.
73. XI:319f.; cf. 401.
74. See *Weltalter Fragmente, Druck I* (1811), 66f. (top margin pagination:

I:121f.), also 84ff. (top margin pagination: I:154ff.). Compare *Philosophie der Mythologie* XII:392.
75. XI:401f., 417f.
76. Ibid., 420; cf. 462ff.
77. Ibid., 475, 483, 557. Schelling makes a pun in describing this reconciled spirit as the "wieder zur Seele gewordene Geist . . . mit Recht ein *seliger* genannt . . . " (475).
78. Ibid., 588; XII:53, 100.
79. XI:566, 568.
80. XII:100f.
81. Ibid.
82. See Von Hartmann, *Gesammelte Studien und Aufsätze gemeinverständlichen Inhalts* (Berlin: C. Duncker, 1876), 717–18.

Chapter 8. Positive Philosophy and the Experiential Proof of God

1. XI:251; cf. 5, 66f., 77, 199, 214f., 219.
2. XIII:114.
3. XI:194; XIII:113f., 119.
4. See, for example, XI:297–302, 326, 380.
5. XIII:128.
6. Cf. XI:189, 197f., 216; XII:127, 130f., 209, 526.
7. XI:9, 183f., 244.
8. Ibid., 251f.
9. Gerbrand Dekker, *Die Rückwendung zum Mythos. Schellings letzte Wandlung* (Munich/Berlin: R. Oldenbourg, 1930), 76–86.
10. Jürgen Habermas, "Das Absolute und die Geschichte. Von der Zwiespältigkeit in Schellings Denken" (Bonn: Ph.D. diss., Rheinische Friedrich Wilhelms Universität, 1954), 100–101. See also my critical commentary on Habermas's interpretation in chapter 9, pp. 164–69.
11. Xavier Tilliette, *Schelling. Une philosophie en devenir*, 2 vols. (Paris: Vrin, 1970), 2:44.
12. Ibid., 49.
13. XIII:156 and 167. See also chapter 6, above, note 17, p. 101.
14. XIII:169.
15. Ibid., 130, note.
16. Ibid., 151, note. Another note, written by Schelling's son and editor, Karl Friedrich August Schelling, mentions that earlier versions of his father's lecture drafts coined the terms "regressive empiricism" and "progressive empiricism" to describe a similar distinction (130). The latter would be the equivalent of *philosophia descendens.*
17. E.g., ibid., 129.

18. XI:571.
19. Tilliette, *Schelling,* 2:50. Cf. Schelling XIII:129.
20. Cf., e.g., XII:152, 263f.; XIII:66ff.
21. XI:240.
22. XII:115.
23. *System des transzendentalen Idealismus* III:604; cf. P. Heath, trans., *System of Transcendental Idealism (1800)* (Charlottesville: University Press of Virginia, 1978), 211f. See also VII:432f.; XIII:204, 261, 270.
24. XIII:131f.; cf. also XIV:8f.
25. XI:124; XIII:154.
26. XI:569.
27. Ibid., 239f., 474f., 557ff., 564ff., esp. 569; XIII:93, 160. Walter Kasper brings out this dimension of dialogue in Schelling's philosophical theology, contrasting it nicely to the dialectic of Hegel. Cf. *Das Absolute in der Geschichte. Philosophie und Theologie der Geschichte in der Spätphilosophie Schellings* (Mainz: Matthias-Grünewald, 1965), 22, 141, 368.
28. XIII:126f. One is reminded, in this connection, of Martin Buber's conception of the "I-thou" mode of relationship between the individual and God.
29. XI:402, 418; cf. 386f., 412f.
30. Ibid., 565. This statement may seem to conflict with those at XI:402 and elsewhere, which insist to the contrary that the *Daß* must be separated from the *Was.* Schelling's explanation is that although the *Was,* as the conditioned, predicative being, cannot be without the *Daß,* yet the *Daß,* for its part, as the transcendently causal being, is in principle free of the *Was.* Cf. XI:314f., 570.

Chapter 9. Representative Issues: Habermas and Schulz

1. Michael Theunissen, "Die Idealismuskritik in Schellings negativer Philosophie," in *Ist systematische Philosophie möglich? Hegel-Studien, Beihelf 17,* ed. D. Henrich (Bonn: Bouvier Verlag Herbert Grundmann, 1977), 185.
2. Jürgen Habermas, "Dialektischer Idealismus im Übergang zum Materialismus—Geschichtsphilosophische Folgerungen aus Schellings Idee einer Contraction Gottes," in *Theorie und Praxis* (Frankfurt a. M.: Suhrkamp, 1971, c. 1963), 172–227, esp. 215–19. (Unfortunately, this chapter has been omitted from the translation by J. Viertel.)
3. Jürgen Habermas, "Das Absolute und die Geschichte. Von der Zwiespältigkeit in Schellings Denken" (Bonn: Ph.D. diss., Rheinische Friedrich Wilhelms Universität, 1954).
4. Ibid., 7ff.
5. Habermas bases his discussion primarily on the recently discovered first draft of the *Weltalter* (1811), published as *Die Weltalter. Fragmente in den Urauffassungen von 1811 und 1813,* ed. Manfred Schröter (Munich: Biederstein Verlag und Leibniz Verlag, 1946). Habermas regards this manuscript as having

taken a more daring and original approach than Schelling's subsequent works did to the ontological foundations of human historicity and freedom.

6. Recall again Schelling's striking statement in the *Freiheitsschrift*, "There is, in the last and highest instance, no other Being *(Sein)* at all than Will *(Wollen)*. Will is primordial Being *(Ursein)* . . . " VII:350; cf. trans. J. Gutmann, *Philosophical Inquiries into the Nature of Human Freedom* (La Salle, Ill.: Open Court, 1986), 24.

7. "Das Absolute und die Geschichte," 313ff.; cf. 380.

8. Ibid., 315.

9. *Weltalter Fragmente*, 94 (top margin pagination: I:172).

10. Ibid., 96 (top margin pagination: I:175).

11. Schelling is fully cognizant of this danger, but regards a developmental conception of the Deity as especially necessary for Christianity. See XIV:162.

12. "Das Absolute und die Geschichte," 10.

13. Ibid., 118. Habermas's interpretation of Schelling's development is controversial. Manfred Durner, for example, has argued to the contrary that it was only after Schelling's Erlangen phase (1821–25) that he was finally able to break out of the tendency to logicize actuality and freedom. Cf. *Wissen und Geschichte bei Schelling. Eine Interpretation der ersten Erlanger Vorlesung* (Munich: J. Berchmans, 1979), 248ff.

14. "Das Absolute und die Geschichte," 101. See also chapter 8, above, p. 154.

15. "Das Absolute und die Geschichte," 91. Cf. Schelling: XI:249, 317, 412; XIII:292.

16. In addition to earlier texts like VII:432f., emphasizing that change and becoming are fundamental to a living Deity, see also such striking passages as XIII:204, 261, and 270, where Schelling insists that God's being is essentially a future-being.

17. "Das Absolute und die Geschichte," 111. Along similar lines, Joseph A. Bracken notes a "fundamental tension" in Schelling's thought between the principles of freedom and causality. See his *Freiheit und Kausalität bei Schelling* (Freiburg/Munich:: K. Alber, 1972), 110–11, 121–22.

18. "Das Absolute und die Geschichte," 387, 115.

19. Walter Kasper, *Das Absolute in der Geschichte. Philosophie und Theologie der Geschichte in der Spätphilosophie Schellings* (Mainz: Matthias-Grünewald Verlag, 1965).

20. For two representative examples of Schelling's endorsement and use of empirical methods, see XII:263 and 527.

21. See the important arguments in the foreword and introduction to his *Freiheitsschrift* VII:333–57; cf. trans., 3–31.

22. Walter Schulz, *Die Vollendung des Deutschen Idealismus in der Spätphilosophie Schellings*, 2d ed. (Pfullingen: Neske, 1975). The 1st ed. appeared in 1955. Schulz summarized his arguments and conclusions in a paper of the same name delivered at the centennial Schelling convention at Bad Ragaz, Switzerland. See *Verhandlung der Schelling-Tagung in Bad Ragaz (Schweiz) vom 22. bis 25.*

September 1954, vol. 14 of *Studia Philosophica, Jahrbuch der schweizerischen philosophischen Gesellschaft* (Basel: Verlag für Recht und Gesellschaft, 1954), 239–55. In the second, 1975 edition of his book, Schulz republished this paper as the concluding chapter, 321–33.

23. Walter Schulz, "Macht und Ohnmacht der Vernunft," in *Schelling. Seine Bedeutung für eine Philosophie der Natur und der Geschichte: Referate und Kolloquien der Internationalen Schelling-Tagung in Zürich, 1979*, ed. L. Hasler (Stuttgart-Bad Cannstatt: Frommann-Holzboog, 1981), 21–33.
24. *Vollendung*, 287ff.
25. Ibid., 327.
26. Ibid., 323.
27. Ibid., 324.
28. Ibid., 290–91.; see also "Macht und Ohnmacht," 27.
29. X:276.
30. See, for example, Hegel's *Enzyklopädie der philosophichen Wissenschaften*, vol. 8 of *Werke: Theorie Werkausgabe*, 20 vols., ed. E. Moldenhauer and K. M. Michel (Frankfurt am Main: Suhrkamp, 1970), secs. 192 and 204, pp. 344–45, 359–61; cf. W. Wallace, trans., *The Logic of Hegel*, 2d ed. (London: Oxford University Press, 1892), pp. 327–29, 343–46. Also *Enzyklopädie*, vol. 10 of *Werke*, sec. 552, pp. 354–55.; cf. A. V. Miller, trans., *The Philosophy of Mind* (Oxford: Clarendon Press, 1977), 282–83.
31. XIII:165f.
32. *Vollendung*, 333.
33. Ibid., 314, note.
34. Ibid., 290.
35. Ibid., 72.
36. "Macht und Ohnmacht," 33.
37. See, for example, Schelling's comments at XI:463, note; also XIII:153.
38. *Vollendung*, 324. Schulz is on solid ground at least as far as the rejection of sense-data empiricism is concerned; see XI:298ff.
39. *Vollendung*, 325.
40. XIII:119ff.
41. Ibid., 113.
42. Xavier Tilliette, *Schelling. Une philosophie en devenir*, 2 vols. (Paris: Vrin, 1970), 2:70–77, esp. 74.
43. XI:316. Schelling frequently writes in this vein: see, for example, XI:326.
44. *Vollendung*, 296.
45. See Kant's *Kritik der reinen Vernunft* (1787), vol. 3 of *Gesammelte Schriften*, ed. Preussische Akademie der Wissenschaften, 20 vols. (Berlin: G. Reimer, 1900–1942), 385ff. (B599ff.); cf. Norman Kemp Smith, trans., *Critique of Pure Reason* (Toronto: Macmillan, 1929), 487ff.
46. *Vollendung*, 333.
47. XI:285.

48. *Vollendung,* 326.
49. Ibid., 292. For other passages in Schulz tending to equate Schelling's God with absolute reason, cf. 68, 79–80, 82, 89–90.
50. Ibid., 296.
51. Ibid.

Chapter 10. From Uranus to Cronus

1. There is a potentially confusing discrepancy in Schelling's technical nomenclature as between the "Historical-Critical Introduction" and the main body of the *Philosophie der Mythologie.* In the former work, the god of the first Potency is designated as "god A," whereas the god of the second Potency is called "god B," the third Potency being there left unnamed. See XI: 130, 136f., 148f. The source of the discrepancy seems to lie in the different orders of appearance of the principles in question. Thus, because the god of the first Potency was the first to emerge on the stage of human history, he is labeled "god A" in the "Historical-Critical Introduction." In purely logical terms, however, this was a secondary product of a transcendental inversion from A^1 (the first Potency at rest) to B (the same Potency in a condition of tension); hence, from the "Philosophical Introduction" onward, the god of the first Potency is redesignated as "god B." Names of the god of the second Potency are also modified accordingly.

For the sake of greater clarity and consistency, the present study will use throughout the terminology of the "Philosophical Introduction" and following volumes.

2. The thesis that Greek mythology was paradigmatic, and therefore suitable to use as the prime example for the study of all pagan religions, was also central to Creuzer's *Symbolik und Mythologie der alten Völker, besonders der Griechen,* 6 vols. (Leipzig und Darmstadt: Heyer & Leske, 1819–23), which greatly influenced Schelling. The latter's adoption of this (admittedly dubious) thesis is the reason I have followed him in concentrating on Greek religion to illustrate his philosophy of mythology.

3. XII:279.

4. Ibid., 278. Herodotus also made the following other identifications: Amon = Zeus, Min = Pan, Set = Ares, Isis = Demeter, Bast = Artemis, Neith = Athena, Hathor = Aphrodite. Cf. *Histories,* bk. 2, chaps. 41, 42, 49, 50, 59, 83. Herodotus is among the most frequently cited authorities in Schelling's lectures on mythology.

5. See above, p. 122–23.

6. XII:127f. For Schelling's appraisal of Hermann, see chapter 2, above, note 4, p. 258.

7. For a fuller discussion of this traditional approach to non-Christian religions, see chapter 1, above, pp. 17–23.

8. (Georg) Friedrich Creuzer, *Symbolik und Mythologie der alten Völker,*

besonders der Griechen, 1:6ff. See also chapter 1, above, p. 22. Creuzer drew upon Herodotus as one of his primary sources of evidence for this theory. See the *Histories,* bk. 2, chaps. 49–57.

9. Creuzer, *Symbolik* 2:428. Yet cf. 1:523, n. 307; and compare Schelling's critical comment, XII:288.
10. XI:76f., 89ff., 137ff., 177.
11. XII:289.
12. Ibid., 125ff. For the relation of mythology to language, see XI:50ff., 65.
13. XI:100ff., 111, 129. For further references see below, note 33.
14. XI:110f.
15. Ibid., 65, 109; cf. V:287.
16. XII:247, 254, 277, 311.
17. Ibid., 592, 671.
18. Karl-Heinz Volkmann-Schluck, *Mythos und Logos. Interpretationen zu Schellings Philosophie der Mythologie* (Berlin: de Gruyter, 1969), offers a more or less Heideggerian reading of Schelling's treatment of mythology, emphasizing especially those principles and deities that symbolize undifferentiated Being. (Schelling's ideas about the opposed deities that represent differentiation and civilization receive relatively scant attention from this writer.)
19. XII:190ff. The term "real" does not imply that any other gods would be "unreal." It serves, rather, to emphasize the sheer spatiotemporal existence of B. A^2, by contrast, will be described as "the relatively spiritual god."
20. Schelling frequently writes of the "analogy between the epochs of nature and the successive periods or moments of mythology" (XI:216; cf. XII:356). For more on Kielmeyer, see chapter 3, above, note 18, pp. 264–65.
21. XI:178; cf. 119.
22. Ibid., 103f.
23. Ibid., 251; cf. 9, 219, 251.
24. Ibid., 127f.
25. XII:35ff. The term *potentia existendi* obviously harks back to the designation of the first Potency as *das sein Könnende.*
26. Ibid., 43f.
27. XI:29f., 59, 76f., 178; see also chapter 2, above, p. 39 and note 43, p. 261.
28. XIII:386; cf. XII:267, 356; XIII:398, 435.
29. XI:103f., 233f.; XII:35ff., 182ff.
30. XI:94ff.; XII:182.
31. XI:101ff., 133ff.; XII:541ff. According to Schelling, ancient Chinese was the closest descendant in historical times from this primitive *Ursprache* (XII: 541ff.). His primary source on the Chinese and other Eastern languages was the work of Jean Pierre Abel Rémusat, *Éléments de la grammaire chinoise* (Paris: Imprimerie royal, 1822). The same Rémusat also had a considerable influence on the linguistic theories of Wilhelm von Humboldt.
32. XI:127, 144.
33. Ibid., 121; XII:172.

34. XI:89, 137; XII:643.
35. XI:139f., 164.
36. For more on the "Great Spiritual Crisis," cf. XI:19, 24, 100ff., 233.
37. XII:205ff.
38. XI:145ff., 161ff.; XII:47f., 95, 165, 304.
39. XII:156ff.
40. See above, pp. 117, 119.
41. See above, pp. 130–32.
42. XII:171, 253. Much later in the dialectical development, Schelling will argue that the first Potency must return to the position of the "Center." At that point, however, it will no longer be there for the sake of self-aggrandizement, nor will it any longer be in the role of an "actual" being, but will have voluntarily returned to the subordinate status of being an eternal "potentiality." Cf. ibid., 579, 643f.
43. Ibid., 173.
44. Ibid.; cf. XIII:388.
45. XII:179f. A more customary form of the same word is "Sabeism," but Schelling offers reasons why the other spelling is preferable.
46. Ibid., 174f.
47. Ibid., 174; cf. 187.
48. See, e.g., Wilhelm Schmidt, *The Origin and Growth of Religion. Facts and Theories,* trans. H. J. Rose (London: Methuen, 1935, c. 1931), 251–90; E. E. Evans-Pritchard, *Nuer Religion* (New York and Oxford: Oxford University Press, 1956), 1–27; Mircea Eliade, *Myth and Reality* (New York and Evanston: Harper & Row, 1963), 92–113; Geoffrey Parrinder, *African Traditional Religion* (New York: Harper & Row, 1976, c. 1962), 31–43; John S. Mbiti, *African Religions and Philosophy* (Garden City, N.Y.: Anchor Books, 1970), 37–96.
49. XI:168; XII:182, 637; XIII:419, 436f.
50. XI:99f., 108.
51. See above, p. 117.
52. XII:273f., 300. Compare 182ff., where Schelling describes the sense of well-being associated with the originally unencumbered Zabism.
53. Ibid., 269.
54. Ibid., 274, 288, 323.
55. Ibid., 271, 286ff.
56. Cf. Hesiod's *Theogony,* lines 154–89.
57. XII:292. In contrast, cf. Aristotle, *De mundo,* chap. 7. For a modern structuralist attempt to interpret the Cronus motif in relation to time, see Edmund R. Leach, *Rethinking Anthropology* (London: Athlone Press, University of London, 1961), 124ff. Leach notes, however, that there is no close etymological connection between the Greek words κρόνος and χρόνος. To that extent, but probably no further, Schelling would have agreed.
58. XII:288.
59. Ibid., 293, 298ff., 340. Schelling does not appear to distinguish clearly

between El and Baal. A principal source of information regarding the Phoenician religion was Sanchuniathon (fl. 14th–13th centuries B.C.E.), fragments of whose works were transmitted via Philo of Byblos (64–141 C.E.) and Eusebius (260–340 C.E.); cf. the latter's *De evangelica praeparatione.* Schelling cites these authorities at XII:303, 306, 312.

60. XII:300.
61. For Herakles, see ibid., 308; for Melkart, 307; for Isaac, 304.
62. Ibid., 298, 321f.
63. XIII:401.
64. XII:275, 307, 311, 372.
65. Cf. ibid., 304, 312f., 335, 371.
66. Ibid., 313, 324.
67. Cf. ibid., 315ff.
68. Ibid., 321ff.
69. Cf. Sigmund Freud, *Totem und Tabu* (c. 1913), in vol. 9 of *Gesammelte Werke. Chronologisch geordnet,* ed. A. Freud et al. (London: Imago, 1961), chap. 4, paras. 5–7, pp. 169–94; cf. J. Strachey, trans., *Totem and Taboo,* in vol. 13 of *The Standard Edition of the Complete Psychological Works of Sigmund Freud* (London: Routledge & Kegan Paul, 1950), 141–61.
70. Cf. above, pp. 11, 102.
71. XII:298.
72. Ibid., 238ff., 248f., 299, 363.
73. Ibid., 299f.; cf. 369, 646; XIII:432. In the last of these passages, Schelling indicates that the word derives from a character named Deisidæmon in Theophrastus's *Characters.*

Chapter 11. From Dionysus to Iakchos

1. XII:193, 616.
2. Ibid., 173.
3. Ibid., 193.
4. Ibid., 194, 200, 249, 253ff., 261, 274; XIII:390. Despite the Greek name conferred on her by Herodotus and adopted by Schelling, this goddess is not to be confused with one of the Greek Muses. She was, rather, an ancient Middle Eastern deity known variously as Ishtar, Asherat, Astarte, and Alilat. Worshipped as the goddess of fertility, sexuality, motherhood, and life in general, she was associated by Schelling with the first agricultural civilizations; cf. XII:254.
5. XII:352ff., 570; XIII:395.
6. Cf. XII:262, 353; XIII:396.
7. XII:261, 616. In the final stages, however, the gender roles of the progressive versus the regressive were reversed, according to Schelling. This explains why Hera was always represented as anxious and mean-spirited, the implacable enemy of A^2 in his manifestation as Herakles; cf. XII:261, 335.

8. See above, pp. 124–25.
9. XII:616, 626.
10. Ibid., 628ff.; XIII:411ff.
11. XII:616.
12. Cf. ibid., 194, 249, 349f., 363, 381.
13. Ibid., 274.
14. Ibid., 254. It is unclear exactly who these ancient people were. Schelling observes that they evidently practiced agriculture and built cities, for which reason he designates them as "Arabians," in contradistinction to the nomadic "Arabs" of the desert. Possibly these "Arabians" were Amorites.
15. Ibid., 255. Cf. Herodotus, *Histories,* bk. 3, chap. 8. A modern English translation by H. Carter has: "They acknowledge no gods other than Dionysus and Urania . . . " Quoted from *The Histories of Herodotus* (New York: Heritage Press, 1958), 169. On this reading, of course, the intriguing linguistic clue that Schelling fastens upon would lose its significance.
16. XII:340f.
17. Ibid., 293f.
18. XI:168; XII:637; XIII:436f.
19. XII:306f., 380; XIII:437.
20. XII:275.
21. Ibid., 337.
22. Ibid., 254.
23. Ibid., 288f.
24. Ibid., 255, 348. Schelling also says something very similar with respect to the myths of Persephone (ibid., 161) and Demeter (ibid., 631), but this is hardly surprising in view of the fact that he also identifies these goddesses with aspects of Dionysus himself.
25. Ibid., 208.
26. Friedrich Wilhelm Nietzsche, *Die Geburt der Tragödie. Oder: Griechenthum und Pessimismus* (Leipzig: E. W. Fritzsch, 1871); cf. trans. W. Kaufmann, *The Birth of Tragedy* (New York: Vintage Books, 1967).
27. XII:386f., 638f.; XIII:421, 436. See also chapter 2, above, especially pp. 38–39.
28. XIII:436f. Note that Cronus was himself one of the Titans.
29. Ibid., 435. Some corroboration of this view may be found in an article on the Maenads in the *Encyclopedia of Religion and Ethics* (Edinburgh: T. & T. Clark, 1908–26), 8:240. The writer observes that alcoholic intoxication played no part in the original rites.
30. Schelling observes in passing that Socrates had a similarly maddening effect on Athenian society, XII:285.
31. Ibid., 276. The line of Horace comes from book 3 of his *Carmina* (Odes), no. 25: "Whither, Bacchus, dost thou hurry me . . . ?"
32. Cf. *Die Stuttgarter Privatvorlesungen,* VII:469ff., and *Die Weltalter,* VIII:337ff.; cf. trans. F. de Wolfe Bolman, Jr., *The Ages of the World* (New York:

AMS Press, 1967 c 1942), 227ff. In the latter passage, he characterizes the absence of all capacity for such controlled madness as the condition of idiocy.

33. Plato, *Phaedrus,* 244a–45d.
34. XII:351.
35. XI:103f., 178; XII:368, 380; XIII:388. See also above, pp. 133 and 186–88.
36. Cf. XIII:435f.
37. XII:321, 341, 343. These passages refer primarily to the Heraklean myth cycle. Recall that Herakles is for Schelling a form of Dionysus himself (348).
38. XIII:386f.
39. Ibid., 468f.
40. Ibid.
41. Ibid., 496. "Typhon" is a Greek name used by Herodotus for the Egyptian god Set, the fierce enemy of Osiris. For Schelling, Set was the Egyptian equivalent of Cronus, just as Osiris corresponded to Dionysus. For more on the connection between the "Titans" and "tension," cf. XII:385.
42. XII:88, 124; XIII:473.
43. Anna Freud, *Das Ich und die Abwehrmechanismen* (Vienna: Internationaler psycho-analytischer Verlag, 1936), 127; cf. C. Baines, trans., *The Ego and the Mechanisms of Defense* (New York: International Universities Press, 1946), 119.
44. XIII:435f.
45. XII:385.
46. Ibid., 276.
47. Ibid., 391.
48. Ibid.
49. See especially pp. 118–19, 127.
50. Schelling designates this ultimate vocation of the reintegrated first Potency as the "God-positing consciousness" *(das Gott-setzende Bewußtsein),* XI:197f. Cf. also ibid., 391; XII:85.
51. XII:623ff.
52. Ibid., 634.
53. XIII:483f.
54. XII:569f.
55. XIII:476.
56. Ibid., 477.
57. XII:642; XIII:507. Cf. Pausanias, *Description of Greece,* bk. 8, chap. 31, (4); trans. J. G. Frazer (New York: Biblo & Tannen, 1965), 1:414.
58. Cf. XII:582, 664.
59. XIII:481.
60. Edward Geoffrey Parrinder, *African Traditional Religions* (New York: Harper & Row, 1976, c. 1962), 36ff.
61. Mircea Eliade, *Myth and Reality,* trans. W. R. Trask (New York: Harper & Row, 1963), 92–113.
62. Ibid., 109.

63. Ibid., 99.
64. Ibid., 95f.
65. XII:587ff.
66. Ibid., 589f.
67. XIII:428f.; cf. *Weltalter* VIII:268, 339; cf. trans., 156, 229f.
68. Xavier Tilliette, *La mythologie comprise* (Naples: Instituto Italiano per gli studi filosofici, 1984), 105.
69. Ibid., 107.
70. *Weltalter* VIII:337; cf. trans., 227. Also cf. XII:427.
71. VII:439.
72. XII:649; cf. XIII:471.
73. Schelling's theory that the Homeric world was based on the Mysteries should be compared to Friedrich Creuzer *Symbolik under Mythologie der alten Völker, besonders der Griechen,* 6 vols. (Leipzig and Darmstadt: Heyer & Leske, 1819–23), 1:111, 113, 121, 206, 208.
74. Cf. Freud's essay, "Das Unheimliche" (1919), in vol. 12 of *Gesammelte Werke* (London: Imago, 1952–68), 235–36, 254–55; cf. A. Strachey, trans., "The Uncanny," in vol. 17 of *The Standard Edition of the Complete Psychological Works of Sigmund Freud* (London: Hogarth Press, 1955), 225–26, 241. (The original version of the essay attributed this idea to Schleiermacher rather than Schelling. The error was corrected in later editions.)

Further anticipations by Schelling of Freudian concepts—in particular the theories of inhibition and repression as functionally constitutive of conscious life—can be found in Odo Marquard, "Schelling—Zeitgenosse incognito," in *Schelling. Einführung in seine Philosophie,* ed. H. M. Baumgartner (Freiburg/Munich: K. Alber, 1975), 21–22. See also chap. 3, note 9, p. 263.

75. Cf. Paul Ricoeur, "The Critique of Religion," trans. R. B. DeFord, first published in *Union Seminary Quarterly Review* 28 (1973): 205–12; reprinted in *The Philosophy of Paul Ricoeur,* ed. C. E. Reagan and D. Steward (Boston: Beacon Press, 1978), 213–22.
76. Ricoeur, too, advocates a return to faith, but faith of a special kind. "No longer, to be sure, the first faith of the simple soul, but rather the second faith of the one who has engaged in hermeneutics, faith that has undergone criticism, postcritical faith." See his *De l'interpretation: Essai sur Freud* (Paris: Seuil, 1965), 36–37.; cf. D. Savage, trans., *Freud and Philosophy: An Essay on Interpretation* (New Haven and London: Yale University Press, 1970), 28.

Chapter 12. The Self-Overcoming of Mythology

1. XI:125, 198. See also the discussion of "metaphysical empiricism" in chapter 8, above, p. 148. Unlike dramatic scripts or musical scores, of course, myths are not the productions of individual artists.
2. XI:420, 463.

3. XII:84ff., 122, 144, 266; XIII:499. See also above, pp. 133–34.
4. XII:91.
5. VII:459, 482; *Die Weltalter* VIII:266ff.; cf. F. de Wolfe Bolman, Jr., trans., *The Ages of the World* (New York: AMS Press, 1967, c. 1942), 154ff. Also XII:38, 582. Baader's influence is much in evidence here; see chapter 5, above, 79–82.
6. XII:260f.; XIII:454.
7. XII:127f.
8. XIII:388; cf. XII:173f.
9. See chapter 7, above, pp. 136–42.
10. X:276.
11. XI:586ff.
12. XII:90.
13. Paul Tillich, "Die religionsgeschichtliche Konstruktion in Schellings positiver Philosophie, ihre Vorassetzungen und Prinzipien" (Ph.D. diss., Universität Breslau; Breslau: H. Fleischman, 1910), 37–38. Cf. V. Nuovo, trans., *The Construction of the History of Religion in Schelling's Positive Philosophy: Its Presuppositions and Principles* (Lewisburg, Pa.: Bucknell University Press, 1974), 67–69..
14. XII:571.
15. XI:566.
16. XII:100.
17. XI:315f. Recall, in this connection, the discussion of Walter Schulz's differing interpretation in chapter 9, above, pp. 169–75.
18. Cf. Christian August Lobeck, *Aglaophamus; sive, De theologiae mysticae Graecorum causis libri tres* (Königsberg: Borntraeger, 1829); Johan Friedrich Voß, *Mythologische Briefe*, 2d ed. (Stuttgart: J. B. Metzler, 1827–34; c. 1794). Schelling discusses Voß's and Lobeck's views at XIII:443, 453, 457, 479, 486, 505.
19. Discussion of Creuzer is provided at pp. 22 and 183–84, above. See also Guillaume Emmanuel Joseph Guilhem de Clermont-Lodève, Baron de Sainte-Croix, *Recherches historiques et critiques sur les mystères du paganisme* (Paris: De Bure, 1817, c. 1784). For Schelling's evaluations of Creuzer's and St. Croix's opinions, cf. XIII:453, 460, 475, 488, 498f., 503, 516.
20. XIII:501. Cf. William Warburton, Bp. of Gloucester, *The Divine Legation of Moses Demonstrated*, in nine books, 4th ed. (London: Millar & Tonson, 1765), 1:188–392.
21. XIII:453.
22. Ibid., 500–506.
23. Ibid., 494, cf. 443.
24. Ibid., 503.
25. Ibid., 463. On the mystical identification of the god of the underworld with the god of life, the testimony of Heraclitus (though not mentioned by Schelling) gives independent confirmation: "If it were not in honor of Dionysus that they conducted the procession and sang the hymn to the male organ, their activity would be completely shameless. But Hades is the same as Dionysus, in whose honor they

rave and perform the Bacchic revels . . . " (DK, fr. 15, in *Ancilla to the Pre-Socratic Philosophers: A Complete Translation of the Fragments in Diels, "Fragmente der Vorsokratiker,"* trans. K. Freeman (Cambridge: Harvard University Press, 1956), 25. See also W. K. C. Guthrie, *A History of Greek Philosophy* (Cambridge: At the University Press, 1962), 1:473–82, esp. 475–76.

26. XIII:482–90.

27. Ibid., 490.

28. Cf. Manfred Frank, *Der kommende Gott. Vorlesungen über die Neue Mythologie* (Frankfurt a. M.: Suhrkamp, 1982), 296.

29. Christoph Jamme has observed that on this point Schelling's interpretation of the Melkart-Herakles myth motif most sharply diverges from the views of his contemporaries, including Hegel. Cf. Jamme, *Neuzeit und Gegenwart*, vol. 2 of *Einführung in die Philosophie des Mythos*, by Luc Brisson and Christoph Jamme (Darmstadt: Wissenschaftliche Buchgesellschaft, 1991), 70.

30. XII:317. For Schelling's extensive discussion of Christianity, see the *Philosophie der Offenbarung*, in *Sämmtliche Werke*, vol. XIV. Brief synopses of the role of Christ may be found in Paul Tillich, *Die religionsgeschichtliche Konstruktion in Schellings positiver Philosophie* (Breslau: M. Fleischmann, 1910), 119–22, 164–68; cf. V. Nuovo, trans., *The Construction of the History of Religion in Schelling's Positive Philosophy: Its Presuppositions and Principles* (Lewisburg, Pa.: Bucknell University Press, 1974), 109–12, 154–58. See also Xavier Tilliette, *La mythologie comprise* (Naples: Instituto Italiano per gli studi filosofici, 1984), 118–22.

31. XIII:406; cf. 511f. and XII:346.

32. XIII:488.

33. XI:198; XII:120f.

34. See Brunner's 1934 essay, *Natur und Gnade; zum Gespräch mit Karl Barth* (Zurich: Zwingli Verlag, 1935); cf. P. Fraenkel, trans., *Natural Theology; comprising "Nature and Grace" by Emil Brunner and the reply "No!" by Karl Barth* (London: G. Blecs: Centenary Press, 1946); Brunner's essay, 15–64.

35. Karl Barth, *Nein! Antwort an Emil Brunner* (Munich: C. Kaiser, 1934); cf. P. Fraenkel, trans., *Natural Theology*, 67–128. For a good summary and analysis of the Brunner-Barth controversy, cf. Garrett Green, *Imagining God: Theology and the Religious Imagination* (New York: Harper & Row, 1989), 28–40. It should be noted that Barth's position changed considerably after 1934, but I am addressing only his classical, neo-orthodox period.

36. XI:566.

37. XII:439ff., 570f.; XIII:127, 403, 405f.

38. XIII:126f. For more on the relation between intuitive insight and rationally mediated knowledge in Schelling, see above, pp. 100–109.

39. XII:646f.

Bibliography

Bibliographies and Bibliographical Studies

(Entries in this first section are arranged chronologically. Brief statements indicate the periods and selective principles employed by the respective bibliographies.)

Schneeberger, Guido. *Friedrich Wilhelm Joseph von Schelling. Eine Bibliographie.* Bern: Francke, 1954. A virtually complete listing of works by and about Schelling up to 1953.

Sandkühler, Hans Jörg. *Friedrich Wilhelm Joseph Schelling,* 24–41. Stuttgart: Metzler, 1970. Extends Schneeberger's list, covering the years 1954 to 1969, with much useful supplementary material.

Zeltner, Hermann. *Schelling-Forschung seit 1954.* Darmstadt: Wissenschaftliche Buchgesellschaft, 1975. Covers works published between 1954 and 1975.

Schieche, Walter. "Bibliographie." In *Schelling. Einführung in seine Philosophie,* edited by Hans Michael Baumgartner, 178–201. Freiburg/Munich: Alber, 1975.

O'Meara, Thomas Franklin. "F. W. J. Schelling: A Bibliographic Essay." *Review of Metaphysics* 31, no. 2 (Dec. 1977): 283–309. Provides a fine overview of Schelling studies up to 1977, including a critical evaluation of other Schelling bibliographies. Concludes with a discussion of works done in English.

Procesi-Xella, Lidea. "Filosofia e Mitologia in Schelling. Le interpretazioni del '900." *Annali della Scuola Normale di Pisa,* ser. 3, vol. 9, no. 3 (1979): 1293–1323. Reviews the reception and critical reactions in twentieth-century scholarship to Schelling's philosophy of mythology.

Major Editions of Schelling's Collected Works

(In this section, the three major editions of Schelling's collected works are listed chronologically in relation to each other. Their respective strengths, organizational principles, and aims are also briefly noted.)

Schelling, Friedrich Wilhelm Joseph von. *Friedrich Wilhelm Joseph von Schellings sämmtliche Werke.* Edited by Karl Friedrich A. Schelling. 14 vols. Stuttgart/

Augsburg: J. G. Cotta'scher Verlag, 1856–61. Issued in two divisions, but with continuously numbered volumes in Roman numerals I–XIV. This is still the standard edition of Schelling's works, to which the scholarly literature regularly refers. Following are the titles of individual works cited from this edition, preceded by their volume numbers. Dates in parentheses are the approximate dates of completion by Schelling, not necessarily dates of publication.

I: 43–83. *Über Mythen, historische Sagen und Philosopheme der ältesten Welt* (1793).

III: 327–634. *System des transzendentalen Idealismus* (1800).

IV: 333–510. *Fernere Darstellungen aus dem System der Philosophie* (1802).

V: 207–510. *Vorlesungen über die Methode des akademischen Studiums* (1802).

VI: 11–70. *Philosophie und Religion* (1804).

VII: 331–416. *Philosophische Untersuchungen über das Wesen der menschlichen Freiheit und die damit zusammenhängenden Gegenstände* (1809).

VII: 417–84. *Denkmal der Schrift von den göttlichen Dingen usw. des Herrn Friedrich Heinrich Jacobi und der ihm in derselben gemachten Beschuldigungen eines absichtlich täuschenden, Lüge redenden Atheismus* (1812).

VIII: 195–244. *Die Weltalter* (1813).

VIII: 345–69. *Über die Gottheiten von Samothrake* (1815).

IX: 207–52. *Erlanger Vorträge* (1821).

X: 1–200. *Zur Geschichte der neueren Philosophie* (1827).

X: 225–86. *Darstellung des philosophischen Empirismus* (1830).

XI: 1–252. *Historisch-kritische Einleitung in die Philosophie der Mythologie* (1842).

XI: 253–572. *Philosophische Einleitung in die Philosophie der Mythologie oder Darstellung der rein-rationalen Philosophie* (1847ff.).

XI: 575–90. *Abhandlung über die Quelle der ewigen Wahrheiten* (1850).

XII: 1–132. *Philosophie der Mythologie. Erstes Buch, Der Monotheismus* (1842).

XII: 133–674. *Philosophie der Mythologie. Zweites Buch, Die Mythologie* (1842).

XIII: 1–174. *Einleitung in die Philosophie der Offenbarung oder Begründung der positiven Philosophie* (1841).

XIII: 177–530. *Philosophie der Offenbarung. Erster Teil* (1841ff.).

XIV: 1–344. *Philosophie der Offenbarung. Zweiter Teil* (1841ff.).

Schelling, Friedrich Wilhelm Joseph von. *Schellings Werke. Nach der Original Ausgabe in neuer Anordnung.* Edited by Manfred Schröter. 6 vols. and 6 supplementary vols. Munich: C. H. Beck and R. Oldenbourg, 1927–59. Somewhat arbitrarily rearranged according to the whims of the editor, this edition fortunately retains the volume and page numbers of the Cotta edition in the margins.

———. *Friedrich Wilhelm Joseph Schelling. Historisch-kritische Ausgabe.* Edited by H. Krings and W. Jacobs. Stuttgart: Frommann-Holzboog, 1976– . A meticulously detailed work, projected eventually to number eighty volumes, of which only the first few have appeared. Unfortunately, this critical edition is not expected to reach Schelling's late period, including his final *Philosophie der Mythologie,* until the mid-twenty-first century.

Further Writings by Schelling, Not Included in Collected Works

(Listed chronologically in order of composition.)

Schelling, Friedrich Wilhelm Joseph von, *Aus Schellings Leben. In Briefen.* Edited by G. L. Plitt. 3 vols. Leipzig: S. Hirzel, 1869–70.

———. *F. W. J. Schelling: Briefe und Dokumente.* Edited by H. Fuhrmans. 3 vols. Bonn: H. Bouvier, 1962–73.

———. *Die Weltalter. Fragmente in den Urauffassungen von 1811 und 1813.* Edited by Manfred Schröter. Munich: Biederstein and Leibniz, 1946.

———. *Einleitung in die Philosophie* (1830). Edited by Walter E. Ehrhardt. Stuttgart/Bad Cannstatt: Frommann-Holzboog, 1989.

———. *Grundlegung der positiven Philosophie: Münchner Vorlesung WS 1832/33 und SS 1833.* Edited by Horst Fuhrmanns. Turin: Bottega D'Erasmo, 1972.

———. *F. W. J. Schelling: Das Tagebuch 1848.* Edited by Hans Jörg Sandkühler. Hamburg: Meiner, 1990.

English Translations of Schelling

(Listed chronologically in order of composition.)

Schelling, Friedrich Wilhelm Joseph von, *Ideas for a Philosophy of Nature* (1797). Translated by Errol E. Harris and Peter Heath. Cambridge: Cambridge University Press, 1988.

———. *System of Transcendental Idealism* (1800). Translated by Peter Heath.

———. *Bruno; or, On the Natural and the Divine Principles of Things* (1802). Edited and translated by Michael G. Vater. Albany: SUNY Press, 1984.

———. *On University Studies* (1802). Translated by E. S. Morgan. Athens: Ohio University Press., 1966.

———. *The Philosophy of Art* (1803). Translated by Douglas W. Stott. Minneapolis: University of Minnesota Press, 1989.

———. *Schelling: Of Human Freedom* (1809). Translated by James Gutmann. La Salle, Ill.: Open Court, 1986.

———. *Schelling: The Ages of the World* (1813). Translated by Frederick de Wolfe Bolman, Jr. New York: Columbia University Press, 1942; reprint New York: AMS Press, 1967.

———. *Schelling's Treatise on "The Deities of Samothrace"* (1815). Translated by Robert F. Brown. Missoula, Mont.: Scholars Press for the American Academy of Religion, 1976.

———. *On the History of Modern Philosophy* (1827). Translated by Andrew Bowie. Cambridge: Cambridge University Press, 1984.

———. *On the Source of the Eternal Truths* (1850). Translated by Edward A. Beach. In the *Owl of Minerva* (Fall 1990): 55–67.

Additional Sources

(Listed alphabetically by author.)

Baader, Franz von. *Sämtliche Werke*. Edited by Franz Hoffmann. 16 vols. Aalen: Scientia Verlag, 1963. Reprint of Leipzig edition, 1850–60.

Baumgartner, Hans Michael, ed. *Schelling. Einführung in seine Philosophie*. Freiburg: Alber, 1975.

Beach, Edward A. "Absolute Knowledge and the Problem of Systematic Completeness in Hegel's Philosophy." Ph.D. diss. in Philosophy, Northwestern University; Ann Arbor, Mich.: University Microfilms International, 1980. Order no. 8104687.

———. "The Paradox of Cognitive Relativism Revisited: A Reply to Jack W. Meiland." *Metaphilosophy* 15, nos. 3 & 4 (July/October 1984): 157–71.

———. "Schelling's Philosophy of Mythology: A Critical Analysis." Ph.D. diss. in Religious Studies, Stanford University; Ann Arbor, Mich.: University Microfilms International, 1988. Order no. 8826096.

———. "Schelling's Conception of Dialectical Method: In Contradistinction to Hegel's." *Owl of Minerva*, Fall 1990, 35–54.

Beiser, Frederick C. *The Fate of Reason: German Philosophy from Kant to Fichte*. Cambridge, Mass., and London: Harvard University Press, 1987.

Böhme, Jakob. *Sämtliche Schriften*. Edited by Will-Erich Peuckert. 11 vols.

Stuttgart: F. Frommanns, 1955–61; a facsimile reprint of the 1730 edition, *Theosophia Revelata. Das ist: Alle Göttliche Schriften des Gottseligen und Hocherleuchteten Deutschen Theosophi Jakob Böhmes*. English translations edited by William Law, *The Works of Jacob Behman*. 4 vols. London: Richardson, 1764.

Bolman, Frederick de Wolfe, Jr. Translator's introduction to Schelling's *Ages of the World*, 3–79. New York: AMS, 1967, c. 1942.

Bowie, Andrew. *Schelling and Modern European Philosophy: An Introduction*. London: Routledge, 1993.

Bracken, Joseph A. *Freiheit und Kausalität bei Schelling*. Freiburg/Munich: K. Alber, 1972.

———. "Schelling's Positive Philosophy." *Journal of the History of Philosophy* 15 (1977): 324–30.

Brown, Robert F. Translator's introduction to *Schelling's Treatise on "The Deities of Samothrace."* Missoula, Mont.: Scholars Press, 1977, c. 1974.

———. *The Later Philosophy of Schelling: The Influence of Böhme on the Works of 1809–1815*. Lewisburg, Pa.: Bucknell University Press, 1977.

Cassirer, Ernst. *Sprache und Mythos. Ein Beitrag zum Problem der Götternamen*. Leipzig & Berlin: B. G. Teubner, 1925. Translated by Susanne K. Langer under the title *Language and Myth*. New York: Dover, 1953.

———. *Philosophie der symbolischen Formen*. Darmstadt: Wissenschaftliche Buchgesellschaft, 1973–79, c. 1923. 3 vols. Translated by Ralph Manheim under the title *The Philosophy of Symbolic Forms*. 3 vols. New Haven: Yale University Press, 1953–57.

Creuzer, (Georg) Friedrich. *Symbolik und Mythologie der alten Völker, besonders der Griechen*. 2d edition. Leipzig: Heyer & Leske, 1819–23. Facsimile reprint, New York: Arno Press, 1978.

———. *Symbolik und Mythologie . . . im Auszüge von Dr. Georg Heinrich Moser*. Edited and abridged by Georg Heinrich Moser. Leipzig: C. W. Leske, 1822.

———. *Über einige mythologische und artistische Schriften Schellings, Ouwaroffs, Millins und Welckers*. Heidelberg: Mohr and Winter, 1817.

Dekker, Gerbrand. *Die Rückwendung zum Mythos. Schellings letzte Wandlung*. Munich/Berlin: R. Oldenbourg, 1930.

Dietzsch, Steffen, ed. *Natur-Kunst-Mythos. Beiträge zur Philosophie F. W. J. Schellings*. Berlin: Akademie, 1978.

Donougho, Martin. "Hegel and Friedrich Creuzer; or, Did Hegel Believe in Myth?" In *New Perspectives on Hegel's Philosophy of Religion*, edited by David Kolb, 59–80. Albany: SUNY Press, 1992.

Düsing, Klaus. "Spekulative Logik und positive Philosophie. Thesen zur Auseinandersetzung des späten Schelling mit Hegel." In *Ist systematische Philosophie möglich?* edited by Dieter Henrich. Vol. 17 (Beiheft 17) of *Hegel-Studien*, 117–28. Bonn: Bouvier Verlag Herbert Grundmann, 1977.

Durner, Manfred. *Wissen und Geschichte bei Schelling. Eine Interpretation der ersten Erlanger Vorlesung.* Munich: J. Berchmans, 1979.

Feldman, Burton, and Robert D. Richardson. *The Rise of Modern Mythology, 1680–1860.* Bloomington: Indiana University Press, 1972.

Feuerbach, Ludwig. "Zur Kritik der Hegelschen Philosophie." Series of essays (30 Aug. to 9 Sept. 1839). In *Hallische Jahrbücher für deutsche Wissenschaft und Kunst.* Edited by Arnold Ruge and Theodore Echtermeyer. Nos. 208–16, pp. 1657–1725. Reprinted in Glashütten im Taunus: D. Auvermann, 1972.

Fischer, Kuno. *Schellings Leben, Werke und Lehre.* Heidelberg: C. Winter, 1899.

Frank, Manfred, and Gerhard Hurz, eds. *Materialien zu Schellings philosophischen Anfängen.* Frankfurt am Main: Suhrkamp, 1975.

Frank, Manfred. *Der unendliche Mangel an Sein: Schellings Hegelkritik und die Anfänge der Marxschen Dialektik.* Frankfurt am Main: Suhrkamp, 1975.

———. *Der kommende Gott. Vorlesungen über die Neue Mythologie.* Frankfurt am Main: Suhrkamp, 1982.

———. *Gott im Exil. Vorlesungen über die Neue Mythologie.* Frankfurt am Main: Suhrkamp, 1988.

Frantz, Gustav Adolph Constantin. *Schellings positive Philosophie. Nach irhem Inhalt wie nach ihrer Bedeutung für den allgemeinen Umschwung der bis jetzt noch herrschenden Denkweise dargestellt.* In 3 parts. Köthen: P. Schettler, 1879. Reprinted in Aalen: Scientia, 1968.

Frauenstädt, Julius. *Schellings Vorlesungen in Berlin. Darstellung und Kritik der Hauptpunkte derselben.* Berlin: A. Hirschwald, 1842.

Fuhrmans, Horst. *Schellings letzte Philosophie. Die negative und die positive Philosophie im Einsatz des Spätidealismus.* Berlin: Junker & Dünnhaupt, 1940.

———. *Schellings Philosophie der Weltalter. Schellings Philosophie in den Jahren 1806–1825. Zum Problem des Schellingschen Theismus.* Düsseldorf: L. Schwann, 1954.

———. "Dokumente zur Schellingforschung." *Kant-Studien* 47 (1955–56): 182ff., 273ff., 378ff.; *Kant-Studien* 48 (1956–57): 302ff.

———. "Der Ausgangspunkt der Schellingschen Spätphilosophie (Dokumente zur Schellingforschung)." *Kant-Studien* 48 (1956–57): 302–23.

———. "Der Gottesbegriff der Schellingschen positiven Philosophie." In *Schelling-Studien. Festgabe für Manfred Schröter zum 85. Geburtstag.* Edited by Anton M. Koktanek, 9–47. Munich/Vienna: R. Oldenbourg, 1965.

Gutmann, James. Translator's introduction to Schelling's *Philosophical Inquiries into the Nature of Human Freedom,* xi–lii. La Salle, Ill.: Open Court, 1986, c. 1926.

Habermas, Jürgen. "Das Absolute und die Geschichte. Von der Zwiespältigkeit in Schellings Denken." Bonn: Ph.D. diss., Rheinische Friedrich Wilhelms Universität, 1954.

―――. "Dialektischer Idealismus im Übergang zum Materialismus. Geschichtsphilosophische Folgerungen aus Schellings Idee einer Kontraction Gottes." In *Theorie und Praxis*, 172–227. Frankfurt am Main: Suhrkamp, 1971, c. 1963.

Harris, Errol E. *An Interpretation of the Logic of Hegel.* Lanham, Md.: University Press of America, 1983.

Hartkopf, Werner. *Studien zur Entwicklung der modernen Dialektik.* 3 vols. Meisenheim am Glan: Anton Hain, 1972–76.

Hartmann, Eduard von. *Schellings positive Philosophie als Einheit von Hegel und Schopenhauer.* Berlin: O. Loewenstein, 1869.

―――. *Schellings philosophisches System.* Leipzig: H. Haacke, 1897.

Hasler, Ludwig, ed. *Schelling. Seine Bedeutung für eine Philosophie der Natur und der Geschichte: Referate und Kolloquien der Internationalen Schelling-Tagung in Zürich, 1979.* Stuttgart/Bad Cannstatt: Frommann-Holzboog, 1981.

Hayes, Victor C. "Myth, Reason and Revelation: Perspective on and a Summary Translation of Three Books from Schelling's Philosophy of Mythology and Revelation." Ph.D. diss., Columbia University, 1970.

Hegel, Georg Wilhelm Friedrich. *Werke, in Zwanzig Bänden. Theorie Werkausgabe.* 20 vols. Edited by Eva Moldenhauer and Karl Markus Michel. Frankfurt am Main: Suhrkamp, 1971–78.

Heidegger, Martin. *Schellings Abhandlung über das Wesen der menschlichen Freiheit.* Lectures presented in 1936. Edited by Hildgard Feick. Tübingen: M. Niemeyer, 1971. Translated by J. Stambaugh, under the title *Schelling's Treatise on the Essence of Human Freedom.* Athens: Ohio University Press, 1985.

Hemmerle, Klaus. *Gott und das Denken nach Schellings Spätphilosophie.* Freiburg/Basel/Vienna: Herder, 1968.

Hennigfeld, Jochem. *Mythos und Poesie. Interpretationen zu Schellings "Philosophie der Kunst" und "Philosophie der Mythologie."* Meisenheim am Glan: Hain, 1973.

Henrich, Dieter, ed. *Ist systematische Philosophie möglich?* Vol. 17 (Beiheft 17) of *Hegel-Studien.* Bonn: Bouvier Verlag H. Grundmann, 1977.

Holz, Harald. *Spekulation und Faktizität. Zum Freiheitsbegriff des mittleren und späten Schelling.* Bonn: Bouvier, 1970.

Howald, Ernst. *Der Kampf um Creuzers Symbolik. Eine Auswahl von Dokumenten.* Tübingen: J. C. B. Mohr, 1926.

Jamme, Christoph. *Neuzeit und Gegenwart.* Vol. 2 of *Einführung in die Philosophie der Mythos,* by Luc Brisson and Christoph Jamme. Darmstadt: Wissenschaftliche Buchgesellschaft, 1991.

Jaspers, Karl. *Schelling. Größe und Verhängnis.* Munich: Piper, 1955.

Jung, Carl Gustav, and Károly Kerényi. *Einführung in das Wesen der Mythologie. Das göttliche Kind, das göttliche Mädchen.* Zurich: Rascher, 1942. Translated by R. F. C. Hull, under the title *Essays on a Science of Mythology: The Myth of the Divine Child and the Mysteries of Eleusis*. New York: Pantheon Books, 1949.

Károly Kerényi. *Die Eröffnung des Zugangs zum Mythos*. Darmstadt: Wissenschaftliche Buchgesellschaft, 1967.

Kasper, Walter. *Das Absolute in der Geschichte. Philosophie und Theologie der Geschichte in der Spätphilosophie Schellings*. Mainz: Matthias-Grünewald, 1965.

———. "Die Freiheit als philosophisches und theologisches Problem in der Philosophie Schellings." In *Glaube und Geschichte*, 33–47. Mainz: Matthias-Grünewald Verlag, 1970.

———. "Krise und Neuanfang der Christologie im Denken Schellings." *Evangelische Theologie* 33 (1973): 366–84.

Kile, Frederick O. *Die theologischen Grundlagen von Schellings Philosophie der Freiheit*. Leiden: E. J. Brill, 1965.

Koktanek, Anton Mirko, ed. *Schelling-Studien. Festgabe für Manfred Schröter zum 85. Geburtstag*. Munich/Vienna: R. Oldenbourg, 1965.

Kondylis, Panajotis. *Die Entstehung der Dialektik. Eine Analyse der geistigen Entwicklung von Hölderlin, Schelling und Hegel bis 1802*. Stuttgart: Klett-Cotta, 1979.

Krings, Hermann. "Das Prinzip der Existenz in Schellings 'Weltaltern'." *Symposion, Jahrbuch für Philosophie* 4:337–47. Munich: K. Alber, 1955.

Lawrence, Joseph P. *Schellings Philosophie des ewigen Anfangs*. Würzburg: Königshausen & Neumann, 1989.

Lukács, György. *Die Zerstörung der Vernunft*. 3 vols. Darmstadt & Neuwied: Luchterhand, 1973, c. 1954. Translated by P. Palme, under the title *The Destruction of Reason*. Atlantic Highlands, N.J.: Humanities Press, 1981.

Marquard, Odo. "Schelling—Zeitgenosse incognito." In *Schelling. Einführung in seine Philosophie*, edited by Hans Michael Baumgartner, 21–22. Freiburg/Munich: K. Alber, 1975.

———. "Über einige Beziehungen zwischen Ästhetik und Therapeutik in der Philosophie des neunzehnten Jahrhunderts." In *Materialien zu Schellings philosophischen Anfängen*, edited by Manfred Frank and Gerhard Kurz, 341–77. Frankfurt am Main: Suhrkamp, 1975.

Marx, Werner. *Schelling: Geschichte, System, Freiheit*. Freiburg im Br./Munich: K. Alber, 1977. Translated by Thomas Nenon, under the title *The Philosophy of F. W. J. Schelling: History, System, and Freedom*. Bloomington: Indiana University Press, 1984.

Oesterreich, Peter Loth. *Philosophie, Mythos und Lebenswelt: Schellings universalhistorischer Weltalter-Idealismus und die Idee eines neuen Mythos*. Frankfurt am Main: Peter Lang, 1984.

O'Meara, Thomas Franklin. *Romantic Idealism and Roman Catholicism: Schelling and the Theologians.* Notre Dame, Ind.: University of Notre Dame Press, 1982.

Orth, Johannes. *Der psychologische Begriff des Unbewußten in der Schelling'schen Schule.* Ludwigshaven a. Rh.: Weiss & Hameier, 1914.

Poser, Hans, ed. *Philosophie und Mythos. Ein Kolloquium.* Berlin and New York: de Gruyter, 1979.

Schellings Philosophie der Freiheit. Festschrift der Stadt Leonberg zum 200. Geburtstag des Philosophen. Stuttgart: W. Kohlhammer, 1977.

Schmidt, Friedrich W. *Zum Begriff der Negativität bei Schelling und Hegel.* Stuttgart: J. B. Metzler, 1971.

Schröter, Manfred. "Vorwort" and "Einleitung des Herausgebers." Introductory essays to Schelling's *Die Weltalter. Fragmente in den Urauffassungen von 1811 und 1813,* edited by Manfred Schröter, ii–lviii. Munich: Biederstein Verlag and Leibniz Verlag, 1946.

———. *Kritische Studien über Schelling und zur Kulturphilosophie.* Munich: R. Oldenbourg, 1971.

Schulz, Walter. "Die Vollendung des Deutschen Idealismus in der Spätphilosophie Schellings." In *Verhandlungen der Schelling-Tagung in Bad Ragaz (Schweiz) vom 22. bis 25. September 1954,* vol. 14 of *Studia Philosophica, Jahrbuch der schweizerischen philosophischen Gesellschaft,* 239–55. Basel: Verlag für Recht und Gesellschaft, 1954.

———. *Die Vollendung des Deutschen Idealismus in der Spätphilosophie Schellings.* 2d ed. Pfullingen: Neske, 1975, c. 1955.

———. "Freiheit und Geschichte in Schellings Philosophie." Introductory essay to Schelling's *Philosophische Untersuchungen über das Wesen der menschlichen Freiheit und die damit zusammenhängenden Gegenstände,* 7–26. Frankfurt am Main: Suhrkamp, 1975.

———. "Macht und Ohnmacht der Vernunft." In *Schelling. Seine Bedeutung für eine Philosophie der Natur und der Geschichte. Referate und Kolloquien der Internationalen Schelling-Tagung in Zürich, 1979,* edited by Ludwig Hasler, 21–33. Stuttgart/Bad Cannstatt: Frommann-Holzboog, 1981.

Schulze, Wilhelm A. "Zum Verständnis der Stuttgarter Privatvorlesungen Schellings." *Zeitschrift für philosophische Forschung* 11 (1957): 575–93.

Sedlar, Jean W. *India in the Mind of Germany: Schelling, Schopenhauer and their Times.* Washington, D.C.: University Press of America, 1982.

Snow, Dale Evarts. "The Role of the Unconscious in Schelling's *System of Transcendental Idealism.*" *Idealistic Studies* 19, no. 3 (September 1989): 231–50.

Theunissen, Michael. "Die Idealismuskritik in Schellings negativer Philosophie." In *Ist systematische Philosophie möglich?* edited by Dieter Henrich, 173–91. Vol. 17 (Beiheft 17) of *Hegel-Studien.* Bonn: Bouvier Verlag H. Grundmann, 1977.

Tilliette, Xavier. "Schelling contre Hegel." *Archives de Philosophie* 29 (Jan.–Mar. 1966): 89–108.

———. *Schelling. Une philosophie en devenir.* 2 vols. Paris: Vrin, 1970.

———. "Schelling." In *Histoire de la philosophie,* vol. 2, edited by Y. Belavel, 947–93. 3 vols. Paris: Pleiade, 1969–74.

———, ed. *Schelling im Spiegel seiner Zeitgenossen, Ergänzungsband.* Turin: Bottego d'Erasmo, 1981.

———. *La mythologie comprise.* Naples: Instituto Italiano per gli studi filosofici, 1984.

Tillich, Paul. *Die religionsgeschichtliche Konstruktion in Schellings positiver Philosophie.* Breslau: H. Fleischmann, 1910. Translated by Victor Nuovo under the title *The Construction of the History of Religion in Schelling's Positive Philosophy: Its Presuppositions and Principles.* Lewisburg, Pa.: Bucknell University Press, 1974.

———. *Mystik und Schuldbewußtsein in Schellings philosophische Entwicklung* (1912). Vol. 1 of *Gesammelte Werke,* edited by R. Albrecht. 14 vols. Stuttgart: Evangelisches Verlagswerk, 1959. Translated by Victor Nuovo under the title *Mysticism and Guilt-Consciousness in Schelling's Philosophical Development.* Lewisburg, Pa.: Bucknell University Press, 1974.

Uslar, Detlev von. "Die Aktualität Schellings für Tiefenpsychologie und Psychologie." In *Schelling. Seine Bedeutung für eine Philosophie der Natur und der Geschichte,* edited by Ludwig Hasler, 163–66. Stuttgart/Bad Cannstatt: F. Frommann and G. Holzboog, 1979.

Vater, Michael. Introduction to Schelling's *System of Transcendental Idealism (1800),* xi–xxxvi. Translated by Peter Heath. Charlottesville: University Press of Virginia, 1978.

Vries, Jan de. *Forschungsgeschichte der Mythologie.* Freiburg/Munich: Karl Alber, 1961.

———. *Perspectives in the History of Religions.* Berkeley: University of California Press, 1977.

Volkmann-Schluck, Karl-Heinz. *Mythos und Logos. Interpretation zu Schellings Philosophie der Mythologie.* Berlin: de Gruyter, 1969.

White, Alan. *Schelling: An Introduction to the System of Freedom.* New Haven and London: Yale University Press, 1983.

———. *Absolute Knowledge: Hegel and the Problem of Metaphysics.* Athens: Ohio University Press, 1983.

Christoph Wild. *Reflexion und Erfahrung. Eine Interpretation der Früh- und Spätphilosophie Schellings.* Freiburg/Munich: K. Alber, 1968.

Zeltner, Hermann. *Schelling.* Stuttgart: F. Frommann, 1954.

Index

A^0, A^1, A^2, A^3. *See* Potencies
Absolute, 98, 101, 103, 105, 106, 141, 166, 170, 171, 174, 232; absolute *Prius*, 153, 155, 156–57, 170
Absolute (Hegel). *See* Hegel
Absolute monotheism, 188, 191, 192, 220, 232, 242, 250. *See also* Relative monotheism; Religion: monotheism
Absonderung (of the Potencies from the *Daß*), 140–41, 237–38. *See also Daß:* divestiture of Potencies
Abyss *(Ungrund)*. *See* Böhme: abyss
Actuality, 5, 9, 10, 12, 20, 35, 52–53, 54, 56, 61, 62–63, 65, 71–74, 80, 81, 84, 86, 88–89, 96–98, 99, 101–2, 103–4, 106–8, 112, 113, 114–16, 118–19, 126, 129–46, 147–49, 150, 152–54, 154–62, 165, 166–67, 171, 172, 174, 175, 187, 188–89, 193, 194, 196, 197, 200, 205, 208, 211, 213, 216, 218, 221, 223, 225, 233, 235, 284; degrees of reality, 117–18; experiential proof of God's actuality, 147–62; in relation to existentializing activity of the *Daß*, 107, 136–42, 147, 148, 149, 150, 152, 155–61, 171, 233, 235; in relation to ground of existence, 52–53, 176, 196, 197, 213, 216; in relation to inverted first Potency (B), 131–35, 144, 145, 187, 188–89, 193, 194, 196, 197, 200; in relation to pure principles of potentiality, 54, 113–14, 115, 116, 117–20, 125, 129, 144–45, 147–49, 152–53, 173, 174, 208, 218, 223; insofar as transcending conceptual determinations, 9, 12, 101–2, 103–4, 106–8, 115, 129–31, 143, 151, 155, 160, 162, 166–67, 171, 172, 174, 176, 277, 278, 280; transition from pure Potencies to extra-ideal actualities, 129–36, 142, 233, 277n. 48; ultimate (unconditioned) Actuality, 117, 131, 139. *See also* Creation; *Daß;* Ground; Potentiality
Actus purus (pure act). *See* Potencies: A^2, second Potency
Adamite religion, 183, 184
African religions, 19, 225
Aggressive impulses in religious motifs. *See* Psychology of religion
Ain Soph (Kabbala), 72. *See also* Judaism
Alchemy, 69, 75, 78. *See also* Böhme
Allegorical interpretations of religion. *See* Euhemerism; Mythology; Naturalism; Religion
Ambivalence. *See* Psychology of religion
American religions, Native, 19
Anaxagoras, 25, 28, 258
Animism. *See* Religion
Anquetil-Duperron, Abraham Hyacinth, 21, 255
An-sich-Seiendes (being-in-itself). *See* Potencies: A^1, first Potency
A posteriori. *See* Philosophy
A priori. *See* Philosophy
Arabian religion, 194–95, 210. *See also* Gods, goddesses, and legendary heroes: Arabian
Archetypes. *See* Psychology of religion
Arian heresy, 81
Aristotle, 54, 65, 66, 81, 86, 87, 101, 122, 126, 128, 139, 199, 206, 222, 240, 242, 266, 273, 278n. 72, 285. *See also Seiende, das*
Art, 32–33, 34, 51, 53, 149, 156, 210, 260, 262, 289. *See also* Freedom: free creative expression
Asian religions, 21, 180 (table 2). *See also* Indian religions

303

Assyrio-Babylonian religion, 179, 180 (table 2), 186, 203, 224. *See also* Gods, goddesses, and legendary heroes: Assyrio-Babylonian
Astral religion. *See* Cronus/Uranus: Zabism
Atheistic interpretations of religion, 27, 40, 44
Aufhebung (for Schelling), 171, 189, 269–70, 277, 278. *See also* Hegel
Aufhebungsdialektik. See Hegel
Ausscheidung (of the Potencies from the *Daß*), 140–41, 237–38. *See also Daß:* divestiture of Potencies
Ausschließende Kraft. See Potencies: B, inverted first Potency
Außer-sich-Seiendes. See Potencies: A², second Potency
Awe. *See* Psychology of religion

B. *See* Potencies: B, inverted first Potency
Baader, Franz von, 14, 36, 69, 75–82, 115, 260, 266–69, 277, 290; creation, 69, 76–77, 79, 82; dialectic of cooperation *(Kooperationsdialektik)*, 75–77; eternity, 76, 77; evil, 78, 79–82; God, 69, 76–82; Schelling's critique of, 80–82
Babylonian religion. *See* Assyrio-Babylonian religion
Bacon, Francis, 148
Barth, Karl, 247, 291
Beach, Edward Allen, 87, 263–64, 270, 272
Begriff. See Concept
Being-for-self. *See* Individuality
Being-in-itself. *See* Potencies: A¹, first Potency
Being-outside-itself. *See* Potencies: A², second Potency
Being-that-must-be. *See* Potencies: A², second Potency
Being-with-itself. *See* Potencies: A³, third Potency
Beiser, Frederick C., 273
Bei-sich-Seiendes. See Potencies: A³, third Potency
Bellah, Robert, 8, 252
Berger, Peter, 8, 252
Bettelheim, Bruno, 11, 253
Bible, 20, 21, 30, 31, 184, 188; Pentateuch, 18. *See also* Christianity; Judaism

Bochart, Samuel, 27, 28, 259
Böhme, Jakob, 14, 33, 36, 37, 69–75, 78, 79, 98, 144, 172, 260, 266–68; abyss *(Ungrund)*, 70–72; alchemical motifs, 69, 75, 78; chaotic ground *(Grund)* of being, 71, 72–73; creation, 37, 69, 70–75, 79; dialectic, 70, 74; eternity, 71, 72, 74; God and Godhead, 70–75; Schelling's critique of, 74–75; wrath within God, 72–75. *See also* No-thing; *Überseiendes*
Bolman, Frederick de Wolfe, Jr., 260–61 n. 32
Bracken, Joseph A., 273, 281
Braga. *See* Martin of Braga, Saint
Brosses, Charles de, 19, 26, 254
Brown, Robert F., 70, 260–61n. 32, 268n. 32
Brunner, Emil, 246–47, 291
Buber, Martin, 280
Buddhism. *See* Indian religions
Bultmann, Rudolf, 12, 253

Canaanite religion. *See* Phoenician and Canaanite religions
Carlyle, Thomas, 28, 29, 259
Cassirer, Ernst, 7, 29, 252, 259
Chaos, primordial principle of, 33, 107, 132–34, 144, 186, 193, 199, 200, 232. *See also* Böhme: chaotic ground of being; Ground; Potencies: B, inverted first Potency
Christ, 3, 31, 81, 116, 201, 211–12, 242–43, 245
Christianity, 2, 3, 4, 6, 12, 17, 19, 20, 23, 28, 31, 39, 42, 43, 44, 61, 70, 75, 78, 81, 116, 139, 163, 191, 201, 203, 211–12, 232, 242–43, 246–48, 291 n. 30
Colebrooke, Henry Thomas, 21, 22, 149, 256, 257
Coleridge, Samuel Taylor, 38, 261
Concept, 2–3, 9–10, 31–35, 38, 41–43, 53, 63–64, 83–91, 96–98, 101–3, 104, 106, 107–9, 127, 128, 129, 130, 131, 143, 150, 154, 155, 161, 167, 171, 172, 173, 175, 176, 184, 196, 231, 238, 246, 247. *See also* Essence; *Figur des Seienden;* Philosophy: negative philosophy; Reason; *Was*
Concrete Universal. *See* Hegel

INDEX 305

Creation, 69, 79, 82, 156–57, 160, 166, 174, 189, 223; creative fiat of the existentializing *Daß*, 107–8, 136–42, 155, 160, 233, 235; creative "inversion" of the Potencies, 129–36; critique of Schelling's theory, 108–9, 142–46; nonrational Ground of creation, 97–99, 108–9, 197–98; Potencies prior to creation, 116–30; table 1, representing phases of creative activity, 141. *See also* Actuality; Baader; Böhme; *Daß*; God; Ground; Time; *Überseiendes*

Creuzer, (Georg) Friedrich, 2, 22, 36, 37, 149, 183–84, 191, 239, 256–57, 261, 262, 265, 283–84, 289, 290; Schelling's critique of, 183–84, 191, 257n. 24

Crisis. *See* Great Spiritual Crisis

Cronus/Uranus (god B), lord of natural existence, 27, 179, 180 (table 2), 183–84, 186–201, 205-7, 207 (table 3), 209–25, 227–28, 234, 240, 285, 287, 288; *agkylometes* (crooked-minded), 183–84, 199; conflict with Dionysus, 193, 197–202, 203–4, 211–12, 215–20, 223; *Deus otiosus*, 223, 225–26; feminine counterparts in Persephone/Urania/Cybele, 192, 205–9, 207 (table 3), 240–41, 241 (table 5), 287n. 24; identification with divine antagonist (Dionysus), 200–201, 203, 216–19, 227–28, 234, 240, 245; peripheralization (subordination) of, 193–94, 205, 217–19, 223, 225–26, 234, 237, 240, 243, 249; preliminary phase as relatively undifferentiated pantheism, 181, 185, 186–92, 205, 211, 220, 223; principle of resistance to differentiation and order, 193–94, 196–204, 205, 211–12, 215–18, 219–20, 221, 223; principle of unity qua subordinated to differentiated order (Hades/Zeus), 220–21, 223–25; psychoanalytic interpretations of, 201–2, 218–19, 227–30; the "real god," 187, 200, 211, 219, 221, 284n. 19; Zabism (star-worship), 8–9, 191–97, 198, 205, 210, 217, 219, 220, 223, 224, 225, 234, 240, 250, 285n. 52; Zagreus as symbolic expression of Cronus, 56, 216–18, 224, 225, 240, 241. *See also* Gods, goddesses, and legendary heroes: Baal, Brahma, Cybele, Elohim, Ishtar, Mithras, Moloch, Mylitta, Persephone, Set, Urania, Zagreus; Potencies: B, inverted first Potency

Daß (thatness, or *quodditas*), 74, 107–8, 116, 136–42, 147–62 passim, 171, 173, 233, 235–38, 243, 248, 278n. 71; provisional investiture, subsequent divestiture of Potencies from God's true *Daß*, 136–42, 161, 233, 235–38, 240–43, 247–49, 278n. 71, 280n. 30; table 1, representing phases of the *Daß* in relation to the Potencies, 141. *See also* Actuality; Creation; Potencies: A^0; *Was*

De Brosses. *See* Brosses, Charles de

Deisidaemonia. *See* Psychology of religion

Dekker, Gerbrand, 150, 252, 260, 279

De Polier. *See* Polier, Marie Elisabeth de

Descartes, René, 60

Determinism, 59–62, 65, 74, 164–69, 223, 265n. 5. *See also* Providence

Developmental models of religion. *See* Religion: evolution of

De Vries. *See* Vries, Jan de

Dialectic, 1, 2, 4, 9–10, 50, 60–62, 64–65, 80, 83, 274; dialectic in mythology, 2, 9–10, 13, 61, 187, 193, 194, 196, 198, 205, 206, 221–22, 225, 226–27, 232, 234–35, 246; dialectic in Schelling's *Potenzenlehre*, 96, 100, 109, 116, 119, 123, 125, 126, 127–29, 130, 134, 151, 154, 155, 157, 158, 160, 163, 166, 167, 169–70, 171, 173, 175, 176, 225, 275n. 6, 285n. 42; dialectic of production (*Erzeugungsdialektik*), 84, 85–86, 90–91, 99, 111, 113–14, 116, 117, 119, 120, 124, 125, 126, 127–29, 136, 139, 142, 143, 144, 147, 186, 188, 222, 269–70nn. 50 and 51, 275n. 6; dialectic of time and eternity, 59, 60–62, 64–65, 83, 235–36; dialectical materialism (anticipated), 88, 164, 270–71n. 58. *See also* Baader: dialectic of cooperation; Böhme: dialectic; Hegel: dialectic; Logic; Reason

Dionysus (god A²), champion of humanity and civilization, 56, 180 (table 2), 186, 191, 197–202, 203, 205–25, 207 (table 3), 227–28, 234, 240–42, 241 (table 5), 245, 264, 287, 288, 290–91; Bacchanalia, Bacchantes, 213–14; Bacchus, 215, 224, 227–28, 240–41; celebration in Dionysian and Eleusinian Mysteries, 217, 227–29, 240–44; conflict with Cronus, 193, 197–202, 203–4, 211–12, 215–19; deity of differentiated structure and rationality, 197–99, 200, 211–13, 216; Demeter as feminine counterpart, 208, 240–42, 241 (table 5), 287n. 24; grapes, wine, and intoxication, 211, 213–14, 224, 227; Herakles as prototype, 200, 201, 210, 211; identification with divine antagonist (Cronus), 201, 216, 217–19, 228–29, 234, 240, 245; liberating god, 211–15, 227; loosener of social inhibitions, 213–14; madness and orgiastic pantheism, 212–20, 227, 264; martyrdom, 200–201, 203, 216–17, 242; Nietzsche's interpretation compared, 213, 228; provisionally appropriated guise of undifferentiated monism, 212–19; psychoanalytic interpretations of, 217–19, 221, 227–30; resurrection, 212, 219, 241, 242; the "relatively spiritual god," 211, 212, 219, 221, 284n. 19; triune aspects of Dionysus as Zagreus/Bacchus/Iakchos, 56, 216–18, 224–25, 240–41, 241 (table 5), 290–91n. 25; ushered into consciousness by Urania/Cybele, 205–11, 207 (table 3); Zagreus as symbolic internalization of Cronus, 216–18, 224–25, 241. *See also* Gods, goddesses and legendary heroes: Demeter, Herakles, Isaac, Isis, Melkart, Osiris, Shiva; Mystery cults; Potencies: A², second Potency

Displacement. *See* Psychology of religion

Divestiture (of the Potencies from the *Daß*), 140–41, 237–38. *See also Daß*: divestiture of Potencies

Donougho, Martin, 256

Durner, Manfred, 273, 281

Early theories of religion (prior to Schelling), 2–4; corrupted truth hypothesis, 18–19; developed superstition hypothesis, 19; imaginative fiction hypothesis, 3, 5, 6–7; nonreligious hypotheses, 17–18, 23, 25, 40; primordial revelation hypothesis, 20–23, 183–84, 191; progressive revelation hypothesis, 19–20; Schelling's criticisms of, 2–8, 17–45. *See also* Euhemerism; Naturalism; Religion

Eckhart, Johannes (usually known as Meister Eckhart), 78

Ecstasy of reason, 103, 104, 105, 106, 159, 161, 162, 176, 249, 273n. 28. *See also* Philosophy: metaphysical empiricism; Transrational

Ego. *See* Individuality

Egyptian religion, 22, 26, 27, 34, 180 (table 2), 181, 183, 208, 212, 213, 214, 224, 225, 257n. 24, 283n. 4, 288n. 41. *See also* Gods, goddesses, and legendary heroes: Egyptian

Ehrenreich, Paul, 26, 259

Eleusinian Mysteries. *See* Mystery cults; Dionysus

Eliade, Mircea, 202, 225–26, 285, 288

Empiricism, 149–54, 167–69, 170, 172, 282n. 38. *See also* Philosophy: metaphysical empiricism; Philosophy: positive philosophy

Epistemology, 96–109, 112, 146, 147–62, 168–69, 170–73, 175–76. *See also* Dialectic

Erzeugungsdialektik. See Dialectic: dialectic of production

Essence, 12, 32, 33, 37, 42, 54, 60, 71, 72, 73, 76, 77, 78, 86–91, 101, 104, 105, 107–8, 111–13, 115, 116, 124, 127, 128, 129–32, 133, 134, 136–39, 142–45, 166, 167, 171; temporalization of essence, 55, 59–60, 64–65, 85–86, 91, 111–13, 125, 127, 147, 164–67, 188. *See also* Concept; *Figur des Seienden; Seiende, das; Was*

Eternity, 50, 53, 55, 59–67 passim, 71, 72, 74, 76, 77, 81, 82, 83, 89–91, 95, 97, 101, 111–14, 116, 117, 120, 125, 127, 155, 156, 160, 163–67, 196, 235, 243;

INDEX 307

temporality within eternity (proto-time), 64–65, 81, 82, 83, 90–91, 116, 117, 120, 125, 127, 165–67, 265n. 11. *See also* Concept; Time
Euhemerism, 25–29, 30, 34, 38, 39–40, 45, 239, 261
Euhemerus of Messene, 26–27, 28, 29, 39, 259
Evans-Pritchard, Edward E., 202, 285
Evil, 53, 59, 65, 78, 79–82, 132–34, 233, 277n. 60. *See also Felix culpa;* Original Sin
Evolutionary models of religion. *See* Religion: evolution of
Existence. *See* Actuality
Existentialism, 104, 163, 165, 169–70, 171, 226
Extrarational. *See* Intellectual intuition; Irrational principle; Noncognitivist theologies; Transrational; Unconscious

Fall, The, 22, 62–63, 115, 192–93, 233, 237 (table 4)
Felix culpa, 79, 80, 233, 269n. 38, 277n. 60. *See also* Evil; Original Sin
Fetishism, 19, 26, 189, 254
Feuerbach, Ludwig, 2, 3, 88, 244, 270–71n. 58
Fichte, Johann Gottlieb, 32, 48, 123, 164, 254, 260, 274n. 37
Fideism, 100–103, 104
Figur des Seienden (figure of [determinate] being), 129–30. *See also* Potentiality; *Seiende, das*
First World Age, 187, 190. *See also* Great Spiritual Crisis; Second World Age
Fischer, Kuno, 265
Frank, Manfred, 271, 291
Frantz, Gustav Adolph Constantin, 253–54
Freedom, 14, 53–54, 59–67, 91, 95, 98, 100, 108–9, 119, 125, 130–31, 134, 137, 138–39, 140, 141, 142, 163, 164–66, 182, 186, 189, 192, 200, 215, 216, 221–22, 223, 226–27, 228, 233; absolute vs. historical freedom, 164–66, 168, 280–81; formal (as compared to real) freedom, 61, 265n. 4; free creative expression, 31, 38, 43, 182, 186, 226–27, 228; God and freedom, 53, 59–67, 71–72, 73, 82, 98, 137, 141, 167–68, 171, 174, 176, 233, 235–36, 280n. 30; human freedom, 53, 56, 61, 80, 82, 84, 91, 98, 108, 141, 165–66, 168–69, 176, 189, 192, 200, 233; in relation to reason and rationality, 53, 98, 100, 104, 106, 119, 138–39, 166–67, 168, 169, 171, 174, 175, 200, 215, 216, 221–22; in relation to time and eternity, 59–67, 95, 164–69; real freedom of will in relation to the source or ground of existence, 53–54, 56, 98, 100, 109, 130, 133–34, 137, 192, 216, 221–22, 226, 265n. 4. *See also* Voluntarism; Will
Freud, Anna, 218, 288
Freud, Sigmund, 56, 201–2, 229, 234, 244, 245, 286, 289
Fuhrmans, Horst, 108, 164, 270, 274
Functionalism, 47

Geist. See Spirit
Geworfenheit. See Thrownness
God, 3, 6, 12, 32, 53, 59–67, 69, 70–75, 76–82, 87–91, 97–99, 101, 107–08, 116, 131, 133–34, 136–42, 147, 149, 150, 152–62, 164, 166, 167–68, 170–75, 183, 191, 195, 232–50; *causa sui,* creator, or absolute *Prius,* 60–63, 66, 67, 69, 70–75, 76–77, 79–82, 97–99, 107–8, 115, 116, 134, 136–42, 153, 155, 156–57; 160, 166, 174, 189, 223, 233, 235, 275n. 10; early theories about the nature of Deity, 3–4, 6–7, 17, 18, 20, 21, 23, 32–33, 50–51, 53–54, 164; essence of God, 32–33, 42, 44, 60–62, 71–72, 76, 87–89, 101, 107–8, 136–42, 152–53, 154, 158–61, 167–68, 171, 172, 173–75, 234, 235–36, 247; experiential proof of God, 152–62, 232; God and the possibility of freedom, 53, 59–67, 98–99, 134, 168, 171, 233, 235–36; Godhead, 12, 70–75, 101, 155, 160, 162, 235, 243; God-positing consciousness *(Gott-setzende Bewußtsein),* 246–50, 288n. 50; in relation to human spirit, 54, 61–63, 65–66, 139–40, 141, 155, 156–61, 233, 246–50, 280n. 28; knowability of God,

God *(continued):*
    100–108, 137–38, 172–73; ontological proof, 101, 107, 152, 272n. 17; personhood of God, 137–38, 140, 155–61 passim, 174, 236–38, 240, 247–48, 250, 278n. 71, 280n. 28; prototemporal activity in eternity, 62–65, 81, 82, 83, 90–91, 116, 167–68; provisional investiture, subsequent divestiture of Potencies from God's true self, 136–42, 161, 233, 235–38, 240–43, 247–49, 278n. 71, 280n. 30; theogony of (or development within) God's nature, 62, 75, 81–82, 134, 166, 167–68, 233, 235–38, 250, 281nn. 11 and 16; transcendence of, 3, 11–13, 36, 51, 53, 62–63, 66, 71, 77, 79, 82, 103, 107, 136–42, 155, 160, 162, 171–72, 173–75, 191, 192, 232, 236–38, 249–50, 280n. 30; *das Überseiende,* 103, 108, 155–61, 247. *See also* Absolute: absolute *Prius; Daβ;* Early theories of religion; Religion; *Überseiendes*
Goddesses, as compared to gods, 180 (table 2), 192, 205–9, 207 (table 3), 210, 240–42, 241 (table 5). *See also* Cronus/Uranus; Dionysus; Great Mother Goddess
Godhead. *See* God
Gods, goddesses, and legendary heroes:
    Arabian:
        Alilat, 210, 287n. 15)
        Orotal, 210, 211, 287n. 15
    Assyrio-Babylonian:
        Ishtar, 179
        Mylitta, 180 (table 2), 203
        Unnamed god, 180 (table 2), 186
    Egyptian:
        Anubis, 27
        Apis, 27
        Horus, 180 (table 2), 208
        Isis, 208, 283
        Osiris, 26, 27, 180 (table 2), 181, 201, 211, 213, 214, 217, 224, 225, 242, 245, 288
        Set, 27, 180 (table 2), 181, 201, 224, 225, 283, 288
    Greco-Roman:
        Achilles, 26, 77
        Adonis, 27
        Apollo, 213
        Argus, 26
        Athena, 213, 283
        Atlas, 32
        Axieros, 36, 37
        Axiokersos, 211
        Bacchus, 215, 224, 227–28, 240–41
        Cronus *(see main entry* Cronus/Uranus)
        Daedelus, 30
        Danaus, 27
        Demeter, 31, 37, 208, 238, 240–42, 283, 287
        Dionysus *(see main entry* Dionysus)
        Eros and Psyche, 34
        Hades, 25, 39, 192, 223, 241, 290–91n. 25
        Hera, 286
        Herakles, 26, 200, 201, 210, 211, 286, 288, 291
        Hermes, 26, 27
        Iakchos *(see main entry* Iakchos)
        Io, 26
        Kadmos, 27
        Kore *(see below,* Persephone/Kore)
        Laius, 201
        Maenads, 41, 214, 287
        Numa, 39, 244
        Oedipus, 201
        Omphale, 210
        Persephone/Kore, 25, 37, 39, 192, 240, 241 (table 5), 243, 287 *(see also main entries* Cronus/Uranus; Iakchos)
        Phaëthon, 25
        Prometheus, 211
        Remus, 39, 244
        Rome, 244
        Romulus, 39, 244
        Semele, 242
        Titans, 214, 216, 217
        Urania, 207, 209–10, 286n. 4, 287n. 15
        Uranus *(see main entry* Cronus/Uranus)
        Zagreus, 56, 216–18, 224, 225
        Zeus, 26, 27, 201, 224–25, 283
    Hebrew:
        Abraham, 201

INDEX 309

Adam and Eve, 80, 192
Elohim, 192
Enosh, 192
Isaac, 200, 201
Jehovah, 192
Methuselah, 30
Moses, 21, 27, 259
Noah, 18, 30, 244
Samson, 32
Indian:
Brahma, 180 (table 2), 181
Buddha, 180 (table 2)
Shiva, 180 (table 2), 211, 214, 242
Vishnu, 180 (table 2)
Persian:
Ahriman, 192
Mithras, 180 (table 2), 191, 192
Ormuzd, 192
Zoroaster, 27
Phoenician and Canaanite:
Baal, 180 (table 2), 199, 203, 286
El, 199, 201, 286
Melkart, 180 (table 2), 200, 201, 211, 242, 286, 291
Moloch, 180 (table 2), 181, 199
Taaut, 27
Phrygian:
Attis, 204
Cybele, 180 (table 2), 181, 207 (table 3) *(see also main entry* Cronus/Uranus)
God(s) to come, 180 (table 2)
Syrian:
Adonis, 27
See also Early theories of religion; Mythologies; Religion; *specific religious traditions*
Görres, Johann Joseph, 22, 257–58
Great Mother Goddess, 206–9, 207 (table 3). *See also* Cybele; Cronus/Uranus; Goddesses, as compared to gods; Urania;
Great Spiritual Crisis, 185, 191. *See also* Kataboles
Greek religion, 2, 18, 19, 22, 25, 26, 27, 37, 39, 41, 55–56, 95, 179, 180 (table 2), 181, 183–84, 186, 192, 194–95, 200, 204, 208, 211, 212, 213, 214, 221–22, 224–25, 226–29, 238–44, 248, 257–58, 276, 283n. 2, 285, 286, 288. *See also*

Gods, goddesses, and legendary heroes: Greco-Roman; Mystery cults
Green, Garrett, 7, 252, 291
Grotius, Hugo, 18, 254
Ground *(Grund)* of existence, 52–57, 80, 97–100, 103, 104, 107, 113, 119, 130–34, 143–44, 165, 166–67, 171, 176, 189, 196, 197, 213. *See also* Actuality; Böhme; Chaos
Gutmann, James, 268n. 32

Habermas, Jürgen, 75, 100, 142, 150, 154, 163, 164–69, 175, 268, 272, 279, 280–81
Haeckel, Ernst, 264
Harris, Errol E., 271
Hartmann, Eduard von, 144, 279
Hebrew language, 36, 194. *See also* Judaism
Hegel, Georg Wilhelm Friedrich, 2, 3, 4, 9, 14, 22, 41, 42, 44, 45, 47, 48, 52, 69, 75, 76, 77, 80, 83–91, 97, 104, 108, 109, 151, 158, 166, 171, 196, 231–32, 246, 251, 254–82 passim, 285, 291; Absolute (Reason), 42, 52, 75, 86–91, 98, 158; Concept *(Begriff),* 41–43, 83–91, 101, 112, 120, 128–29, 231–32, 246; conceptual circles, 84, 88, 90; Concrete Universal *(das konkrete Allgemeine),* 41, 42, 83, 86–89, 129; critique of Schelling's *Potenzenlehre,* 128; dialectic, 45, 47, 83–91, 113, 120, 128–29; dialectic of sublation *(Aufhebungsdialektik),* 76, 84–85, 86, 91, 97, 112, 113, 125, 126, 269–70, 275; God, 87–91; religious representations *(Vorstellungen),* 41–42, 47, 231–32, 246, 262; Schelling's critique of, 9, 41–44, 86, 88–91, 97, 98, 101, 108, 158, 270–71nn. 57 and 58; time and eternity, 42, 83, 89–90, 91, 112, 113
Heidegger, Martin, 100, 104, 142, 169, 171, 175, 272, 273, 284
Hennigfeld, Jochem, 258
Henrich, Dieter, 275, 280
Heraclitus, 74, 114, 125, 290
Hermann, Gottfried, 26, 28, 31, 182, 258, 262
Hermeneutics, 1–13, 25–49, 95–96, 100, 147, 149, 162, 179–82, 184–86, 192, 197, 212, 219, 227–30, 231, 238, 244–50, 257, 287n. 24, 289

Hermeticism, 69, 266
Herodotus, 149, 181, 210, 257, 283–88 passim
Hesiod, 31, 34, 183–84, 186, 199, 285
Heyne, Christian G., 26, 31, 258, 262
Hinduism. *See* Indian religions
Historical-critical method, 5, 6, 44, 54, 146, 148, 150, 188
Historicism, 60, 164–69
Holz, Harald, 70, 266
Homer, 31, 227–29, 289
Horace, 215, 287
Horton, Robin, 26, 259
Howald, Ernst, 262
Huet, Pierre Daniel, 27, 259
Hume, David, 254

Iakchos (god A³), harmonizing reintegration of Cronus and Dionysus, 180 (table 2), 218, 220–25, 227–29, 234; celebration in Dionysian and Eleusinian Mysteries, 240–43; *ieros gamos* (holiest wedding, to Kore), 243; Kore as feminine counterpart, 240–43; principle of spirit *(Geist),* 221. *See also* Gods, goddesses, and legendary heroes: Horus, Kore, Vishnu; Potencies: A³, third Potency
Ichheit. See Individuality
Idealism, 1, 2, 48, 49, 61, 66, 77, 79, 86, 88, 104, 108–9, 115, 117, 169–70, 175, 208, 231
Idea-world *(Ideenwelt),* 62, 97–98, 115, 131, 134, 196, 265
Identitätsphilosophie, 48, 52, 164
Inbegriff (all-inclusive rational ideal), 174. *See also Seiende, das*
Indian religions, 2, 21–22, 180 (table 2), 181, 183, 212, 214, 224, 248, 255–56, 257; Buddhism, 72, 224; Hinduism, 21–22, 255–58, 276. *See also* Gods, goddesses, and legendary heroes: Indian
Individuality, 53, 54, 56, 59, 63, 65, 66, 77, 84, 87, 89, 90, 91, 97, 98, 104, 108, 115, 117, 119, 122, 126, 128, 130–31, 133–34, 138–39, 140–41, 157–58, 161, 164–66, 168–69, 189, 197; being-for-self, 194; ego, egoity *(Egoität),* egotism, 63, 98, 119, 193, 199, 234; I-ness *(Ichheit),* 32, 140; selfhood *(Selbstheit),* 193–94, 196, 197; soul *(Seele)* as distinguished from spirit *(Geist),* 140–41, 279 n. 77. *See also* Spirit
Intellectual intuition *(Intellektuelle Anschauung),* 12, 101–7. *See also* Philosophy: metaphysical empiricism; Transrational
Inward-drawing, collapsing power *(zusammenziehende Kraft). See* Potencies: B, inverted first Potency
Irrational principle, 2, 9, 14, 47, 52–57, 97–98, 100, 106, 108, 132–34, 136, 142–44, 147, 175, 196, 197–98, 213, 231–32, 245, 264. *See also* Intellectual intuition; Transrational

Jacobi, Friedrich Heinrich, 102, 273
Jamme, Christoph, 291
Jaspers, Karl, 142, 274, 164, 175, 274
Jesus. *See* Christ
Jevons, Frank Byron, 26, 259
Jones, William, 21, 22, 255, 256
Judaism, 3, 21, 27, 192, 195, 200, 201, 258; Kabbala, 69, 72, 266. *See also* Bible; Gods, goddesses, and legendary heroes: Hebrew
Jung, Carl G., 11, 184, 253

Kabbala. *See* Judaism
Kant, Immanuel, 47, 48, 53, 62, 66, 101, 103, 107, 112, 118, 137, 142, 151, 174, 253, 263, 264, 265, 266, 282; noumenon, 48, 63, 66
Kasper, Walter, 100, 108, 164, 168, 175, 272, 274, 280, 281
Kataboles, 180 (table 2), 207 (table 5). *See also* Great Spiritual Crisis; Second World Age
Kaufman, Gordon D., 7, 252
Kerényi, Károly, 11, 253, 257
Kielmeyer, Carl Friedrich, 187, 264–65n. 18, 284n. 20
Kierkegaard, Søren, 43, 247, 262
Kile, Frederick O., 70, 266
Kooperationsdialektik. See Baader: dialectic of cooperation

Lawrence, Joseph P., 274, 278
Leach, Edmund, 10, 253, 285

Leibniz, Gottfried Wilhelm von, 47, 60, 61, 263, 265
Lessing, Gotthold Ephraim, 20, 255
Lévi-Strauss, Claude, 10, 252, 253
Lobeck, Christian August, 239, 290
Logic, 59–67 passim, 82, 83–91 passim, 100, 102, 106, 107, 111, 113, 115–16, 118–19, 120, 121–23, 125, 126–27, 128–30, 134, 137–38, 144, 145, 147, 152–54, 155–56, 158, 159, 162, 163, 166–67, 168, 170–71, 176, 196, 197, 269, 278, 281; in mythology, 3, 47; in relation to extra-rational truth, 63–64, 96, 98, 100, 127, 129–30, 134, 137–38, 147, 170–71, 176; in relation to the unconscious, 50, 51, 176. See also Dialectic; Philosophy; Reason
Logical rudeness, 105, 274n. 37
Lukács, György, 100, 264, 272

Madness. See Psychology of religion
Malinowski, Bronislaw, 8, 252
Marquard, Odo, 263, 289
Martin of Braga, Saint,18, 254
Marx, Karl, 88, 163, 170, 229, 270–71 n. 58
Marx, Werner, 70, 164, 267, 268, 271
Me on (relative not-being), 120. See also Plato
Messiah, 201. See also Christ
Metaphysical empiricism. See Philosophy: metaphysical empiricism
Milton, John, 18, 254
Monism. See Religion
Monotheism. See Absolute monotheism; Relative monotheism; Religion: monotheism
Moralistic or doctrinal interpretations of religion. See Religion.
Moritz, Karl Philipp, 34, 260, 261
Müller, Max, 27, 254
Mystery cults, 37, 38, 55, 56, 217, 228–29, 238–44, 289; Dionysian Mysteries, 214, 227, 241, 242, 264; Eleusinian Mysteries, 37, 39, 208, 238–44; fusion of archetypal "causal gods" as moments of supreme Godhead, 240–42; *ieros gamos,* the holiest wedding, 243; Samothracian Mysteries, 29, 37. See also Dionysus
Mythology 1, 78, 80, 81, 95, 98, 107, 108, 133, 145, 146, 147, 149, 150, 162, 179–250; allegorical interpretations of, 25–49, 194, 199, 262n. 49; "complete" vs. "incomplete" mythological systems, 180 (table 2), 205, 211–12, 224, 226; cross-cultural identifications of deities, 179–86, 180 (table 2), 211–12, 224–25, 242; cross-gender identifications of deities, 180 (table 2), 192, 205–9, 207 (table 3), 210, 240–42, 241 (table 5); demythologization, 12–13; free versus unfree uses of, 31, 38, 182, 186, 226–27, 228; functional adaptations of, 8–9; fusion of archetypal "causal gods" as moments of supreme Godhead, 240–42; hermeneutical principles for interpreting myths, 1–13, 25–49, 95–96, 100, 147, 149, 162, 179–82, 184–86, 192, 197, 212, 219, 227–30, 231, 238, 244–50, 287n. 24; illusory fabrications, 2, 5, 6–8, 11, 39–40, 202, 229–30, 235–36, 244–45; implicit logic of, 47, 56, 107–8, 133, 139, 145; mythical deities as stages in God's theogonic, self-revelatory process, 3–4, 11–13, 43, 61–62, 81–82, 95, 139, 149, 160–61, 231–50; myths in relation to the unconscious, 10–11, 13, 47, 51, 54–57, 143, 145, 182, 184–85, 194, 196–97, 201–2, 203–4, 218, 227–30; origins of pagan myths, 17–23, 81, 182–86, 201; scientific *(wissenschaftlich)* study of, 1, 4–5, 184; self-transcendence of mythology, 231–50; stages in evolution of mythological consciousness, 237 (table 4); uncanny secrets beneath the surface of myths, 226–30. See also Early theories of religion; Goddesses, as compared to gods; Gods, goddesses, and legendary heroes; Mystery cults; Psychology of religion; Religion: polytheism; Tables representing comparative mythology. *See also specific religious traditions*

Naturalism, 25–29, 31–34, 38–39, 40, 45, 47, 77, 189, 194, 214, 239
Naturphilosophie, 48, 52, 55, 260n. 19
Negative philosophy. See Philosophy

Nicht sein Sollendes. See Potencies: B, inverted first Potency
Nicht wollender Wille. See Potencies: A¹, first Potency; Will
Nietzsche, Friedrich, 213, 228, 229, 234, 244, 287
Noncognitivist theologies, 102, 106. *See also* Intellectual intuition; Transrational
Nonrational. *See* Intellectual intuition; Irrational principle; Noncognitivist theologies; Transrational; Unconscious
Norse religion, 27
No-thing, 72, 137. *See also Ain soph;* Böhme: abyss; Buddhism
Noumenon, 48, 63, 66

Objectivity, 5, 11, 33, 35, 38, 48–50, 63–64, 73–74, 75, 87–88, 96–97, 101, 102, 103–6, 114, 116, 117, 118–20, 121–24, 135, 141–42, 144–45, 132–34, 234, 240, 244, 272, 277. *See also* Potencies: A², second Potency; Subject/object relation; *Subjekt-Objekt*
O'Meara, Thomas Franklin, 258, 268
Ontology, 3, 10, 14, 19, 23, 40, 41, 44, 55, 57, 59–67, 69, 75, 82, 83, 84, 86, 95–98, 100–101, 103, 107–9, 111–46, 147, 149, 163, 164–69, 170–71, 174, 175–76, 179, 232, 233–35, 238, 281; Potencies, 111–46; representation of Potencies in relation to the *Daß* (table 1), 141. *See also* Potencies
Original Sin, 192. *See also* Evil; *Felix culpa*
Orth, Johannes, 263
Ouk on (absolute nonbeing), 120. *See also* Plato
Over-being. *See Überseiendes*
Over-existing. *See Überexistierendes*

Paganism. *See* Early theories of religion (prior to Schelling); Mythology; Religion.
Pantheism. *See* Religion
Pantheismusstreit, 102, 273
Paracelsus, 69, 78, 266
Parmenides, 125
Parrinder, (Edward) Geoffrey, 225, 285, 288
Particular, 33, 35, 60–61, 96–98, 103, 115, 119, 120, 121, 122, 128, 130–31, 138, 144, 164, 166, 168, 238. *See also* Universal
Paul, Saint, 39
Paulus, Heinrich Eberhard Gottlob, 31
Pausanias of Lydia, 149, 224, 239, 288
Persian religion, 27, 180 (table 2), 183, 191–92, 195, 224, 257n. 24. *See also* Gods, goddesses and legendary heroes: Persian
Philosophy: *a posteriori,* 107, 146, 168, 170; *a priori,* 61, 107, 118, 145–46, 150, 162, 163, 164, 166–67, 170, 172, 202, 203, 246, 264; metaphysical empiricism, 148–62, 172–73, 176, 202, 238, 267n. 22; negative philosophy, 107–9, 111, 139, 147–62, 167, 170, 172–73, 175, 179, 251; *per posterius,* 153, 157, 161; *philosophia ascendens* (regressive empiricism), 153, 279n. 16; *philosophia descendens* (progressive empiricism), 154, 279n. 16; philosophy of religion, 95–176, 231–50; positive philosophy, 107–9, 147–62, 163, 167, 170, 172–73. *See also* Concept; Dialectic; Empiricism; Logic; Reason
Phoenician and Canaanite religions, 27, 36, 183, 199, 200, 203, 212, 254, 286. *See also* Gods, goddesses, and legendary heroes: Phoenician and Canaanite
Phrygian religion, 180 (table 2), 181, 183, 203–4, 207 (table 3). *See also* Gods, goddesses, and legendary heroes: Phrygian
Pindar, 234, 265
Plato, 31, 64, 97, 112, 118, 239, 242, 258, 265, 276, 277, 288; distinction between *ouk on* (absolute nonbeing) and *me on* (relative not-being), 120, 215, 276n. 24
Plutarch, 26, 34, 149, 239, 258, 260
Polier, Marie Elisabeth de, 21, 255
Polycleitos, 224
Polytheism. *See* Religion
Positive philosophy. *See* Philosophy
Potencies, 111–46, 168, 170, 260, 276n. 14, 277, 283n. 1, 284, 285, 288; applications to mythology, 39, 44, 95, 108, 133, 179, 180 (table 2), 181–86, 187, 188, 205, 215, 219, 223–24, 226–

27, 232–38, 237 (table 4), 240–43, 241 (table 5), 248–49, 271; debt to Böhme, 70, 74; early definitions of, 32–33, 36–37; inversion and displacement of, 129–42, 233–37, 237 (table 4); ontology of, 67, 95, 108, 111–46; provisional investiture, subsequent divestiture of Potencies from God's true *Daß,* 136–42, 141 (table 1), 161, 233, 235–38, 240–43, 247–49;

A^0 (the *Daß*): true Godhead as distinguished from Potencies, 137, 141. *See also Daß;* God: Godhead

A^1, first Potency, amorphous principle of sheer possibility, 117, 120–35, 141, 147, 237 (table 4), 240–43, 241 (table 5); as *das An-sich-Seiende* (the being-in-itself), 117, 122, 132; *der nicht wollende Wille* (the wantless will), 120, 123, 276n. 23; *potentia pura,* 122; principle of original subjectivity, 117, 119–21, 122–26; pure subjectivity, 117, 122, 124; *das Sein Könnende* (the being-able-to-be), 117, 120, 124, 126, 132, 147, 284n. 25; *der unendliche Mangel an Sein* (the infinite lack of being), 117, 123

B, inverted first Potency, basis of existence yet provisional antagonist to true order, 37, 74, 133–35, 141, 142–44, 164, 179, 180 (table 2), 181–204, 205–8, 207 (table 3), 209–25, 227–28, 234, 236–37, 237 (table 4), 240–43; as *die ausschließende Kraft* (the excluding power), 133; god B, 179–230; *das nicht-sein-Sollende* (that-which-ought-not-to-be), 133, 134; *potentia existendi,* 188, 284n. 25; principle of recalcitrant objectivity, 132–34; *die verneinende Kraft* (the negating power), 133; *die zusammenziehende Kraft* (the inward-drawing, collapsing power), 37, 133, 144, 186–87, 193. *See also* Cronus/Uranus; Ground

A^2, second Potency, principle of objective order, 122–33, 135, 141–42, 144–45, 180 (table 2), 186, 191, 197–203, 205–25, 207 (table 3), 227–28, 237, 240–43, 241 (table 5), 277; as *actus purus* (pure act), 122; *das außer-sich-Seiende* (the being-outside-itself), 122; condition of inversion, 135, 144–45, 179, 182; god A^2, 179, 180 (table 2), 186, 191, 197–204; principle of original objectivity, 121–23, 277n. 48); principle of secondary subjectivity, 135, 144–45; *das rein Seiende* (the pure being), 121, 125; *das sein Müssende* (the being that must be), 122, 126, 135; *das willenlose Wollen* (the unwilled wanting), 123, 124, 276n. 23. *See also* Dionysus

A^3, third Potency, principle of harmonious integration, 125–30, 135–36, 137, 141, 144–45, 208, 218, 220–25, 227, 237, 240–43, 241 (table 5); *das bei-sich-Seiende* (the being-with-itself), 126, 137; condition of inversion, 135–36, 145; *Geist* (spirit), 127, 137, 221, 277n. 45), 279 n. 77; god A^3, 179, 180 (table 2), 182; *das sein Sollende* (the being that ought to be), 126; *Subjekt-Objekt* (subject-object), 126, 127, 139. *See also* Iakchos

Potentiality, 112, 113–14, 115, 117–21, 122, 123, 124–25, 126, 127, 128–31, 135, 137, 144, 173, 206, 208, 218, 223, 243; in relation to need, 113–14; of Potencies prior to actualization, 116–29; relative not-being, 120, 130, 135, 136, 144. *See also* Actuality; *Figur des Seienden;* Potencies (esp. A^1, first Potency)

Potenzenlehre (theory of Potencies). *See* Potencies

Predestination. *See* Determinism; Providence

Primordial consciousness *(Urbewußtsein),* 54–55, 187. *See also* Unconscious

Prius. See Absolute: absolute *Prius;* God

Projections, 99, 194, 234–37, 243, 244–50. *See also* Sublimated projection theory

Proto-time. *See* Eternity; Time

Providence, 3, 43, 52, 62, 77, 82, 133, 134, 155, 157, 158, 159, 160, 196, 238, 246, 250. *See also* Determinism

Psychologism, 11, 102, 104, 202
Psychology of religion, 1, 2, 3, 6, 10–11, 34, 47–57, 102, 104, 143, 195–204, 205, 218, 219–20, 221, 227, 232; ambivalences in religious attitudes, 1–2, 56, 193, 196–97, 201–2, 203–4, 217–18, 227–30, 231, 232, 233–35, 236, 245, 249–50; archetypes, 10, 31, 39, 56, 127, 202, 213, 220, 221, 235, 244; cathartic reenactment of religious conflicts, 217, 240, 245; cross-identifications between aggressors and victims in religion, 199–201, 203, 216–20; destructive impulses and motifs, 192, 198–204, 205, 211–12, 214, 216–19; *Deisidaemonia* (neurotic religious doubt), 204, 223, 286 n. 73; displacement of emotions, 201–4, 219–20, 233–35, 236; dissimulated motives in religion, 196, 199, 219–20, 227–30, 244; dynamics of sacrifice, 199–201, 211, 216–19, 242, 245; existential anxiety, 200, 203; hysterical response to unwelcome new divinity, 214–15; inspired madness, 212–20, 227, 264, 288; repressed meanings in religious symbolism, 48, 50, 55–56, 227–29; sense of awe and wonder, 11, 28, 39, 101–2, 159–60, 188–89, 193, 197–98; "uncanny" *(unheimliche)* secrets beneath surface phenomena, 226–30. *See also* Psychologism; Unconscious

Pure being *(rein Seiendes). See* Potencies: A², second Potency

Pythagoras, 128

Quidditas. See Was
Quodditas. See Daß

Reason, 20, 23, 30, 32, 41–43, 47, 50–51, 52–53, 56–57, 60, 86–91, 96–109, 115, 132–33, 134, 136, 142, 143, 144, 151, 152–54, 158, 159, 169–76, 197, 213, 216, 221, 232, 234, 239, 247, 248. *See also* Concept; Dialectic; Ecstasy of reason; Logic; Philosophy

Reductionism, 28, 29, 39, 40, 88, 90, 229–30

Reimarus, Hermann Samuel, 255

Rein Seiendes. See Potencies: A², second Potency

Relatively spiritual god. *See* Dionysus

Relative monotheism, 186–91, 193, 195, 198, 205, 220. *See also* Absolute monotheism; Religion: monotheism

Relative not-being. *See* Potentiality

Relativism, 53, 59, 60, 99–100, 106, 114

Religion, 1–109 passim, 111, 116, 138, 139, 142, 145–46, 147, 149, 150, 159, 160–61, 162, 169, 170, 179–250 passim; allegorical interpretations of, 25–49, 69, 194, 199; animism, 19, 254n. 6; evolution of, 3–4, 13, 19–20, 42–44, 50, 55, 59, 60, 61–62, 69, 73, 74, 76, 81–82, 85, 95, 98, 111, 136, 139, 149, 154, 158–61, 168, 184, 187–88, 206, 208, 216, 222, 232, 237 (table 4), 239–40, 246, 247–48; integrity (reality) of religious phenomena, 4–5, 19, 35–38, 42–44, 47, 54; moralistic or doctrinal interpretations of religion, 40–45; monism, 21, 32, 105, 187–88, 213; monotheism, 18, 20, 21, 22, 23, 44, 61, 89, 141, 186–91, 192, 193, 195, 198, 205, 220, 232, 239, 242, 250, 257; mysticism, 69, 70, 75, 78, 138, 238, 248, 249; pantheism, 22, 23, 76, 77, 80, 102, 188–89, 192, 195, 199, 202, 205, 219, 220, 255, 276; philosophy of religion, 95–176, 231–50; polytheism (paganism), 2–4, 7, 8, 21, 22, 43, 44, 61, 81, 88, 95, 139, 179–250, 256, 257, 271, 283n. 2; projection theory, 99, 194, 234–37, 243, 244–50; religion and the unconscious, 10–11, 13, 47, 52–57, 184–85, 201–4; sublimated projection theory, 244–50; *Urreligion*, 184, 188, 195. *See also* Atheistic interpretations of religion; Early theories of religion (prior to Schelling); Euhemerism; God; Goddesses, as compared to gods; Gods, goddesses, and legendary heroes; Mystery cults; Mythology; Naturalism; Psychology of religion; Revelation; *also specific religious traditions*

Resurrection: 212, 219, 224

Revelation, 1, 4, 6, 18–19, 20, 21, 43, 70, 71, 72, 73, 75, 78, 79, 80, 81, 98–99, 108, 116, 117, 138, 140–41, 149, 154–61 passim, 171, 184, 191, 212, 232, 238, 243, 246–48, 255 n. 10, 271; pre-Christian or non-Christian conceptions of, 18–23, 28–29, 37
Ricoeur, Paul, 12, 29, 229–30, 253, 259, 289
Romanticism, 21, 31, 40, 41, 47, 215, 242
Roman religion, 18, 19, 21, 39, 244. *See also* Greek religion; Gods, goddesses, and legendary heroes: Greco-Roman
Roy, Rammohun, 21, 256

Sacrifice, human, 199–201, 211, 217–19. *See also* Psychology of religion
Sainte-Croix, Guillaume Emmanuel, Baron de, 239, 290
Saint-Martin, Louis Claude de, 78
Samothracian religion, 29, 36–37. *See also* Gods, goddesses, and legendary heroes: Greco-Roman: Axieros
Sartre, Jean-Paul, 104
Schelling, Friedrich Wilhelm Joseph von
  Works cited by title in main text:
    Philosophie der Mythologie, 1, 22, 54, 55, 139, 186, 228, 250
    Philosophie der Offenbarung, 234
    Philosophie und Religion, 97
    Philosophische Untersuchungen über das Wesen der menschlichen Freiheit und die damit zusammenhängenden Gegenstände [Freiheitsschrift], 53, 66, 78, 80, 84, 97, 98, 165
    Stuttgarter Privatvorlesungen, 54, 86, 287
    System des transzendentalen Idealismus, 48, 66
    Über die Gottheiten von Samothrake, 36, 260, 261
    Über die Methode des akademischen Studiums, 31
    Über Mythen, historische Sagen und Philosopheme der ältesten Welt, 30
    Weltalter, 36, 54, 64, 97, 139, 166, 167
    Weltalter Fragmente, 165
Schlegel, August von, 2
Schlegel, Friedrich von, 2, 21, 34, 149, 255, 260, 262

Schleiermacher, Friedrich David Ernst, 102, 289
Schopenhauer, Arthur, 21, 254
Schröter, Manfred, 108, 164, 274
Schubert, Gotthilf Heinrich, 56, 265
Schulz, Walter, 108, 163, 169–75, 272, 273, 274, 278, 280, 281–83, 290
Schulze, Wilhelm A., 260, 268, 269
Second World Age, 191, 193, 197. *See also* First World Age; Great Spiritual Crisis
Sedlar, Jean W., 256
Seele. See Individuality; Spirit
Seiende, das (determinate being), 138–39, 152, 154, 155, 159, 160, 173, 174, 276 n. 20, 277 n. 49; That which IS *das Seiende,* 139, 173. *See also Figur ses Seienden; Inbegriff; Was*
Sein Könnendes. See Potencies: A^1, first Potency
Sein Müssendes. See Potencies: A^2, second Potency
Sein Sollendes. See Potencies: A^3, third Potency
Selfhood. *See* Individuality; Spirit
Sin. *See* Evil; *Felix culpa;* Original sin
Snorri. *See* Sturlason, Snorri
Snow, Dale Evarts, 264, 273
Soul *(Seele). See* Individuality; Spirit
Spinoza, Baruch, 32–33, 60, 63, 102, 141, 164, 264
Spirit *(Geist),* 127, 136–42, 221, 277 n. 45, 279 n. 77; self-determined causality of, 59–67, 137, 140, 164–66, 168. *See also Daß;* Individuality; Potencies: A^3, third Potency
Star-worship (Zabism). *See* Cronus/Uranus
Storr, Georg Christian, 31
Stoudt, John Joseph, 75, 267
Strauß, David Friedrich, 2, 3, 244
Sturlason, Snorri, 27, 259
Suber, Peter Dain, 105, 274 n. 37
Subjection (subordination) of Potencies, 117, 190, 216, 217–18, 219, 220, 221, 222, 223–24, 225, 226, 228, 243
Subjectivity, 6, 10, 11, 32, 35, 41, 42, 101, 115, 117, 119–27, 132, 135, 144–45, 148, 170, 184, 193, 208, 234, 240, 244, 260, 272; see also Individuality; Potencies: A^1, first Potency; Spirit; Subject/object relation; *Subjekt-Objekt*

Subject/object relation, 12, 32, 48–52, 73–74, 87–88, 96–97, 103–6, 115, 117, 123–28, 208. *See also* Objectivity; Subjectivity; *Subjekt-Objekt*

Subjekt-Objekt (subject-object), 126, 127, 139. *See also* Objectivity; Potencies: A³, third Potency; Subjectivity; Subject/object relation

Sublation *(Aufhebung),* 171, 189, 269–70n. 51. *See also* Hegel

Sublimated projection theory, 244–50. *See also* Projections

Suprarational. *See* Transrational

Symbol, 1, 2, 6–13, 14, 17, 22, 25, 31–45, 47, 51, 56, 61, 69, 73, 83, 95, 183, 186, 194, 196, 199, 201–2, 203, 209, 211, 213–14, 216, 217, 219, 224–25, 226–30, 244, 245, 250, 260–61; symbolic reenactments in the Mysteries, 239–41. *See also* Psychology of religion: repressed meanings in religious symbolism; Religion: allegorical interpretations

Syrian religion, 27, 224. *See also* Gods, goddesses, and legendary heroes: Syrian

Tables representing comparative mythology:
Table 1, phases of the *Daß* in relation to the Potencies, 141;
Table 2, cross-cultural parallels among deities, 180;
Table 3, successive "kataboles" via feminine deities, 207;
Table 4, stages of potentiality versus actuality in evolution of mythological consciousness, 237;
Table 5, parallel personas of Demeter and Dionysus as successive manifestations of the One True God, 241

Tauler, Johannes, 78

Thatness. See *Daß*

Theagenes of Rhegium, 25, 28, 29, 47,

Theosophy, 69, 70, 75, 78, 172

Theunissen, Michael, 163, 280

Thrownness *(Geworfenheit),* 99, 171, 272

Tieck, Ludwig, 268

Tillich, Paul, 142, 236, 273, 291

Tilliette, Xavier, 108, 109, 119, 151, 157, 164, 172–73, 227–28, 257, 260, 261, 274, 275, 276, 279, 280, 282, 291

Time, 59–67 passim, 69, 75, 83, 89, 90, 91, 111–13, 114, 116, 130, 131, 139, 157, 158, 164–66, 168, 184, 185, 187, 199, 223, 235–36, 243, 285; beginningless beginning of, 55, 111–13, 137; and eternity, 55, 64–65, 73, 81, 82, 83, 90, 95, 164–69 passim; principle of temporal/ontological parallelism, 55, 57; proto-temporal, 64, 65, 90–91, 116, 117, 120, 125, 127, 165–66, 265n. 11. *See also* Creation; Essence: temporalization of; Eternity; Hegel: time and eternity

Transrational (nonrational or suprarational), 1, 3, 11–12, 13, 23, 36, 48–52, 53, 101–7, 136, 142–44, 147, 170, 171, 172–73, 175, 176, 231–32, 238, 246, 247–48. *See also* Ecstasy of reason; Intellectual intuition; Irrational principle; Philosophy: metaphysical empiricism; Noncognitivist theologies; Unconscious

Überseiendes (over-being), 103, 108, 155, 156–57, 159, 160, 171, 247, 273n. 30; *Überexistierendes* (over-existing), 136–37, 278n. 68. *See also Daß;* God

Uncanny *(das Unheimliche). See* Psychology of religion

Unconscious, 2, 10–11, 13, 14, 43, 47–57, 95, 98, 143, 145, 175, 176, 182, 184–85, 194, 196–97, 201, 203, 211, 216, 218, 220, 226, 227–30, 231. *See also* Irrational principle; Primordial consciousness; Psychology of religion; Transrational

Ungrund. See Böhme: abyss

Unheimliches. See Psychology of religion

Universal, 33, 35, 60–61, 84, 85, 115, 128–29, 131, 136–38, 141, 153, 159, 161, 168, 173, 182, 191, 194, 196, 199, 238, 276, 278; actual universalia *(wirkliche Universalia),* 89; universals and particulars, 96–98. *See also* Actuality; Hegel: concrete universal; Individuality; Particular

INDEX   317

Universal, Concrete. *See* Hegel
Uslar, Detlev von, 263

Vater, Michael, 263
Verneinende Kraft. See Potencies: B,
    inverted first Potency
Void (in Buddhism), 72. *See also* No-thing
Volkmann-Schluck, Karl-Heinz, 273, 284
Voluntarism, 75, 84–86, 108, 111, 114–16,
    119–20, 123–24, 125, 126–27, 129,
    134, 138, 140, 142–43, 145, 147, 148,
    155–57, 165, 176. *See also* Freedom;
    Will
Voß (Vossius), Gerhard, 18, 254
Voß, Johann Heinrich, 239, 262, 290
Vries, Jan de, 29, 47, 254–59 passim, 263

Warburton, William, bishop of Gloucester,
    239, 290
Was (whatness or *quidditas*), 107, 136–37,
    138, 140, 142, 143, 145, 147, 148, 149,
    152–53, 155, 160, 161, 165, 235–36,
    238, 248, 278n. 72, 280n. 30. *See also*
    Daß; Seiende, das
Whatness. See *Was*
White, Alan, 100, 272 nn. 13 and 17
Will, 14, 38, 59, 62, 65, 70–75, 77, 80, 84,
    86, 89, 98, 107, 108, 111, 114–16, 120,
    121, 123–24, 127, 134, 135, 138, 141–
    42, 142–43, 144, 145, 148, 155, 156–
    57, 158, 165–66, 189, 196, 226, 233,
    234, 235, 281n. 6; *der nicht wollende
    Wille* (wantless will), 119, 120, 123,
    127, 276n. 23; *willenloses Wollen*
    (unwilled wanting), 123–24, 127,
    276n. 23. *See also* Freedom;
    Voluntarism

Zabism. *See* Cronus/Uranus
Zend Avesta, 191
Zeno of Elea, 112
Zusammenziehende Kraft. See Potencies: B,
    inverted first Potency